SHAKESPEARE
STUDIES

EDITORIAL BOARD

SHAKESPEARE STUDIES
VOLUME XXVI

EDITED BY
LEEDS BARROLL

BOOK-REVIEW EDITOR

Susan Zimmerman

Madison • Teaneck
Fairleigh Dickinson University Press
London: Associated University Presses

Associated University Presses
440 Forsgate Drive
Cranbury, NJ 08512

Associated University Presses
16 Barter Street
London WC1A 2AH, England

Associated University Presses
P.O. Box 338, Port Credit
Mississauga, Ontario
Canada L5G 4L8

The paper used in this publication meets the requirements
of the American National Standard for Permanence of Paper
for Printed Library Materials Z39.48-1984.

International Standard Book Number 0-8386-3782-5 (vol. xxvi)
International Standard Serial Number 0582-9399

All editorial correspondence concerning *Shakespeare Studies* should be addressed to the Editorial Office, *Shakespeare Studies*, Fine Arts 447, University of Maryland (Baltimore County), Baltimore, Maryland 21250. Manuscripts submitted without appropriate postage will not be returned. Orders and subscriptions should be directed to Associated University Presses, 440 Forsgate Drive, Cranbury, New Jersey 08512.

Shakespeare Studies disclaims responsibility for statements, either of fact or opinion, made by contributors.

PRINTED IN THE UNITED STATES OF AMERICA

Contents

6 Contents

Articles

Responses: Forum: A Funeral Elegy by W. S.

Reviews

Contents

8   *Contents*

                            Errata

Foreword

IN keeping with the new directions of *Shakespeare Studies*, this issue includes a fourth in the series of Forums initiated in Volume XXIV with "Editing Early Modern Texts," and continued in Volume XXV with "Studying Early Modern Women," and "A Funeral Elegy by W.S." Our Forum for this issue, "Race and the Study of Shakespeare," has been organized by Margo Hendricks and includes the commentaries of six scholars: Dympna Callaghan, Peter Erickson, Nancy A. Gutierrez, Judith A. López, Francesca T. Royster, and Jyotsna G. Singh. An essay by Linda E. Merians, adapted from her forthcoming book and entitled "'Hottentot': the Emergence of an Early Modern Racist Epithet," provides an interesting complement to this Forum.

Volume XXVI is also pleased to introduce the first two in a new series of essays detailing the status of particular fields of early modern studies. John Drakakis examines the development of Robert Weimann's Marxist-based analytical paradigms as well as the impact of his work; and Jean E. Howard evaluates four recent studies in early modern sexuality, especially as they defamiliarize and "make new" our view of the early modern period itself.

In our next volume, the fifth *Shakespeare Studies* Forum will focus on the scholarly corpus of Harry Berger, Jr. Organized by Lena Cowen Orlin, this Forum will feature Stanley Cavell, Lynn Enterline, Stephen Greenblatt, Marshall Grossman and Lois Potter. Volume XXVII will also include review essays by S. P. Cerasano, William Ingram, and Constance Jordan.

LEEDS BARROLL

Contributors

RICHARD ABRAMS is Associate Professor of English at the University of Southern Maine, Portland. He is completing a book entitled *Another Shakespeare: Essays in Speculative Biography.*

JOEL B. ALTMAN is Professor of English at the University of California, Berkeley. He is currently completing a book on Shakespeare and rhetorical anthropology in the Renaissance.

DYMPNA CALLAGHAN, Associate Professor of English at Syracuse University, is author of *Women and Gender in Renaissance Tragedy* and coauthor with Jyotsna Singh and Lorraine Helms of *The Weyward Sisters: Shakespeare and Feminist Politics.*

THOMAS CARTELLI is Chair of the Department of English at Muhlenberg College. He is the author of *Marlowe, Shakespeare, and the Economy of Theatrical Experience* and of *Repositioning Shakespeare: National Formations, Postcolonial Appropriations.*

MARGRETA DE GRAZIA is Professor of English at the University of Pennsylvania. She is currently working on Hamlet's epochal status in the modern age.

JOHN DRAKAKIS is currently Professor of English Studies at the University of Stirling. He is the General Editor of the Routledge *New Critical Idiom* and is currently working on the New Arden edition of *The Merchant of Venice*, and on a book entitled *Shakespearean Discourses.*

PETER ERICKSON is author of *Patriarchal Structures in Shakespeare's Drama* and *Rewriting Shakespeare, Rewriting Ourselves.* He is co-editor of *Shakespeare's "Rough Magic": Renaissance Essays in Honor of C.L. Barber,* and of a forthcoming collection, *The Visual Culture of Early Modern England.*

DONALD W. FOSTER, Jean Webster Professor of Dramatic Literature at Vassar College, is completing a two-volume collection of medieval and early modern writing by women while restructuring Shaxicon, his text-analysis database, for access on the World Wide Web.

PATRICIA FUMERTON is Associate Professor of English at the University of California, Santa Barbara. She is author of *Cultural Aesthetics: Renaissance Literature and the Practice of Social Ornament,* coeditor of a forthcoming collection of essays entitled *Renaissance Culture and the Everyday*, and currently at work on a book entitled *Spacious Voices/Vagrant Subjects in Early Modern England*.

NANCY A. GUTIERREZ is Associate Professor of English at Arizona State University. She is currently at work on a book on women's refusal of food in certain early modern English plays and pamphlets.

MARGO HENDRICKS teaches at the University of California, Santa Cruz. She is at work on a project tentatively titled *Shakespeare and/in the African-American Community*.

JEAN E. HOWARD is Professor of English at Columbia University and Director of the Institute for Research on Women and Gender. Her most recent books include *The Stage and Social Struggle in Early Modern England* and, with Phyllis Rackin, *Engendering a Nation: A Feminist Study of Shakespeare's English Histories*. She is also one of the coeditors of the Norton *Shakespeare*.

LORNA HUTSON is Reader in Renaissance Studies at Queen Mary and Westfield College, University of London. She is the author of *The Usurer's Daughter* and of various articles on Renaissance literature and culture.

MACDONALD P. JACKSON is Professor of English at the University of Auckland. For seven years (1985–1991) he wrote *Shakespeare Survey's* annual review of editions and textual studies.

HEATHER JAMES is Assistant Professor of English at the University of Southern California. She has published *Shakespeare's Troy: Drama, Politics and the Translation of Empire* as well as articles on Shakespeare and Milton.

THEODORA A. JANKOWSKI teaches English at Washington State University. Author of *Women in Power in the Early Modern Drama* and articles on Lyly, Shakespeare, and Webster, she has completed a book on queer virgins in the early modern drama and is now working on definitions of middle-class identity in Thomas Heywood's plays.

NORA JOHNSON is Assistant Professor of English at Swarthmore College. She is at work on a book about acting and authorship in early modern England.

IAN LANCASHIRE is Professor of English at the University of Toronto. He is currently undertaking studies of Shakespeare's idiolect with the Early Modern English Dictionaries Database and *TACT*, computer tools he is developing.

JUDITH A. LÓPEZ teaches in the Department of Literature at the University of California, Santa Cruz.

LAWRENCE MANLEY is Professor of English at Yale University and the author of *Literature and Culture in Early Modern London*. His current project, "Reading Repertory," examines relationships between acting and the composition of Shakespeare's plays.

LINDA E. MERIANS is Associate Professor of English at La Salle University and editor of *The Secret Malady: Venereal Disease in Eighteenth-Century Britain and France*. Her forthcoming book examines social and rhetorical strategies for constructing the "Hottentot" in early modern Britain.

DAVID LEE MILLER is Professor of English at the University of Kentucky. He is currently preparing a study of filial sacrifice and masculinity.

KAREN NEWMAN is University Professor and Professor of Comparative Literature and English at Brown University. She is the author of *Shakespeare's Rhetoric of Comic Character, Fashioning Femininity and English Renaissance Drama*, and most recently, *Fetal Positions*. She is at work on a new project on cultural production in early modern London and Paris tentatively entitled "Cultural Capitals."

LOIS POTTER is Ned B. Allen Professor of English at the University of Delaware. She is currently working on a book on *Othello* for the Shakespeare in Performance Series (University of Manchester Press), and a critical biography of Shakespeare.

NICHOLAS F. RADEL is Professor of English at Furman University in South Carolina. He has written articles on Renaissance literature and queer theory.

FRANCESCA T. ROYSTER is Assistant Professor of English at Pennsylvania State University. She is currently completing a book manuscript entitled *Becoming Cleopatra: Cross-Cultural Appropriation and Shakespearean Tactics*.

JYOTSNA G. SINGH is Associate Professor of English at Southern Methodist University. She is the author of *Colonial Narratives/Cultural Dialogues*, and co-author of *The Weyward Sisters: Shakespeare and Feminist Politics*.

BRUCE R. SMITH, Professor of English, Georgetown University, is the author of *Homosexual Desire in Shakespeare's England*, and most, recently, of "L[o]cating the Sexual Subject" in *Alternative Shakespeares 2*.

GRACE TIFFANY is Associate Professor of English at Western Michigan University. She is at work on a novel about Shakespeare, time travel, and spinach.

GUSTAV UNGERER, Professor of English Literature at the University of Berne, retired, has done archival research into Elizabethan prostitution and is currently preparing papers on Falstaff and the sexual transgressions of the Brookes; Moll Newborough and the Bridewell scandal of 1598–1601; and Moll Cutpurse and her fictional autobiography.

VALERIE WAYNE is Professor of English at the University of Hawai'i at Mānoa. She has edited *The Matter of Difference: Materialist Feminist Criticism of Shakespeare* and Edmund Tilney's *The Flower of Friendship: A Renaissance Dialogue Contesting Marriage*. Her current work includes a contextual edition of *The Winter's Tale* for the Bedford Shakespeare Series and a critical edition of *Cymbeline* for the Arden Shakespeare, third series.

LINDA WOODBRIDGE, Professor of English at Pennsylvania State University, is completing her third book, which deals with homelessness in English Renaissance literature and history.

GEORGIANNA ZIEGLER is Louis B. Thalheimer Reference Librarian at the Folger Shakespeare Library. She has published various articles on women in the Renaissance and in Shakespeare's plays, and has forthcoming an annotated bibliography of writings on how to research early modern women.

SHAKESPEARE STUDIES

FORUM:
RACE AND THE STUDY
OF SHAKESPEARE

Introduction

Margo Hendricks

WHEN ASKED to organize this forum, "Race and Shakespeare Studies: Is There a Future," I was both honored and hesitant. Did we, Shakespearean and early modern scholars and critics, truly need another discussion on "race" and its importance to Renaissance and/or early modern English studies? Has the argument for attention to the "matter of race" not already been made? Yet, after I invited the six contributors to offer their thoughts and had read their essays, I realized that there remains much to be done. In very different ways each of the contributors arrives at the same general conclusion: despite the appropriation of post-structuralist and post-modern theoretical apparati, critics of early modern English culture have yet to comfortably situate the "problem of race" in an early modern historiography that fully adumbrates the complexity, fluidity, and problematic nature of the discourses of race that prevailed in the sixteenth and seventeenth centuries.

Each of the essays that follow suggestively acknowledges, as David Theo Goldberg has argued in his seminal work *Racist Discourse: Philosophy and the Politics of Meaning*, that "race is a fluid, transforming, historically specific concept parasitic on theoretic and social discourses for the meaning it assumes at any given moment" (74). What this means is that in order for race to be understood, it must pretend to universality, engendering commonality by negating or effacing the disparate interests of disparate subjectivities. However, there is an inherent paradox in this activity: in order to inflect race with meaning, modern social formations must frame visible (and, quite frankly, minor) differences among people in terms of antithesis: race is simultaneously transcendentally immutable and historically mutable. This at-times-contradictory "truth" becomes preternaturally productive in sustaining itself in and through an illusion of essentialism.

Comprehension of this theoretical avatar produces different sets of questions than one might normally ask with regard to early mod-

19

ern English literature: for example, we might well inquire why literary works such as Shakespeare's *Othello* and *Titus Andronicus* or John Webster's *The White Devil* are treated as texts that deal almost exclusively with race and racism, while Philip Sidney's *Arcadia* or Edmund Spenser's *Faerie Queene* are treated as primarily concerned with matters of nationalism and Englishness. On this and related issues, we might also ask whether modern cultural and social critics of early modern literature, by extending the racial taxonomies and ideologies that have shaped post-Enlightenment social subjectivity to pre-Enlightenment subjectivity, fashioned earlier social formations in our own image?

Questions such as these, of course, as Nancy Gutierrez astutely contends, must become the catalyst for additional epistemological problems and queries in the discourses of race in Shakespeare and early modern studies. Readers, all of the contributors posit, must become interrogators of the varied racial implications of any early modern text and must also inquire into how audiences (then and now) might have construed and recognized the concept of race and its linguistic inflections.

Race, as it surfaces in Shakespeare's and other early modern texts, reveals itself to be a multiplicity of loci, of axes of determinism, as well as of metaphorical systems to aid and abet its deployment across a variety of boundaries in the making. As an expression of fundamental distinctions, race's meaning varied depending upon whether a writer wanted to specify difference born of a class-based concept of genealogy, a psychological (and essentialized) nature, or a group typology. Nonetheless, in all these variations, race is envisioned as something fundamental, something immutable, knowable, and recognizable, "seen" only when its boundaries are violated, and thus race is also, paradoxically, mysterious, illusory, and mutable. The contributions of Dympna Callaghan, Peter Erickson, Nancy Gutierrez, Judith López, Francesca Royster, and Jyotsna Singh mark an emerging awareness of this deeply complex system of meaning. And, in distinct but correlated, and often polemical, ways, each contributor's thoughts represent a challenge to prevailing wisdom about how we address the question of race in Shakespeare and early modern studies.

Works Cited

David Theo Goldberg. *Racist Discourse: Philosophy and the Politics of Meaning.* (Oxford: Basil Blackwell, 1994).

Margo Hendricks, "Obscured by Dreams: Race, Empire, and Shakespeare's *A Midsummer Night's Dream*," *Shakespeare Quarterly* 2, no. 1 (summer 1996): 37–60.

What's at Stake in Representing Race?

Dympna Callaghan

"ENTER BLACKAMOORS with music," reads the stage direction in act 5, scene 2 of *Love's Labors Lost*. Unlike "Exit, pursued by a bear" in *The Winter's Tale* (3.3.58), which scholars believe may have involved a real trained bear rather than an actor in a bear suit, (though not, of course, a bear actually in deathly pursuit), "Enter Blackamoors" undoubtedly signals the entrance not of actual Africans but of English minstrels in blackface. For all that, "Blackamoors with music," holds forth a prospect that stage directions like "A street in Athens," "A Tavern in Eastcheap," and so forth, cannot, namely that of a perfect coincidence between dramatic representation and reality: the tantalizing possibility of presence. Of course, the direction "Enter Blackamoors with music," dating at the latest from 1597, was not available to Shakespeare's audience any more than the expectation that, even if impersonated ad vivum by virtue of mimetic and cosmetic proficiency, these musicians might be real Africans. There is a wealth of evidence about how early modern performers achieved racial impersonation by means of theatrical integument, and although English monarchs employed black musicians from the reign of Henry VIII—Henry had a "blacke trumpet," while Elizabeth I is depicted with a group of black minstrels and dancers in a painting dated ca. 1577 and attributed to Gheeraerts the elder, and James I later had a troupe of black minstrels—there is no record of black performers being borrowed from royal or aristocratic households to play roles on stage.[1] The stage direction, then, signals not that the players borrowed royal musicians but that they are dramatizing the richness and exoticism of court culture.

However problematic or fleeting, the possibility of presence offered by this stage direction shares an epistemological affinity with Stanley Cavell's account in *Must We Mean What We Say?* of the apocryphal incident of the southern yokel "who rushes to the stage to save Desdemona from the black man."[2] The "joke" is not so much that the yokel thinks that Desdemona—a white actress performing in the old South—is really being killed, but rather, that he believes that the white actor playing Othello is really black. Though he nowhere remarks upon it, Cavell's yokel is not simply a naive spectator who contrasts with "the state of mind in which we find the events in a theatre neither credible nor incredible," but a racist spectator whose fear of miscegenation inhibits his capacity to distinguish between dramatic representation and reality. That is, the problem of representation in this incident coincides with specific problems attendant upon the dramatic depiction of gender and race.

What is significant about the blackamoors in the stage direction from *Love's Labors Lost* and Cavell's yokel is that they bespeak fantasies of presence about people who for reasons far in excess of problems of geography and practicality could not possibly have been onstage. *Love's Labors'* blackamoors and Cavell's yokel thereby exemplify the specifically political dimension of the dense philosophical problems posed by dramatic representation. In what follows, I want to suggest some of the ways in which Shakespeare's racially homogenous stage can serve as a site from which to address the stakes of representation, especially for those who in spite, or perhaps because, of their hypervisibility have been historically its objects and not its subjects.

* * *

Despite the absence of women and Africans from early modern public theater, the only visual depiction we have of a Shakespearean performance, Henry Peacham's drawing of *Titus Andronicus*, contains a vivid depiction of conspicuous racial and gendered difference and seems to point to the inclusivity of Shakespeare's stage. One has the sense that Peacham's depiction of Tamora and Aaron reflects the fact that they captured his attention so as to make an enlarged and more vivid impression on his imagination than that of the other characters. A Roman spear marks center stage, while to its right (stage left) a kneeling Tamora pleads for her sons' lives. Aaron is the only standing figure on this side of the drawing. Black and gesticulating, he offers a stark contrast with the outlines of the nondescript Romans lined up stage right. The picture emphasizes Africans as visibly different from Europeans, which has been the intriguing phenomenon in Western art history: in the fifteenth century existing white images were painted over with the figure of the

Black Magus, and in the nineteenth century depictions of Ham, which had been white hitherto, suddenly were rendered as black. It seems, indeed, that, as Don Hedrick has observed in the Marxist literary journal *Mediations*: "the ideology of the visual image . . . pertains to race in ways that differ from the discursive meaning of race or ethnicity."[3]

In the context of the iconography of racial representation, Peacham's picture, and especially Aaron's hypervisibility within it, makes for a fascinating juxtaposition with an observation made by the late Betty Shabazz, Malcolm X's widow: "Malcolm said if you are looking at a picture of the world and you don't see yourself in it, your task should be obvious: to get in the picture."[4] That Aaron, a villain, a distorted image of African identity, *is* in the picture is itself problematic and constitutes evidence of the troubled contiguity between cultural representation and representation understood in the broader political sense. Certainly, as Shabazz's comment indicates, we in the twentieth century have come to equate sheer visibility with power.

Many of Shakespeare's contemporaries did not share our faith in representation. Both theatricalists and antitheatricalists feared the encroachments mimetic representation made upon the real. When in 1642, with the advent of the Commonwealth period, those who had been the nonentities of English history gained representation for the first time, the site of that representation, singularly, was not in the theaters. Indeed, far from equating cultural representation with political power, the Puritans, who were, in Marxist terms, the vanguard class of the new economic and social order, deplored as lewd and idolatrous what went on at the playhouse, and did so despite the fact that representational practices of all kinds became necessary as part not only of an economy based on increasingly abstract systems of exchange, but also on a social system that replaced what Richard Halpern calls "the visible or patent form of sovereign power with an invisible and resolutely *latent* form of economic domination."[5] That is, the coercion that inheres in social relations whereby the aristocracy takes and maintains power gives way to an invisible function of the economic system itself. Thus, visibility, which at a later historical moment comes to signify representation in its political sense (that is, representing the interests of a particular constituency rather than mere depiction) becomes prominent precisely at the moment when crucial aspects of power and economic exchange become invisible.

The perils of cultural representation seem to have been much more apparent in pre-Hollywood eras. The status of actors like Nathan Field, who was barred from receiving communion in his parish church, makes it clear that the practice of theatrical representation was parlous. In stark contrast to the dangers of visibility in early modern England and to Cleopatra's fears about squeaking boys, certain groups in the twentieth century, especially, as we see from Shabazz's comment, people of color, but also gays and lesbians and other marginalized groups, have tended to regard even misrepresentation as the necessary cost of visibility: "Representation at any price."[6]

My point here is, first, that it is necessary to maintain a certain philosophical skepticism about the mechanisms of dramatic representation as well as a specifically political skepticism about the benefits of representation, understood as cultural visibility, for marginalized groups. Secondly, on Shakespeare's stage as a result of both all-male mimesis and the production of racialized others in racially homogenous acting companies, the problem of representation in general—that it necessarily represents what is not actually there—thus becomes exacerbated in historically specific relation to femininity and racial difference.

Historically, however, in relation to Shakespeare, marginalized groups have not felt underrepresented and invisible. Indeed, generations of readers and playgoers, many of them racial and cultural "others," have experienced the powerful and pleasurable perception that in Shakespeare, they are indeed represented. This may be because, as Stephen Greenblatt observes in his introduction to *The Norton Shakespeare*, "[S]o absolute is Shakespeare's achievement that he has himself come to seem like great creating nature: the common bond of humankind, the principle of hope, the symbol of the imagination's power to transcend time-bound beliefs and assumptions, peculiar historical circumstances, and specific artistic conventions."[7] Roberto Fernandez Retamar, for instance, writes in a tradition of reading in *The Tempest* the script for resistance to colonialism: "I know no other metaphor more expressive of our cultural situation, of our reality. . . . [W]hat is our history, what is our culture, if not the history and culture of Caliban?"[8] Pioneering theater director Joseph Papp recalls: "I grew up in a home where Yiddish was spoken, and English was only a second language, I was acutely sensitive to the musical sounds of different languages and had an ear for lilt and cadence and rhythm in the spoken word. . . . Although Shakespeare lived and wrote hundreds of years ago, his name rolls off my tongue as if he were my brother."[9] In the complex structure of Papp's distinctly humanist identification, it is notable that he does not identify with a particular character: Shylock, for instance. Indeed, identifications regularly entail rather elusive correlations of self and Shakespearean character or situation. At a conference I attended in Providence, Rhode Island, a woman in the audience, responding to a paper on Shakespeare's histories, stood up and explained the powerful impact the plays had on her as an adolescent reader struggling with her sexual identity. "I came out," she declared, "with *Henry V.*"

It would be futile and anachronistic to indict Shakespeare for failing to engage in twentieth-century casting practices or to blame him for the sex and race prejudices of his era, or, indeed, for those of our own. I neither know nor, frankly, do I much care to speculate about whether it would have been "better" if Shakespeare had used a real African rather than Richard Burbage to play Othello or Aaron. (If there *must* be an answer, it is that it would have been "different".) I am suggesting that *presence cannot be equated with representation any more than representation can be equated with inclusion.*

Let me explain what I mean by briefly examining what, on the theoretical register, we might describe as an instance of the instantiation of presence: the introduction of black actors. Representation, as Horkheimer and Adorno point out in *The Dialectic of Enlightenment*, is always one step forward and two steps back: "the capacity of representation is the vehicle of progress and regression at one and the same time."[10] Thus, when actors of genuinely African heritage finally began to play Shakespeare, these performers could not redeem a character such as Aaron because of the increasing racism of audiences and directors alike in the face of an actual black actor. Othello, for instance, often became less sympathetic than he had ever been when played by Richard Burbage. As he becomes less of a hero and more of a savage, his tragedy was simply that of reverting to his uncivilized ways. In a more recent example of the limits of corporeal presence, a director who chose to dramatize the figure of the Indian boy in *A Midsummer Night's Dream* (a figure who is alluded to but does not have a role in Shakespeare's play) did not manage to represent the role of race in the play but, as Margo Hendricks has shown in a recent article in *Shakespeare Quarterly*, to reenact and solidify its orientalist fantasies.[11]

Thus, the realization of the fantasy of "presence" in the body of performer serves more to uncover the limits of representation rather than undo them. That we expect otherwise is testimony to the hold of the fantasy itself, to our enormous investment in cultural representation, and, crucially, to its conflation with political power.

Notes

1. Peter Fryer, *Staying Power: The History of Black People in Britain* (London: Pluto Press, 1984), 4; 9. James Walvin, *Black and White: The Negro and English Society 1555–1945* (London, Allen Lane: The Penguin Press, 1973), 9. See also Alden T. Vaughan and Virginia Mason Vaughan, "Before *Othello*: Elizabethan Representations of Sub-Saharan Africans," *The William and Mary Quarterly*, 3d Series, LIV, 1 (January 1997): 19–44; 35–6.

2. Stanley Cavell *Must We Mean What We Say?* (Cambridge, Cambridge University Press, 1969), 327.

3. Don Hedrick, "Framing O. J.: Tabloidation and 'Tragedy,' or Analog Racism and Digital Racism," *Mediations*, 19, 2 (Fall 1995): 4–14; 2.

4. "All things considered," PBS, May 1997.

5. Richard Halpern, *The Poetics of Primitive Accumulation* (Ithaca: Cornell University Press, 1991), 5.

6. Harvey Firestein in *The Celluloid Closet* (1996) Dir. Rob Epstein and Jeffrey Friedman. Distributed by Sony Picture Classics.

7. Stephen Greenblatt, "General Introduction," Stephen Greenblatt et. al. eds., *The Norton Shakespeare* (New York: W. W. Norton, 1997), 1.

8. Roberto Fernandez Retamar, *Caliban and Other Essays*, trans. Edward Baker (Minneapolis, Minn.: University of Minnesota Press, 1989), 14.

9, Joseph Papp, Forward to *A Midsummer Night's Dream*, David Bevington, ed. (New York: Bantam, 1988), ix; xiv.

10. Max Horkheimer and Theodor W. Adorno, *Dialectic of Enlightenment*, Trans. John Cumming (New York: Continuum, 1972), 35.

11. Margo Hendricks, "'Obscured by Dreams': Race, Empire, and Shakespeare's A Midsummer Night's Dream," *Shakespeare Quarterly*, 47, 1 (1996): 37–60.

The Moment of Race in Renaissance Studies

PETER ERICKSON

I KNOW OF no other area of scholarly investigation in which the overall interpretive stance and conceptual framework so directly and completely hinge on the status and legitimacy of a single word. But it is not too much to say that the very existence of race as a valid topic in Renaissance studies depends on the outcome of a definitional crisis concerning the term *race.*

Simply put, we have three options in considering how to formulate the issue of race in the early modern period: race in the modern sense is present in the Renaissance; race is not applicable to the Renaissance because it is unhistorical to trace the idea back so far; race is relevant for the Renaissance but the concept has to be redefined to make it appropriate for the specific historical context prior to plantation slavery in the Americas. Too much energy seems tied up in the unproductive, all-or-nothing debate between the first two positions. The third possibility, though more promising, plunges us into a double quandary that forces us to clarify not only what we mean by race but also how we define history. The historical/unhistorical division is too crude. Everyone now wants to be historical, but this is not sufficient to produce agreement on a common approach. Evidently we have to choose among different ways of being historical.

I

To begin with a specific example, I have chosen the writing of Kwame Anthony Appiah because of its currency and prominence as well as its elegance. In his 1990 article "Race" in *Critical Terms for Literary Study* and in the 1996 restatement and elaboration in his contribution to *Color Conscious: The Political Morality of Race*, Appiah presents a three-part historical model that turns on the nineteenth century as the point of origin of a modern concept of race. On one side of this central point is the subsequent history of struggles against racism, including the future freed from racial limitations toward which Appiah aims. On the other side is a pre-nineteenth-century past, with Shakespeare as a primary reference point, in which Appiah finds that race is largely absent. Since my criticism involves Appiah's characterization of the sixteenth- and seventeenth-century past, I would like explicitly to note my positive response to his vision of the future. In particular, I want to acknowledge that I have been a beneficiary of Appiah's work in helping to open up a cross-racial discussion of race by creating a critical discourse free from rigidly separatist identity protocols.

The chief difficulty of Appiah's narrative of the past is that its overemphasis on the nineteenth century produces an excessive downplaying of race in the early modern period. This extreme degree of contrast between nineteenth and seventeenth centuries is not necessary or inevitable; one could grant proper emphasis to the nineteenth century while also according due weight to seventeenth-century developments. The problem is that Appiah's analysis willfully insists on dismissing the latter. His exclusive reliance on G. K. Hunter's 1967 essay "Othello and Colour Prejudice" conveys just this quality of denial by ignoring critical work in the thirty-year period since.

Appiah's benign view of Shakespeare's historical context is influenced by his perspective on present-day politics of the literary canon. Rightly opposing the racial division of academic labor that would assign black culture to black scholars while reserving traditional high culture for white critics, Appiah observes:

> Because Homer and Shakespeare are products of Western culture, they are awarded to white children who have never studied a word of them, never heard their names. And in this generous spirit the fact is forgotten that cultural geneticism deprives white people of jazz and black people of Shakespeare. This is a bad deal—as Du Bois would have insisted. "I sit with Shakespeare," the Bard of Great Barrington wrote, "and he winces not." (*Color Conscious*, 90)

I support the cross-racial cultural access for which Appiah is arguing here. But I would also stress a distinction between access and content that I believe Appiah conflates. There is no necessary connection between the proposition that black people should be able to study Shakespeare and the premise that the content of Shakespearean texts will be positive.

In promoting contact with Shakespeare, there is a tendency to oversell the positive valuation of the treasure to which one is gaining access. But I would rewrite the oft-cited passage from Du Bois that Appiah complacently adopts. Shakespeare—symbolically speaking—does wince! What he is wincing at is not the racial identity of any of his readers but rather the degree of critical bite that the reader, irrespective of color, brings to bear against his work. We need to hold open, for black and white students alike, the possibility of a sophisticated negative assessment of a play such as *Othello*.

But this possibility is ruled out because Appiah's historical framework gives Shakespeare an exonerative blank check by effectively making race a historical nonissue in the early modern period. There is an unacknowledged catch-22 in the operation of Appiah's historical argument: race is defined according to nineteenth-century specifications; the Renaissance cannot meet this stringent definition; therefore race is not a salient issue in the Renaissance. But surely it is unhistorical to impose a monolithic definition, derived from a single period, across the entire historical spectrum. Instead of one definition fits all, we should expect fluctuating, multiple definitions, each one appropriate to its specific period. This historical variation is precisely what Appiah's fixed nineteenth-century derivation blocks. The full richness and burden of history are thus lost to view, and the resulting version of the past is incomplete, inadequate, and impoverished.

II

Countering Appiah's model, I posit a broader historical scope for the study of race that includes early modern Europe, beginning with the sustained Portuguese contact with West Africa in the fifteenth century. Returning to the question of terminology I raised at the outset, I address two tactical matters: First, should we use quotation marks around the word *race*? Second, would it be preferable to find a substitute that would enable us to avoid the term race altogether?

Quotation marks can be used to convey a variety of messages. For example, they may signify that the term race is understood not as biological fact but as a cultural construct; they may signal awareness of the difference between race as defined in the linguistic usage of the early modern period and race as a concept defined by the critic. While both these points are important, quotation marks are not strictly necessary to make them. Sophisticated verbal explanation can accomplish the task equally well and, I would argue, even better. Because quotation marks appear to operate as a hedge or dodge, they confuse as much as clarify. It is difficult, if not impossible, to eliminate or control the connotations of skepticism that quotation marks communicate; it is as if not just the word *race* but the entire scholarly project were placed in quotation marks. This bracketing effect implies a skittishness or apologetic tone that undercuts the inquiry before it begins. In my view, the disadvantages associated with quotation marks are great enough to warrant their rejection. A historically nuanced definition of the term goes without saying it in quotation marks.

One alternative to the race-versus-"race" dilemma might be to find another word. *Ethnicity* is an appealing possibility because, compared to the highly charged term race, it comes across as analytically neutral. A further benefit is that ethnicity suggests a wider frame of reference that encompasses a global perspective. The image of diverse ethnic interactions holds up a historical mirror to the multicultural nature of our own society and, in the spirit of Stuart Hall's landmark 1988 essay "New Ethnicities" in *Black Film, British Cinema* (London: Institute of Contemporary Arts), encourages a comprehensive, fully international exploration of Renaissance ethnicities.

The expanded vision made possible by the term ethnicity has a price, however. In the shift from race to a more inclusive ethnicity, the specificity of black-white power relations is in danger of disappearing. When all ethnicities are implicitly placed on the same footing, the tendency is to imagine a system of equivalencies that produces misleading analogies. To take a specific case, one can see interesting parallels in the respective treatments of Africans and Irish in Ben Jonson's *Masque of Blackness* and *Masque of Beauty* and in his *Irish Masque at Court*. On the other hand, Jonson's representations of blacks and Irish, though overlapping, are not identical. The argument for parallel ethnicities is pushed too far when the notion that the Irish are portrayed as nonwhite is turned into the assumption that the Irish are therefore black. The differences are as important as the similarities: the concept of blackness stands out as a separate category even at this point in historical time.

One consequence of a switch to the term ethnicity is the risk that the special prominence and pressures of strongly marked black-white color lines are minimized or lost. This is a price I am unwilling to pay. Instead, my recommendation is that ethnicity be used as an adjunct, not a replacement, and that the primary commitment to the term race be retained. The full particularity of the meanings of blackness can be activated only if the specific resonance of the term race is heard. Moreover—bearing in mind that race refers to white as well as black identities—race is also indispensable because it gives better access and sharper focus to the formation of white identity.

To give an example, I shall argue that we need to put the whiteness back in *Othello*: that is, we should read it as a play in which the purview of race is not limited to images of blackness but also very much involves the fashioning of a discourse of racial whiteness. The haunting resonance of Othello's desperate phrase "ocular proof" comes from its double meaning. The phrase refers not only to Desdemona's sexual betrayal, a delusion for which the imagined proof disintegrates. The ironies run deeper because the play offers a second ocular proof in the form of Othello's visually evident racial identity. The first proof is false, but the second is upheld. The play demonstrates that Othello's race is a mainspring of the tragic action: what is dramatized is not the aggression of a man who happens to be black but rather a quite specific version of black male violence against a woman seen explicitly as white. Registering the role of Desdemona's racial identity is important to the recognition that *Othello*'s racially inflected language involves the interplay of black and white.

Although the drama begins by disrupting and temporarily suspending racially based stereotypes, it ends by reimposing them. In theory, the automatic link between external color and internal moral worth is broken. Yet the pressure of the play's unfolding action produces a conventional alignment: Desdemona enacts the equation of white skin and inward innocence while Othello confirms the link between black skin and a predisposition to moral dislocation and depravity. This convergence of moral value and skin color is anticipated by Othello's tangled premonition: "I'll have some proof, my name, that was as fresh / As Dian's visage, is now begrim'd, and black / As mine own face." Othello's color is not only ocular proof but also verbal proof against himself. Every time he tries to make his language bear down on sexual purity, his words boomerang and point back toward the racial impurity he embodies.

The play's loaded language of color serves as a switch point that converts sexual meaning into inadvertent racial significance. At the very moment that Othello seeks to condemn Desdemona as black for her presumed sexual duplicity, his own language turns against him by reinforcing racial connotations:

> O thou black weed, why art thou so lovely fair? . . .
> Was this fair paper, this most goodly book,
> Made to write "whore" on? . . .
> I should make very forges of my cheeks,
> That would to cinders burn up modesty,
> Did I but speak thy deeds.

Othello's accusatory language—"black weed," the implied image of black print on white paper, the burnt cinders (even if the first element in the series is disallowed as a questionable emendation, the second two are sufficient to carry the black-white imagery)— escapes the intended target of Desdemona's transgression and fixes on his own blackness in a self-indicting rhetoric that is ultimately realized in Othello's suicide.

My reason for pointing to this passage is that it shows how the black-white counterpoint operates as a mutually dependent pair: the rhetoric of blackness is seen against, and calls attention to, a prior background of whiteness. The "fair paper" that Othello experiences as lost here translates directly into "that whiter skin of hers" that he approaches with such reverence in the final scene. Unlike the fair paper with the black marks, Othello's image of Desdemona's skin as "monumental alabaster" struggles to restore and preserve an unmarred field of pure white. But the accent of this final image of whiteness is as much racial as sexual: the inscription of Desdemona's body wrought by Othello's black hands now fulfills his previous image of the black ink applied to Desdemona's white paper. The play thus presents ocular proof of Othello's involuntary motivation by a racial discourse that intertwines black with white.

III

I conclude by delineating three aspects of the word *moment* in my title. "The Moment of Race in Renaissance Studies" refers to what I see as a new critical development. As the writings of Eldred

Jones, Elliot Tokson, Jack D'Amico, and Anthony Barthelemy show, the study of race is not new in an absolute sense. My claim is rather that more recent work has established a distinctly new stage characterized by the attainment of a critical mass absent from previous scholarship.

The two earlier and current phases are marked by significant differences in scale and impact. In the first phase, the study of race was conducted by comparatively few scholars on a basis of individual interest and effort; in the present phase, the growth in the number of scholars committed to the topic of race has created the sense of a more concerted collective level of activity with a more powerful cumulative force. Seen in the context of the overall field of Renaissance studies, the scholars of the first phase succeeded in putting race on the map but as a relatively peripheral, even marginal, topic. What is new about more recent work is the way it places race at the center of attention as a major organizing category for the period as a whole.

The principal body of second-phase work includes: Ania Loomba's *Gender, Race and Renaissance Drama* (1989); *Women, "Race," and Writing in the Early Modern Period*, the 1994 collection edited by Margo Hendricks and Patricia Parker; Kim F. Hall's *Things of Darkness: Economies of Race and Gender in Early Modern England* (1995); *Race, Ethnicity, and Power in the Renaissance*, edited by Joyce Green MacDonald (1996); and the special issue of the *William and Mary Quarterly* 54, no. 1 (January 1997) entitled "Constructing Race: Differentiating Peoples in the Early Modern World" (I have discussed the last two items in *Shakespeare Quarterly* 48 (1997): 363–66). Ania Loomba's book is set apart; it anticipates but predates the current burst of research. The link, however, is clear. Loomba's work as precursor is recognized and honored by her position as lead essayist in *Women, "Race," and Writing*. Within this context, the emergence of systematic, intensive investigation of race can be assigned to the period 1994–97.

This dating leads to the second aspect of my use of the word *moment*. The idea that race in the Renaissance is a topic whose time has come needs to be counterbalanced by other questions about timing. We should ask not only why the issue of race should emerge so strongly at this particular moment, but also why it did not arise with this force earlier. If in 1980 *The Woman's Part: Feminist Criticism of Shakespeare* called attention to gender as the concern of a visible critical movement, then *Women, "Race," and Writing in the Early Modern Period* in 1994 may be seen as a com-

parable symbolic moment for the concept of race. But what explains the time lag of nearly fifteen years between addressing
gender and turning to race?

Key words in the list of titles I cited above—Loomba's *Gender*,
Hendricks and Parker's *Women*, Hall's *Gender*—suggest that the
study of race has often originated in and grown out of feminist
criticism. The differential time frames might then be explained
partly as a function of this interrelationship. In the overall history
of American feminist Shakespeare criticism, two time gaps stand
out. First, as the distance between Kate Millett's pioneering *Sexual
Politics* in 1970 and the appearance of *The Woman's Part* in 1980
indicates, it takes a significant amount of time for a new conceptual
framework to be incorporated into the scholarship of earlier historical periods. Second, feminist criticism of Shakespeare required
another substantial block of time to establish itself through an exclusive focus on gender. Only after completing this first phase devoted to gender (1980-85) did feminist criticism begin to make the
transition to a second wave in which other cultural variables were
brought to the fore to expand and complicate the initial picture.
Though the names of these multiple variables have been carica-
tured as a mantra that intones a ready-made formula, in fact it has
been an extraordinarily difficult as well as illuminating process to
put combinations of these terms to the test of detailed critical
analysis.

The foregoing account ought to lead to the confident conclusion
that it is only a matter of time before race attains the same acceptance as a standard category in Renaissance studies as, we can see
in retrospect, gender has achieved. However, I want to place pressure on this optimistic scenario by invoking the uncertainty contained in the third meaning of the term *moment*: will the current
interest in race be only a momentary phenomenon or will it have
lasting scholarly effect? The reason for hesitation in answering this
question involves more than the generalized caution that the un-
predictability of the future makes it premature to draw any long-
term conclusions at this early stage of scholarship. Rather, there is
a specific perception that gender may be easier to assimilate into
Renaissance criticism than race. Without in any way wishing to
underestimate the opposition occasioned by feminist criticism's
sponsorship of gender, I think the argument for race faces additional obstacles.

The first obstacle concerns the historical differences that prevent
gender and race from being exactly parallel. Compared to the large

numbers of women undeniably present in early modern England, the actual population of blacks was tiny. Similarly, the number of female characters and the amount of gendered language are greater than those for black figures and racially inflected rhetoric. Simply put, the study of gender is easier in the sense that it has a wider historical and literary base with which to work. I say this not to discourage the study of race, only to note its degree of relative difficulty.

The second obstacle involves the more problematic, intractable status of the term race in our own time. Quite simply, it continues to prove easier to make political progress with respect to gender than to race. This disparity is reflected even in the social structures of Shakespeare studies as a professional discipline. The overall representation, advancement, and prominence of women Shakespeare scholars constitute a driving force in the development of feminist Shakespeare criticism. The emergence of Shakespeareans of color has occurred more recently and on a far smaller, slower, and perhaps more precarious scale. The concept of identity politics, long since a staple in defensive conservative ridicule, has lately been discredited and misconstrued in liberal-to-left discourse, a process exemplified at its best by Todd Gitlin's *The Twilight of Common Dreams* (1995). Though this across-the-board reaction makes it difficult to communicate the precise nuances that comprise the positive value of identity politics, I believe it is imperative to preserve the intellectual distinction between reductive and subtle versions of identity politics against critics who insist on collapsing all discussion into the former category. I explicitly reject an oversimplified model that implies that all black Shakespeareans share an identical point of view or that black critics as a group have monopoly control over the interpretation of race to the exclusion of others. The study of race in the Renaissance to date shows that black critics disagree and that the overall effort is multiracial. However, the story cannot end here because it is also necessary to recognize that the presence of Shakespeareans of color is a significant change in the profession and a major factor in providing the impetus to direct attention to race.

There is no formularized one-to-one correspondence between contemporary American politics and the interpretation of Renaissance history, but there are correlations, reverberations. Our research activities in the Renaissance are doubly historical: they refer to the history of the early modern period, but they are also expressions of the history of criticism in our own time. It is this second meaning of history to which the title word *moment*, with an emphasis on the sense of opportunity associated with it, alludes. The current effort to add race to the agenda of major Renaissance topics holds open the potential for reframing the Renaissance on a scale not yet envisioned in the early initiatives of feminist criticism or new historicism. Even as we modify our history of the Renaissance, our own critical history is changing. We need to be as conscious as possible about our roles in shaping this latter history, and we need actively to develop its larger connections with a contemporary politics of antiracism.

King Arthur, Scotland, Utopia, and the Italianate Englishman: What Does Race Have to Do with It?

NANCY A. GUTIERREZ

EXACTLY what does it mean that race is a category of analysis for early modern writings? In most cases, the word race suggests a "color"/whiteness binary, in which whiteness is privileged. However, in the first half of the sixteenth century, color was not yet the dominant "other" within the English culture. So the task of using race as a category of analysis in this early, early modern period means that configurations other than the color/whiteness binary should be explored, configurations, I would argue, that are contained within the emergence of English nationalism and Tudor hegemony. As a way into exploring this issue, I offer a kind of sideways preamble—three representative texts from three different moments within the Tudor period.

Sir Thomas Malory's *Le morte d'Arthur*, published in 1485, is a nostalgic view of a political and social ideal lost in past time. Sir Ector's lament for his dead brother, Sir Lancelot, provides a recital of the values that age held dear:

> And thou were the courteoust knight that ever bore shield! And thou were the truest friend to thy lover that ever bestrode horse, and thou were the truest lover of a sinful man that ever loved woman, and thou were the kindest man that ever struck with sword. And thou were the goodliest person that ever came among press of knights, and thou was the meekest man and the gentlest that ever ate in hall among ladies, and thou were the sternest knight to thy mortal foe that ever put spear in the rest. (157)

The chivalric code exemplified by Lancelot's life shows us a social system based on an elaborate code of manners, both in battle and out—an exclusive and elitist "club" that only the highest-born men could enter. Certainly not the reality in the war-ravaged England of 1485, it nevertheless was an attractive paradigm that Henry VII utilized in his crafting of the Tudor myth as an overlay upon his pragmatic consolidation of political and economic power.

Seventy-five years later, in 1560, William Baldwin, an outspoken reformer and pamphleteer, published a poem entitled *The Funerals of King Edward the Sixth*. Written shortly after the death of the sixteen-year-old king in 1553, it depicts England as a kind of Sodom and Gomorrah, which God punishes by taking away its virtuous king. In this poem, England is put in opposition to "the maynland . . . With Mahometrie and Idol blud embrewed" and found to be even more depraved. Baldwin appeals to the people of England to change their ways so that God may again, by his "speciall grace / [Make England] his wurd and chosens resting place" and "[power] on it such store / Of welthy giftes as none could wish for more" (69). In the years since the publication of *Le morte d'Arthur*, the picture of an idealized England has shifted from an emphasis upon social relations among the aristocracy to that of a wished-for Protestant-shaped morality displayed by all classes of people. Further, this morality is provided a counterpoint by the introduction of the "other" of Moslem and idolatry.

In 1588, Queen Elizabeth reviews her troops before the onslaught of the Armada. She calls her people "faithful and loving," in whose loyal hearts and goodwill is placed her chiefest strength. She asserts she is "resolved . . . to live or die amongst [them] all, and to lay down for my God and for my kingdom and for my people, my honour and my blood." Elizabeth's words provide yet another view of England and its people: she depicts not a social system, not a moral order, but a united culture, with a common God, a common code of ethics, and a common polity.[1]

Within this emerging national identity, as it is rendered in these three discursive "snapshots," we can also chart an emerging awareness of racial difference. However, this difference rests not on differences of color, but on differences within the concept of "whiteness." To begin exploring this idea, I would like first to call attention to three sites of debate within current scholarship. Whereas, prior to the early 1990s, the books and articles that addressed race as a category of analysis were scarce—and most started with the examination of the Moor as a character type in Renaissance drama—in the last several years, the situation has changed: one single-authored book and two edited collections, as well as numerous other articles in major Renaissance journals have appeared; the Modern Language Association and national and international conferences on Renaissance studies have featured sessions dedicated solely or partly to the topic; and conception of racial and race issues in early modern culture has extended itself beyond the figure of the Moor to representations of American Indians, Turks, Jews, and numerous peoples of Asian descent, as well as to an examination of "white" and "black" as ideological counterpoints in the culture. Issues of class and gender are recognized as important relatives to this research. Within the expanding inquiry of this topic, three questions concerning both content and methodology remain a constant presence:

1. A question grappled with in virtually every piece of scholarship on the subject, the interest in defining "race" itself as it has meaning in the early modern period cannot be neatly labeled, despite the disinterested scholar's desire to define terms clearly. Rather, this interrogation is a recurrent microcosm of our own culture's uneasiness with this particular aspect of difference. That race is a construct is a starting place for us all, and we all then "construct" what it is we mean by the term. One of the inherent ambiguities is the prevalent recognition that "race becomes more or less visible in early modern culture in the degree to which it is articulated through and articulates some other hegemonic category" (MacDonald 13)—such as gender, class, or nationality. If race is generally recognized only in relation to something else, exactly what is it we mean when we use the term? Kim Hall passionately argues that understanding such ambiguity and instability are as much a necessary aspect of our understanding of race in the early modern context as they are when we consider gender or class or any other category of analysis. While I am singularly attracted to this argument, it is important to remember that, as always, when flexibility rather than concreteness of idea is privileged, the category in question becomes susceptible to either erasure or appropriation.

2. We seem to have moved past the initial objection that race is a modern term that may not be anachronistically applied to early modern writing without an invalid reading. However, while we are theoretically aware that the construction of race includes the term whiteness as well as color, examination of whiteness in and of itself, without its binary of blackness or darkness, is absent. As Toni Morrison and others have persuasively argued, the category of whiteness must also be recognized and studied as the opposing other for racial categories. Substantial and excellent work is being

done on the other in race issues in early modern culture, but, with certain exceptions, the dominant and the primary culture that can be represented by the term whiteness is an unexamined site, unless it is brought in to define and clarify the "other."

3. A commonplace opening (or closing) for articles on the topic of race in early modern writings is a nod to critics' concentration on drama and, more specifically, on Shakespeare. Partly, this is due to the acceptance of the 1550s as the period when a discursive record about Africans in England first appears. While a scholar or two at times suggest alternatives to this time sequence, nevertheless, most students of the period find themselves mining works— and mostly dramatic works—written during the late-sixteenth and early-seventeenth centuries.

If we take seriously these three recurrent concerns in the scholarship about race in the early modern period—the indeterminacy of the term, the lack of attention to the racial question of whiteness, and the disproportionate attention on drama—I would suggest that an important next step in our collective intellectual enterprise is to contextualize and historicize the racialized texts in the Elizabethan period by foregrounding both Henrician and Edwardian discourse, especially humanist discourse. It is in the spirit of this reexamination that I spotlighted the three texts that opened this essay. Humanism as an intellectual movement was neither monolithic nor stable, so examining such texts using race as a critical term is fraught with minefields. However, humanism's importance as one of the significant cultural determinators for the period is critical, and therefore seminal, in the current effort to establish a scholarly discourse that addresses the racialized forces existing during the sixteenth century. The three texts I cited earlier—late medieval, mid-Reformation, and late Elizabethan—are interesting moments in the process by which the English nation began to consider itself a single collective: privileged (i.e., white), divinely blessed, and culturally and politically a unified entity.

While the discovery of the New World most manifestly inculcated an awareness of race in the English of the later-sixteenth century, its effect occurred within a world conditioned by the tenets of humanism in its variety of guises: as an educational regimen; as a return to origins, both biblical and classical; as a revaluing of public life and works. The elitism and conservatism of humanism in general meant that the few, rather than the many, were privileged, and this in turn resulted in a hierarchy closed to those who were not male, not educated, and not in the higher levels of society. Further, the rise of humanism was concurrent with a period of political and social flux in which feudal relationships were being redefined in terms of a centralized court and the nation-state. Such a world resulted in a discursive tendency to compartmentalize, to establish concrete identities, to build walls, to shut out. (Of course, the fact that this was also a period in which fluidity of movement characterized class structure serves only to reinforce this discursive evidence.) As the English began to be aware of themselves as a single entity with its own national identity, the culture simultaneously began to define anything "not-English" as dangerous and other. In other words, this world established itself as civilized, chosen—as white.

A cursory examination of seminal texts of this period reveal that the English national identity was being created in opposition to a series of threats to its culture, and these threats were presented both directly through polemic and indirectly through not-so-hidden fictions. As the English national identity was crystallized, the psychic boundaries of the people were also being circumscribed—against cultures, ideologies, even other national borders.

"The New Learning" of humanism, by its very name, puts into opposition forms of education and intellectual endeavor prevalent in England during the fifteenth century, especially prior to the accession of Henry VII, the first monarch to patronize fully those men who had been trained in the new philosophy. In counterpoint to the system of chivalry advanced in Malory's stories of King Arthur as elegant and courtly, the early humanists characterized the middle ages as barbarous and Gothic. As Roger Ascham said in his introduction to *Toxophilus*:

> "In our fathers tyme nothing was red, but bookes of fayned cheualrie, wherin a man by redinge, shuld be led to none other ende, but onely to manslaughter and baudrye." (xiv)

After the Reformation, English humanists literally demonized the influence of Roman Catholicism on humanist learning.

> "And yet ten *Morte Arthures* do not the tenth part so much harme, as one of these bookes, made in *Italie*, and translated in England. They open, not fond and common wayes to vice, but such subtle, cunnyng, new, and diuerse shiftes, to cary yong willes to vanitie, and yong wittes to mischief, to teach old bawdes new schole poyntes, as the simple

head of an English man is not hable to inuent, nor neuer was hard of
in England before, yea when Papistrie ouerflowed all." (231)

The Englishmen who are tempted to give in "to the inchantments
of Circes, brought out of Italy" have this said of them:

"And so, beyng Mules and Horses before they went [to Italy], returned
verie Swyne and Asses home agayne: yet euerie where verie Foxes with
suttle and busie heades; and where they may, verie wolues, with cruell
malicious hartes. A meruelous monster, which, for filthines of liuyng,
for dulnes to learning him selfe, for wilinesse in dealing with others,
for malice in hurting without cause, should carie at once in one bodie,
the belie of a Swyne, the head of an Asse, the brayne of a Foxe, the
wombe of a wolfe." (228)

In sum, this beast is not an Englishman: *Englese Italianato, e vn
diabolo incarnato*, that is, "The Italianate Englishman is the devil
incarnate."

Proponents of the new learning were also able to exploit political
or military events in such a way as to privilege English rule and
righteousness against an "other" entity. The relations with Scotland
provide several illustrations. In the early part of his reign, for example, Henry VIII made several moves to establish himself as one of
the leading sovereigns of Europe, invading France in 1513 in order
to reestablish England's claim on that country. This excursion into
France was perceived by the larger European community as largely
superfluous, and his minor victories at Therounne and Tournay in
some ways damaged rather than improved his reputation as a great
warrior king. However, a border skirmish with the Scots at Flodden
Field while Henry was in France, a skirmish resulting in the death
of King James IV and most of the Scottish aristocracy, became the
occasion for Henry's paid publicists, his court humanists, to situate
their monarch as a divinely appointed regent thwarting a vassal's
treason. More important, the victory provided the opportunity to
paint the Scots as uncivilized barbarians: John Skelton, for example, describes them as "rough-footed," as "drunken," as "ranke"
(i.e., coarse, crude, wanton), as ultimately as "gups" (cart horses).
The racist inflections in Skelton's several poetic diatribes against
the Scots, with few exceptions such as a short essay by Valerie
Allen, have generally received no comment, although Skelton repeatedly bestializes and demonizes the English enemy. While Skelton bestializes the Scots, his fellow humanists are even more
chauvinistic. Peter Carmeliano vilifies James IV because he has

violated a treaty with Henry, having entered England "veluti tur-cus / Saracenus / et Indus"—like a Turk, a Saracen, and Indian. In this case, the Scots, who look like the English and who speak the same language, are depicted as the most extreme "other." Ten years later, when the duke of Albany invaded England and then with-drew in apparent apprehension and concern about the English army's potency, Skelton reiterated his abuse in a court-commissioned piece that was clearly written to influence promi-nent nobility and gentry, not only of English military might and readiness, but also of its exceptional divine favor.

Political advice books address Englishness as well, although per-haps not as flagrantly. In his 1516 *Utopia*, Thomas More depicts an island people so remote from the rest of the world that they are virtually unknown. An obvious analogue to England, the country of Utopia is ostensibly an ideal as presented by Raphael Hythlo-daeus. Its isolation is the direct result of the action taken by Utopus, the country's conqueror and first king, who, immediately after his conquest, ordered a channel to be dug that would separate the land entirely from that of its neighbors: "the channels are known only to the Utopians, so hardly any strangers enter the bay without one of their pilots; and even they themselves could not enter safely if they did not direct themselves by some landmarks on the coast" (31). While there is a certain humor in the idea that the native sailors themselves have difficulty navigating the channels around their own island, More accurately identifies an inherent solipsism and cultural inward-lookingness that endangers any kind of sympa-thy and tolerance of other cultures. And indeed, Utopia is charac-terized by an extreme kind of solipsistic synergy: it enslaves its people who try to leave; it rewards conformity and compliance and punishes idiosyncrasy and individuality; it has no curiosity about other peoples or cultures. This fiction is England to the extreme, perhaps England only as it was in danger of becoming, but England nevertheless.

Once Henry VIII breaks from the Roman church in the 1530s, Protestant polemics continue the process of creating a reformed and divinely marked England, particularly by demonizing any-thing and anyone connected with the Catholic church. Hence, in one ribald polemic by Luke Shepherd, the Mass is personified as the granddaughter of Pluto, illegitimate daughter of the pope, and niece of Mohammed (*The Upcheringe of the Messe*, ca. 1548), "oth-ering" the principal ritual of the Roman church by applying three different categories: pagan, Roman Catholic, and Moslem. In William Baldwin's *Beware the Cat* (1552), Ireland is the antithesis of right religion and civilized behavior, embracing superstition and heathen ritual; in fact, Baldwin's Ireland here parallels the England of his *Funerals of Edward VI.* Roger Ascham's well-known vilification of Italians, a part of which I quoted above, turns on the tendency of Englishmen to be corrupted and thus to lose their "Englishness."

Later in the century, awareness that England was unique from other European countries in its lack of internal strife prompted numerous popular ballads and pamphlets to be printed, extolling England as God's chosen country. For example, in 1579, Thomas Churchyard published a work entitled *The Miserie of Flaunders, Calamities of Fraunce, Misfortune of Portugall, Vnquietnes of Irelande, Troubles of Scotlande: And the blessed state of Englande.* A series of tedious poems in fourteeners, the subject and theme of the work is manifest in its title. A consciousness of difference permeates the work, which ends with these lines:

> O Englande, thou art blest in deede,
> Thy necke is free from yoke:
> Thy armes are strong, thy body sounde,
> And in good howre be spoke . . .
> More blessed than thy neighbours all,
> By proof thou art as yet,
> More likely art thou by that cause,
> In peace and reste to sit.   (sig. Eii^v)

Other like publications were precipitated by various crises in the reign, such as Elizabeth's excommunication from the Roman Church and the Ridolfi Plot in 1570, the Babington Plot in 1586, the Essex Rebellion in 1601, and, of course, the threat of the Spanish Armada in 1588, the latter of which precipitated Elizabeth's (possibly apocryphal) words, which I quoted earlier.

These various texts collectively depict whatever opposes the humanist regimen as monstrous, depraved, and treacherous. On the other hand, English identity is evinced as normal, virtuous, and loyal. Englishness is civilized and cultured; not-English is rude and barbaric. The cultural, ideological, and religious space in which humanist discourse situates Englishness, a space that relies on hierarchies of whiteness, is a precondition against which "race" as a construct may be defined. Such a consciousness of a national and cultural identity, even as it is in the process of being forged, shapes the construction of race we see in texts produced in the late-sixteenth and early-seventeenth centuries.

We are currently experiencing a renaissance of sorts in scholarship on the reigns of the early Tudors. Perhaps sparked by John King's *English Reformation Literature* in 1982, which focuses on the literature written during King Edward VI's brief reign, we also now have available several books on the Henrys, but particularly Henry VIII: Alistair Fox's *Politics and Literature in the Reigns of Henry VII and Henry VIII* and Greg Walker's *Plays of Persuasion: Drama and Politics at the Court of Henry VIII* and *Persuasive Fictions: Faction, Faith, and Political Culture in the Reign of Henry VIII*, as well as edited collections by Alistair Fox and John Guy, by Daniel Williams, and by Peter C. Herman. Several books have focused solely on single authors, such as John Skelton (Walker's *John Skelton and the Politics of the 1520's* and Arthur Kinney's *John Skelton, Priest as Poet*), Thomas Starkey (Thomas Mayer's *Thomas Starkey and the Commonwealth*), and Thomas Wolsey (Peter Gwyn's *The King's Cardinal*), while others have examined discrete aspects of the culture of the late-fifteenth and early-sixteenth centuries: David Carlson's *English Humanist Books* and John King's *Tudor Royal Iconography*, to cite two particular examples. There have also been numerous books reconsidering the reformation in England: to name just a few, Anne Hudson's *The Premature Reformation*, Peter Lake and Maria Dowling's edited *Protestantism and the National Church in Sixteenth-Century England*, and Joseph S. Block's *Factional Politics and the English Reformation, 1520–1540*.

In very few cases do any of these books call attention to the production and reception of racial texts created during this earliest part of the early modern period. Roland Greene calls attention to how Petrarchism's intense interest in desire, domination, and conquest is paradigmatic of the colonial enterprise, thus contextualing Wyatt's lyrics within his native country's contacts with the New World; Thomas Mayer notices that, in his description of an ideal commonwealth, Thomas Starkey sets up binaries between a people who live "lyke wylde bestys in the woodys wythout lawys & rulys of honesty" and "a polytyke ordur of a multytude conspyryng togyddur in vertue & honesty" (120); Peter Gwyn notes how discourse in the early decades of the sixteenth century depicts the Irish and the Welsh as "wilde men," uncivilized and barbaric in looks, language, and custom, and consequently separate from the English (237). However, these discussions are the exception. The various antithetical forces of the period have simply not been examined as examples of racialized or preracialized polarities. For example, the Tudor Myth, which espouses that Henry VII is the literal descendant of the legendary King Arthur, whose prophesied return was promised to ignite a British resurgence, also works to legitimize and celebrate the colonized natives of England in opposition to the rule of the Norman French. Further, while in apparent opposition to the humanist view of history as secular and human-centered, this "myth" contributed to the rise of Anglo-Saxon studies later in the century, which more firmly established the English national people as ancient and distinguished descendants of Germanic peoples, and as uniquely equipped to provide leadership to the various peoples of the world. These cultural ways demarcating the English cooperated with the efforts of the early reformers to mark themselves as followers of the one true church, but this antagonism, too, is not discussed as a kind of antecedent acknowledgment of racial difference. Likewise, the on-again, off-again battles between England and France, and England and Scotland, and the incipient threat of the Holy Roman Empire in the person of Philip II receive considerable attention, but again, not within the bounds of race analysis. If cultural reception has been the focus of race analysis of early modern texts up to this point, it is necessary to review cultural production as well, and not just cultural production at the moment of composition or of publication, but actual creation of the culture itself as much as it can be recalled and reconstituted.

The racialized discourse of the late-sixteenth century and later was not generated spontaneously, but was a constituent piece in a culture that had long been fraught with tensions between itself and "others" in areas of religion, politics, language, and custom. As hierarchies of whiteness were established, such as English/Scottish, English/Italian, and English/Irish, a kind of racial awareness began to emerge. How the more familiar concept of racial difference itself connects to these older tensions is a question that we have only begun to ask with any frequency. In asking and in finding answers to such a question, we continue to demarcate this fascinating and rather new (to us) aspect of the early modern period, and in the process, discover anew the world we think we know.

Note

1. Susan Frye has recently initiated a lively debate concerning the authenticity of this very famous speech (see both Frye and Green in Works Cited). Whether

the speech is apocryphal or authentic, my principal point stands—and in fact, if the speech indeed was later invented and ascribed to the queen at this moment of national crisis, it makes all the more convincing my comments regarding the English national identity at the turn of the seventeenth century.

Works Cited

Allen, Valerie. "'Scot' as a Term of Abuse in Skelton's *Against Dundas*." *Studia Neophilologica* 59 (1987): 19–23.

Ascham, Roger. *The Scholemaster*. 1904; rpt. *Roger Ascham: English Works*, edited by William Aldis Wright. Cambridge: Cambridge University Press, 1970.

———. *Toxophilus*. 1904; rpt. *Roger Ascham: English Works*, edited by William Aldis Wright. Cambridge: Cambridge University Press, 1970.

Baldwin, William. *Beware the Cat: The First English Novel*. Edited by William A. Ringler, Jr., and Michael Flachmann. San Marino, Calif.: Huntington Library, 1988.

———. *Beware the Cat* and *The Funerals of King Edward the Sixth*. Edited by William P. Holden. New London: Connecticut College, 1963.

Block, Joseph S. *Factional Politics and the English Reformation, 1520–1540*. Woodbridge, Suffolk: Boydell Press, 1993.

Carlson, David R. *English Humanist Books: Writers and Patrons, Manuscript and Print, 1475–1525*. Toronto: University of Toronto Press, 1993.

Carmeliano, Peter. "Epitaphium Iacoobi Regis Scotorum." In "Print into Manuscript: A Flodden Field News Pamphlet (British Library MS Additional 29506)." By Nancy Gutierrez and Mary Erler. *Studies in Medieval and Renaissance History* 8 (1987): 189–229. [Carmeliano's poem appears on p. 229.]

Churchyard, Thomas.*The Miserie of Flavnders, Calamitie of Fraunce, Misfortune of Portugall, Vnquietnes of Irelande, Troubles of Scotland: And the blessed State of Englande*. 1579.

Fox, Alistair. *Politics and Literature in the Reigns of Henry VII and Henry VIII*. Oxford: Basil Blackwell, 1989.

Fox, Alistair, and John Guy, eds. *Reassessing the Henrician Age: Humanism, Politics and Reform, 1500–1550*. Oxford: Basil Blackwell, 1986.

Frye, Susan. "The Myth of Elizabeth at Tilbury." *Sixteenth Century Journal* 23 (1992): 95–114.

Green, Janet M. "'I My Self': Queen Elizabeth I's Oration at Tilbury Camp." *Sixteenth Century Journal* 28 (1997): 421–45.

Greene, Roland. "The Colonial Wyatt: Contexts and Openings." In *Rethinking the Henrician Era: Essays on Early Tudor Texts and Contexts*, edited by Peter C. Herman, 240–66. Urbana: University of Illinois Press, 1994.

Gwyn, Peter. *The King's Cardinal: The Rise and Fall of Thomas Wolsey*. London: Barrie and Jenkins, 1990.

Hall, Kim F. *Things of Darkness: Economies of Race and Gender in Early Modern England*. Ithaca: Cornell University Press, 1995.

Hendricks, Margo, and Patricia Parker, eds. *Women, "Race," and Writing in the Early Modern Period*. London: Routledge, 1994.

Herman, Peter C., ed. *Rethinking the Henrician Era: Essays on Early Tudor Texts and Contexts*. Urbana: University of Illinois Press, 1994.

Hudson, Anne. *The Premature Reformation: Wycliffite Texts and Lollard History.* Oxford: Clarendon Press, 1988.

King, John N. *English Reformation Literature: The Tudor Origins of the Protestant Tradition.* Princeton: Princeton University Press, 1982.

——. *Tudor Royal Iconography: Literature and Art in an Age of Religious Crisis.* Princeton: Princeton University Press, 1989.

Kinney, Arthur F. *John Skelton, Priest as Poet: Seasons of Discovery.* Chapel Hill: University of North Carolina Press, 1987.

Lake, Peter, and Maria Dowling, eds. *Protestantism and the National Church in Sixteenth-Century England.* London: Croom Helm, 1987.

MacDonald, Joyce Green, ed. *Race, Ethnicity, and Power in the Renaissance.* Madison, N.J.: Fairleigh Dickinson University Press, 1997.

Malory, Thomas. *Malory: Le morte d'Arthur. (Pts. 7 and 8).* Edited by D. S. Brewer. Evanston, Ill.: Northwestern University Press, 1974.

Mayer, Thomas. *Thomas Starkey and the Commonwealth.* Cambridge: Cambridge University Press, 1989.

More, Thomas. *Utopia.* Translated and edited by Robert M. Adams. 2d ed. New York: W. W. Norton and Company, 1992.

Morrison, Toni. *Playing in the Dark: Whiteness and the Literary Imagination.* Cambridge: Harvard University Press, 1992.

Skelton, John "Agaynst the Scottes," "A Ballade of the Scottysshe Kynge," and "Howe the Douty Duke of Albany." *The Complete English Poems,* edited by John Scattergood. Harmondsworth, Middlesex: Penguins Books, 1983.

——. "Chorus de Dys contra Scottos." In *The Latin Writings of John Skelton.* Edited by David Carlson. *Studies in Philology,* Texts and Studies, LXXXVIII, no. 4 (1991).

Shepherd, Luke. *The Upcheringe of the Messe.* Ca. 1548.

Walker, Greg. *John Skelton and the Politics of the 1520s.* Cambridge: Cambridge University Press, 1988.

——. *Plays of Persuasion: Drama and Politics at the Court of Henry VIII.* Cambridge: Cambridge University Press, 1991.

——. *Persuasive Fictions: Faction, Faith, and Political Culture in the Reign of Henry VIII.* Aldershot, Hants: Scolar Press, 1996.

Williams, Daniel, ed. *Early Tudor England: Proceedings of the 1987 Harlaxton Symposium.* Woodbridge, Suffolk: Boydell Press, 1989.

"Black and White and 'Read' All Over"

JUDITH A. LÓPEZ

IN 1992, prompted by the most recent Los Angeles riots, *Time* magazine published an article written by George J. Church entitled "The Fire This Time" (11 May 1992). The subtitle to this article read, "As Los Angeles smolders, black and white Americans around the country try to comprehend the verdict and the future of race relations" (24). What followed was a narrative piece on "race" interspersed with questions such as, "If you had been on the jury, how would you have voted?" and "Before the verdict was announced, what did you think it would be?" Those asked to respond to these questions were either "black" or "white." I found myself so irritated by this article, that I did something I rarely do. I wrote an angry letter in response to what I believed was a ridiculous inability to recognize the existence of more than two "races." Almost a month later, an associate editor wrote to thank me for my letter and to defend the article as representing the opinions of those most involved. This response seemed strange to me, largely because, it seemed as though network television had gone out of its way during the riots, to produce numerous images of Korean shopkeepers with guns and Latinos looting disposable diapers.

Nevertheless, both the *Time* article and their response to my letter enacted a reductive binarism that continues to persist in American discussions of race, despite the current and somewhat bewildering willingness to acknowledge the existence of persons of mixed race. Even so, this "new" conversation is usually framed as a continuing story, as though mixed heritage is a recent phenomenon. In May of 1997, *Time* magazine published an article written by Jack E. White entitled "I'm Just Who I Am" (5 May 1997). The subtitle to this article read, "White Black Asian Other, Race is *no longer* as simple as Black or White. So, what does this mean for America?" (emphasis mine). White observes,

> In one grandiose vision, shared by conservative analyst Douglas Besh-
> arov of the American Enterprise Institute and communitarian sociolo-

gist Amitai Etzioni of American University, the ambiguous racial identity of mixed-race children may be "the best hope for the future of American race relations," as Besharov puts it. Letting people define themselves as multiracial, Etzioni argues, has the potential to soften the racial lines that now divide America by rendering them more like economic differences and less like harsh, almost immutable, caste lines." Those who blend many streams of ethnicity within their own bodies, the argument goes, will render race a meaningless concept, providing a biological solution to the problem of racial justice. (33)

Contrary to the opinions expressed above, mixed heritage is not some "new technology" whereby race can someday be eliminated altogether. People of mixed heritage have always existed, and thankfully, I see no evidence of the bizarre racial "progress" to which both Besharov and Etzioni aspire. Whereas their vision attempts to erase race, George J. Church attempts to contain it.

In the middle of his article, Church makes the following curious comment: "To many blacks, the fact that the non-guilty verdicts were handed down by a jury that included no blacks (though it did have one Asian and one Hispanic) virtually proves that the criminal-justice system is ruled by bias and that they cannot look to it for fair treatment" (23). Church's statement oddly posits that the nearest thing to a "black" is an "Asian" or a "Hispanic." In fact, in like discussions of race, blacks are frequently represented as prototypically "other" and serve as "stand-ins" for all people of color. As a friend and colleague reminds me, its seems as though we as "postmodern" subjects should understand and readily accept contradictory and fragmented identity. In other words, we in the late-twentieth century are poised to see beyond black and white; however, somehow, our work the arrangement of our academies into departments, continues to retreat to the comfortable binarism of black and white.

One of the obvious limitations of race as it is discussed and understood in much of America is its contribution to our inability to see the complexity and importance of a developing discourse of race in the pre-and early modern periods, and the subsequent characterization of such a study as yet another ridiculous outcome of curriculum devoted to multiculturalism. Furthermore, the reductive and contemporary view of race also allows for the designation of a handful of pre-and early modern texts as "race" texts—that is to say, texts that are assumed "appropriate" to the discussion of race. The most obvious examples in the Shakespeare canon include, *Othello*, *The Tempest*, and *The Merchant of Venice* (hereafter

Merchant). In fact, *Othello* has come to represent "black experience"; *The Tempest* is believed to represent the colonization of the New World; and *Merchant* is regarded as a text of choice for those studying the representation of Jews. What I hope to illustrate is that even the reading of a so-called race text such as *Merchant* requires the recognition of multiple and fragmented identities and pushes a conventional modern understanding of"race" beyond its limitations of some prototypical other versus white. In fact, a consideration of race in the pre-and early modern period eventually necessitates a reconsideration of the boundaries of race in the modern and postmodern period. Ultimately, my objection to a discussion of race that begins by establishing a dichotomy between black and white is that it obscures the prominent intersection between race and religion, which is perhaps more obvious in the pre-and early modern period, but is nonetheless still evident in the modern.

*   *   *

> *Racism of the modern type only began in the 15th century, when Portuguese ships started to outflank Islamic power by sailing round the coast of West Africa and immediately began kidnaping anybody they could find and taking them back to Portugal to sell as slaves. Their justification for this was that they were prisoners of a just war and any war fought by Christians against non-Christians qualified as a just war. Quite soon however, a new justification grew up, that of racism.*—Martin Bernal, "Race in History" (82).

> Race is one of the central conceptual inventions of modernity. . . . By modernity, I will mean throughout that general period emerging from the sixteenth century. . . . The modern project accordingly emerges as and in terms of a broad sweep of sociointellectual conditions. These include the commodification and capital accumulation of market-based society, the legal formation of private property and systems of contract, the moral and political conception of rational self-interested subjects, and the increasing replacement of God and religious doctrine by Reason and Nature. David Theo Goldberg, *Racist Culture: Philosophy and the Politics of Meaning* (3).

Critics and theorists often segregate the discussion of race from the discussion of religion. After all, many of those critics theorizing race posit its origin in modernity and the modern move toward the secular and physical, away from the religious and metaphysical. Other commentators suggest that the grouping of people by shared features prior to modernity is "ethnicity" and the grouping of people after modernity is "race." In this regard, "ethnicity" includes features usually characterized as "cultural," and "race" includes features usually characterized as "physical." In his summary of this critical trend, Bernal notes that religion falls among those features usually regarded as cultural:

> I shall begin with the concept of "race" in history but before I do so, I should like to try to distinguish ethnicity from racism. The word "ethnicity" is commonly used to denote the consciousness of solidarity beyond real or fictitious kinship, based on shared symbols or images; a particular territory, history, religion, flag, currency, law, etc. (75).

In addition, among the definitions of "cultural" found in *Webster's Third International Dictionary*, is the citation: "all humans are strongly influenced by cultural inheritance as well, which is transmitted *outside* the body, such as language, custom, education and so on—L. C. Dunn." (532), emphasis mine). Similarly, Goldberg observes that "[E]thnicity is the mode of cultural identification and distinction. . . . the interpretation of race seemingly most antithetical to this construal [is] the biological" (74–75). He concedes that "assigning significance to biological or physical attributes . . . is a cultural choice," and that "the biological in a sense becomes one among the possible cultural criteria for determining ethnicity," but insists on a delineation of ethnicity as "socially defined on the basis of cultural criteria" and race as "socially defined, but on the basis of physical criteria" (75). Neither Goldberg nor Bernal consider religion, particularly Christianity, as precisely that discourse which, by mandate, attempts to arbitrate between what is defined as "physical" and what is defined as "cultural." However, by concerning itself with the struggle between body and spirit, religion is, in a sense, mediating between the physical and cultural, and therefore figures prominently in any consideration of race.

In my current research, I am pursuing an explanation for the deviation between what I self-consciously call "a Catholic fantasy of race and miscegenation" and "a Protestant fantasy of race miscegenation" that borrows its scheme of ideological difference from theological understandings of sacrament. I say self-consciously because I acknowledge the urgent need to describe *discourse(s)* of Catholicism and Protestantism even as I make this argument. In short, I am intrigued by representations of religious conversion that both reflect theological differences among Christians during the Reformation and either transform or confirm a character's existing "racial" status. In several Catholic texts, conversion is portrayed as fixed and lasting. In addition, it is far more common to see conversion staged in literal terms. That is, a spiritual transformation is often registered physically. By contrast, Protestant texts more often separate the figurative from the literal in representations of conversion. Moreover, conversion in these texts is often avoided, challenged, temporary, or impossible. Ultimately, I want to suggest that the comparison of Catholic and Protestant fictional texts that portray conversion reveals a trend: Catholic representations of conversion conflate the figurative and the literal and Protestant texts maintain the boundary. This, in combination with what Goldberg argues is a growing association of race with phenotype (76), creates a scenario in which we can begin to see a difference between a Catholic racialized body and a Protestant racialized body. Interestingly, this "dialogue" does not take place on the bodies of Protestants or Catholics, but on the bodies of a third group: non-Christians.

To illustrate this point, I want to turn briefly to *Merchant*. This play has often been described as a play that moves toward the reconciliation of contradictory mythologies. Both Walter Cohen and to a greater extent, Lawrence Danson have argued that the play works toward and ultimately achieves a final resolution and reconciliation of disparate ideological beliefs. One imagines that Besharov and Etzioni might be impressed by such readings, for they render difference meaningless. However, with its overriding thematic emphasis on the difference between the spirit of the law and letter of the law, appropriate to read the *Merchant* as a play that instead articulates the anxiety of reconciliation or, more specifically, a particular Protestant anxiety about incorporation. In other words, *Merchant* expresses the fear that "to incorporate the alien. . . . is to admit poison into the body: the dualism of eater/ eaten is not transcended or sublimated through internalization, but perpetuated" (Kilgour 13). As Maggie Kilgour observes, incorporation begins with the absolute distinction between inside and outside and ends with the obliteration of this separation. In *Merchant*, the breakdown of the initial boundary between inside and outside threatens the perceived integrity of an existing body. Indeed, the whole symbolic economy of the play seems concerned with the maintenance of a distinction between inside and outside.

By order of her father's will, Portia, an heiress, is to marry that suitor who correctly selects one of three caskets. Each casket is made of a different material (gold, silver, lead) and bears an inscription that will assist only the most appropriate suitor. As the scroll inside the winning casket indicates, the riddle is predicated on a recognition of the difference between what the box *appears to be* on the outside and what it *is* on the inside: "You that choose not by the view, / Chance as fair and choose as true!" (3.2.131–132). Furthermore, those contestants, the princes of Morocco and Aragon, coming from areas geographically and culturally *outside* of Italy, are unable to make this distinction, while he who is already *inside* Italy and has been *inside* Belmont—Bassanio—solves the puzzle by upholding the delineation.

Among the "outsiders" on the "inside" is Shylock, a Jew, and as such a member of a group that defies many attempts to construct a verifiable difference between race and religion. As Paul Cantor notes,

> if we come to sympathize with Shylock, it will interfere with our feeling of comic resolution. Above all, if we feel that Shylock stands for a genuine principle, we will have at least something of a tragic impression at the end of the play. We will sense that the community has re-established itself only at the cost of excluding a legitimate point of view and thus narrowing its horizons. (240)

Moreover, by sympathizing with Shylock, we might also come to blur the distinction between "merchant" and "usurer" in which so many surrounding Shylock are invested. Even this distinction is tinged by the difference between literal and figurative. That is to say, merchants are perceived as exchanging something intangible, a service, for money. By contrast, usurers exchange money for more money. In addition, with his desire for an actual "a pound of flesh," and his declaration "But yet I'll go in hate, to feed upon / The prodigal Christian," (2.5.14–15), it seems as though Shylock resembles yet another group of purported literalists, the Catholics. The Protestant reading of Catholic transubstantiation critiques the inability to distinguish between an object's literal properties and its symbolic meaning (i.e., during the act of transubstantiation, the bread and wine used in the sacrament become rather than symbolize the body and blood of Christ, who is therefore truly present). Indeed, to insist on the presence of Christ's body during Eucharist was, to a Protestant, cannibalism. As Kilgour notes, "during the Middle ages the Jews were accused of cannibalism, after the Reformation the Catholics were" (5). In summary, both Catholics and Jews have been reproached for their inability to distinguish between what is said and done literally and what is said and understood symbolically. Nowhere in *Merchant* is this theological conflict more profound that in its depiction of conversion.

In *Merchant,* there are two significant conversions or, as I contend, "non conversions." It has been suggested that the action of *Merchant* moves toward the transformation of Jews and their replacement with newly converted Christians. I would argue the contrary: that conversion in this text is not easily confirmed.

In act 3, scene 5, Jessica, Shylock's daughter and his former servant, Launcelot Gobbo, engage in the following dialogue:

> *Launcelot Gobbo.*   Yes, truly, for, look you, the sins of the father are to be laid upon the children. Therefore, I promise ye, I fear you. I was always plain with you, and so now I speak my agitation of the matter. Therefore be of good cheer, for truly, I think you are damned. There is but one hope in that can do you any good, and that is but a kind of bastard hope neither.
>
> *Jessica.* And what hope is that, I pray thee?
>
> *Launcelot Gobbo.* Marry, you may partly hope that your father got you not, that you are not the Jew's daughter.
>
> *Jessica.* That were a kind of bastard hope, indeed. So the sins of my mother should be visited upon me.
>
> *Launcelot Gobbo.* Truly then I fear you are damned both by father and mother. Thus when I shun Scylla, your father, I fall into Charybdis, your mother. Well, you are gone both ways.
>
> *Jessica.* I shall be saved by my husband; he hath made me a Christian.
>
> *Launcelot Gobbo.* Truly, the more to blame he. We were Christians enow before, e'en as many as could well live, one by another. This make of Christians will raise the price of hogs. If we grow all to be pork-eaters, we shall not shortly have a rasher on the coals for money.
>
> (3.5.1–23)

In this brief scene, a number of religious discourses are in conflict. This is, after all, a text ostensibly about Jews and Venetian Christians (Catholics) written by an author from a Protestant nation. From a Catholic point of view, Launcelot Gobbo is quite wrong; Jessica can be converted to Christianity. However, from a Jewish perspective, he is both right and wrong. Within this faith/race, lineage is inherited not through the father, but through the mother. In other words, Jessica is Jewish not because her father is Jewish, but because her mother is. Therefore, at least in some sense, tricking, leaving, and renouncing her *father* is not enough to "get the job" of conversion "done." But from a Protestant point view, Launcelot Gobbo is quite correct. Within Protestant theology, marriage is not a sacrament as it is in Catholicism. Jessica and Lorenzo's union is not "the outward and visible sign of an internal and spiritual grace" (Goring, 449). There is no "change involving a transformation and reorientation [that] affects every aspect" of her life (118). Therefore, from a Protestant perspective, Jessica is not truly converted or transformed.

In the middle of this conversation between Jessica and Launcelot Gobbo, Lorenzo enters. Jessica summarizes their discussion and Lorenzo responds,

> Lorenzo. I shall answer the better to the commonwealth than you can the getting up of the negro's belly. The Moor is with child by you, Launcelot.
> Launcelot Gobbo. It is much that the Moor should be more than reason. But if she be less than an honest woman, she is indeed more than I took her for. (3.5.33–38)

With this exchange, yet another faith/race is added to the multivehicle pileup of religion and kind. Interestingly, the theological *custom* of Jessica's lineal faith is made *visible* by reference to the *invisible* and unrepresentable female Moor. Lynda Boose has observed that

> In terms of the ideological assumptions of a culture such as that of early modern England, the black male-white female union is not the narrative that requires suppression. What challenges the ideology substantially enough to require erasure is that of the black female-white male, for it is in the person of the black woman that the culture's pre-existing fears both about the female sex and about gender dominance are realized. . . . [N]not only was black more powerful than white and capable of absorbing and coloring it, but that in this all-important arena of reproductive authority, the black women controlled the power to resignify all offspring as the property of the mother. (46)

The "identities" of both women suggest that lineage is matrilineal. Therefore, Launcelot Gobbo's denial of Jessica's conversion is an expression informed by Protestant theology and a defense of male parthenogenesis. It also potentially constructs a "logic" by which Launcelot Gobbo might deny he is the father of the Moor's child. Furthermore, by diverting the discussion to Launcelot Gobbo's situation, Lorenzo is relying on the power of *visibility* to disguise and distance what is *theologically* true of his own situation.

The conversion of Shylock also raises issues about what is visible and invisible. In this regard, it seems rather significant that there are no textual directions requiring the enactment of Shylock's conversion onstage. In fact, the Duke's comment, "Get thee gone, but do it" (4.1.393), would suggest that Shylock could leave the stage immediately after he signs half his wealth over to Antonio. Moreover, there are no textual directions returning Shylock to the stage after his "conversion." Therefore, it can be argued that the ordered and forced spiritual transformation is never made visible.

Ultimately, the threat posed by Shylock and his potential incorporation has to do with the act of "delineation" itself. To allow Shylock into the social body is to expose how similar "his" practices *already* are to "theirs." Shylock argues,

> What judgement shall I dread, doing no wrong?
> You have among you many a purchas'd slave
> Which, like your asses and your dogs and mules,
> You use in abject and in slavish parts
> Because you bought them. Shall I say to you,
> "Let them be free, marry them to your heirs!"
>
> (4.1.89–94)

As Kilgour observes, the risk of incorporating the other is a threat not only to national identity, but also to individual identity—that is, the inability to tell who's who. Rather than moving toward the absorption and reconciliation of disparate ideologies, both these "non-conversions" suggest that the text allows for the alienation of "Jews" and other "foreign" beings, thereby successfully preventing both their incorporation and the recognition of how much they are already the same. Moreover, it does so by attempting to distinguish what is physically and literally so from what is theoretically, spiritually, and figuratively so.

My point is simply this: *Merchant of Venice* is no more a play specifically and only about Jews and Christians than the Los Angeles riots were a struggle simply between blacks and whites. Just as Church encourages us to read the story of the Los Angeles riots as a conflict between blacks and whites, there is a discouraging trend in criticism of the pre-and early modern period to read *Merchant* as a story only about Jews and Christians. Similar examples can be found for all "race" texts, and indeed can be said to participate in the characterization of some texts as appropriate to the study of race whereas others are not. In my own work, I speculate that the representation of non-Christian bodies is never only about the difference between non-Christians and Christians, but also an attempt to delineate between types of Christianity. I also suggest that it is difficult, perhaps impossible, to distinguish between racial and religious identities. What I see in *Merchant* is a struggle to construct and maintain competing claims of what is outside a community and what is inside a community. However, any attempt to define the community is slippery at best, because it cannot account for the multiple and fluid attempts to change identities throughout the play. What I see in Church's article is the assumption that fixed and definable communities already exist, and that people are obviously and happily divided into prototypically black and white groups. The failure to see a pre-and early modern discourse of race informed by more than just color is a consequence of a rather obvious but effective modern binarism that is read back onto the past. The ultimate irony is that an American contemporary mind framed by the insistent dichotomy of black and white interferes with the also present postmodern goal of reading texts multifariously.

Works Cited

Bernal, Martin. "Race in History." In *Global Convulsions: Race, Ethnicity, and Nationalism at the End of the Twentieth Century.* edited by Winston A. Van Horne, 75–92. Albany: State University New York Press, 1997.

Boose, Lynda. "The Getting of a Lawful Race": Racial discourse in early modern England and the Unrepresentable Black Woman." In *Women, "Race," and Writing in the Early Modern Period,* edited by Margo Hendricks and Patricia Parker, 35–54. London: Routledge, 1994.

Cantor, Paul. "Religion and the Limits of Community in The *Merchant of Venice.*" *Soundings* 70 (1987): 239–58.

Church, George J. "The Fire This Time." *Time* 139 (11 May 1992): 18–25.

Cohen, Walter. "The *Merchant of Venice* and the possibilities of Historic Criticism." *English Literary History* 49 (1982): 765–89.

Danson, Lawrence. *The Harmonies of The Merchant of Venice.* New Haven: Yale University Press, 1978.

Goldberg, David Theo. *Racist Culture: Philosophy and the Politics of Meaning.* Cambridge, Mass: Blackwell Publishers, 1993.

Goring, Rosemary, ed. *The Wordsworth Dictionary of Beliefs and Religions.* Hertfordshire: Wordsworth Editions, 1995.

Kilgour, Maggie. *From Communion to Cannibalism: An Anatomy of Metaphors of Incorporation.* Princeton: Princeton University Press, 1990.

Shakespeare, William. *The Merchant of Venice.* Edited by John Russell Brown. London: Methuen and Co., 1955.

White, Jack E. "I'm Just Who I Am." *Time* 149 (5 May 1997): 32–35.

The "End of Race" and the Future of Early Modern Cultural Studies

FRANCESCA T. ROYSTER

TIGER Woods's twelve-shot victory at the 1997 Masters Golf Tournament took place at the Augusta National, "'a club that no black man was allowed to join until six years ago, at the tournament whose founder, Clifford Roberts, once said, 'As long as I'm alive, golfers will be white, and caddies will be black'" (Reilly 1977, 35). At twenty-one, Woods has clearly shaken up the popular image of golf—both with his precocious skills and with his race. The reality may be that golf is played on public courses, taken for college credit, and enjoyed by a variety of men and women all around the world. But it is no revelation that the sport's mystique is maintained by its association with the Exclusive Country Club, the rare but not obliterated site of racial segregation and carefully policed class boundaries.

Indeed, some commentators have embraced Tiger Woods as a spokesperson for race relations in the 1990s. There have been a number of comparisons made in the press between Woods and Jackie Robinson. But more than taking on the legacy of Robinson and other color-line breakers, Woods became an icon for all sides: for race, nonrace, and mixed race. After Frank "Fuzzy" Zoeller publicly dismissed Woods as "boy," along with other racial slurs, a boycott campaign ensued against K-Mart, which carried a line of golf clothing and equipment endorsed by Zoeller. Without fanfare, K-Mart dumped the line. Soon after his coup at the Masters, Woods set off a flurry of controversy on *The Oprah Winfrey Show* by insisting that he was "Cablinasian" (his own Caliban-like acronym for his Caucasian, black, American Indian, Thai, and Chinese roots). In a story that followed the *Oprah* episode, *Time* magazine used Woods's acronym as an example of how America is becoming a "melding [sic] pot"—the sign of a future where race may be so ambiguous as not to matter (White 1997, 33).

It is not clear to me that Woods's identification with several racial identities is an indication that we have reached a point in history when race does not matter (though *Time's* representation of mixed race as "news" caters to a general public ignorance of the history of race and its social construction). Wood's racial fluidity has lent itself to the marketing of his image as an icon of race "neutrality." I cannot help but notice how quickly Woods's success has been sculpted into an orthodox and "colorless" narrative of uplift. In contrast to the racialist images of deadbeat dads and welfare mothers that occupy America's imagination, Tiger's parents, Earl and Kultida, gave steady attention and discipline to their young prodigy, beginning his golf swing lessons in the high chair. Earl Woods, whose child-rearing techniques are described in his recent book, *Training a Tiger*, credits Tiger's success to consistent shows of affection combined with lessons of military discipline culled from Earl's Green Beret training (Woods 1997). Kultida stayed home from work to raise their child full-time. Not surprisingly, as smoothly as Tiger slipped into his green Masters' champion jacket, Woods's upbringing has been shaped into an exemplar of race-neutral family values. The battle of the country clubs fades into the background.

Tiger's formula for success, it turns out, is one that any family could follow: discipline, affection and family involvement. Even Earl Woods' confession that Tiger asked him to check out the pretty women among the spectators while he plays smacks of the banality of a rock video. This is not to say that it does not matter to America that Tiger Woods is not white, but that America's stamina for reflexive racial analysis is short.

Why bring up Tiger Woods in this context of the future of race in Shakespeare and early modern English studies? In the essay that follows, I want to suggest that the narrative of racial transcendence in the Tiger Woods story betrays a larger impatience with race and race studies. Like golf, until early modern English studies relatively recently has been an "unraced" enterprise. (I put "unraced" in quotation marks to call attention to the deceptiveness of the term and those like it, including those words that I have just used: *race neutral* and *colorless*.) As recently as 1992, critic Kim Hall could describe black studies in early modern literature as "Writing What Isn't There." Hall was responding to the widespread critical assumption that there was no such thing as racial identity in early modern England.

Frustratingly enough, at the same historical moment when early modern cultural studies has accepted race, or at least "race," as a viable paradigm to explore the construction of identity, other public intellectuals—some from within the American academy and some without—have proclaimed that "race" has run its course: from Dinesh D' Souza (*The End of Racism*) and Ellis Cose (*Color-Blind: Seeing Beyond Race in a Race-Obsessed World*) to theater critic Robert Brustein, who has debated with August Wilson on color blind-casting and the African American Theater. (Perhaps it is telling that in the past twenty years we have seen the publication of two books titled *The End of Culture* and five separate books called *The End of History.*) This desire to declare the ending of race and, with it, history and culture, seems to be a mass end-of-the-century phenomenon to wipe the slate clean of the cultural and political conflicts and tensions engendered by past inequities.

In his essay "The Cultural Logic of Late Capitalism," Frederic Jameson has argued that the we are living in a moment where the subject has lost its ability to organize its past and its future into coherent experience (Jameson 1995, 25). The result is a crisis in historicity—in effect, a "libidinal historicism." For Jameson, libidinal historicism is "an elaborated symptom of the waning of our historicity, of our lived possibility of experiencing history in some active way" (21). As I will discuss, the backlash against multiculturalism in academia and the popular press has exacerbated this crisis in historicity.

As I noted earlier, some critics have already proclaimed the "death knell" of race studies in academia, or at least sounded the warning bell of atrophy. For example, in his review of Henry Louis Gates's most recent work, including *The Norton Anthology of African American Literature*, Vince Passaro warns that African American studies may face the constraints of orthodoxy at the very moment of its greatest influence in American universities and the culture at large. Passaro argues that Gates in particular has been able to make great changes in publishing and in the shape of African American studies departments, but all the while undergoing "a continual, quick-footed dance with political orthodoxy—an orthodoxy now less obviously tilted toward a distinct ruling class than it once was, yet more often riddled with internal contradictions" (Passaro 1997, 71).

While early modern race studies has not enjoyed the wide public recognition of African American studies, there too has been some suggestion that early modern race studies is already in danger of losing its radical edge. The newest *Norton Shakespeare*, edited by Stephen Greenblatt, Walter Cohen, Jean E. Howard, and Katherine Eisaman Maus, includes a five-page section in its introduction entitled "The English and Otherness." ("Otherness" in this case includes racial difference, though the editors do not choose to isolate race in the subtitle.) Topics include early modern England's flailing colonial efforts in Ireland, the trial of Elizabeth I's doctor, Roderigo Lopez, the use of blackamores in Jacobean entertainments, and Drake's expedition to the New World. In the *Chronicle of Higher Education*, James Shapiro writes that the new *Norton Shakespeare* "is testament to a revolution in Shakespeare studies over the past twenty years, as textual scholars, feminists, theater historians, and cultural historians have overturned prevailing orthodoxies. Now they constitute the orthodoxy" (Shapiro 1997, B36).

If early modern race studies and other forms of multiculturalism have lost their critical edge, some could not be happier. At least that seems to be the sentiment behind the recent hullabaloo spawned by the National Alumni Forum's study "The Shakespeare File: What English Majors are *Really* Studying." The study reported that less than half of seventy surveyed universities required their English majors to take a Shakespeare course. The report was released to the public in January 1997 and stirred the passions of many critics of multiculturalism. Jonathan Yardley, a writer for the *Washington Post*, seemed particularly disturbed by what he perceived was the replacement of Shakespeare by writers like Toni Morrison, Aphra Behn, and Jane Anger. Castigating universities like Dartmouth and Georgetown as "academic whorehouses," Yardley exclaimed, "The sheer vulgarity of that is beyond description: Shakespeare and Toni Morrison as equals!" (1997, 2). On the heels of the National Alumni Forum's report came several stories reassuring the public that Shakespeare is more popular than ever. Norton publishers released the statistic that more than fifty thousand copies of Shakespeare editions were purchased for academic study last year alone.

In David Gates's opinion piece "Dead White Man of the Year," he similarly misconstrues the project of race studies and other forms of multiculturalism while dismissing their impact. As represented in pieces such as Gates's and Yardley's, considerations of race in early modern studies are often linked to affirmative action and thus have to do with quotas and "representation": with killing Shakespeare, the consummate "dead white Male," and replacing him with women, people of color, queer writers, and other under represented figures. Gates characterizes recent theoretical innovations in Shakespeare studies as a kind of hostage crisis—though at least the captive has been kept alive: "though a couple of years ago multiculturalists had supposedly frog-marched" Shakespeare out of school curriculums, the "postcolonialists, feminists and specialists in 'queer studies'" have kept Shakespeare studies alive by "rop-[ing] him in as either a fellow subversive or No. 1 whipping boy" (Gates 1996–1997, 52). The proliferating images of erotic debasement that appear in Gates's and Yardley's pieces (Shakespeare roped-in and whipped by academic subversives, students serviced by "academic whorehouses") threaten to overcome the coherence of their arguments and reduce the larger issues of historical and literary representation to emotional responses like shock, fear, and shame.

Rather than succumb to the "hysteria" of individuals like Gates and Yardley, I want to argue that the future of race studies in early modern literature depends on our ability to negotiate the larger public's suspicion of multiculturalism's relevance to the past and with it, to historicize the gendered and racialized aspects of these suspicions. In other words, the future of Shakespeare studies and early modern English studies depends on engagements with this moment of libidinal historicity—not by forcing coherence between the present and the past, but precisely by exposing the points of crisis with our own sense of racial categorization. The insistence of the past's relevance to the present is at the foundation of early modern race study's formative texts. Seminal studies of race in early modern culture, including Ania Loomba's *Gender, Race, Renaissance Drama*; Margo Hendricks and Patricia Parker's edited volume *Women, "Race" and Writing in Early Modern England*, Kim Hall's *Things of Darkness*, Joyce Greene MacDonald's edited *Race, Ethnicity, and Power in the Renaissance*, have already begun the project. The authors of these texts share an interest in bridging the historical gulf between early modern studies, postcolonial theory, and other disciplines such as African American studies, gender studies, and cultural studies, for example. And, in doing so, this work also foregrounds the slipperiness of terms like race as we make that bridge. We must continue such vigilance as we juggle the demands of historical accuracy with present cultural currency. When we look at the cultural history of *Othello*, for example, we see a proliferation of black masculinities. As my later remarks will illustrate, comparative analyses of productions, commentaries, criticisms, and so on that bridge the early modern and the postmodern demonstrate that the public reception of Ira Aldridge's nineteenth-century Othello and Lawrence Fishburne's 1995 Othello share a propensity to link black sexuality with violence. But while for Aldridge's audience this propensity for violence was what makes Othello "natural," authentic, and therefore knowable, for 1995 audiences Othello was sexy precisely because of the ways that he resisted being known or understood. Contradictory images of what "black is and black ain't" (in the words of Ralph Ellison) can coexist in our histories, even as they disrupt the linearity of our chronologies.

In the paragraphs that follow I would like to highlight the different representations of Othello and their usefulness for thinking about the cultural place of black American men in the Shakespeare industry. When Ira Aldridge, the first internationally successful African American actor to play Othello, debuted in Russia in 1836, the audience's reaction was ecstatic. It was reported that after one particularly successful performance, Russian students seized a carriage carrying Aldridge, removed the horses, and transported the actor themselves through the snowy streets. The wonder of an "authentically black" Othello clearly gave new power to the role, creating a delicious frisson between theater and real life. Certainly, by watching an African American Othello kiss and kill a white actress on stage, Aldridge's viewers were watching social change take place before their eyes. The Russian audience's willingness and enthusiasm to think of Aldridge as Othello did have negative consequences, however. In one cartoon from a Russian newspaper contemporary to Aldridge's Russian tour, we see Aldridge hurtling Iago over his head. In another contemporary cartoon, Othello and Desdemona appear in court. The distraught actress begs the judge, "Please sir, I'm afraid that some day, he really will kill me." It was in particular the staging of interracial desire, the intimacy of gestures shared between black and white actors, that lent Aldridge's performances their particular charge. Aldridge's audience insisted on seeing his savage passion as "real," as the authentic and essential sign of his blackness. Not unrelated is the fact that when Aldridge married a white English actress, the European theater world followed the event with great interest. Aldridge's Othello, in essence, confirmed the fantasy of murderous black passion, one that can scarcely be contained within the fragile structures of the theater. Othello's stage history, and Aldridge's version, has engendered an ideology that there is a "natural" black acting style (especially among black Americans who perform the role), conflating black acting with the perception of black masculinity as sexy and violent.

In 1995, the year that Oliver Parker came out with his film *Othello*, public passion and outrage at interracial romance, marriage, and murder was still possible, as the various news media were obsessed with the ongoing drama of the turbulent marriage of O. J. and Nicole Simpson. That year, O. J. could be seen everywhere: on magazine covers in his prison blues, on C-Span's marathon trial reports, even on late-show revivals of the *Naked Gun* films, which featured Simpson in cameo roles. The Simpson trial lent *Othello* an aura of contemporality. The trial also stimulated public appetite for the image of the menacing black male body. Parker's production is noteworthy not only in its inclusion of Kenneth Branagh, currently the reigning popular king of Shakespeare on film, as Iago, but more significantly because of its casting of Lawrence Fishburne in the starring role. Fishburne had already given an explosive performance as abusive husband Ike Turner in the film *What's Love Got to Do with It?* (1993). While productions of *Othello* starring actors of African descent were not new (in addition to Aldridge, Ignatio Sancho performed the role in the eighteenth century, and in the twentieth century Paul Robeson, James Earl Jones, and John Kani have performed the role), Fishburne was the first African American to be cast as Othello in a mainstream film production.

Interestingly, as one discovers from the Fishburne depiction, the means by which black male sexuality is controlled in 1995 proved to be quite different from those particular to Aldridge's nineteenth-century context. As I have argued earlier, the novelty of Aldridge's Othello for many of his audience was that Aldridge's actions and emotions were viewed as "natural"—the authentic inner life of a black man, captured on stage. This concept and discourse of a "natural" black acting style was relatively new in the nineteenth century. Italian actor Tomaso Salvini, one of Aldridge's contemporaries, was one of the first actors to shape his characterization of Othello with research on African and Islamic culture; significantly, he downplayed Othello's associations with blackness: he robed himself in an Arabic costume and browned his skin to a "tawny" rather than black color. Even further from a conceptualization of performing Othello's "natural" blackness were actors in the seventeenth-and eighteenth-century London theater. Actors playing Othello wore blackface, but there was little interest in replicating the physical specificities of London's growing black population. In fact, actor Samuel Foote feared that blackface and blackness in general were distracting and would make the character less sympathetic. In an eighteenth-century actor's handbook, Foote warned other Othello actors that blackface obscured the subtleties of the facial expressions and argued that performing Othello would be more convincing without it.

In the Hollywood of the 1990s, such acts of racism are usually expressed more covertly. The audience for Oliver Parker's film is encouraged to enjoy his (and Fishburne's) physical Othello, to take pleasure in his body, in his rages and even in his murder of the play's heroine. All this, conveniently, is accomplished by reducing Othello's black identity to an appetizing and culturally acceptable icon: the athletic black male body. Throughout the film, we see much of Fishburne's body either open shirted, shirtless, or nude. Fishburne's portrayal of Othello combines physical power with reticence. More often than not, Othello's response to the characters around him are glares, grunts, or lapses into feverish sexual fantasy. Broodingly sexual in a way that is most often associated with the warrior's violent lifestyle, Fishburne's Othello is most evocative of a cultural figuration of the American black male in the 1990s. From Robert Mapplethorpe's black nudes to the late Tupac Shakur, the black male body is most readily and easily consumed by the American public when it is posed with its muscles flexed, when his voice, if heard at all, confirms the subject's nihilism—that nothing can be known or communicated except the body itself.

Parker makes the most of Fishburne's commanding physical presence—his height, his warrior build—but does little with Fishburne's vocal range and performative skills. The question we might ask is, what is the "cultural logic" of an Othello production where Othello is thus reduced to nothing more than a stereotypical black male icon? If we turn back to Frederic Jameson's concept of "libidinal historicism," we can understand the image and importance of black masculinity as unknowable as the extension of our changing relationship with the visual as well as with the past. In this moment, Jameson suggests, the present as well as the past is endowed "with the spell and stance of a glossy mirage" (Jameson 1995, 20). The history of aesthetic style has displaced real history. Jameson's libidinal historicism describes quite neatly *Pulp Fiction*'s brand of nostalgia, or the marriage between style and ethnography in MTV's *Real World,* or perhaps the pearlized Michael Jackson and Bubbles statue of Jeffrey DeKoons, as well as Parker's *Othello.* But it would also follow that a libidinal historicism would have a significant impact on the fetishistic relationship between contemporary Anglo-American cultures and the theatricality of Shakespeare, whether onstage, on film, or in the printed text, as an artifact of the past with relevance for the present.

Paradoxically, by telegraphing Othello's ultimate unreadability through iconic representations, Parker engages with the history of the many ways that Othello has been read in the past. It is precisely Parker's 1995 Othello's stimulation of cultural memory through the replication of past images of black masculinity that places it in the postmodern moment. Whether Othello has been presented as Moorish converso, as black rapist, as slippery diplomat, assimilationist, Tom, or Buck, there has always been the invitation to give up on meaning by play's end. Desdemona's murder and Iago's plot revealed, Othello becomes his own enemy, the "circumcised dog," the Spartan other who once defined his own insider status. Othello stabs this enemy—that is, stabs himself, and as Gratiano says in response, "All that's spoke is marr'd" (5.2.358).

The videotape of Othello has been accompanied by a lengthy preview of Kenneth Branagh's production of Hamlet, as well as information on an interactive Othello CD-ROM. More than a craving for all things Shakespeare in this high-tech age, Parker's ambiguously located Moor (is he African? Is he Venetian?) presents an alternative narrative of blackness for a media that is perhaps a little too weary of the cultural specifics of black villains and heroes from Los Angeles's South Central or Chicago's Cabrini Green. Othello, loyal leader of the Venetian army's march against the Turkish threat, provides relief from the mass "misbehavior" of the Million Man March or from Clarence Thomas's orchestrated protest against his "high-tech lynching." Moreover, Othello kills, but he has the sense to punish himself. He commits suicide at the end. No more of the messy, yearlong trials. No getting off free to avenge his killer and to sell videotapes describing the reasons that he did not kill his wife. Othello assumes the personal responsibility to end the danger with himself; he presents a racial menace to society that can ultimately be controlled.

In Oliver Parker's 1995 production of William Shakespeare's Othello, the history of race matters. In this essay, I have sought to link the attempted erasure of the race paradigm in the public sphere with a larger suspicion of multiculturalism and of much of academic discourse in general. Parker's Othello illustrates that this very act of racial erasure has its link to a history of racist strategies of containment of the other. In the meantime, early modern constructions of racial difference continue to influence contemporary narratives of black masculinity in particular and black subjectivity in general.

Epilogue

Tiger Woods has a golf ball tee smelted from the gold of his father's bridgework. He carries it whenever he plays, but he says he will not actually use it until his father is dead. This is the biographical tidbit that most sticks with me in the recent deluge of cover stories about the young golf genius. The intimacy and perhaps morbidity of the gesture from father to son (a gift for his eighteenth birthday?) jar with the placid narratives of suburban childhood represented in cover stories in *People, Golf Digest, Sports Illustrated,* and *Time.* It is as though a black man (a father) has to die in order for a black "boy" to become a man. Perhaps more than has been done with any other recent athlete, the selling of Tiger Woods has been the selling of Tiger's upbringing—the construction of black masculinity from boy to man. Woods's public image is one of breezy confidence and success, as casual and as winsome as a nicely pressed pair of khakis. He has the smile of Bellafonte and the poise of Poitier, and more, he is very good at what he does. We are told in several of the recent interviews with his parents that Woods's appetite for golf came "naturally." This talent was drawn out and nurtured on the manicured lawns of his childhood home. So far, Woods has done a great job of making his break into a historically white sport very digestible to an American stomach already churning with the bile of past and present racial tensions.

But that golf tee has its own story to tell. Even transmogrified from its coarser function, the tee speaks of sacrifice. The golf tee links Tiger Woods to a history that *Golf Digest* and *People* have not told us: to the history of Earl Woods, a semi pro golfer himself who never "made it" like his son, and to the history of other black men, including the caddies and the players barred in the past from many country clubs. But all of that history has now been melted down; purified into one small and gleaming scruple.

While we have certainly not reached the end of race studies in early modern discourse, in some ways "race" is at risk of becoming like Tiger Wood's golf tee: smelted in the hot fires of past injustices, loaded with psychic meanings. What was once early modern race studies' cruder function—to bridge once separate critical traditions like Shakespeare studies and African American studies—has now become more fully integrated. However, in doing so, we may be at risk of losing a complex view of historical context as we, Shakespeare scholars and cultural critics, seek to make contact with the present. Scholars interested in the study of race in Shakespeare and early modern English studies need to continue our archival research to give us fresh materials and to provide new narratives. We need to continue to expand our interrogations of canonical texts like Shakespeare and to go beyond them. If not, we risk losing a critical distance from the discipline of early modern studies. As race studies is becoming, theoretically and intellectually, a familiar point of departure in Shakespeare and early modern English studies, we must be careful not to lose something as we expand the contours of the game.

Works Cited

Cose, Ellis. 1997. *Color-Blind: Seeing beyond Race in a Race-Obsessed World.* New York: Harper Collins.

D'Souza, Dinesh. 1995. *The End of Racism: Principles for a Multicultural Society.* New York: Free Press.

Gates, David. 1997. "Dead White Male of the Year: Shakespeare." *Newsweek,* 30 December/6 January.

Hall, Kim F. 1995. *Things of Darkness: Economies of Race and Gender in Early Modern England.* Ithaca: Cornell University Press.

Hendricks, Margo, and Patricia Parker. eds. 1994. *Women, "Race," and Writing in the Early Modern Period.* London: Routledge.

Jameson, Frederic. 1995. *Postmodernism, or The Cultural Logic of Late Capitalism.* Durham: Duke University Press.

Loomba, Ania. 1989. *Gender, Race, Renaissance Drama.* Manchester: Manchester University Press.

MacDonald, Joyce Green, ed. 1997. *Race, Ethnicity, and Power in the Renaissance.* Madison, N.J.: Fairleigh Dickinson University Press.

Passaro, Vince. 1977. *Harpers,* April.

Reilly, Rick. 1997. *Sports Illustrated,* 21 April.

Shapiro, James. 1997. *Chronicle of Higher Education,* 31 January.

White, Jack E. 1997. "'I'm Just Who I Am.'" *Time,* 5 May.

Woods, Earl. 1997. "How to Raise a Tiger." *Golf Digest,* June.

Yardley, Jonathan. 1997. *Washington Post,* 5 January.

Racial Dissonance/Canonical Texts: Teaching Early Modern Literary Texts in the Late Twentieth Century

JYOTSNA G. SINGH

I

IN TEACHING Shakespeare's *Othello* and Aphra Behn's *Oroonoko* (1688) to American students in the late 1990s, one quickly notes the racial fault lines in the class and in the United States. Despite the prolific—almost feverish—use of terms like "multiculturalism" and "multi-ethnic," most Americans recognize "race" as a catchall term for the relationship between African Americans and those of European descent—a relationship that is inseparable from the origins of American national identity in a period that spawned both the concept of democratic rights and the institution of slavery. Questions touching upon this complex history inevitably emerge in my fairly multiracial and urban classroom, as, for instance, when we discuss the following passage from *Oroonoko*:

(this passage deals with the female [European] narrator's description of Oroonoko, the "noble slave"):

This great and just character of Oroonoko gave me an extreme curiosity to see him, especially when I knew he spoke French and English and that I could talk with him. . . . He was pretty tall, but of a shape the most exact that can be fancied. The most famous statuary could not form the figure of a man more admirably turned from head to foot. His face was not of that brown, rusty black which most of that nation are, but a perfect ebony, or polished jet. His eyes were the most aweful that could be seen and very piercing, the white of 'em being like snow, as were his teeth. His nose was rising and Roman, instead of African and flat. His mouth, the finest shaped that could be seen, far from those great turned lips, which are so natural to the rest of the Negroes. The whole proportion and air of his face was so noble and exactly formed that "bating [excepting] his colour" there could be nothing in nature more beautiful, agreeable, and handsome. (11–12)

Whether I discuss *Oroonoko* in a course structured by the ideological underpinnings of colonial history or focus on the formal aspects of the novel in an introductory fiction/literature course (and I have done both), the students' racially coded responses to this passage are quite remarkable in their predictability. Not only do African American students respond more subjectively—and often with some anxiety and anger—to the narrator's implicit denigration of physical features "so natural" to "Negroes," but they also frequently interpose experiential narratives of their own interracial relations into Oroonoko's story. And if I do not keep the reins on the class discussion, it can stretch the limits of intellectual debate and elide ideological issues into students' personal concerns. Quickly recognizing that the criteria of beauty used by the narrator to extol Oroonoko's nobility are entirely European and Caucasian, black students reflect concerns and anxieties about their own appearance, skin color, and body types. Of course, the Europeans and other groups in the classroom also pick up the implicit racism of the passage and link it to the narrator's earlier matter-of-fact description of the enslavement of Africans in the West Indian plantation economy. However, when they frequently introduce their *own* narratives of race relations into the discussion, these are often different and even antagonistic to the African American accounts. And more importantly, students of European descent find it easier to relegate the early modern representations of "race" and racism to the *past*, marking easy historical divisions between "then" and "now." While cultural conflicts often remain unresolved in these discussions of texts such as *Othello* and *Oroonoko*, the students nonetheless learn that we inevitably interpret the past in terms of the present.

My aim here—in this glimpse into my classes—is *not* to essentialize the identities and responses of *all* students in terms of their race or to stress the experiential as the basis for theorizing the economic and political production of racial divisions; rather, I wish to address New Critics and others who complain that literary works have been reduced to "sociological documents" by those of us who teach literature in the context of history and ideology. My point is that while teaching *Oroonoko* in today's United States, I do not even have to introduce a historical perspective into the class discussion. Rather, the students who interpret this passage bring their *own* histories to the discussion—histories that are *inseparable* from their own class and race positions, even though they may describe them in the most intimate and subjective terms. Thus, whether one teaches *Oroonoko* or *Othello* (as most Shakespeareans discover) many early modern literary texts lend themselves to contemporary debates about racial divisions and hierarchies quite easily and unavoidably. In fact, given the general interest in studying the historical, psychoanalytical, and political underpinnings of literature in the past two decades, it is not surprising that early modern studies—in disciplines ranging from history and literature to anthropology—have generated a considerable body of work devoted to "race."

Thus, by now it has become a critical commonplace that the rich collection of Renaissance texts can no longer be considered autonomous artifacts impermeable to shifts in history and in interpretive conventions. Within this context, the period from 1500 to 1800 is seen as crucial to colonial and postcolonial history, as has been pointed out by, Hendricks and Parker, the editors of *Women, "Race," and Writing in the Early Modern Period* in their introduction to this volume: "the early modern period . . . saw the proliferation of rival European voyages of 'discovery' as contacts with what from a Eurocentric perspective were 'new' and different worlds, the drive toward imperial conquest and the subjugation of indigenous peoples, and the development (and increasingly 'racial' defense) of slavery" (2). Considering that the more politically oriented criticism of the 1980s and 1990s has placed early modern European literature within this history, the landscape of these canonical texts seems to have changed—peopled more visibly now by characters previously in the shadowy margins: "Moors," "Jews," New World "natives," "Indians," and "others." In looking afresh at the colonial contexts of early modern literature, critics have produced work with powerful political ramifications. Among recent studies, for instance, Kim Hall's seminal book, *Things of Darkness*, exposes the racialized *language* of light and dark—"tropes of darkness"—in which the social and sexual hierarchies of the period were encoded. In her extended discussions of lyric poetry, court masques, and portrait paintings, among other cultural forms, Hall reveals the history and power of the black/white binary opposition that was inherited from classical and Christian imagery (drawn from medieval iconography, doctrine, and literature) and that spawned English notions of 'self' and 'other' so well known in [contemporary]

Anglo-American racial discourses" (2). An interest in "race" has also led scholars further, beyond considerations of Western imperialist discourse to historicist analyses of non-European intrusions into European Christendom such as those of the Ottoman Turks', as described in Daniel Vitkus's compelling essay "Turning Turk in *Othello*" (146–47). This essay looks afresh at the Venetians' racial and cultural anxieties within Shakespeare's play by bracketing them within European fears of being engulfed within an Ottoman empire. For instance, as Vitkus shows, the general European feelings of fascination and revulsion toward the Turks and Islam were intrinsic to the English Protestant's misreading of Islam's "ethnic and political complexity." Thus, the critic explains how in "early modern parlance" the "words *Moor* and *Turk*, for example, were sometimes used to refer specifically to the people of Morocco or Turkey, but more often they signified a generalized Islamic other. English popular culture, including drama, rarely distinguished between Muslims" (161); hence, the figure of Othello in Shakespeare's play evokes a range of negative associations, even though he is a Christian. Readings such as Vitkus's, and, earlier, Virginia Vaughan's *Othello: A Contextual History*, reinterpret *Othello* by historicizing English culture in relation to its non-European others in the Middle East and Africa. Thus, collectively, such studies have made an important intellectual and conceptual breakthrough as critics can no longer elide race within general considerations of human nature. Rather, we see it as a shifting category in multiple histories in which the language of "race" performs different modes of cultural work.

Furthermore, early modern work expands the chronological scope of our perspective on East-West racial struggles. Theorists of African origin such as Henry Louis Gates, Jr., remind us that contemporary conversations about race—replete with metaphors and mystifying tropes and, sometimes, biological misnomers, often have their source in typologies established in eighteenth-and nineteenth-century philosophical and pseudoscientific theories. As he explains that "while the Enlightenment is characterized by its foundation on man's ability to reason, it simultaneously used the absence and presence of reason to delimit and circumscribe the very humanity of the cultures and peoples of color which Europeans had been 'discovering' since the Renaissance" (8). In illuminating these earlier European "discoveries"—both literal and metaphoric or geographical and imaginative—early modern studies have shown, among other things, the racialized antecedents of Enlightenment attitudes.

The effects of these historical reevaluations and attendant critical shifts are most apparent in the classroom: these fresh observations on early modern representations of race and self often, and sometimes willy-nilly, generate a new kind of critical consciousness that transcends the disciplinary and temporal limits of early modern studies. Most typically, students draw on these new historical materials to reappraise "race" and racism within contemporary identity politics in the United States (often in terms of neocolonial global struggles), frequently relating traditional literary works to headlines of the "trial of the century," to images of the "black man" in the national and world media, and to the vexed issue of interracial sexual politics in the United States. These analogies, not surprisingly, remind us of the extent to which popular-identity politics have dismantled liberal humanism with its attendant, gender-inflected claims of universalism. Since the mid-1980s when students demonstrated at Stanford and elsewhere against a curriculum composed of the works of "dead white males," we have witnessed an expansion of the curriculum to include works by women and non-European minorities. Yet even today, despite the misrepresentation by some alarmist groups and sections of the media, students in most major universities and four-year colleges continue to be exposed to a basic fare of traditional Western canonical works, ranging from Chaucer to Milton, Shakespeare, and Pope, among numerous others. What has changed, however, to the dismay of the earlier New Critics and idealists, is the way in which these traditional works are seen through the prism of the history and ideology. Hence, "race" is no longer ignored, and Prospero's sense of colonial entitlement does not go unchallenged in most standard readings of Shakespeare's *The Tempest*. Repeatedly, the racial concerns of the *present* impinge on the *past*.

II

Herein lies the conceptual/theoretical as well as pedagogical impasse for the teacher and students. In a post-Foucauldian world, it would be naïve to consider history in terms of a "seamless web of yesteryear" leading slowly and inexorably into the present (Poster, 74). In studying present-day racial inequities and conflicts, it is tempting for some in a multiracial, frequently tense classroom to "ransack history in order to rediscover the play of anticipations or echoes, to go right back to the first seeds or to go forward to the last traces" (Foucault, 144). How to avoid such a totalization of the *past* and the *present* is truly a challenge for the teacher of early modern texts in contemporary North America. One way out of this impasse, I believe, is offered by Foucault's own perspective on history—one that in stressing discontinuity has nonetheless opened multiple frames of reference for historians. For Foucault, history is both a means of knowledge and of power at the same time. Thus history is a "means of controlling and domesticating the past in the form of knowing it" (Poster, 75). In approaching early modern literature, students as historians visibly engage in this process of "domestication" according to racial divisions: by the different questions they raise and by the continuities or discontinuities they perceive between past and present racial inequities. One way to study whether early modern discourses converge with or diverge from current racialist ideas and practices is via a broad power/ knowledge nexus: this historical/literary analysis would approach any social formation as a multiplicity—and to "explore each discourse/practice separately, unpacking its layers, decoding its meanings, tracing its development wherever its meandering path may lead" (Poster, 88). Such a methodology productively translates into a classroom discussion of *Oroonoko*, for instance, not by stressing a one-to-one correspondence between the seventeenth-century slave plantation and contemporary forms of "slavery" in the inner-city meltdown across the United States, but rather by emphasizing the *specificity* and *difference* of the two discourses/practices even while pointing to the *interplay* of their relationships and dependencies. In thus exploring collisions as well as continuities between past and present practices and institutions of slavery and racism, students of different racial groups learn to challenge the "rationality" and inevitability of the phenomena being explored.

The challenges of creating an antiracist pedagogy have rarely been the direct concern (at least explicitly) of most groundbreaking work on race in the past two years—with some exceptions, of course, like Kim Hall's book, for instance. But even this book, as Crystal Bartolovich has pointed out in her astute review of it, could have done with a "more specific detailing of modern examples [which] would have encouraged . . . more careful differentiation of early modern troping of blackness from current practices, [and] which would strengthen the case for such continuities as do pertain" (Bartolovich, 236). Bartolovich's concerns about the chasm between historicized readings of race and contemporary racist discourses and practices are well founded. Though we can chart some curricular/critical shifts in approaches to Renaissance literature, we can observe little change in the *demographic landscape of early modern studies* as a discipline. At conferences, at the major research libraries, and among the job candidates at the Modern Language Association, we discover little correspondence between the inclusion of race as a category of analysis and the actual growth in the number of African Americans in Renaissance studies. The most recent data produced by the United States Department of Education, National Center for Education Statistics (published in 1996) shows (in its most recent field study) that among the 1,344 English language and literature candidates awarded their doctorates in 1993–94, only 32 were black, (non-Hispanic) candidates—a total of 2.4 percent. The further split was between 6 black men and 26 black women who received their doctorates in English. This demographic chasm between white and black doctoral students is evident across the disciplines, covering both the sciences and the humanities, and speaks volumes in itself. In all cases the black population is clearly underrepresented in the entire pool of doctoral candidates.

In this demographic context, we in Renaissance studies cannot assume that we have made any significant break in bridging this chasm between the two races, especially in the United States. Furthermore, among the minuscule numbers of black doctoral candidates, we can also assume that few have chosen to specialize in the works of canonical authors—the "dead white males," as it were. The demands of identity politics and capitalist multiculturalism have pushed African American scholars toward recovering new archives of black authors. They also experience, no doubt, considerable pressures to legitimate their cultural/intellectual identities in their "own" field. While this cultural specialization and a proliferation of subfields must be welcomed, it is also unfortunate that black scholars do not choose to intellectually intervene in the discourses/ practices of European racism in the early modern period; instead, as is obvious, new forms of ghettoization have emerged, giving the *appearance* of inclusion, while leaving intact the demographic chasm between black and white doctoral candidates. In Howard University's English department, for instance, only a few students over a period of many years have received the doctoral degree in the early modern period.

This demographic crisis in the doctoral arena is cruelly (and some would say ironically) contrasted by the disproportionate numbers of African American males caught in the maze of under-education, unemployment, and the criminal justice system. This crisis of contemporary America calls for the aid of *history* as a necessary component in recognizing the cause and effect of this urban meltdown. Thus, as teachers of Renaissance texts, as we take our students on a journey through the European past, we must try to develop a viable, antiracist pedagogy that can point to the political import of historical knowledge. And as we recover racialized discourses in the rich body of earlier texts—lyrics, plays, travel accounts, religious treatises, aesthetic theory—we can follow the powerful discursive mechanisms, ever evolving and intractable, constantly energized by the resilient tropes of otherness, that take the form of familiar and present-day binaries: black/white, Christian/heathen, nurture/nature, civilization/savagery. In this exercise, we can often recognize racial fault lines distinct yet not wholly dissimilar from our own period. Such reading practices have been a part of the larger prerogative of "cultural studies" as a field—practices that have undoubtedly created a crisis in the European hegemony even as the racial inequities persist.

I recognize that my reflections may suggest a polemical pedagogy, whereby the study of the racial inflections of texts may become central, not peripheral, to the task of literary analysis. But given the bleak conditions of inequity we face in United States cities, we must consider the needs of the present, the commonplace, the local as much our intellectual domain as the Renaissance. As we end the century here in the United States, we can look back, via Renaissance literature, to the literal and symbolic geography of the sixteenth and seventeenth centuries in a profusion of names: the Americas, the New World, the world of gold and "cannibals," the Virginia Colony, and the Caribbean Islands. And as we reflect on the past in the present tense of the American classroom, slavery and its effects inevitably assert their presence in the multiracial classroom. Thus, the political is hard-pressed to defer to the aesthetic, even in a course on early modern literature.

Finally, as we grapple with the pressures of political forces on literary work in the American classroom, we can perhaps see some of the promise and conflicts of our task in the ideas and words of Thomas Jefferson, the "father" of American democracy. A proponent of classical and humanist learning, in which he was proficient, Jefferson often promoted literature for its moral lessons. Writing to his nephew, Robert Skipworth, in a letter accompanying a catalog of a "general collection" of books that the latter might "find convenient to procure," Jefferson does not promote these books for their "utility," but rather because they "fix us in the principles and practice of virtue" (Peterson, 349). Then he goes on to explain the processes of this moral edification via great books:

> When any signal act of charity or of gratitude, is presented either to our sight or imagination, we are deeply impressed with its beauty and feel a strong desire in ourselves of doing charitable and grateful acts also. On the contrary, when we see or read of any atrocious deed, we are disgusted with its deformity and conceive an abhorrence of vice. Now every emotion of this kind is an exercise of our virtuous dispositions; and dispositions of the mind, like limbs of the body, acquire strength by exercise. But exercise produces habit; and in the instance of which we speak, the exercise being of the moral feelings, produces a habit of thinking and acting virtuously. We never reflect whether the story we read be truth or fiction. If the painting be lively and a tolerable picture of nature, we are thrown into a reverie. . . . I appeal to every reader of feeling and sentiment whether the fictitious murder of Duncan by Macbeth does not excite in him . . . a great horror of villainy. . . . Does he not in fact feel himself a better man while reading [such works] and privately covenant to copy the fair example? (350).

In carefully charting such a formation of moral feelings via fictional examples, Jefferson expresses his abiding faith in the moral power of literature as he goes on to assert in the same letter: "The spacious field of imagination is thus laid open to our use, and lessons may be formed to carry home to the mind every moral rule of life. Thus, a lively and lasting sense of filial duty is more effectually impressed on the mind of a son or daughter by reading *King Lear*, than by all the dry volumes of ethics and divinity" (351).

While he discusses moral issues with ease and fluency in his analysis of the power of literature, he is less at ease at other times. For instance, when Jefferson, both as a political leader and a slave owner, grapples with the possibilities of ending slavery, he does not seem to find any guidance or lessons in the classics he loved. In his letter to his neighbor Edward Coles, he is not averse to the "hour of emancipation" "advancing" in the "march of time," but defers this task "for the young" of the next generation. He desires a "gradual extinction" of the institution of slavery because he views the slaves "as incapable as children of taking care of themselves" and if not "guided" could become "pests in society by their idleness" (546). More pointedly, Jefferson is uneasy about emancipation, which might lead to "their [the blacks'] amalgamation with the other color [which] produces a degradation to which no lover of his country, no lover of excellence in the human character can innocently consent" (546). Given his naturalized fear of miscegenation, what moral lesson, one wonders, would Thomas Jefferson derive from *Othello*? The conflict between the aesthetic and the political are evident in these letters, replicating the pedagogical struggles in contemporary American classrooms. What kind of moral lessons or political work can we generate by our readings of the great works of literature? The answer will depend on our own investment in the great political and economic struggles of our own time.

Works Cited

Bartolovich, Crystal. *Things of Darkness: Economies of Race and Gender in Early Modern England (rev.) Shakespeare Quarterly* 48, (summer 1997): 233-37.

Behn, Aphra. *Oroonoko and Other Writings.* Edited by Paul Salzman. Oxford: Oxford University Press, 1994.

Digest of Education Statistics. Washington, D.C.: U.S. Department of Education; National Center for Education Statistics, November 1996.

Foucault, Michel. *The Archaeology of Knowledge,* Translated by A. M. Sheridan. New York: Pantheon, 1972.

Gates, Henry Louis, Jr. "Writing 'Race' and the Difference It Makes." Introduction to *"Race," Writing, and Difference.* Chicago: University of Chicago Press, 1986: 1–20.

Hall, Kim. *Things of Darkness: Economies of Race and Gender in Early Modern England.* Ithaca: Cornell University Press, 1995.

Parker, Patricia, and Margo Hendricks. eds. *Women, "Race," and Writing in the Early Modern Period.* London: Routledge, 1994.

Peterson, Merrill D., ed. *The Portable Thomas Jefferson.* New York: Penguin Books, 1977.

Poster, Mark. *Foucault, Marxism, and History: Mode of Production versus Mode of Information.* Cambridge: Polity Press, 1984.

Vaughan, Virginia. *Othello: A Contextual History.* Cambridge: Cambridge University Press, 1994.

Vitkus, Daniel J. "Turning Turk in *Othello*: The Conversion and Damnation of the Moor." *Shakespeare Quarterly* 18, no. 2 (summer 1997): 145–176.

REVIEW ARTICLES

Discourse and Authority: The Renaissance of Robert Weimann

JOHN DRAKAKIS

IN THE FINAL sentence of a chapter contributed to Ivo Kamps's recent collection, *Materialist Shakespeare: A History* (1995), Fredric Jameson observes that there is no need to return to matters of greatness, continued relevance, or indeed to posterity as such, "in order to suggest that it is political commitment to the historical originality of late capitalism which is most likely to spur contemporary readers of 'Shakespeare' in new and exciting directions."[1] We may detect here a certain feeling of resignation born. out of the realization that the capacity of capitalism to effect endless self-transformation has raised serious questions about any narrative predicated upon the linear and rational progression of history. As a consequence Jameson is forced to accept a revisionist Marxism through what he now acknowledges to be a "world of multiple causalities" (324). This shift into a more supple form of Marxist criticism is one that we need to keep firmly in mind when considering the impressive body of work produced by Robert Weimann over the last thirty years (including an essay reprinted in Kamps's collection), except that for Weimann, this observation is not entirely without irony. His monumental *Shakespeare and The Popular Tradition in the Theatre* first appeared in German in 1967, but since its translation into English in 1978, it has been enthusiastically rediscovered in the 1980s in Britain and the United States as a seminal work of materialist criticism. This is all the more remarkable at a time when from the point of view of a practical politics as well as theoretical orientation, classical Marxism with its emphasis upon the role of collectivities such as class in the making of history is thought by some to have entered a period of terminal decline. It is also a matter of no little inconvenience to Weimann himself, who is now forced to divide his time between the recently "unified"

Germany and the West Coast of the United States, where, paradoxically, the intellectual cachet of Marxism as a developing discourse
continues to command serious and sustained, although, as Jacques
Derrida has recently indicated, somewhat nervous attention.[2] There
has, of course, been a significant increase in historical research in
Renaissance culture during the last two decades, despite proclama-
tions of "the end of history" and of the alleged triumph of liberal
democracy.[3] This context has proved to be more important than ever
for Weimann, since in his own work he has continued to engage in
a rigorous self-reflexivity in the face of an increasingly feverish
circulation and exchange of professional intellectual capital, refusing to be swayed by fashion, yet receptive to the questions that
advances in critical theory have opened up.

In an early essay that Weimann contributed to Arnold Kettle's
Shakespeare in a Changing World (1964) he had already begun to
question a critical practice that was indifferent to "the facts of
economic and social history."[4] Moreover, some three years later,
and at a time before English translations of Bakhtin had appeared,
Weimann demonstrated in *Shakespeare and the Popular Tradition
in the Theatre* that he was already attuned to the multivocal nature
of theatrical representation and to an implicit politics of signification, and also to the limitations of a positivist model of the theater
as an artistic phenomenon that merely "reflected" its environment.
For Weimann, and very much in keeping with his commitment to
a vibrant Marxism, art was a special mode of production, and this
led him to insist from the outset that "Shakespeare's theatre and
his society were interrelated in the sense that the Elizabethan stage,
even when it reflected the tensions and compromises of sixteenth-
century England, was also a potent force that helped to create the
specific character and transitional nature of that society."[5] Indeed,
he perceived in what he called "the receptivity of the audience"
and "the consciousness and artistry of the drama . . . a new historical synthesis," which remains accessible to us once we become
aware as critics of this "dialectics of interdependence" (xii). Even
at this stage, Weimann was fascinated by what he described as the
"mingle-mangle" of late-sixteenth-century society, and a corresponding mixture in the drama of the period of the styles of "con-
ventionalism" and "naturalism" that "helped constitute the
universalizing pattern in Shakespeare" (251). Nor could this be a
mere formal matter, since it was in precisely that combination of
tension and mutual interrelation between these two modes of rep-

resentation that a much larger, implicitly political, freedom resided (251).[6] The affirmation of a "universalising pattern in Shakespeare," whose origin is ascribed to a security born of the dramatist's access to "the fully developed techniques and values of a popular theatre turned into a national institution," may read, some thirty years on, as a form of special pleading. But this is perfectly consistent with an issue that by the mid-1970s had become one of Weimann's abiding concerns, and that he explored in more detail in his book *Structure and Society in Literary History* (1976). Unhappy with the formalist reading practices of American New Criticism, which depended upon "the postulate of the timelessness of reading and an a-historical conception of the reader and his responses,"[7] Weimann was concerned to maintain a clear distinction between "the reciprocal quality of the most basic historical relationship between the past significance of the work and the present meaning of its revitalised use and interpretation" (32). In the essay he contributed to *Shakespeare in a Changing World* he had already taken severely to task "a certain critically inert type of sociological or even Marxist writing" that did not distinguish between literature as "literature" and as "a medium of sociological reference and exemplification," and he insisted that what cannot be ignored is the contradiction between the historicity of the work and its enduring value as art (18). When he came to reconsider some of these issues a decade or so later, it was against a background of crisis, both in the discipline of literary criticism and also in Western society generally, "in which the revolutionary idea of change, organic and dialectical concepts of evolution, and the liberal and humanist traditions of progress" had all been rendered problematical (18). By this time Weimann was clearly thinking of the United States, where what he called "the most general assumptions about the practical uses of literature as an agent of social change and consciousness," and a critical practice that was characterized by "scepticism and retreat," had been subsumed under a purely self-serving academic discourse designed to fulfil "professional requirements" (30). He has always been stubborn in his resistance to the Leavisite notion of "tradition," on the grounds that such a view of the literature of the past overlooks the historically complex dialectic between "past significance and present meaning" (43). Of course, this is an issue that more recent attempts to historicize the literature of the Renaissance have attempted to address, most notably Stephen Greenblatt's dismissal of "an aestheticized and idealized politics of the imagination" in favor of a study that had forced him "simultaneously to feel more rooted and more estranged in my own values."[8] If we take this together with the contributions of Foucault to the analysis of discourse and with Derrida's account of the durability of the text in history as the consequence of its own "iterability," something "which puts down roots in the unity of a context and immediately opens this non-saturable context onto a recontextualisation,"[9] we can then begin to locate the complexity of the discursive field within which Weimann has been moving over a long period of time. He returned to these issues in some detail in the epilogue to the expanded edition of *Structure and Society in Literary History* (1984), where he renewed his seriously qualified enthusiasms for the post structuralist emphasis on textuality.[10] Indeed, we may perceive his own work as having been, and continuing to be, involved in a dialogue with a variety of positions that have emerged in the wake of poststructuralism, as well as with a range of materialisms that cannot exactly be described as Marxist.

Robert Weimann's most recent book, *Authority and Representation in Early Modern Discourse* (1996), is the culmination of a series of investigations into different facets of what is referred to, perhaps not a little tendentiously, as "the early modern period." This choice of title implies two apparently contradictory things. Firstly, it signals a decisive movement into the very discursive terrain and categories of classification that Marxist historians such as Perry Anderson have come to regard as symptomatic of a withdrawal from history. Indeed, it is Anderson's contention, and in a vein that is similar to Weimann's own, that the legacy of poststructuralism is a reduction of causality to contingency: "Diachronic development, in other words, is reduced to the chance outcome of a synchronic combinatory."[11] Secondly, it continues to hold on to an irreducibly causal logic that seeks in the past coherent explanations for the present.

We may trace the trajectory of Weimann's concern with these issues through a series of essays that he contributed to various books and journals throughout the 1980s. For example, in 1981 in an essay entitled "Society and the Individual in Shakespeare's Conception of Character," he sought to locate in the radically transitional art of Shakespearean drama a relation between "the self" and "the social" that is of historical significance, but that has been for some time a consistent feature of the poststructuralist concern with subjectivity. He argues:

> It is only when these two points of reference—the self and the social—are seen as entering into a dynamic and unpredictable kind of relationship that the most original and far-reaching dimension in Shakespeare's conception of character—the dimension of growth and change—can be adequately understood.[12]

At issue here is something more substantial than the notion of a "character effect" involving "growth" and "change," although later in his argument, Weimann refuses to accede to the traditional humanist assumption that the detail of dramatic representation is symptomatic of a fuller, internally coherent identity. The plenitude he identifies is not designed to produce, as in neo-Bradleyan character criticism, an opposition between "character" and "role," but rather to demarcate a traversable boundary, "where one theatrical part is revealed and evaluated in relation to an ensemble of dramatic identities" that disclose the multiple conflicts and contradictions that function as determinations of social process itself. Here character is something more than the human essence that art liberates and that the spectator or reader glimpses at particular moments in the text or in performance; rather, it emerges as a series of contingent identities. He ascribes to Shakespeare a conception of character that draws upon "that basic contradiction according to which the individual ultimately, in the course of modern history, does not achieve his particularity and individuality in isolation from, but only in connection with, the social process," (30). Moreover, and in a way that returns our attention to the vexed question of universality, he affirms that in the England of the time "it was possible to comprehend the emerging forms of individuality not as the least, but as the most universalised dimension of character" (31). This argument hints at the proposition that, in the words of Ernesto Laclau, "nobody can aspire to be the true consciousness of the world," and that the "endless interaction between perspectives" renders more remote than ever the possibility of "any totalitarian dream."[13] Thus already by the early 1980s Weimann was beginning to wrestle with a series of political problems in his own writing that have become even more germane to the history of Marxism in the light of more recent events in East Germany.

The question of "character" dovetails neatly into two of Weimann's abiding concerns, the relationship between mimesis and ideology, and the question of authority. Between the first appearance of *Structure and Society in Literary History* and its reissue in 1984, he attempted to think through more systematically what he perceived to be the aporias in particular aspects of poststructuralist theory. Here he raises the question of what happens when the concepts of "production" and "reproduction" are "pushed beyond the limits of textuality";[14] he perceives in what he believes to be the "(self)-repressive strategies" of the Derridean critique of metaphysics and logocentricity a privileging of certain textual strategies that occlude what he calls "a referential and pragmatic (non-differential) definition of the links between mimesis and "production" or even theatrical "production," and that it is here, at the point of intersection between text and historical context, that "an opening/or a radically historicizing use of 'mimesis' would have to be sought" (308–9). He goes on:

> To produce is to go beyond the eternal circle of deferment, beyond the limitations of the sign and the permanent displacement of meaning; it is, even more, to break through the textualization of experience and to undermine any hierarchical relationship between writing and speech vis-à-vis discursive practice. The person who makes a watch and reads the time, who plants a tree and harvests its fruit, constitutes himself or herself as a subject; the meaning of his or her activity is not deflected by verbal language as a differential system of signification. The theatrical person who knocks at a door or embraces his or her partner may not, through the production of an object, constitute himself or herself as a subject; but neither can that person's activity be subsumed under the depersonalised modes of textualization. The production of his or her "voice" is both a premise and a product of the particular social activity that a theatrical production re-presents. (309)

This distinction is seminal insofar as it focuses on precisely what Weimann wishes to retain of the classical Marxist logic of labor, production, and appropriation. Texts do not, he insists *produce* themselves, and while it is perfectly legitimate to explode the mirage of its surface univocality, a poststructuralist commitment to the principle of linguistic difference as constitutive remains,"blind to the essential challenge in the link between production and value, as contained in the Marxian concept of *Aneignung* "(310). Following Marx's *Grundrisse: Foundations of the Critique of Political Economy*, Weimann insists that contrary to the view ascribed to commentators such as Julia Kristeva, who argue that it is developed solely with reference to "the capitalist conditions of exchange-value," the concept of production must remain "independent of any specific social form" or class formation as the activity involved in "the production of use values, appropriation of nature for human needs" (311). In his essay "Mimesis in *Hamlet*," which appeared a year after this Epilogue, he sought to distinguish between Marx's Theoretical limitations of "the old mimesis," which had implied that there was a stable connection between "language and meaning, signifier and signified,"[15] and a theater still committed to a culture that was yet to become fully literate and that could not, therefore, "lend itself easily to those semiotic and deconstructive methods which take as their starting point a purely literary definition of the sign or some exclusively textualized concept of language" (276). On the surface such an argument would appear to render impossible any rapprochement with poststructuralist theory, and to some extent Weimann was already aware of this difficulty. In *Shakespeare and the Popular Tradition in the Theater* and in his article "Society and the Individual in Shakespeare's Conception of Character," he had wrestled with the opposing demands of medieval allegory and its commitment to a harmonized relationship between the universal and the particular, on the one hand, and on the other, the new, more openly agonistic ways of figuring the relationship between these two categories that emerged during the Renaissance. He noticed how what he called "principles of homogeneity, 'closure' and authority in representation are constantly undermined and subverted," in order to gain some purchase on the category of ideology, and, in the process, readmitting the possibility of the deconstruction of representation itself but under certain controlled conditions. This is an interesting attempt to address what Weimann perceives as a critical distinction between a discursive, irreducibly textualized definition of mimesis that privileges the constitutive function of difference and a nondiscursive definition in which there is an assumed "continuity and congruity between the act of interpretation, its cultural function, and its unique object, the Shakespearean text" (275–76). If it is assumed that mimesis traditionally involves "relatively stable links between language and meaning, signifier and signified," then the linguistic self-consciousness of the Shakespearean text, by virtue of its exposure of the homogenizing practices of representation, poses a threat to ideology itself, and nowhere more so than at the very point where ideology is being represented. He argues:

> If "representation" is said to homogenize textual production, stabilize hierarchies and privileges (and so void the text of contradictions and

interrogations), then, indeed, the dramatic representations of Shake-speare may well be shown not to exhaust their mimetic potential under these modes of closure and plenitude. On the contrary, although the specular reading or viewing of the plays can of course fix the reader or viewer in the plenitude of some false consciousness, there is ample evidence that, over and beyond its stabilizing functions, Shakespearean mimesis comprehends a self-conscious subversion of authority in representation. (276–77)

Thus Weimann can propose that "the issue of authority in represen-tation need not necessarily preclude its deconstruction *through* representation" (279). It is worth remembering that "authority" in this context is the collective term for all forms of coercive social regulation designed to compel allegiance to the vested interests of a dominant order. Or, to put the matter differently, in focusing on ideology as the means by which these interests are naturalized Weimann halts the slide into the Nietzschean figurations of power that would collapse absolutely his own holistic account (which he was not yet prepared to relinquish in its entirety) into the sphere of a Foucauldian micropolitics. The conclusion to "Mimesis in *Hamlet*" firmly resists any move into a spiraling textuality, which is regarded here as both a necessary and sufficient condition of poststructuralist critical practice, insisting upon a refusal to sepa-rate representation "from some more comprehensive idea of the connectedness of social, economic, and cultural productions" (289). At issue here is the difficult question of the relationship between text and context, narrative and history, whose connections Weimann seeks to reinforce but at the same time to avoid the pit-falls of the concept of expressive causality. There are times when he is in danger of drifting toward the very position that he seeks to avoid, but the general direction of his argument aligns itself with Fredric Jameson's revisionary position, whereby history is perceived *neither* as a text nor as a narrative, but as "an absent cause"[16]

This ingenious compromise, however, does not fully address the question of a referential model of language that haunts Weimann's argument. The readmission of a deconstructive turn, through a Brechtian notion of defamilarization, enables him to postulate a politics of representation. However, in choosing to privilege the discussion of mimesis, Weimann is able to bypass the question of whether or not material production precedes the linguistic sign. There is ample evidence in his writings to suggest that he is entirely sympathetic to the solution to the problem proposed by Fredric Jameson, where "history" is accessible to us only "in textual form, and that our approach to it and to the Real itself necessarily passes through its prior textualization, its narrativization, in the political unconscious" (35).

In a short essay he contributed to *Shakespeare Reproduced: The Text in History and Ideology* (1987), Weimann carried his thinking on the question of textuality a stage further. Here he concludes a short prefatory encounter with New Historicism and Cultural Materialism by observing that where "the mimetic uses of power" either sustain or conflict with "an ideological signified which is already given," but where art is asserted to occupy a register that is no longer mimetic but symbolic in its articulations, then "the work of the mimetic critic must be conceived as altogether irreconcilable with that of the post-structuralist or semiotic critic." This leads to the overwhelming question of how we evaluate "and grapple with the actual non-identity between the referential and the signifying dimensions of the text."[17] Weimann's argument that in the theater there is a contradiction between mimesis and the linguistic sign leads to the following consideration:

> far from obliterating or displacing this contradiction, we need to bring it out into the open, in order to use it with a view to stimulating a materialist and historicist understanding of the mimetic dimensions of the theatrical sign and the signifying dimensions of theatrical mimesis—"mimesis" taken in both its discursive and non-discursive dimensions, in language as well as action. It is at the cross-roads of these two dimensions that, I think, the production and reception of theatrical texts can best be explored as to the strengths and limits of the ideological function involved in them. (266)

The vexed phrase in this quotation is "its discursive and non-discursive dimensions," since Weimann refuses here to give up absolutely the prospect, however attenuated, of a referent that can be separated from its signifier. It is for this reason that he questions "the Derridean terminology of presence and absence" where the representation of *difference* could lead to an incessant relativism, postulating instead, and in a manner that recalls Volosinov's *Marxism and The Philosophy of Language*, an alternative explanation in which difference may be "a function of social conflicts in the sense that it is preceded by existential needs, desires and appropriations." Here difference is perceived not as a primary structural mechanism necessary for the production of meaning, but rather as a representation "of 'difference' in both the social sense of class conflict, gender, and cultural heterogeneity *and* the linguistic sense of the discontinuity between signifier and signified" (268).

This negotiation is important, and cannot easily be dismissed as a casually pragmatic gesture. Weimann's Marxism will not permit him to depart absolutely from the classical tenet that both the act of appropriation of representation itself and "the material reproduction of life precede the problematic of the sign," (269) although there is in this a tacit acknowledgment of the materiality of representation that will allow him occasionally to be more receptive than he is here to the Foucauldian dynamics of discourse. Indeed, at this point in his argument he appears already to have accepted the historical shift from the allegorical to the representational that had been in part the subject of *Shakespeare and the Popular Tradition in the Theatre*. But through the recognition of the crisis of ideology as exemplified in the shift from allegory to mimesis, and along with the circulation of signs facilitated by the advent of the printing press, Weimann can pose the question of how the "unsanctioned social interests" of the public theater were able to *authorize* theatrical discourse.

It is the historical conditions under which certain cultural practices are authorized, or authorize themselves, that have continued to fascinate Weimann, and his investigations have now broadened out considerably from his discussions of the Elizabethan public theater and Shakespearean drama into Renaissance culture generally. In a series of articles he has contributed to learned journals during the past decade, he has taken on a number of issues. These include the canonization of Shakespeare,[18] and the significance of disguise as an index to the conflict between "textual authority" and "performative agency" in Shakespearean drama.[19] He has also considered linguistic instability, and the divisions of authority to which it leads on the medieval stage,[20] and most recently, an analysis of the significance of the endings of Shakespeare's plays that affirms the instability of their authority in performance, while they are, at the same time, enjoining spectators "to recollect, discuss, and re-appropriate the performed play after its theatrical transaction is over."[21] In each of these articles Weimann extends one of a number of themes that continually recur in his work, although it is in the first, "Shakespeare (De)Canonized: Conflicting Uses of 'Authority' and 'Representation,'" that he makes explicit his own theoretical stance:

> Perhaps the best way to avoid any eclectic confusion between semiotic and sociological perspectives is to hint at my own position (which

relates to, but is not quite identical with, the current languages of
[de]canonization) by saying that I propose to use these languages as a
genuine pre-text, in the sense that I find it difficult to subscribe to either
the traditional naturalizing mode of canonization, or, for that matter,
a deconstructionist position which, beyond all considerations of the
cultural uses and values of Shakespeare, presumes to re-write literary
history outside the dialectic of continuity and discontinuity, tradition
and revolution. (67)

Unlike Foucault, Weimann is less concerned with the archaeology
of discourse itself, and the regulative functions of particular discourses, than with the contestation that takes place for particular
positions within a single discourse. His preoccupation with Shakespeare's monumental reputation involves primarily "both its
construction and deconstruction, in terms of those modes of authorization by which differing types of critical discourse engage in
the representation of a representation" (66). Any suggestion that he
has succumbed to a full-blown poststructuralist theory of textuality
here would be to mistake Weimann's purpose. A little later he proposes the conceptual tool of "a notion of discourse as appropriated
language," leaning more in the direction of a Habermasian theory
of communication than toward Foucault: "This would involve inscribed or oral utterances in the form of constative and performative speech acts and would allow us to view, as mutually related,
signification *and* co-operation in the uses of language, the semiotics
of the sign *and* the contingency of communication. Such a notion
of discourse would link the problematic of the sign with the pursuit
of social, cultural, and individual interests and legitimations as
they cut through the specificities of poetic and critical uses of language" (67).[22] He is prepared to subscribe to a poststructuralist
suspicion of any discursive stabilizing of cultural hierarchies, and
attempts in the interests of canonicity to suppress discontinuity,
but he stops short of a full endorsement, fearing that it is history
itself that might ultimately be jettisoned.[23] In attempting to historicize what he calls "the decanonizing gesture itself," Weimann aims
to get under discourse, to explode its claim to irreducible textuality
and to explore its representational properties. Once the concepts
of representation and discursive practice are elided, both demand
to be viewed "as an act of either embodying or intercepting the
commission, the delegation, the mediation of certain powerful or,
indeed, certain underprivileged interests and activities in history."[24] This is little short of a recuperation of the Foucauldian
dynamics of the structure of power for a thoroughgoing dialectical

materialist model of history that preserves, however gingerly, and in conditions which are far from auspicious, some preexistent human identity that demands to be emancipated. The difficulty, however, with seeking to separate out the elements of a structural model is that it lays Weimann open to the danger, so eloquently described by Ernesto Laclau, of inscribing the identity of the forces of oppression within that which searches for emancipation.[25] Thus, having acceded to at least part of the Foucauldian structuration of the dialectics of power at the level of a micropolitics, Weimann cannot escape entirely from some of its larger consequences in relation to totalities. To attempt to recuperate discourse as an instrumental phenomenon, while at the same time conceding that it is also the *object* of struggle, is to try to have it both ways. This is not to say that Weimann is committed to the concept of an absolute knowledge; rather, he is a little less sanguine about what Laclau perceives as "the exhilarating effects" of dispensing with it altogether. More than anyone, Weimann has good reason to suspect the consequences of the "totalitarian dream," but he is unwilling to jettison the concept of totality for the still unnerving prospect of "an endless interaction between various perspectives" (17).

Weimann cannot quite bring himself to what he perceives, in the final analysis, to be the pessimism of deconstruction. Its impact on literary history must be seen, he contends, in relation to "some larger response to the radical unrepresentativeness of cultural discourse in a society in which the appropriation of a usable past in relation to some common pursuit of social purpose in the present has become almost an impossibility."[26] Interestingly, the category of social class as an agency in the process of historical change has given way here to the larger prospect of "some common pursuit of social purpose"; historical transformation is still facilitated by means of collective action, but there appears to be a little less reliance than hitherto on the belief that the future rests with one particular class. And yet, for all that "the newest criticism" has done to expose the reactionary agenda associated with the business of constructing a literary canon, Weimann cannot but conclude that "the proposed alternative smacks of an agnosticism and a pragmatism which I for one do not find very appealing."(75–76) He refuses to dispense with the issue of mimesis because, however seductive some of its formulations might be, he cannot accept the post structuralist premise that fixes representation wholly within the sphere of the formal constitutive operations of a textual difference. "What we need," he proposes, is

> An awareness of the unresolved contradictions between the social history of the uses of the text and the synchronic system of intra-linguistic signs, between its referential and its signifying dimensions, between representation as a historical practice involving some form of subjectivity, and representation as a linguistic process of textual difference and differentiation.(77)

He perceives what he calls "the methodological alliance" and the "contradiction" between history and language as being currently unresolved, but also holds that attempts to resolve them are likely to be crucial to the development of Shakespeare studies in the nineties and beyond.

These, then are the issues, and this is the methodological and theoretical context within which Weimann's most recent book requires to be situated. *Authority and Representation in Early Modern Discourse* (1996) reprises those themes that I have tried to identify and that have been the focus of Weimann's own developing oeuvre during the last thirty years. In concentrating on the broader aspects of early modern culture, he pushes further his insights into the liminal nature of the Elizabethan stage, and reaffirms his interest in the Renaissance as a transitional moment from the medieval to the modern world. The contours of that transformation have long fascinated historians, but Weimann eschews the nostalgia occasionally associated with it for a much more rigorous historiography that simply refuses to make of the past a site upon which the present projects its own identity. Moreover, he is cautious about monological constructions of early modern "authority," while at the same time remaining acutely aware that certain continuities are implicit in discursive and nondiscursive practices of, for example, the language of "legitimation and 'possession,'" which "extend right to our own doorstep." At the same time, he recognizes that this is a world that, "although it made ours possible, is light years removed from the uses of power (and its opposite) in the age of electronic information."[27] The issue, for him, is the historical difference between how early modern culture represents its own concerns to itself, and how modern critics read and interpret those problematical self-representations. In this respect he seems at one with those he labels "(post)modern critics" for whom

> Sixteenth century culture presents itself as a language ruptured by divisions, a language whose configurations need to be read against the grain of early modern meanings. There is an irresistible (some critics would say ethical) urge to look at the Renaissance rhetoric of aggrandisement as a discourse of impoverishment, to read the fame of exploration as infamous news of colonisation, the triumphs of self-liberation as testimony to social fission, the pride in appropriation as a condoning of vast expropriations.(7)

At stake here are two different categories of "authority": first there is the question of the authority from which the historical discourses and practices of colonization derive their own legitimacy, and second there is the authority that particular modern readings seek in order to validate their own practices. In neither case can the appeal be made to "assumptions of any univocal articulation of authority as a given, unitary court of appeal" (8). As a Marxist, Weimann is always interested in those historical conjunctures when hitherto oppressed energy finds and secures its emancipation. He is also interested in the changing relationship between "subject" and "object" during the Renaissance, although he is very wary of the proposition that modern authority "became a product of writing, speaking, and reading, a result rather than primarily a constituent of representation" (5). Fictional discourses in the Renaissance—and he will go on in the book to offer specific examples—carry with them the traces of a range of antecedent cultural practices, and their complexity is exacerbated by an "interiorization and privatization of meaning" consequent upon the social, cultural, and ecclesiastical changes which took place during the Reformation,[29] along with a relatively new means of the circulation and exchange of these ideas, the printing press. Indeed, he identifies a link, which he suspects "(. . . is of unique cultural potency) between the decline of given, unitary, locations of authority and a unprecedented expansion of representational discourses" (4).

In *Authority and Representation in Early Modern Discourse* Weimann picks his way very carefully through a series of positions that have been subjected to serious scrutiny during the past decade. He is no longer content with an Enlightenment "teleology of progress," but he is very much aware that any prospect of similitude between his own personal situation as a nomadic scholar and the disintegration that he detects in Renaissance culture "invites at best self-projection, and at worst self-congratulation" (6). There is far less in this book about the classic Marxist notion of the "appropriation of nature for human needs," and much more about the consequences of the emergence of "the disparate set of relations between language and existence that created the need for . . . several contradictory registers of authority and authorization" (11).

The Elizabethan public theater continues to provide Weimann with the model for diverse and often agonistic representations of authority, although he has now extended his horizons to encompass the literature of sermons, medieval romance, and the writings of Luther and Calvin, Rabelais, Cervantes, and Thomas Nashe. His concern is with the ways in which these discursive sites interconnect, and with the implications of their overlapping. For example, in three public agencies, such as the sermon, the printing press, and the public stage, new sites of authority established themselves on the same textual grounds as those they supplanted. Having acceded to a sense of the power of discourse to effect transformation in the world at large, Weimann is then able to focus upon representation itself as a site of contestation. Criticism, he argues, has consistently underplayed the significance of "the point of discord and interaction between world-picturing representations *in* the text and the text's cultural uses in the circumstantial world of actually achieved cultural transactions and appropriations" (22). In concentrating upon various texts and the dynamics of their production, circulation, and consumption, Weimann neatly circumvents any suggestion that he has capitulated to a poststructuralist insistence upon the primacy of the signifier. Moreover, he is also at pains to stress that Renaissance authority, and by implication Renaissance subjectivity, cannot be reduced to a simple binary opposition between "outward power and inward spirituality (25). However, his concern with "the author function" and the questions of legitimation and authority that arise from it allows him to divert his attention from an extended discussion of subjectivity and this, in certain respects, is one of the few lacunae in the complex thesis he advances.

Weimann begins with a discussion of the transformation that takes place in ecclesiastical discourse, and he offers the writings of Luther and Calvin as examples of two differently inflected responses to "the Reformation crisis of ecclesiastical authority." Luther, for example, positions himself within the ethos of a writing that had become "an officially uncontrolled act of public communication," with the result that "as he half addresses and half creates his audience, the burden of his newly assumed representativity is so great, the unconfirmed authority so precarious, that it tangibly affects his performance, making his utterance sound tentative, self-conscious and defensive, as perhaps never before or after" (32–33). The question of style, which Weimann later takes up in relation to Cervantes and Thomas Nashe, is important in that it allows him to negotiate in some detail both the transition from oral to literate culture, and the resulting linguistic variety in which residual and emergent forms jostle with each other within particular texts. Without subscribing to the constitutive power of the difference in the production of the signifier, Weimann is able to draw a crucial distinction between pre-reformation legitimation practice, in which representation was a "delegated act of institutionalised power and homogeneity, where alterity was affirmed as something given even before the particular acts of writing, thinking, and reading began" (34), and a post-Reformation strategy that foregrounded indeterminacy and "incertitude, between the signifying and the signified levels of prepresentation"; the notion of a "strategy" here, it would seem, leaves open the possibility of a self-fashioning that retains some degree of agency in the process of rendering compatible "political subordination and spiritual freedom" (35). In contrast, Weimann argues, Calvin rejected this Lutheran antinomy, placing emphasis upon "the self-authentication of scripture" and thereby resisting any attempt to subject the Word "to proof and reasoning" (46–48).[30]

In an argument whose ramifications spread into many aspects of Renaissance culture, Weimann analyzes acutely both the linguistic practices within whose aegis authority was produced and also its thematization as a preoccupation of absolutist rulers. Indeed, what began as Reformation became in some instances revolution (the Kett Rebellion of 1549, for example), as the struggle for control of the authorizing of representation in ecclesiastical discourse spilled over into a contest for discourse itself and the power to legitimize meaning. Moreover, and despite the possibilities of physical coercion, the legacy of discord that this contestation bequeathed was connected, so Weimann argues, to "the need to negotiate vital interests ideologically, to shift the medium through which power was appropriated from that of violence and tradition of that of discourse and argument (64). Here Weimann fleshes out the New Historicist perception of the theatricality of identity by demonstrating its imbrication of the fundamentally linguistic performance of a conflict in which signs were then severed from their stable anchoring

points in authorized representations of the world. The public theater becomes, in this argument, symptomatic of "the empty signifier," of the gulf between reality and appearance induced by a new
social mobility (66).

The density of Weimann's argument resists paraphrase as he
picks his way carefully through a series of positions with which
he retains some affinity but not complete agreement. Historical
detail is judiciously mobilized in support of complex, theoretically
sophisticated arguments, which allow him to stage his own encounters with the past. He is alive to any clue to the location of
the inception of modernity, as in his brief championing of the Lord
Protector Somerset's response to the strictures of Bishop Gardiner,
in relation to a discussion of the vice figure "Idolatry" in John
Bale's *Three Laws*; where the latter insisted upon "stable relations
between signs and meanings" that would buttress "the distinction
between 'true' and 'false' representation, between authoritative uses
of 'images and ceremonies' and mere 'idolatry'" (74). Somerset resisted the injunction to gather all forms of unauthorized or unruly
language together as a part of a composite definition of "evil," prof-
fering instead "a vision of varied discursive activities" and thereby
making an "early (possibly the earliest known) attempt to come to
terms with that nascent differentiation of discourses which may
well be said to be constitutive of modernity" (76). The operative
term here is "differentiation," and it is worth recalling in this connection the Heideggerian roots of Weimann's preoccupation with
representation. For Heidegger the notion of a "world picture" is
emphatically not a picture of the world, but "the world conceived
and grasped as picture." Heidegger continues:

> What is, in its entirety, is now taken in such a way that it first is in
> being and only is in being to the extent that it is set up by man, who
> represents and sets forth. Wherever we have the world picture, an essen-
> tial decision takes place regarding what is, in its entirety, the Being of
> whatever is, is sought and found in the latter.
>
> However, everywhere the whatever is, is *not* interpreted in this way,
> the world cannot also enter into a picture; there can be no world pic-
> ture. The fact that whatever is comes into being in and through repre-
> sentedness transformed the age in which this occurs into a new age in
> contrast with the preceding one.[31]

Weimann has no wish to pursue the antihumanist implications of
this Heideggerian position. Rather, he wishes to retain an integrated vision of the totality of the social formation, where each

activity is overdetermined but cannot be reduced to the status of a text. For Weimann, the concept of a radical rupture remains a possibility, although he is perfectly well aware of the historically verifiable fact that revolutionary energy is frequently dispersed across a number of positions that may well be in conflict with each other. However, what is crucial to Weimann's thesis is the emerging notion of authorship whose definition does not hinge upon a Derridean distinction between speech and writing as "a duplicitous attempt to justify the autonomous subject and the subjective world,"[32] or upon the Foucauldian notion of disciplinary regimes. Rather, he sees the emerging category of authorship during the period as an essentially humanist "positioning of the writer as a creative and responsible agent between interior and exterior modes of expression [which] helped fortify the public plane and moral status of authorship" (109). This leads him to the conclusion that there existed a continuity between the verbal articulations of authority and "the political parameters of authority" that could be viewed both "strategically" and, in the case of public theaters, "ironically" (110). This is one of the reasons why Weimann believes that the passage from an oral to a literate culture is so important, and one of his objectives in this book is to tease out in the texts he chooses some of the densely interwoven strands that mark this transition.

It would be misleading to suggest, however, that Weimann's project is the production of a single historical narrative. It is indeed the case that in *Authority and Representation in Early Modern Discourse* he returns regularly to a number of issues that have both a social and economic resonance. For example, linguistic indeterminacy and the impulse to reconstitute and legitimize authority occurs at a historical conjuncture marked by the displacement and volatility of commercial markets (150–179), and as part of a fascinating discussion of Nashe's amalgamation of different registers in his own fiction, he cites Jean-Christophe Agnew's neatly elliptical observation that that market "was made meaningful at the very moment that meaning itself was becoming marketable (179). What are, in effect, a series of anthropological concerns never become obstacles to the respect that Weimann accords the texts he discusses. In this sense he retains a firm commitment to the social value of art as an irrepressible human activity capable of undermining ideology as well as figuring forth its contours. He is doubtful about what he calls "the inverted teleology" behind Foucault's analysis of the history of representation, but he is characteristically generous in his acknowledgment that Foucault's account is persuasive "on the *ends* and *limits* of representation." And yet, when all is said and done, theories of representation are, he argues, ineffective when dealing with "the non-representable dimension of existence" (190). For Weimann the late-sixteenth-century crisis in representation derives from the growing opacity of the sign itself: "There is no representation without taxation," and he sees what he calls "the overtaxing" of representation as the consequence of "exacting from it too much presence in the presentation of too many imaginary articles, actions, and relations in a new, movable order of contingency (197).

It is at the point of intersection between "imagination" and "the imaginary" that Weimann's thesis finally comes to a provisional rest. Taking his cue from Duke Theseus's account of the characteristic features of the early modern poetic imagination in *A Midsummer Night's Dream*, he insists that this faculty, "far from serving as the innermost source and image of subjectivity," was also a "strong vessel for shaping and transfiguring perceptions" (200), a species of "radical imaginary" that could become the vehicle for emancipatory narratives. Moreover, in a bid to shake himself free from the now discredited subversion/containment debate, Weimann seeks to map out briefly a site for a more wide-ranging early modern political unconscious. In a manner that is in some ways similar to Foucault's idea of the rule of the "tactical polyvalence of discourses,"[33] he wants to emphasize the *positive* opportunities within the process of representation itself for change and innovation: "Positively speaking, the sites of conscience, choice, invention, exchange, and the imaginary, especially strong when linked, marked the broadest space for innovative practices in and through representation."[34] It is clear from this that Weimann wishes to hold on to the methodology of Marxist dialectics. And he retains a firm belief in historical materialism: hence his fascination with the Elizabethan theater as a limit case. But what is remarkable about this immensely rewarding but nonetheless difficult book is the extent to which the larger interest in totalities gives way in so many instances during the argument to concentration upon micropolitical activity. If he cannot quite bring himself to map out in detail a psychological account of subjectivity that might negotiate the formidable gulf between the determinations implicit in a totalizing explanation and the imperatives of a postmodern historical contingency, then he has, at least, given us notice that a vibrant, supple, unapologetically Marxist epistemology, especially in the hands of an accomplished writer such as Robert Weimann, is capable of rising to these important challenges.

Notes

I wish to thank Professor Catherine Belsey of the Centre for Critical and Cultural Theory at the University of Cardiff for having read and commented on an earlier draft of this essay.

1. Fredric Jameson, "Radicalizing Radical Shakespeare: The Permanent Revolution in Shakespeare Studies," in *Materialist Shakespeare: A History,* ed. Ivo Kamps (London and New York, 1995), 328.

2. Jacques Derrida, *Specters of Marx: The State of the Debt, the Work of Mourning, and the New International,* trans. Peggy Kamuf (New York and London, 1994), 50: "Very novel and so ancient, the conjuration appears both powerful and, as always, worried, fragile, anxious. The enemy to be conjured away, for those sworn to the conjuration, is, to be sure, called Marxism. But people are now afraid that they will no longer recognize it. They quake at the hypothesis that, by virtue of one of those metamorphoses that Marx talked about so much ("metamorphosis" was one of his favorite words throughout his life), a new 'Marxism' will no longer have the face by which one was accustomed to identify it and put it down. Perhaps people are no longer afraid of Marxists, but they are still afraid of certain non-Marxists who have renounced Marx's inheritance, crypto-Marxists, pseudo-or para-"Marxists" who would be standing by to change the guard, but behind features or quotation marks that the anxious experts of anti-communism are not trained to unmask."

3. Cf. Francis Fukuyama, *The End of History and the Last Man* (London, 1992), 44–51.

4. Robert Weimann, "The Soul of the Age: Towards a Historical Approach to Shakespeare," in *Shakespeare in a Changing World,* ed. Arnold Kettle (London, 1964), 17.

5. Robert Weimann, *Shakespeare and the Popular Tradition in the Theater: Studies in the Social Dimension of Dramatic Form and Function,* ed. Robert Schwartz (Baltimore and London, 1978), xii.

6. *Ibid.* "these techniques helped to define and achieve a social and artistic position more comprehensive and more vital in the areas of both its independence and its relatedness, its skepticism and its freedom."

7. Robert Weimann, *Structure and Society in Literary History: Studies in the History and Theory of Historical Criticism* (London, 1976), 23.

8. Stephen Greenblatt, *Learning to Curse: Essays in Early Modern Culture* (New York and London, 1990), 167.

9. Jacques Derrida, *Acts of Literature,* ed. Derek Attridge (New York and London, 1992) 63.

10. Robert Weimann, *Structure and Society in Literary History,* exp. ed. (Baltimore and London, 1984), 287: "Whereas the communicative functions of the spoken word will again and again establish the signifying principle *aliquid stat pro aliquo,* the textualised stratum of language as inscription can more easily be dissociated from the necessary historicity of such significations. What 'textuality' presupposes, then, is a self-generating mode of interaction within a system of *difference* to which the scriptor (and reader) can relate in response to some unbearable constraint in the socially representative function of language. In relinquishing this function, the poststructuralist critic suspends the need for

continuing to confront the links as well as the contradictions between voice and utterance, life and writing, socio-individual existence and the systematic uses of language. As against the weight of these contradictions, culminating as they do in the triumphs and defeats, the possibilities and impossibilities, of representation, the Derridean textuality shields the inscribed utterance from the historical compulsions of the author in his social acts of cultural representativity."

11. Perry Anderson, *In the Tracks of Historical Materialism: The Wellek Library Lectures* (London, 1983), 50.

12. Robert Weimann, "Society and the Individual in Shakespeare's Conception of Character," *Shakespeare Survey* 34 (Cambridge, 1981), ed. Stanley Wells, 25). Cf. Jonathan Dollimore, *Radical Tragedy; Religion, Ideology and Power in the Drama of Shakespeare and His Contemporaries*, 2d ed. (New York and London, 1989), 70–71.

13. Ernesto Laclau, *Emancipations(s)* (London and New York, 1996), 16–17.

14. Weimann, *Structure and Society* exp. ed. (Baltimore and London, 1984), 309.

15. Robert Weimann, "Mimesis in *Hamlet*," in *Shakespeare and the Question of Theory*, ed. Patricia Parker and Geoffrey Hartman, (New York and London, 1985) 275–76.

16. Fredric Jameson, *The Political Unconscious: Narrative as a Socially Symbolic Act* (London, 1981), 35.

17. Robert Weimann, "Towards a Literary Theory of Ideology: Mimesis, Representation, Authority," in *Shakespeare Reproduced: The Text in History and Ideology*, ed. Jean E. Howard and Marion F. O' Connor (New York and London, 1987), 266.

18. Robert Weimann, "Shakespeare (De)Canonized: Conflicting Uses of 'Authority' and 'Representation'," *New Literary History* 20 (1988–89), 65–81.

19. Robert Weimann, "Textual Authority and Performative Agency: The Uses of Disguise in Shakespeare's Theatre," *New Literary History: A Journal of Theory and Interpretation* 25: no. 4 (Autumn 1994) 789–808.

20. Robert Weimann, "'Moralize Two Meanings' in One Play: Divided Authority on the Medieval Stage, *Medievalia*, 18 (1995): 427–50.

21. Robert Weimann, "Thresholds to Memory and Commodity in Shakespeare's Endings," *Representations* 53 (winter, 1996): 1–20.

22. Cf. Jurgen Habermas, *The theory of Communicative Action: The Critique of Functionalist Reason*, trans. Thomas McCarthy, 2, 68–70 (Cambridge, 1987).

23. It may be that Weimann has in mind statements such as the following from Foucault, which posit a tenuous and irreducibly textual, form of "history": "We must renounce all those themes whose function is to ensure the infinite continuity of discourse and its secret presence to itself in the interplay of a constantly recurring absence. We must be ready to receive every moment of discourse in its sudden irruption; in that punctuality in which it appears, and in that temporal dispersion that enables it to be repeated, known, forgotten, transformed, utterly erased, and hidden, far from all view, in the dust of books. Discourse must not be referred to the distant presence of the origin, but treated as and when it occurs." Michel Foucault, *The Archeology of Knowledge*, trans. A. M. Sheridan Smith (London, 1972), 25.

24. Weimann, "Thresholds to Memory," 70–71.

25. Laclau, *Emancipation(s)*, 17.

26. Weimann, "Threshold to Memory," 73.

27. Robert Weimann, *Authority and Representation in Early Modern Discourse*, ed. David Hillmann (Baltimore and London, 1996), 7.

28. But cf. also *Subject and Object in Renaissance Culture,* ed., Margreta de Grazia, Maureen Quilligan, and Peter Stallybrass (Cambridge, 1996), 5: "The very ambiguity of the word 'ob-ject', that which is *thrown before,* suggests a more dynamic status for the object. Reading 'ob' as 'before' allows us to assign the object a prior status, suggesting its temporal, spatial, and even causal *coming before.* The word could thus be made to designate the potential priority of the object. So defined, the term renders more apparent the way material things—land, clothes, tools—might constitute subjects who in turn own, use and transform them. The form/matter relation of Aristotelian metaphysics is thereby provisionally reversed: it is the material object that impresses its texture and contour upon the noumenal subject. And this reversal is curiously upheld by the ambiguity of the word 'subject', that which is *thrown under,* in this case—in order to receive an imprint." This argument attempts to explode the connection between "the subject" and the Foucauldian "sovereignty of consciousness" at the expense of the object. What is not clear in the introduction to the volume is the extent to which objects here designated are what Bataille would call "raw phenomena" (Georges Battaille, "Materialism," *Visions of Excess: Selected Writings, in 1927–1939,* ed., Alan Stoekl (Manchester, 1985), 15–16. See also Martin Heidegger "The Age of the World Picture," in *The Question Concerning Technology and Other Essays,* trans. William Lovitt (New York, 1977), 128, for a gloss on the term "subject" that is diametrically opposed to that of de Grazia, Quilligan, and Stallybrass. In concerning himself primarily with the process of *representation* Weimann neatly circumvents this complex issue, although it is one of which he is very much aware.

29. Weimann, *Authority and Representation,* 4.

30. Weimann later notes that this attempt "to relocate authority through strengthening the relations of institution and inspiration, state and church, Spirit and Scripture" failed (52).

31. Heidegger, "Age of the World Picture," 129–30. For Heidegger, to represent *(vor-stellen)* "means to bring what is present at hand [das *Vorhandene*] before oneself as standing over against, to relate it to oneself, to the one representing it, and to force it back into this relationship to oneself as the normative realm. Wherever this happens, man "gets himself into the picture" in precedence over what is. But in that man puts himself into the picture in this way, he puts himself into the scene, i.e., into the open sphere of that which is generally and publicly represented. Therewith man sets himself up as the setting in which whatever is must henceforth set itself forth, must present itself *(sich . . . prasentieren],* i.e., be picture. Man becomes the representative [*der Repraseeentant*] of that which is, in the sense of that which has the character of object" (131–32).

32. Weimann, *Authority and Representation,* 108.

33. Michel Foucault, *History of Sexuality,* vol. 1, trans. Robert Hurley (Harmondsworth, 1981), 100ff.

34. Weimann, *Authority and Representation,* 202–3.

The Early Modern and the Homoerotic Turn in Political Criticism

JEAN E. HOWARD

T HE REISSUING in 1995 of Alan Bray's *Homosexuality in Renaissance England* I take as a sign that gay, lesbian and queer criticisms now have an acknowledged place in early modern literary and cultural studies. In the first chapter of *Sodometries*, published in 1992, Jonathan Goldberg wrote that the investigation of early modern sexualities can "transform utterly our sense of what Renaissance texts are about, where produced, and in whose interests" (p. 24). This review will look, a bit in retrospect, at what the four pioneering books discussed below have contributed to the achievement of this ambitious goal, how collectively they have set a complicated and multi-focused agenda for the field, and what it would mean if their insights were incorporated into a wide range of early modern scholarship. Ideally, the new scholarship on sexuality is more than the manifestation of an identity-based set of political commitments. It ought to change the questions generally asked of early modern cultural productions and to shift our understanding of the kinds of behaviours and practices that structured social life.

Examining the domain of sexuality in early modern texts extends the work on gender, class, race, and power that marked the remarkable efflorescence of political criticism in Renaissance studies throughout the 1980's. The by now well-studied emergence of feminism, new historicism, and cultural materialism allowed Renaissance literature to be examined, not for transcendental truth, but for its relationship to historically specific discourses, ideologies, and institutions. This scholarship also often took itself as an object of study, arguing that if literary texts have historical and political causes and effects, so does criticism; further, that the work of collective and ongoing critique was to change not only what Renaissance texts could mean, but also what questions, assumptions, and methods would govern the critical practice of the present.

The new work on early modern sexuality has already had several important effects. One has been to make visible the range of homoerotic discourses and practices that were part of early modern culture, in effect "deheterosexualizing" our collective assumptions about the period and making it possible to read Renaissance texts with a new set of possibilities in mind. We can now see that emphasis on the cultural centrality of early modern marriages, and on love rhetorics that imagine a male lover and a female beloved, has obscured the importance of various kinds of sexual practice to other cultural institutions such as schools, apprenticeships, domestic service, armies, and courts, and has overlooked those love rhetorics in which the lover and the beloved share a sex. At the same time, gay, lesbian, and queer criticism has also focused on current critical practice and the heterosexism that sometimes permeates it, even the supposedly "progressive" criticism written by new historicists and feminists. This review looks at how the books in question address these issues, reconstitute the early modern text as an object of study, and lay the ground for further work.

Foucault's influence is everywhere apparent in this criticism, starting with his insistence that sexuality *has* a history and is not an ahistorical, transcultural given. All make clear that the late nineteenth-century terms *homosexual* and *heterosexual* are anachronistic when applied to early modern subjects (though acknowledging that fact does not solve the problem of terminology) and that in this period people did not have sexual "identities," that is, were not classified according to what we now call "sexual orientation." Rather, depending on their age and social position, they might at different times engage without contradiction in sexual acts involving parties of the same sex and partners of the opposite sex. All agree, however, that at least for men, while homoerotic activity appears to have been significant and not necessarily incompatible with marriage, it was also always dangerously shadowed by the potential charge of sodomy.

These ideas, which have become the commonplace of the new early modern sexuality criticism, had their first powerful expression in Alan Bray's work, first published in 1982 by The Gay Men's Press in London. At the heart of Bray's work is his discussion of the gap between the almost hysterical condemnation of sodomy in some polemical and religious writings and evidence that sexual acts between men were, in some social circumstances, quite widespread. They seem, for example, to have taken place with some frequency between masters and apprentices and masters and servants within the early modern household and between teachers and students within the school and university. Bray's explanation of the gap between the official condemnation of sodomy and the prevalence of same-sex sexuality is also an important one. He argues that since the sexual practices he examines were not expressions of sexual identity but were mapped on to, in fact helped to constitute, some of the important social relations of the culture, these practices were demonized—that is, were called sodomitical—only when they became connected to a disruption of those social relations. In a social crisis involving a breakdown of order, "sodomites" could become the scapegoats; or if sexual relations between men disrupted the sexual relations of husband and wife, such behavior might also be labelled sodomitical. Bray insists that it was not any particular act that was denoted as sodomitical; rather, the context in which an act occurred and the social circumstances in which it was interpreted determined whether the dreaded label was applied. This explains, to Bray's mind, the fact that a monarch such as James I could rail against sodomites while engaging in various homoerotic activities with his male favorites. He did not recognize in his own practices the disorderly beastliness he attributed to others.

It is hard to overestimate the importance of Bray's work. It has been crucial in establishing the difference between the hysterical discourse concerning sodomy (a crime that for a long time had no specific referent but included all unspeakable crimes against order such as treason, atheism, and buggery) and the evidence of widespread homoerotic practice. Bray's work also has limitations and raises problems of method that subsequent investigators have had to address. First, of course, is the absence of attention to female sexual subjects. Foucault, too, primarily presented the sexual subject as male; and Bray's interests and evidence concern relations between men. In the late 1970's and early 1980's early modern gender criticism focused on women, implying that women were the "gendered" sex; Bray is but one of many scholars whose work might give the impression that men are the "sexed" sex. Second, Bray's work raises the difficult issue of what kind of evidence one uses in writing about sexuality in the early modern period. Probably because of his disciplinary home in history, Bray focuses on actual sexual practice. While not naive about the difficulties of interpreting the various texts in which traces of such activity might be encoded, such as court records, Bray nonetheless distinguishes sharply between the greater value to his project of legal records and the lesser value of literary texts. For him, literary representations of homoerotic practice and desire are unreliable as evidence of early modern sexual practice both because they are highly conventional and because they have precedents in imaginative literature stretching back to Greek pastoral. Bray also expresses anxiety that such texts might reflect "political bias" in their descriptions of homosexual practice (p. 37). Consequently, his method of proceeding is to read court records of sexual crimes against what he can construct of the social context in which they occurred, mainly that of rural village life with its hierarchical structures of daily life. Only then does he read the material found in court records against the literary representations found in satire, pastoral, the drama, etc. The evidence Bray uses produces a picture of early modern sexual practice focused mainly on rural communities among people who knew one another, such as parsons and their parishioners or masters and their apprentices. Bray is skeptical that London or other cities contained more same-sex sex than villages, though he does indicate that homosexual prostitution probably was centered in urban milieus.

The three other books here discussed all owe an immense debt to Bray's pioneering study, but they differ considerably in terms of methodology and even in terms of purpose. Each, however, implicitly or explicitly revisits the question of evidence, of what one can learn from different kinds of texts about sexual practices and discourses of sexuality in this period. Jonathan Goldberg's *Sodometries*, the book perhaps most obviously indebted to Bray, puts immediate pressure on the idea that any text is free of "political bias," especially legal documents. Goldberg begins with a chapter in which in part he analyzes the language and logic of *Bowers v. Hardwick*, a contemporary legal case involving the rights of homosexuals, precisely to show how impossible it is to disentangle law and ideology, legal writing and questions of convention. For Goldberg, even in law cases sodomy remains an utterly confused category, one, however, that is often deployed in logically indefensible ways to achieve discriminatory ends. The ruses of legal language, therefore, need as much attention as the thickets of literary representation.

Goldberg's overarching project, however, needs to be distinguished from Bray's. Bray's work clearly emerges from the British movement to gain gay visibility in the 1970's. It attempts to write a history, not of an unchanging homosexual identity, but of the different practices and institutions that have governed sexual relations among men at different cultural moments, in this case the early modern period in England. His is a particular kind of gay history, one stressing epistemic breaks, rather than sameness and continuity. While Goldberg has certainly taken both Bray and Foucault on board, *Sodometries* is ultimately not all that concerned with historicist questions. The geographical and temporal coordinates of *Sodometries* are vast. It moves from the 1990 Iraqi invasion of Kuwait to the humanist circle at the court of Henry VIII to the early 1980's emergence of new historicism to Balboa's sixteenth-century progress across Central America to the internal workings of the Massachusetts Bay Colony in the seventeenth century. But there is no painstaking delineation, as with Bray, of the specific social structures in each of these arenas within which sodomitical discourses played a constitutive role. Rather, throughout *Sodometries* there is a certain flattening of cultural and temporal specificity.

That is, I think, because Goldberg is primarily concerned, not with the "recovery" of the past, but with contesting how it is constructed in the present. He does not offer the reader new archival materials, but rather a mode of reading that critiques homophobic and heterosexist interpretations of the past and offers alternatives. The subtitle of *Sodometries* is *Renaissance Texts, Modern Sexualities*, a tantalizing juxtaposition that suggests, among other possibilities, that there is both a difference and a connection between the two, that is, between how sexuality is conceptualized now and how critics read the texts through which they construct the sexualities of an earlier period. The comma in this subtitle, and what I take to be the deliberate eschewal of the term "early modern," suggest to me that Goldberg is *not* assuming continuity between the Renaissance and the present in terms of sexual practices, but *is* suggesting that contemporary sexual regimes structure discourse about the past. Hence his own strenuous project of reading that involves (1) exposing the illogic and the political interests at work in the languages of stigmatization used to separate licit from illicit sexual acts; (2) critiquing the workings of the straight (and misogynist) mind in contemporary criticism; and (3) offering contestatory readings from an antihomophobic position.

In his work of reading, Goldberg employs the tactics of politicized deconstruction to expose the false binaries that sever the heterosexual from the homosexual, the licit from the sodomitical. A major point of his analysis of *Bowers v. Hardwick*, for example, is to show that fellatio, the sodomitical act for which consenting males were condemned, is exactly the same act as that performed without penalty by consenting married couples. He brilliantly exposes the hypocrisy and misrecognition involved in condemning the one performance of this act and ignoring the other. *Sodometries*, the nonce word Goldberg takes from Phillip Stubbes to use for his title, is, of course, his prime example of the indeterminacy and non-referentiality of terms of demonization. While they may seem to denote specific acts, more often they are gestures toward a politically determined understanding of what is unspeakable or unnatural—in this case, sexual intimacy between consenting male adults, not fellatio per se. Goldberg's reading technique sets the word against the word, dismantles seemingly fixed oppositions, exposes naturalized assumptions within highly ideological discourse. But unlike weak forms of deconstruction in which such tactics seem to be ends in themselves, Goldberg's practice keeps in mind always the effectivity of the word in the world. As he makes clear, sodomitical discourses have had and continue to have their role in legalizing executions, endangering civil rights, and shaming some categories of sexual subjects.

An awareness of the worldly stakes of discourse is undoubtedly what motivates Goldberg's relentless critique of other critics as well as the complex manner in which he pursues multiple lines of argument—and multiple targets—simultaneously. For example, in the first part of the book Goldberg investigates the role of sexuality in establishing social position in the courtly world of Henry VIII and Elizabeth I. Several lines of argument are knotted together in this section. First, Goldberg aims to show the importance of homoerotic relations in the careers of those writers and humanist pedagogues such as Gabriel Harvey, Edmund Spenser, and Sir Philip Sidney considered central to "the golden age" of sixteenth-century literature. He is, in essence, queering the golden age. At the same time Goldberg pursues the theoretical point that desire need not flow only between men and women, or even between those gendered masculine and feminine, respectively. Instead, he argues for the possibility of a broad range of cross identifications and multiple vectors of desire. They are not always structured as heterosexuality is supposedly structured, that is, as the desire between two genders. Third, he takes to task those new historicist and feminist critics who have supposedly "straightened" the Elizabethan golden age by insisting on the primacy of just such structures of desire. He especially critiques those who insist on the "essential" femininity of Elizabeth I, or who subtly denigrate the supposedly effeminizing effects of her court in contrast to the allegedly robust masculinity of the court of Henry VIII. As is typical of most of the book, a critique of contemporary misogyny, homophobia, and hetero-sexism, as exemplified by a range of modern critics, ushers in a rereading of specific Renaissance texts to present their encodings of sexuality in a new light.

Part of the challenge of this theoretically sophisticated book comes from the density of its argumentative strategies. Sometimes, however, that very density produces odd results. In the second part of the book, for example, Chapters 4 and 5, Goldberg turns to the question of sodomy and the Renaissance stage. Again, there are multiple agendas in play. One is to critique those who discuss early modern homoeroticism through representations of cross-dressing, mainly because that way of approaching homoeroticism *can* construct homosexuality as the interaction between a feminized and a masculine man, in other words, as a version of the most common understanding of heterosexuality. Goldberg argues that Marlowe, in particular, in the beginning of *Edward II* explicitly eschews that way of representing sexual relations between men. Rather than investigating cross-dressing, Goldberg, following Bray, turns to representations of friendship as the place where sodomitical discourses are to be found. His most sustained example is Prince Hal's relationship to Falstaff. Criticizing both those who have seen in Falstaff's corporeality a projection of feminine attributes and those who have praised Hal as a maturing exemplar of English manhood, Goldberg reads Falstaff as Hal's bedmate and Hal as a hypocritical sodomite with a small prick. Here, his disdain for those who idealize the prince and relate to him as a paragon of heterosexual masculinity leads Goldberg to both "out" Hal and to abject him. Seizing on the lines when the Prince berates Falstaff for not caring what time it is unless "the blessed sun himself" were "a fair hot wench in flame-coloured taffeta" (1.2.9–10), Goldberg declares that Hal is the "sun/son" and that he is here sodomitically revealing the role reversals that make his follower, Falstaff, his master in bed while also revealing his own desire to go cross-dressed in red taffeta. Here Goldberg's anger at idealizing critics overbalances his desire to produce antihomophobic readings of early modern texts. His deliberately provocative picture of a red taffeta-dressed Prince with a small sexual member assaults the idealizing constructions of certain critics, but fails to secure his own construction from homophobic coloration. His prince is a queen, a rather pathetic, self-deceiving one, and the slim critical pleasure Goldberg takes in Hal

seems largely to be the pleasure of unmasking a fraud and exposing
the misrecognitions of those who are said to invest in him.

Sodometries is a very smart and deliberately provocative book,
though on occasion its complicated tactics seem to go awry, as in
the discussion of Falstaff and Hal; and I think that there are real
drawbacks to zeroing in so persistently on the purported hetero-
sexism of other people's criticism. Naming so many guilty parties
I assume is meant to make the point that the field is saturated with
heterosexist discourse and to alleviate the impression that any one
person is being personally singled out for critique. But touching
briefly on the work of so many critics multiplies the possibilities
for flattening and misrepresenting their arguments and invites a
kind of trivializing interest in who is being called to task and who
is not. Moreover, there is a decontextualizing dimension to Goldberg's discussions of other critics. Whether discussing the production of the Spenser Variorum in the 1940's or the emergence of
second-wave feminism in the 1970's or the ascendancy of new his-
torism in the 80's, Goldberg zooms in only on the conjoined homophobia and misogyny he discerns in them all. He pays almost no
attention to the social contexts in which each arose or to their
quite different political consequences and effects or, in fact, to the
importance of some in enabling the kind of work he himself does.
I am not so much asking for a kinder, gentler criticism as a recognition of the collaborative, ongoing nature of the efforts to combat
the kinds of injustice gestured at by words like homophobia, misogyny, and racism.

The last thing I want to say about Sodometries returns again to
the title. The word Sodometries is carefully chosen to suggest the
illogic of stigmatizing discourses. The point is that fantasmatic hor-
rors, not specific behaviors, are evoked through these discourses,
and so they can be applied in an arbitrary manner. But a further
question is whether a focus on the sodomitical obscures both the
prevalence of homoerotic activity that escaped demonization in the
early modern period and also its importance in structuring social
relations among men, and possibly among women, in a wide variety of circumstances. In short, were men who had sex with other
men sometimes in a privileged position? Was such behavior a constitutive part of certain communities and institutions? Goldberg
would undoubtedly answer yes to both questions, but his primary
focus is on the workings of stigmatization and homophobia. To
understand fully the role of same-sex sex in early modern culture

will also mean attending to the circumstances in which it is culturally central, as well as marginal, valorized, as well as demonized.

Bruce Smith's *Homosexual Desire in Shakespeare's England* offers one route into some of this territory. While Smith gives an account of the development of sodomy law in sixteenth-century England and registers the stigmatizing voices of satirist and moralist, he concentrates primarily on those early modern texts that allow him to construct positive expressions of what he calls, in the key words of his title, homosexual desire. Reading the culture of early modern England as neither homophilic like that of Greece nor homophobic like ours, Smith sees it as one of conflict and contradiction that both encouraged intense forms of male bonding and in certain circumstances stigmatized and punished those who participated in these structures. Smith's emphasis, however, falls not on sodomy or sodometries, but on elaborating the various literary languages and stories through which homosocial and homoerotic desire could be articulated. Unlike Bray, Smith values literature precisely because in it he finds evidence, not of acts, but of desires (p. 17).

Smith structures his book as an examination of certain "myths" expressive, he asserts, of different kinds of homosexual desire in the period, each possessing its own plots and characters, classical sources, and geographical sites, and each correlating to some aspect of actual social life in the period. The most inclusive of these myths is that of "Combatants and Comrades" which idealizes the male bonds that form in conditions of war and intense oppositionality. Not explicitly erotic, the bonds of the myth of combatants and comrades nonetheless in the widest sense underwrite the masculine structures of affiliation and control that structure early modern culture, though interestingly, the stories depicting these bonds also show how they come into conflict with marriage bonds. These narratives, then, become ways of mediating the gaps between the period's multiple sexual practices.

In *Homosexual Desire in Shakespeare's England* Smith examines five other "myths," beginning with those of the "Passionate Shepherd" and the "Shipwrecked Youth" found respectively in pastoral and in Greek romance, arguing that the former, more explicitly sexual than the myth of combatants and comrades, has its social homology in the period when young unmarried men were engaged in education or apprenticeships; while the latter has its analogue in periods of social inversion and carnival when cross-dressing, gender inversion, and same-gender desire were permitted. Chapter

V, by contrast, takes up the explicitly sexual and derogatory discourses of satire, here called "The Myth of Knights in Shifts," that had its counterpart in the supposed dissipation of the urban elites. Chapters 6 and 7 deal with Marlowe and Shakespeare. The former, entitled "Masters and Minions," focuses not on a myth but an image, the moment when Jupiter in the form of an eagle wafts Ganymede to heaven to be his cupbearer. Arguing that this is the most famous homoerotic story in the Renaissance, Smith reads it as central to Marlowe's vision in *Edward II*, a play in which the love between a king and his minion is presented as sodomitical because disruptive of class relations, but also as tragic and heroic. For Smith, the possibility of a homosexual subjectivity, hinted at in Marlowe, reaches its full expression in Shakespeare's sonnets, dominated by the myth of "The Secret Sharer" and having its counterpart in the idea of private life.

Regarded as a literary archive, Smith's book is a treasure trove. It makes reference to a wide range of texts in which desire between men is represented, including Barnfield's homoerotic sonnets to Ganymede, Beaumont's homoerotic epyllia, Sidney's *Arcadia*, and a host of stage plays. Moreover, Smith highlights generic distinctions among texts, inviting readers to recognize the conventions that in each case govern sexual expression. Based on this literary evidence, Smith suggests that in the early modern period sex between men was not depicted as exclusively age determined, that is, a matter of love between an older and a younger man, but could also be gender inflected, that is, could take the form of love between a more masculine and a more feminine male, or be based on similitude of status and gendering (p. 76). Throughout the book the highlighted terms are *desire* and *subjectivity*. While *acts, ideologies, and practices* dominate the vocabulary of many critics working in the field of early modern sexuality studies, Smith forthrightly focuses on the affective and subjective dimensions of sexual life.

Of course, this choice invites a host of questions, many having to do with the key term, *desire*. What is its status? Is homosexual desire simply *there*, a spontaneous expression of a universal passion? Is it something produced and channelled by specific cultural circumstances, specific prohibitions and incitements, particular articulations of power? Despite its centrality, desire itself is a curiously under-theorized term in Smith's book. Moreover, while he lays out a range of forms in which what he calls homosexual desire is expressed in the period, the weakest part of his argument is the attempt to link his six "myths" to their various "homologies" in social practice. Smith's underlying premise is that "myths" reflect something in the typical life cycle of social experience of men of the period. But the "homologies" Smith posits are impressionistic and vague. What, really, is the relationship between romance and Carnival or between pastoral and the life experiences of apprentices?

The relationship between the literary and the social plagued Bray. It remains problematic in Smith's work also. For a start, rather than focusing mainly on the content of these texts, it would also be helpful to situate the literary archive more completely in the social worlds in which it was produced and consumed. What writers wrote in each of the genres Smith explores? When were they popular? Who published which kinds of texts? What other ways did they circulate? Who read or watched them and in what circumstances? Knowing more about these matters would help establish the social provenance of texts in which homoerotic material was prominent. At the same time, it is important to query the assumption that "homosexual desire" is all that might motivate the writing or the reading of these texts. They *are* often conventional expressions, and they could be as easily written to gain patronage or to show the writer's fashionability as to reveal desire. I don't mean to suggest that the manifest content of these texts is irrelevant, only that it is dangerous to count on textual transparency. Finally, I think Smith's book does not fully clarify the status of homosexual subjectivity in the period before, it is generally agreed, one's sexuality constituted an identity. Smith implies that there is a special relationship between subjectivity and what Goldberg would call "sodometries" in the early modern period, but the exact nature of the historical claim being staked remains, to me at least, undefined.

The final book I am considering, Valerie Traub's *Desire and Anxiety: Circulations of Sexuality in Shakespearean Drama*, is distinctive in several ways. Most obviously, it is the only one that focuses on women, rather than primarily on men. And, strikingly, it makes the author's own struggles to find an adequate critical practice part of the narrative of the book. In the course of the work Traub self-consciously maps a movement from a feminist gender criticism to a feminist critique of sexuality, from a preoccupation with the containment of female power to an investigation of female agency, from the genres of tragedy and history to that of comedy. Simultaneously she registers her struggles to modify the languages of psychoanalysis, the traditional discourse for speaking of sexual desire, to take account of the historical dimensions of sexuality and its deployment. Not everything is successful in this book, but it attempts to chart territory into which almost no one has ventured.

Traub's introduction stakes out a great deal of theoretical ground. Her basic thesis is that sexuality is not natural, but is constructed along axes of desire and anxiety that, while deeply culturally coded, are nonetheless sufficiently multiple and contradictory to allow for individual agency and for change. Psychoanalysis alone will not explain the currents of anxiety and desire in the individual psyche. Rather, culture determines how both are shaped and deployed. In the early modern period, Traub argues, the stage had a special relationship to sexuality: it both represented states of erotic desire and anxiety and was itself a site where sexual energies flowed in multiple directions among audience, actors, and characters. She asserts that in this theater desire was not located in characters, but in the scene of performance itself. While this is an important claim in regard to why antitheatricalists reacted to the early modern theater with horror, Traub nonetheless cannot resist speaking in many places of desire and anxiety as in characters, that is, as emotions she attributes to Rosalind and Celia and the other dramatic figures she discusses. Perhaps the most telling aspect of her theoretical program, however, is her remarkably clear explanation of why studies of sexuality need, at least temporarily, to be separated from studies of gender in order to break the common sense notion that "each sex has a necessary gender" and "each gender has a corresponding, 'natural' sexuality" (p. 21). In other words, to be biologically categorized as a man does not guarantee that one's gender is masculine or that one's sexuality inevitably takes the form of desire for a woman. Feminist criticism that has traditionally taken gender as its starting point will not automatically, she argues, give an adequate account of sexuality or modes of oppression based on sexual criteria. Queer criticism, focusing on non-normative sexualities, strategically elides the category of gender precisely to undermine the foundational claims of gender that remain encoded even in the terms "gay" and "lesbian."

In the first half of the book when looking at plays primarily from the perspective of a feminist gender criticism, Traub focuses on the anxiety aroused in men by the erotic desire or the reproductive body of woman. These chapters consolidate feminist assumptions about the misogyny encoded in Shakespearean tragedy and history, though each attempts as well to show the instability of masculine dominance, the need for its endless performance and reperformance. The most original of the chapters is devoted to *Henry IV* and the thesis that Falstaff is not a surrogate father for Hal but a displaced figure of the abjected mother which Hal rejects in order to consolidate his adult, misogynist identity. This reading of Falstaff productively accounts for the conspicuous absence of Hal's mother and Henry's wife in the *Henry IV* plays, and it does not preclude Traub's also seeing Falstaff as Hal's homoerotic companion whose rejection marks Hal's disavowal of homoerotic desire and his eventual embrace of a marriage of alliance. In Traub's reading the link between misogyny and the flight from the homoerotic is made strikingly apparent without, I feel, essentializing and "fixing" the gendering of male-male sexuality as a mirror of heterosexuality.

The most pathbreaking part of the book, however, is the second half in which Traub queries the heterosexist assumptions she sees buried in some contemporary feminist scholarship and then turns to a consideration of how one might use drama to speak about women's desire for women in the early modern period. Gender offenses—such as scolding—and women's heterosexual offenses—such as giving birth to bastards—are documented in court records as well as represented in popular pamphlets and literary works. But of same-sex erotic desire or practice, or of sexual crimes between women such as tribadism or the use of dildos, the record in England in this period is nearly silent. Traub's working hypothesis is that this is not because there was no erotic activity among women, but because female homoeroticism, being neither an identity nor an institution, was virtually invisible as long as it did not disrupt the official institutions of society such as marriage and its reproductive regimes. I would argue that men's homoeroticism has remained more culturally legible because it often *part of*, rather than *opposed to*, dominant institutions. Part of patronage networks, schooling, work practices, it could underwrite power structures as well as disrupt them. Even though men's sexuality was also institutionally structured by marriage, that demand seems not to have precluded men's simultaneous sexual participation in other institutional sites and structures.

Traub uses her final chapter to explore how Shakespearean comedies of cross-dressing can be read in ways that suggest the existence of erotic bonds between women. Drawing on the traditional view of comedy as the genre of sexual possibilities, Traub does a dazzling reading of the multiple vectors of sexual desire in *As You Like It.* By contrast, she argues that *Twelfth Night* is more anxious about same-sex desire largely because of the presence of the aggressively possessive Antonio who threatens to preclude Sebastian's marriage and so his fulfillment of the reproductive imperative. In Traub's view, the boundary between reproductive and non-reproductive sexuality needs to be heavily policed in a culture in which marriages were a primary vehicle for securing and transmitting property, establishing lineage, and, in non-elite families, for providing labor for agricultural and domestic production. Any relationship that threatened permanently to remove a woman—or man—from reproductive possibilities would potentially fall under the category of the sodomitical. Nonetheless, it is also necessary to stress that for men the disorderly potential of homoerotic relations was not defined solely as their ability to disrupt reproduction. Why were things different for women? Were they so relatively unimportant in "public" life that it is *only* disruptions of marriage that are criminalized and stigmatized?

Taken as a whole, *Desire and Anxiety* is an important first step in understanding representations of women's sexuality in a period when most of the attention has focused on men. There are several things, however, that this book does not attempt. One is to bridge the gap between dramatic texts and other domains of social life— even other kinds of texts, such as diaries, letters, and popular pamphlets in which a fuller view of women's life in the family and neighborhood might emerge. If, in a period before sexual identities, eroticized relations among members of the same sex followed the trajectories of power and affiliation, what were those for women? What does one discover in examining the world of the female monarch and her female courtiers? In looking at mistresses and their serving women? In examining particular communities, such as the women in recusant families? In looking at friendship patterns, traced by the exchange of manuscripts, among gentry women? The gains of a gender-based feminist criticism are crucial to maintain and extend if we can hope to answer the questions posed by a feminist queer criticism in the early modern period. Gender is still a crucial category of analysis for historical and literary inquiry. Until more is known about the social life of women of many classes, it will be difficult to know how to make textual intimations of female homoeroticism intelligible in a wider social matrix. And though it is analytically useful to disentangle the study of gender from sexuality, in the end, I feel, the two will need to be rejoined. They are not the same, and they cannot simply be mapped onto one another, but the social meanings of sexuality cannot be fully understood without attending to the gender positionality of different categories of subjects.

Collectively, these four books begin a process of cultural investigation and ideological critique that is far from complete. Since they were written, texts by Jeffrey Masten, Stephen Orgel, Mario DiGangi, and others have appeared, each deepening our understanding of early modern sexuality and its differences from the sexual regime we inhabit today. But the four critics whose works I have too briefly engaged in this review are pioneers in this endeavor, and their books suggest much of what has been accomplished and what yet remains to be done. Clearly, from the work of Alan Bray on, the question of how literary representations are connected to social practice remains a challenging one. It is quite possible to see the job of the literary critic as primarily one of ideology critique. With Goldberg one can read both early modern texts and contemporary criticism to reveal their ideological fault lines, the places where particular interests are concealed beneath the ruse of the "natural." But revealing that even historical constructions are ideological does not obviate the inevitability of, or the need for, historical knowledge, for rigorous narratives of the past that combat the homophobia and the simple ignorance that inflect so many accounts of prior sexualities.

Simultaneously, some of these books are struggling to give an account, not just of sexual acts and institutions in the past, but of desire, affect, and subjectivity, domains to which a psychoanalytic criticism has traditionally given access. Yet *Homosexual Desire in Shakespeare's England* makes more use of cultural anthropology and Foucauldian discourse than psychoanalysis, and *Desire and Anxiety* stresses the limitations of psychoanalysis even in the process of employing it. If one believes, as all these scholars do, that sexuality has a history, and that even affect and desire were configured differently in 1600 than they are now, then it may be necessary to modify the psychoanalytic paradigm more significantly than has yet been done to account for these phenomena in different cultural contexts. Here the affiliated work of Gail Paster, Stephen Mullaney, and Frank Whigham may be of particular usefulness.

I do not believe that studies of early modern sexuality have, as Goldberg hoped, yet transformed our sense of what Renaissance texts are about, who produced them, and what interests they served. I think, unfortunately, that perhaps even more than most political criticisms, queer criticism is taken to be of primary interest only to those who self-identify as gay or lesbian. This seems to me to be an intellectual loss of no small proportions. As with so much else, the early modern period was historically a time of transition in regard to regimes of sexuality and gender. Because compulsive heterosexuality became normative; because it is our common sense; because culture eventually made marriage less an economic and political arrangement than an affective and sexual one, we forget the cultural struggles that led to these outcomes, and we lose the ability to read the codes of sexual alterity in the past. Deheterosexualizing Renaissance culture is politically and intellectually useful not only because it lets gay and lesbian students and scholars find a usable past; it also allows straight students and scholars to see the constructedness of their own sexual positioning, its historicity, its contingency. And it gives to everyone—man, woman, straight, queer—a more complex and historically adequate understanding of early modern culture.

Eventually, sexuality studies in the Renaissance and other fields will not mean, I hope, only the study of what we now consider non-dominant sexualities. Study of the marked sex, women, led, in time, to studies of masculinity; African-American inquiry opened up not only the workings of racism and white privilege, but eventually the construction of whiteness itself. In Renaissance studies we have hardly begun to study heterosexuality; we have taken it for granted. Besides productively defamiliarizing and "making new" the early modern period, each of the four books considered here make it impossible to naturalize any particular set of sexual practices. I hope they are widely read, and widely taught.

Works Cited

Bray, Alan, *Homosexuality in Renaissance England.* 1982; rpt. with new afterword, New York: Columbia University Press, 1995.

Smith, Bruce R., *Homosexual Desire in Shakespeare's England: A Cultural Poetics.* Chicago: University of Chicago Press, 1991.

Traub, Valerie. *Desire and Anxiety: Circulations of Sexuality in Shakespearean Drama.* London: Routledge, 1992.

Goldberg, Jonathan. *Sodometries: Renaissance Texts, Modern Sexualities.* Stanford: Stanford University Press, 1992.

ARTICLES

"Hottentot": The Emergence of an Early Modern Racist Epithet

LINDA E. MERIANS

THROUGHOUT the eighteenth century, calling a fellow Briton a "Hottentot" was understood to be an insult, and writing satirical or straightforwardly serious warnings that the press, the government, or believers in a certain political or religious persuasion threatened to turn the nation into a land of Hottentots was also a commonplace way to express one's worry that British society was degenerating.[1] How did the race constructed by Europeans as the Hottentot race come to be appropriated for such unique domestic application in eighteenth-century Britain? Examining English representations of the people of the Cape of Good Hope written between 1591 and 1630 shows us how the southernmost society in Africa came to represent, literally and figuratively, the exact opposite of English society and its preferred values for itself. The foundation for the negative casting was laid during the early modern period, when the Cape people were not yet constructed as Hottentots and before "race" became a fully articulated reason for marking them, as John Ovington did in 1696: "the very reverse of Human kind . . . so that if there's any medium between a Rational Animal and a Beast, the *Hotontot* [sic] lays the fairest Claim to that Species."[2]

The role "difference" plays in the construction of race in early modern England is complex as well as obvious. The obvious hardly needs to be stated: it is only natural that early modern English travelers saw varieties of skin color, language, customs, clothing, and diet as ways to mark difference. Recognition of difference in any of the above-mentioned categories did not always automatically transform into value judgments or rankings of racial and/or ethnic identities in comparison to one's own, but it generally did. Above all, skin color became one of the most important difference

markers for race. The early modern construction of race was a process that came to depend on the recording of differences, be they
real or imagined, and on the acceptance of impressions, data, and
arguments we now call racist in order to serve or rationalize colonialism and slavery.

In discussions of race, the idea of difference factors as a mode of
constructing individual and collective identities. Such constructions develop concepts of identity formation that depend upon
what Hayden White calls the technique of "ostensive self-definition
by negation."

> in times of sociocultural stress, when the need for positive self-
> definition asserts itself but no compelling criterion of self-identification
> appears, it is always possible to say something like: "I may not know
> the precise content of my own felt humanity, but I am most certainly
> *not* like that," and simply point to something in the landscape that is
> manifestly different from oneself.[3]

As crucial as difference is in such contexts, what is often ignored in
discussions of race is an acknowledgment that lurking somewhere
within difference is the potential for sameness. Early modern representations of the people of the Cape often reveal both the English
preference for difference and their fear of sameness.

It is especially remarkable that the early modern construction of
the people of the Cape played such a crucial role in the formation
of the English consciousness of self/nation and "other." The succes-
sive councils of Elizabeth, James VI, and Charles I, as well as of
the earliest governors of the English East India Company, exhibited
little, if any, colonial interest in the southern region of Africa. Indeed, they gave no orders to claim the Cape as an English possession when they easily could have. Yet despite the fact that the Cape
Colony did not become a "British" colonial territory until the early
nineteenth century, English interest in the people there was keen
and complicated from almost the first moment of contact in 1591.
The body of this essay explores how early modern contact with the
people of the Cape challenged deeply held English values as well
as certain preconceptions and judgments about Africa and Africans
to such an extent that the English reacted by separating them from
the human race almost altogether.

Once English sailors began to use the Cape as a refreshment
station on their voyages to and from the East, the region and the
people of the Cape disturbed English confidence in what had been
their privileged geographical texts. Many scholars have discussed

how the early modern English reliance on classical geographies, be they set in their original languages or in the popular vernacular translations that became especially popular in Elizabethan and Jacobean England, helped to create a bias against Africa and Africans.[4] Late sixteenth- and early seventeenth-century English translations of Pliny provide an excellent example of why English readers would not have been predisposed to see the people of the Cape in any sort of favorable or neutral way. *Natural History* came to life in English in 1556, with *A Summary of the Antiquities and Wonders of the World*. Thomas Hacket published new editions in 1585 and 1587, and Philemon Holland produced three more editions of Pliny's work in 1601, 1634, and 1635. Also, Pliny's work was a source for the chapter on the Ethiope in Boemus's *Omnium Gentium Mores*, and as Margaret Hodgen has shown, it was popular all over Europe, with twenty-three new editions or reissues in five languages between 1536 and 1611.[5]

In England, Boemus's work found its way into English in William Prat's *Description of the Country of Africa* (1554), in William Waterman's *The Fardle of Facions* (1555), and in Edward Aston's *The Manners, Lawes, and Customs of All Nations* (1611). Waterman's translation includes the following representation of what Boemus (and Pliny, of course) imagined as the inhabitants of the southernmost section of Africa.

> The laste of all the Affriens Southewarde, are the Ichthiophagi. A people borderying upon the Troglodites, in the Goulfe called Sinus Arabicus: whiche under the shape of man, live the life of beastes. They goe naked all their life tyme, and make copte of their wives and their children in commune. They knowe none other kindes of pleasure, or displeasure, but like unto beastes, such as they fiele: neither have they any respecte to vertue, or vice, or any discernying betwirte good or badde. They have little Cabanes not farre from the Sea, upon the clieves side: where nature hath made great cases, diepe into the grounde, the hollowe Guttres.[6]

Edward Aston's early-seventeenth-century translation, *The Manners and Customs of All Nations* (1611), includes the same kind of depiction.[7] That these texts had great influence, even on authors of travel narratives, suggests the early modern English need to privilege a literary legacy of traditional fictions even in the face of contravening evidence.

From the fantastical and anxious descriptions of the area's people and landscape included in the classical works as well as from the reports of early-sixteenth-century Portuguese expeditions that met with disaster at the Cape, English sailors and readers expected to find barbarians and a dangerous wasteland at the Cape. This is confirmed by Thomas Stevens's 1579 letter to his father, written from Goa and published in Richard Hakluyt's *The Principal Navigations* (1598–1600). Stevens, the first Englishman to go to India, never set foot on land at the Cape, but from his vantage point of "no more than five miles from the Cape," he reports the following:

> there we stood as utterly cast away: for under us were rocks of maine stone so sharpe, and cutting, that no ancre could hold the ship, the shore so evill, that nothing could land, and the land itselfe so full of Tigers, and people that are savage, and killers of all strangers, that we had no hope of life nor comfort, but onely in God and a good conscience.[8]

An indication of the admiration and authority early modern English readers and writers gave to the classical authors can be seen in Thomas Herbert's *Some Yeares Travel into Divers Part of Africa and Asia the Great* (1634, 1638, 1665, 1677). He quotes Pliny, Solinus, Aristotle, and other classical authors throughout his section on Africa, and in relation to his representation of the people of the Cape, Herbert mistakenly adopted Pliny's use of the word *troglodites* to refer to them.[9]

As Emily C. Bartels and Richard Helgerson have recently argued, Richard Hakluyt's intention to celebrate and glorify England partially determined the editorial decisions he made for his *Principal Navigations*. The inclusion, for example, of Drake's "The Two Famous Voyages" certainly testifies to this desire. This narrative challenged traditional conceptions of the Cape in a revolutionary way. England's master sailor proclaimed it "a most stately thing, and the fairest Cape we saw in the whole circumference of the earth" (3:742).[10] The "fair" Cape rescued many English sailors from the deathly grip of scurvy and other illnesses picked up and/or exacerbated by a several-months-long sea journey, and other Englishmen besides Drake were generous with their praise for the region. Patrick Copland, chaplain of an English East India fleet in 1612–14, employed language befitting a man of his profession: "The Bay of Soldania and all about the Cape is so healtfull [sic] and fruitfull as might grow a Paradise of the World; it well agrees with English bodies; for all but one in twentie dayes recovered as at the first day they set forth."[11] Such generous statements about the place were not followed by similar comments about the people. Indeed, many of the earliest English visitors to the Cape judged the people to be unworthy and undeserving of the land.

The English desire to construct their trading partners at the Cape negatively is evident in the persistent topos of difference in their written descriptions of them. It was important to the English to maintain a narrative fiction of their own society as Europe's finest. In this narrative, their use of language testified to their intellectual abilities, and their customs, particularly those related to dress, diet, and social behavior, were proof of their civility and their developed talents for cultivating and creating products given to them by God and nature. Early English visitors to the Cape preferred to see only differences between themselves and the people who lived at the Cape. What was spoken by the people of the Cape, the English refused to recognize as language; what was worn, they could not consider as clothing; what was danced and sung to, they did not see as worthy of religion; and the food or shelter that sustained existence, they could not judge according to its appropriateness. The Standish-Croft journal kept on a voyage begun in 1612 provides a good example:

> the Counttrey being firtille ground and pleasantt and a counttrey verie temperatt but the people bruitt and sauadg, without Religion, without languag, without Lawes or gouernment, without manners or humanittie, and last of all withoutt apparell, for they go naked saue onelie a ppees of a Sheepes Skyn to cover their Members that in my opinion yt is a greatt pittie that such creattures as they bee should injoy so sweett a counttrey.[12]

The strategy to see difference and to separate the people of the Cape from their rich landscape accomplished two objectives at once. Firstly, it provided a way to consider the trusted geographical sources as still more correct than incorrect in the face of new evidence. Secondly, and most obviously, it established English superiority over the people of the Cape.

English awareness of the people of the Cape also challenged them to revisit the theories that sought to explain how and why there were different human skin colors. Sixteenth-century debates about skin color were often highly charged, but they remained largely unresolved. Interestingly, the people of the Cape came to occupy an important place for the next two centuries in the debate about skin color. For example, they play a central role in the discussion of it in The History and Description of Africa (1600), where it is located in one of the sections that John Pory added to Leo Africanus's text.

> The people of this place called in the Arabian toong Cafri, Cafres, or Cafates, that is to say, lawlessee or outlawes, are for the most part exceeding blacke of colour, which very thing may be a sufficient argument, that the sunne is not the sole or chiefe cause of their blacknes; for in divers other countries where the heate thereof is farre more scorching and intolerable, there are tawnie, browne, yellowish, ash-coloured, and white people; so that the cause thereof seemeth rather to be of an hereditarie qualitie transfused from the parents, than the intemperature of an hot climate, though it also may be some further-ance thereunto.[13]

Kim Hall argues convincingly that this section and other editorial intrusions reveal Pory's own "anxiety about difference" and his strategy to "protect the unwary reader from the narrator."[14]

The majority of early modern English representations of the people of the Cape depict them as "black" and often call them "Negroes," but their skin color was not automatically a negative issue.[15] For example, a representation, dating from the initial landing in 1591, refers to the people of the Cape as "blacke salvages, very brutish," but English navigator John Davis, who served on a 1598 Dutch expedition and later worked for the English East India Company, made no judgment in his representation of their skin color: "The people are not circumcised, their colour is Olive blacke, blacker than the Brasilians, their haire curled and blacke as the Negroes of Angola."[16] One anonymous hand on the first English expedition sponsored by the English East India Company recorded the people of the Cape as being "of a tawnie colour,"[17] but another on the same expedition saw them as "blacke."[18] Yet, a representation written during the Sir Edward Michelbourne-led expedition in 1605 asserted the people of the Cape to be "a most savage and beastly people as ever I thinke God created" without any reference to their skin color at all.[19]

The different editions of Thomas Herbert's *Some Yeares Travels into Divers Parts of Asia and Afrique* (1634, 1638, 1665, 1677) illustrate how discussions of skin color and character merged into a racist construction of race during the seventeenth century. In the first edition, Herbert writes that the people of the Cape are of a "swarthy darke colour," but this phrase is changed in the second edition to read, "their color is ugly black, [sic] are strongly limbd, desperate, crafty, and injurious."[20] The third and fourth editions present a completely different description, reporting that "the Natives being propagated from Cham [*sic*], both in their Visages and Natures, seem to inherit his Malediction, their stature is but indifferent, their coller olevaster, or that sort of black we see the *American* that live under the Aequator; their faces be very thin, their body as to limbs well proportioned."[21] Herbert's employment of George Best's widely accepted theory is indicative of two extremely important trends in early modern England; namely, it shows the public's attraction to what James Walvin calls "biblical explanation" as well the cultural acceptance of a negative reading of blackness.[22] Walvin contends that "the power of an alleged biblical explanation—however imperfect, garbled or distorted that explanation might be—was a potent force in a post-Reformation society where preaching and biblical exegesis took place in the contemporary vernacular."[23] Indeed, early modern England was eager to accept Best's theory. In a fascinating essay, Benjamin Braude points out that English (and European) acceptance of what has been called the "Curse of Ham" is based on a misinterpretation of Mandeville's *Travels* that amounted to a mistaken and "willfull Africanization of Ham," and he suggests that Purchas's acceptance of it in *Hakluytus Posthumus, or Purchas His Pilgrims* (1625–26) demonstrates how slavery "started to make it credible."[24]

That Herbert's text returns to this mid-sixteenth-century theory as he revisits his own prose in the last quarter of the seventeenth century suggests how skin color began to dominate in the modern racist construction of race. According to Philip Curtin, the Restoration and eighteenth century mark the time when "culture prejudice . . . slid off easily toward color prejudice."[25] Ironically, many travelers at this time described the skin color of the people of the Cape in relation to whiteness and compared it with English and European skin tones. Indeed, the confusion over the skin color of the people of the Cape would be one of the reasons for their racial classification as Hottentot rather than "Negro." Evidence of this can be found in John Maxwell's "An Account of the Cape of Good Hope," read to the members of the Royal Society on 18 and 25 June 1707.

> The *Hottentots*, Natives of the Place, are a Race of Men distinct both from the *Negroes* and *European Whites*, for their Hair is Woolly, Short and Frizled, their Noses flat, and their Lips thick, but their Skin is naturally as White as ours, as appear'd by a *Hottentot* Child brought up by the *Dutch* in their Fort here.[26]

Toward the end of the eighteenth century, however, some in England began to regard them again as Negroes.[27] For example, Oliver Goldsmith wrote in his *A History of the Earth and Animated Nature* (1774): "The fourth striking variety in the human species, is to be found among the Negroes of Africa. This gloomy race of mankind is found to blacken all the southern parts of Africa, from eighteen degrees north of the line, to its extreme termination, at the Cape of Good Hope. I know it is said, that the Caffres, who inhabit the southern extremity of that large continent, are not to be ranked among the Negroe race; however, the difference between them, in point of color and features, is so small, that they may very easily be grouped in this general picture."[28]

Another crucial factor besides blackness (or black skin color) that carried negative weight in England during the early modern period was an association with the Irish. English contact with the people of the Cape occurred at a crucial time in England's attempts to pacify and to squash rebellion in Ireland, and evidence suggests that this historical coincidence placed the people of the Cape, in the collective English imagination, alongside the native Irish as a beastly society. There is great resemblance between late-sixteenth- and early-seventeenth-century English representations of the native Irish and the people of the Cape, and, in some cases, the association between the two is made quite directly.[29] Once again Thomas Herbert can be our source. He found similarities, for example, between the native Irish language and that of the people of the Cape: "their pronunciation is like the Irish: their customs not much unlike the rude ones of antique times."[30] In the 1638 second edition, Herbert revised this passage about the language of the people of the Cape to lay the groundwork for an even more damning assertion about their sexual practices: "Their language is apishly sounded (with whom tis thought they mixe unnaturally) . . . being voyced like the Irish.[31]

Clothing also served as a point of comparison. For the English, the mantle became a signifier of native Irish otherness. For example, in Spenser's *A View of the Present State of Ireland*, Irenius says that it was "a fit house for an outlaw, a meet bed for a rebel, and an apt cloak for a thief." Interestingly, when Eudox and Irenius debate the origins of the mantle, Irenius maintains that Africans have adopted it: "the Africans succeeding, yet finding the like necessity of that garment."[32] The male figure in Herbert's drawing is wearing something extremely reminiscent of an Irish mantle. Additionally, certain body parts of the people of the Cape were

Herbert, A Relation of Some Yeares Travaille, "Man and Woman at Cape of Good Hope," 1634. Courtesy of The Library Company of Philadelphia.

also described in the same way as those of the native Irish. Herbert's female figure is depicted as a sort of she-devil nursing a child over her shoulder. His prose explanation, "The women give their Infants sucke as they hang on their backes, the uberous dugge stretched over her shoulder," is very reminiscent of a like-minded assertion about "meere Irish" women made by Fynes Moryson, who reports that the women "have very great Dugges, some so big as they give their Children suck over theire shoulders."[33]

Perhaps the long unrest in Ireland necessitated that the English construct another race that was, literally and figuratively, beyond the pale as an outlaw race. Quite possibly, the idea of the people of the Cape offered the English a less threatening "primitiveness" to contemplate. In the early modern English mind, geography determined that the idea of human progress or development did not have to be granted to the people of the Cape. On the other hand, the problems the English had in Ireland, especially with subduing the rebellious native and Anglo-Irish populations, were particularly unsettling because the English thought them to be groups that had degenerated from a higher European state to an almost beastly one. Since the English considered these groups as races coming from within their own family, the evident degeneration or rejection of values they considered essential to their own sense of racial and cultural superiority was deeply upsetting to them. Debora Shuger points out that pro-English authors often decried the native Irish and the Anglo-Irish as especially threatening because they manifested little, if any, sense of civility, and civility was an especially treasured value of the early modern English.[34] It is interesting, therefore, that the English often applied the same standards to the people of the Cape as they did to the Irish (and thus themselves).

The English were quick to use what they saw as a lack of civility on the part of the people of the Cape to the English who stopped there as proof that the society was barbaric, beastlike, and, thus, very different from themselves. A pamphlet detailing the 1604 English East India Company expedition led by Henry Middleton shows how the English would record the incivility of the Cape society.[35] So many sailors were sick with scurvy that, contrary to the orders issued to him, Middleton ordered his ships to stop at the Cape for refreshment. Middleton himself led a party of men ashore on 18 July 1604. Some of his men began to set up tents while others went to where "the Negroes had their houses" to bargain for beef and sheep. The description works hard to establish Middle-

ton's evident civility in opposition to the rudeness of the people
of the Cape.

> Our Generall and the captains went to barter with them for small peeces
> of Iron, and bought some 12. sheep, and more would have sold us, till
> that they saw us begin to set up our tents, which as it seemed, was to
> their disliking; for that incontinent they pulled downe their houses,
> and made them fast upon their Beasts backes, and did drive away; yet
> all meanes possible was sought to drawe them to sell us more: but in
> no case they would abide any longer with us, but drove away with all
> the speed they might. It lay in the generals power to have taken them
> all from them, as some counselled him to doe, but he in no case would
> give eare thereunto; but let them depart, not doubting but that they
> would returne again, seeing we offered them no wrong, when it was in
> our powers to dispossesse them of all their cattell.

After the sick men were brought ashore, Middleton again tried to
bargain with the people of the Cape for "fresh victuals, but the
people of the countrey seeing so many in company fled." Middleton
then ordered his company to stand still, and he sent four men
forward to the Cape people with a bottle of wine, other food, a
"taber," and a pipe. The people of the Cape "seeing no more in
company came to them, and did eate, drinke, and daunce with
them so they seeing with what kindes they were used, tooke hart
unto them and came along with our Generall to our tents, where
they had many toyes bestowed upon them."

After this encounter, trading increased substantially. On 26 July,
the people of the Cape brought the English forty-four sheep, and
over the next five days brought them more than two hundred sheep
and some cattle, yet the narrative does not compliment the people
of the Cape for being civil hosts. By August, the English needed
additional food, and so Middleton ordered a dozen men to go out in
a trading party. They returned with only two sheep, which caused
Middleton concern. When he asked the Purser of the *Hector*, who
was in charge of the party, why they returned with so few cattle,
the Purser maintained that he had paid for more, but the Cape
people snatched the cattle back. In response to this, Middleton
planned an ambush against them. He and 120 of his men would
hide in the woods while the Purser's team of men would engage
the people of the Cape in negotiations once again. On a prearranged
signal from the English traders, Middleton and his troop would
come forward and drive the people of the Cape away. The plan
went awry, however, because three armed sailors who had "tast of

a bottell of wine they carried for their captaine" became separated from the company. When the unarmed English traders came into the kraal to begin the faux negotiations, the sailors were somehow discovered, and a scuffle ensued.

Middleton and his party came out from their hiding places to "rescew his men," but one man was wounded. The narrative reports the people of the Cape as taking "to their heeles and al the cattel before them, as fast as they could drive to the mountaines." Remarkably, the subsequent sentence literally and figuratively depicts the English sailors as riding over an inferior society: "Our men, as then, having the raines in their owne handes, pursued after them in such scattering manner, that if the people of the countrey had been men of any resolution, they might have cut off most of them." Strikingly, the conclusion of this section insists on adding that the English were able to secure some livestock despite the fact that they were in retreat. Such a "victory" should demonstrate to the readers the power and moral superiority of the English force over the local inhabitants.

English confidence about their own racial and cultural superiority over the people of the Cape seems to have grown in direct proportion to their demonization and categorization of them as a beastly society. This "truth" became evident to them partly because of a story or myth—for that is how it should be regarded—of the man called "Cory." Cory exemplifies the kind of evidence the English created and used to prove that the people of the Cape were not capable of being "civilized."[36] According to available records, Cory arrived in England in September 1613, having been carried there on the East India Company's *Hector*, captained by Gabriel Towerson.[37] Another man from the Cape was seized along with him, but he died before the ship arrived in England. Cory was kept at the house of Sir Thomas Smith, then the head of the English East India Company, from September 1613 to March 1614. He was returned to the Cape of Good Hope in June 1614, sailing from England in early March on the *New Year's Gift*, the flagship of an English East India Company expedition led by Nicholas Downton. This is the extent of the information that can be regarded as certain.

Early modern English readers could find references to Cory in only two published works, the third and fourth editions of *Purchas His Pilgrimage* (1617, 1626) and in the extracts of Nicholas Downton's journal included in *Purchas His Pilgrimes* (1625). The first printed account of Cory in *Purchas His Pilgrimage* is noteworthy for its brevity. Significantly, it does not include any mention or description of Cory's residence in London, but it does depict him as being helpful to the English after his return home.

The *Hector* brought thence one of these Salvages, called *Cory*, which was carried againe, and there landed by the *Newyeeres-gift, June 21. 1614.* in his Cooper Armour, but returned not to them whiles the Shippes continued in the Roade, but at their returnes in *March* was twelvemonth after, hee came, and was ready to [do?] any service, in helping them with Beeves and Sheepe.[38]

The subsequent representation of Cory in Downton's journal, which was included in *Purchas His Pilgrimes* (1625), is similarly brief, but there is a striking change.

In this later source, Cory is unhelpful to the English sailors. It records that on 18 June 1614, "the Saldanian departed from us, carrying with him his Copper Armour and Javelin, with all things belonging to him, promising to come againe to us the third day after, but he never came againe."[39] A letter Downton wrote to the home office of the English East India Company confirms the published journal account. More importantly, it also suggests the English emotional investment in Cory: "For Cory, soone after our comeing thither, we in hope of his better performance and nothing doubting of his love I lett him goe awaye with his rich armour and all his wealth in the companie of his freindes; but what become of him after we know nor neither could ever understand."[40] The remarkable diction testifies to the falsely placed English confidence in Cory's "love" for them and any material objects they gave him.

Cory's homecoming was described even more emotionally in a letter written by Thomas Elkington, also on the expedition. There he records his opinion that Cory and all the people of the Cape of Good Hope should be regarded as "ingratefull dogges":

Wee landed ther the Saldanian . . . but after he once gott ashore with such things as your Worships bestowed on hym wee could never see hym more; so doe greatly fear he mought be cause of our worser intertaynment, for which he had no ocation given, being all the voyadge more kindly used then he any waies could deserve, but being ingratefull dogges all of them not better to be expected; and would have bynn much better for us and such as shall come hereafter yf he never had seene Ingland, which your Worships hearafter may please to give order to prevente.[41]

Interestingly, Elkington's representation is not the only one that would use the dog metaphor. The English tendency to interpret

Cory's absence from them as a sort of betrayal not only ensured the construction of the people of the Cape as humanity's most irrecoverable and beastly society, but, as we shall see, it helped to shape the figurative levels of meaning subsequently associated with Hottentot in English domestic discourse.

The most descriptive version of Cory's story, and the one that came to be accepted as historical "truth," did not actually appear in published form until Edward Terry's A Voyage to East-India (1655). On its most superficial level, Terry's work records the experiences he had as a chaplain to Sir Thomas Roe and his delegation sent by King James to the court of Jehangir, the mogul emperor of Hindustan.[42] It shows him to be more negative about the people of the Cape than he was about any other indigenous society encountered on the voyage: "but the Sun shines not upon a people in the whole world more barbarous than those which possess it; Beasts in the skins of men, rather than men in the skins of beasts, as may appear by their ignorance, habit, language, diet, with other things, which make them most brutish."[43] The volume combines Terry's travel narrative with his own philosophical, religious, and political reflections concerning the present state of England and, by implication, the Civil War. These digressions make it clear that Terry hopes his work would instruct and reform his readership in regard to England's collective falling away from monarchy and Christianity. His use of the Cory story, in particular, proves Cory's and the people of the Cape's usefulness for political allegory.

The reflection immediately preceding his first discussion of Cory presents the conclusion the readers should draw from the story that would follow:

> Me thinks when I have seriously considered, the Dresses, the Habitations, and the Diet of this people, with other things, and how these beasts of Mankind live all like Brutes, nay worse, I have thought that if they had the accommodations we enjoy (to make our lives more comfortable) by good dwelling, warm clothing, sweet lodging, and wholesome food, they would be abundantly pleased with such a change of their condition; For as Love proceeds from Knowledge, and liking, and we can neither love nor like any thing we cannot know: so when we come to a sensible understanding of things wee knew not before; when the Belly teaches, and the Back instructs, a man would believe that these should work some strong convictions.[43] (19–20)

Terry then begins what he calls a "short story," describing Cory's residence at Sir Thomas Smith's house in London. (It is doubtful that Terry ever saw Cory in London, nor was he present at the Cape when Cory was returned home.)[44]

Terry tries to control the reader's response throughout the representation by inserting phrases that imply how differently an English person would have reacted under the same circumstances.

> he had good diet, good clothes, good lodging, with all other fitting accommodations; now one would think that this wretch might have conceived his present, compared with his former condition, as Heaven upon earth, but he did not so, though he had to his good entertainment made for him a Chain of bright Brass, an Armour, Breast, Back, and Headpiece, with a Buckler all of Brass, his beloved Metal; yet all this contented him not; for never any seemed to be more weary of ill usage, than he was of Courtesies; none ever more desirous to return home to his Countrey than he: For when he had learned a little of our Language, he would daily lie upon the ground, and cry very often thus in broken English, *Cooree home go, Souldania go, home go*; And not long after, when he had his desire, and was returned home, he had no sonner set footing on his own shore, but presently he threw away his *Clothes*, his *Linnen*, with all over *Covering*, and got his sheeps skins upon his back, guts about his neck, and such a perfum'd Cap (as before we named) upon his head; by whom that Proverb mentioned, 2 Pet 2.22. was literally fulfill'd, *Canis ad vomitum; The dog is return'd to his vomit, and the swine to his wallowing in the mire*. (21)

Terry's strategic employment of a biblical citation, one that includes the degrading metaphors of the dog and the pig, effectively exiles the people of the Cape from the human race.

The most dubious and unreliable moments in Terry's narrative are when he "recounts" a conversation he says he had with Cory: "It was here that I asked *Cooree* who was their God? he lifting up his hands answered thus, in his bad English, *England God, great God; Souldania no God*" (23). It seems odd that Cory apparently gained additional skill in English after his return to the Cape, but, of course, the point Terry wrote the section to make is contained in the long reflection it prompted. First, and briefly, Terry considers the people of the Cape:

> Now if any one desire to know under whose Command these brutes live or whether they have any Superiority & Subordination amongst themselves, or whether they live with their females in common, with many other questions that might be put, I am not able to satisfie them; (23–24)

He very quickly, however, moves the discussion to his real subjects, his own head and heart as well as "his" England, when he congratulates himself on his good fortune in contradistinction to the pitiable and unenlightened world around him.

> But this I look upon as a great happiness not to be born one of them and as great nay a far greater misery to fall from the loyns of *Civill & Christian Parents*, and after to degenerate into all brutishness as very many doe, *qui Gentes agrunt sub nomine Christianorum*; the thing which *Tertullian* did most sadly bewail in many of his time, who did act *Atheisme* under the Name of *Christianity*, and did even shame Religion by their light and loose possessing of it. When *Anacharis* the Philosopher was sometime unbraided with this, that he was a *Scythian* by birth he presently returned this quick and smart answer until him that cast that in his teeth; *Mihi quidem patria dedecus, tu autem Patriae*, my Country indeed is some disparagement to me, but thou art a disgrace to thy Country, as there be many thousands more beside, who are very burdens to the good Places that give them *Breath* and *Bread*. Alas, *Turkie*, and *Barbary*, and these *Africans*, with many millions more in that part of the world & in *America*, and in *Asia*, I and in *Europe* too, would wring their hands into peeces, if they were truly sensible of their condition, because they know so little. (24)

The "they" in the reflection's last sentence is very suggestive. It has a powerful resonance and possible connection to those English citizens who fought against the royalist forces during the Civil War. Terry concludes this section with a prophetic warning that would make sense only to a Christian audience, and it might very well have carried special meaning to his English audience.

> And so shall infinite numbers more one day born in the visible Church of God, *in the valley of visions*, Es. 22.1. have in their very hearts broken into shivers, because they knew so much, or might have known so much, and have known and done so little; for without all doubt, the day will one day come, when they who have sinned against the strongest means of Grace and Salvation shall feel the heaviest miserie, when their means to know God, in his will revealed in his Word, shall be put in one Balance, and their improvement of this means by their Practice in the other, and if there have not bin some good proportion betwixt these two, manifested in their lives, what hath been wanting in their *Practice* shall be made up in their *Punishment*. (23–24)

With his sermon delivered, Terry returns to his narration, but not to offer more descriptions of the place and its people. In fact, he never returns to the story of Cory. Instead he prefers to close the Cape interlude by making a connection between the sinners he contemplated in the reflection and some English criminals who had been banished to the region. Terry devotes four pages to recount an experiment conducted in 1614, which saw the delivery to the Cape of ten English convicts sentenced to death. It is remarkable that the lengthy allegorical tale he relates here is far longer than his actual description of the Cape people, nor should it be overlooked that Terry makes a point of mentioning that the criminals who returned to England were hanged for committing another crime. In this way, he underscores the meaning of his pointed political reflection.

Although Terry dropped Cory's story when it no longer served his allegorical purpose, it was what other English authors and editors remembered. Indeed, they rushed to steal it, suggesting its great appeal to the collective English imagination. Peter Heylyn, for example, borrowed the story for the second edition of *Cosmography*, published in 1657. Significantly, Heylyn's passage asserts that Cory helped English sailors, albeit at a higher price.

> I have heard that some of our *English* ships in their return from the *East-Indies*, seized on two Savages, living near this Bay, whom they brought on ship boord, with an intent to carry them into *England*, to the end that having learned the *English* tongue, we might be more particularly informed by them of the Estate and Affairs of this Countrey. One of these who was called *Coore*, being brought to *London* (for the other died upon the way) was dieted and cloathed according to the *English* fashion, gratified also with brasse Rings, Beads and such other things, by which they thought they might most gain upon him to affect the change of his condition. But *home, is home, though it be but homely*, as the saying is. For this poor wretch having learned so much *English*, as to bemoan his own misfortunes, would throw himself upon the ground, and cry out with great anguish, and vexation of spirit, *Coore home go, Soldania go, Coree home go*, out of which unquietnesse of humour, when they could not get him, they sent him back in the next ships which were bound for the *Indies*. After which time, as oft as he saw any ship with *English* colours, he would very joyfully make toward the Bay with Guts and Garbage hanging about his neck (as their custome is) and readily perform all good Offices towards them; yet so that it was found withall; that by discovering to the Natives how low esteem the *English* had of Brasse and Iron, they thenceforth raised the value of those richer Metals, which formerly they had parted with for such sorry trifles, as have been spoken of before.[45]

This account of Cory would appear in all subsequent reissues and or new editions of *Cosmography* (1665, 1666–67, 1669, 1670, 1674, 1677, 1682). Moreover, its appearance in *Cosmography* guaranteed that other Restoration and eighteenth-century travel collections, geography books and encyclopedias of knowledge would also include representations of Cory. Indeed, during the Restoration and the first half of the eighteenth century, versions of the Cory story appeared in Samuel Clark's *A New Description of the World* (1689, 1708, 1712); John Harris's *Navigantium atque Itinerantium* (1705); Thomas Astley's *A New General Collection of Voyages and Travels* (1745–47); and Thomas Salmon's *Modern History* (vol. 5, 1755).

Even more remarkably, versions of the Cory story were repeated in travel narratives that did not make any claim to have seen him. Thomas Herbert mentioned "Cory" in the third and fourth editions of his *Some Yeares Travels into Divers Parts of Asia and Afrique* (1665, 1677), but he gave the story a much "happier" ending for the English. He depicts Cory as being successfully "civilized," only to be murdered by his uncivilized countrymen at his return. Interestingly, Herbert inserts his representation of Cory in a paragraph with an anti-Dutch thrust.

> An example we have in *Cory*, a Savage brought thence into *England* in the year 1614. where being civilized, he returned in a few years after to his Country, where to express how nobly he had been treated, entring the Woods in a copper gilt armour; whether in revenge of his departure, or to be possest of so great a treasure, is not known; but instead of a kind reception which he thought he should have had, they butchered him.[46]

There is no textual precedent for Herbert's version, and while later British texts made allowances for it, the Terry-Heylyn representation was the most copied one. Another retelling of the Cory story appeared in Alexander Hamilton's travel narrative *A New Account of the East Indies* (1727, 1737). Cory lived in the nation's memory into the nineteenth century. It might well be his specter we find in Maria Edgeworth's novel *Leonora* (1806), where one character says to another about a third: "It is lost labor to civilize him, for sooner or later he will hottentot again."[47]

The value of examining these early representations is that they show us the process by which race began to be constructed in early modern England. This process produced two interdependent narratives: the story of the people of the Cape, and a later development of this story which foregrounded the relationship between the Cape people and the English and England. These narratives connect in increasingly complex ways. In the simple story, the descriptions of the Cape people were not, at first, racist. However, as the concept of difference developed around the image and idea of the Hottentot, both the people and the word began to signify a racist ideology that stabilized the more crucial and complex fictions of England and of a superior English race. Ultimately, the demonization of the people who came to be called Hottentot, whether they lived in southern Africa or in Britain, helped to legitimate the xenophobia of the nation, and serves as a screen through which we may identify a newly emergent racist ethos in modern British political discourse.

Notes

1. I discuss this phenomenon in my essay "What They Are, Who We Are: Representations of the 'Hottentot' in Eighteenth-Century Britain," *Eighteenth-Century Life* 17 (November 1993): 14–39 as well as in my forthcoming book on British representations of the Hottentot.

2. John Ovington, *Voyage to Suratt* (1696), 489.

3. Hayden White, *Tropics of Discourse: Essays in Cultural Criticism* (Baltimore: Johns Hopkins University Press, 1978) 151.

4. See, for example, Eldred D. Jones, *The Elizabethan Image of Africa* (Charlottesville: University of Virginia Press, 1971); and Alden T. Vaughan and Virginia Mason Vaughan, "Before *Othello:* Elizabethan Representations of Sub-Saharan Africans, "*William and Mary Quarterly*, 3d. ser., 54, no. 1 (January 1997), 19–44.

5. Margaret Hodgen, *Early Anthropology in the Sixteenth and Seventeenth Centuries* (Philadelphia: University of Pennsylvania Press, 1964), 132–33.

6. William Waterman, *The Fardle of Facions* (1555; reprint, Amsterdam and New York: De Capo Press, 1970), chap. 6, n.pa.

7. Aston's translation of the section reads: "The last people, and the utmost towards the South bee the Ichthiophagi, which inhabite in the gulph of Arabia, upon the frontiers of the Trogloditae, these carry the shape of men, but live like beasts: they be very barbarous and go naked all their lives long, using both wives and daughters common like beasts: they be neither touched with any feeling of pleasure or griefe, other then what is naturall: Neido the [sic] discerne any difference betwixt good and bad, honesty and dishonesty." See his *This Manners and Customs of All Nations* (1611), 48–49.

8. Richard Hakluyt, *The Principle Navigations, Voyages, Traffiques and Discoveries of the English Nations* (London, 1598–1600), 2:100.

9. Interestingly, Herbert's citations from classical sources would increase with each subsequent edition. In relation to a name for the people of the Cape, only Herbert's fourth edition (1677) employed a form of the word *Hottentot*. This is indicative of how Herbert revised his narrative over time. The first time *Hottentot* appeared in print in England was in 1670.

10. See Emily C. Bartels, "Imperialist Beginnings: Richard Hakluyt and the Construction of Africa, *Criticism* 34, no. 4 (fall 1992): 517–38; and chap. 4 of Richard Helgerson, *Forms of Nationhood: The Elizabethan Writing of England* (Chicago: University of Chicago Press, 1992). Hakluyt, *Principal Navigations*, 3:742.

11. Patrick Copland, quoted in R. Raven-Hart, *Before Van Riebeeck: Callers at South Africa from 1488 to 1652* (Cape Town: C. Struik, 1967), 59.

12. Standish Croft Journal, in Raven-Hart, *Before Van Riebeeck*, 57–58.

13. *The History and Description of Africa. Written by al-Hassan Ibn-Mohammed Al-Wezaz Al-fasi, . . . but Better Known as Leo Africanus. Done into English by John Pory*, 3 vols. (London: Hakluyt Society, 1896), 3, 68.

14. Kim F. Hall, *Things of Darkness: Economies of Race and Gender in Early Modern England* (Ithaca: Cornell University Press, 1995), 30–31.

15. Alden T. Vaughan and Virgnia Mason Vaughan believe that Elizabethan era representations of "black" African societies have a negativity that distinguishes them from European depictions of New World "otherness." See "Before *Othello,*" 19–44.

16. *The Voyages and Works of John Davis, the Navigator,* ed. Albert Hastings Markham (London: Hakluyt Society, 1880), 135.

17. *The Voyages of Sir James Lancaster to Brazil and the East Indies, 1591–1603,* ed. Sir William Foster (London: Hakluyt Society, 1940), 3. An account of this journey appeared in the second edition of Hakluyt's *Principal Navigations.* The account from the second journey is also printed in the Foster edition (81).

18. *A True and Large Discourse of the Voyage of 20 April 1601,* London, 1603. Account is published in Foster's *Voyages of Sir James Lancaster,* 123.

19. Edward Michelbourne, quoted in Raven-Hart, *Before Van Riebeeck,* 32.

20. Thomas Herbert, *Some Yeares Travels into Divers Parts of Asia and Afrique* (London, 1638 and 1638), 14 and 16.

21. Herbert, *Some Yeares Travels,* 1665 ed. 17.

22. In Best's *The Three Voyages of Martin Frobisher* (1578) he maintains the Bible proves that blackness is a punishment from God, a sign of the "natural infection" in the blood of the first "Ethiopians," and consequently, "the whole progenie of them descended are still polluted with the same blot of infection.

23. James Walvin, *England, Slaves, and Freedom, 1776–1838* (University: University of Mississippi Press, 1986), 73.

24. Benjamin Braude, "The Sons of Noah and the Construction of Ethnic and Geographical Identities in the Medieval and Early Modern Periods," *William and Mary Quarterly,* 3d. ser. 54, no. 1 (January 1997): 103–42 and 138.

25. Curtin makes this point in *The Image of Africa: British Ideas and Action, 1780–1850* (Madison: University of Wisconsin Press, 1964), 30. Also, see Emmanuel Chukwudi Eze's introduction to *Race and the Enlightenment: A Reader* (Oxford: Blackwell Publishers, 1997) where he calls the period the "Racist Enlightenment" (1) as well as my own "What They Are, Who We Are." Many recent discussions of race also identify the Restoration and eighteenth century as being the crucial period in the construction of race.

26. *Philosophical Transactions of the Royal Society,* 25 (1706–7): 2424.

27. Ethnographically speaking, the people of the Cape of Good Hope are more correctly referred to as the Cape Khoikhoi (also spelled Khoekhoe). They are considered as part of the Khoisan societies of southern Africa. See Alan Barnard's *Hunters and Herders of Southern Africa: A Comparative Ethnography of the Khoisan Peoples* (Cambridge: Cambridge University Press, 1992).

28. Oliver Goldsmith, *An History of the Earth and Animated Nature* (London, 1774), 2:226.

29. See, for example, Nicholas Canny, *The Elizabethan Conquest of Ireland: A Pattern Established, 1565–1576* (New York: Barnes and Noble, 1976), and *Kingdom and Colony: Ireland in the Atlantic World, 1650–1800* (Baltimore: Johns Hopkins University Press, 1988); David Quinn, *The Elizabethans and the Irish* (Ithaca: Cornell University Press, 1966); Joep Leerssen, *Mere Irish and Fíor-Ghael* (Amsterdam and Philadelphia: John Benjamins Publishing Co., 1986) and "Wildness, Wilderness, and Ireland: Medieval and Early-Modern Patterns in the Demarcation of Civility," *Journal of the History of Ideas* 56, no. 1 (January 1995); 25–39; Ann Rosalind Jones and Peter Stallybrass, "Dismantling Irena: The Sexualizing of Ireland in Early Modern England," in *Nationalisms and Sexualities,* ed. Andrew

Parker, Mary Russo, Doris Sommer, and Patrician Yaeger, 157–71 (London and New York: Routledge, 1992).

30. Sir Thoams Herbert, *A Relation of Some Yeares Travaile* (London, 1634), 16. Interestingly, the first edition of his narrative was published six years after his own voyage and the year after the first printed edition of Spenser's *A View of the Present State of Ireland* (1633).

31. Herbert, *A Relation* 1638, ed. 18.

32. Edmund Spenser, *A Present View of the State of Ireland*, ed. W. L. Renwick (Oxford: Clarendon Press, 1970), 51.

33. Herbert, *A Relation*, 17, and Moryson, from unpublished chapters of his *Itinerary* (1617), printed in *Shakespeare's Europe: A Survey of the Condition of Europe at the end of the 16th century*, 2d. ed. introduction and biographical account by Charles Hughes (New York: Benjamin Blom, 1967), 485.

34. Shuger uses Irish tracts to argue that the "organizing polarity" of Tudor/ Stuart critiques of artistocratic warrior society was civility versus barbarism, and that the Irish were regarded as northern European barbarians. See "Irishmen, Aristocrats, and Other White Barbarians," *Renaissance Quarterly* 50 (1997): 494–525.

35. *The Last East-India Voyage* (London, 1606). The title page and a note to the reader makes clear that Walter Burre arranged for the publication of the narrative. In his note he says that the man who began the narrative died during the journey, but Burre promises that the continuation of it is accurate. Middleton's expedition returned in May 1606. Burre worked quickly to get the text ready, and it was entered on the Stationers' Company's Register on 20 May 1606 (STC #17869 or 7456). All quotations from the narrative come from the microfilm (Early English Texts, STC 1, reel 218). The page signatures of the section of the narrative devoted to the stop at the Cape are faulty. The section begins on B4 and continues to C3. The pamphlet is reprinted for the first time in its entirety in *The Voyage of Sir Henry Middleton to the Moluccas*, edited with an introduction by Sir William Foster (London: Hakluyt Society, 1943). Foster's introduction is especially informative. Although there is no room to do so in this essay, I hope to work out in greater detail elsewhere how moments in this narrative find resonance in early-seventeenth-century English drama. An obvious example that comes to mind is the drunken behavior of Stephano, Trinculo, and Caliban in *The Tempest* 3.2.

36. How he received the name Cory is a matter of debate. Early accounts maintain that Cory was his name, but this is doubtful. See Hans Werener Debrunner, *Presence and Prestige: Africans in Europe* (Basel: Afrika Bibliograhien, 1979), 58. That the English thought the people of the Cape beyond recovery sets them in stark contrast to the English construction of native American societies. In this regard, the English story of Pocahontas provides us with a neat opposite to the Cory story. It is an understatement to say that when she and other Virginia Algonquians were in London in 1616–17, they made a far different impression on the English than did Cory. For an interesting reading of the Pocahontas story, see chapter 2 of Kathleen M. Brown's *Good Wives, Nasty Wenches, and Anxious Patriarchs: Gender, Race, and Power in Colonial Virginia* (Chapel Hill: University of North Carolina Press for the Institute of Early American History and Culture, 1996).

37. The minutes of the English East India Company are not extant for the period from 1610 to 1613, which makes it difficult to reconstruct the orders and events surrounding the actual capture and abduction of the man who became known as Cory.

38. Samuel Purchas, *Purchas His Pilgrimage* (London, 1617), 867. The account of Cory in *Purchas His Pilgrimes* (1625) also does not mention his stay in London. Many unpublished representations and letters written to the governors of the English East India Company mention him after his return to the Cape.

39. Nicholas Downton, quoted in Raven-Hart, *Before Van Riebeeck*, 66.

40. Ibid.

41. Thomas Elkington, quoted in Raven-Hart, *Before Van Riebeeck*, 67.

42. Terry explains that after the delegation's return to England in 1619, he wrote his narrative and presented it in manuscript form to Charles, Prince of Wales, in 1622. It appears to have circulated in that form. Purchas, for example, included sections of Terry's narrative in *Purchas His Pilgrimes* (1625), although the excerpts did not feature any descriptions or reflections about Cory or the Cape of Good Hope.

43. Edward Terry, *A Voyage to East-India* (London, 1655), 16. Subsequent quotes from this edition will be noted in the text. A version of Terry's narrative, reduced by the deletion of all the reflections, appeared in 1665 as an afterword to *The Travels of Sig. Pietro della Valle*. It is curious that the full original text reappeared in 1777, especially since eighteenth-century printers did not usually reprint works after such a long period of time. This edition provides no explanation as to its existence.

44. Terry was most likely residing in Oxford when "Cory" was in London. Moreover, he makes no claim to having seen Cory in London. I question the story's reliability, but the point is that the English found a way to use it, whatever its derivation.

45. Peter Heylyn, *Cosmography* (London, 1657), 994.

46. Herbert, *A Relation* (1665, ed.) p. 20.

47. Maria Edgeworth, *Leonora*, cited in the *OED* definition of *Hottentot* (Oxford: Clarendon Press, 1933), 5:414.

Juan Pantoja de la Cruz and the Circulation of Gifts between the English and Spanish Courts in 1604/5

Gustav Ungerer

T HE PRESENT article has been undertaken to show how the English and Spanish courts exploited portraiture and jewellery to advance both their political and dynastic aims in the context of the peace negotiations and celebrations of the new alliance that was signed in London (1604) and in Valladolid (1605). Thus the English and the Spanish monarchs indulged in a diplomatic interchange of miniatures and full-length royal portraits. In London, Queen Anna harnessed Isaac Oliver's ability as court painter; in Valladolid, Juan Pantoja de la Cruz, court painter to King Philip III, was commissioned to paint the miniatures and the portraits of the Spanish monarchs as well as of the infanta Ana de Austria. The article, moreover, takes up the unresolved debate about the contested authorship of *The Somerset House Conference*, a memorial painting acquired by the National Portrait Gallery in 1882.

The political settlement initiated by the archdukes in Brussels and concluded between England and Spain in 1603/4 was signed in Whitehall Chapel, London, on 19/29 August 1604, by the constable of Castile and King James I and was ratified in the Salon Grande of the Royal Palace in Valladolid, on 30 May/9 June 1605, by the earl of Nottingham and King Philip III.[1] The peace favored the resumption of the old cultural intercourse that had been forged by the dynastic policy of the early Tudor monarchs and had been flourishing until severed by Queen Elizabeth and her brother-in-law, Philip II.[2] Both courts in 1604 and 1605 put on brilliant shows of cultural self-representation with a view to strengthening the process of reconciliation. The prestige of painting played as important a role as the splendor of the court celebrations and the codified ritual of gift exchange.

The Somerset House Conference, 1604. By Juan Pantoja de la Cruz. Reproduced by permission of the National Portrait Gallery.

In 1601 the Spanish court had moved to Valladolid, and for the following five years the presence of the court and government transformed the town into the cultural center of Spain. Town and court, in honor of the English embassy, mounted festivities on an unprecedented scale during a period of three weeks in May/June 1605. Among the 560 English and Scottish retainers chosen to accompany the earl of Nottingham on his mission to Valladolid, a good many were qualified to respond to the cultural encounter and even to take up the challenge issued by the Spanish court mythographers to outdo the celebrations staged in London in August 1604. Besides the earl of Nottingham, patron of the Admiral's Men until 1603, I am thinking of Sir George Buc, deputy master of the Revels Office; of Dudley Carleton, on the threshold of a brilliant career as a diplomat and purchasing art agent; of the essayist Sir William Cornwallis, the son of the English ambassador to the Spanish court, Sir Charles Cornwallis; of the physician Robert Marbeck, the author of a discourse on the descent on Cádiz in 1596 that contains an anecdote about Richard Tarlton, "condemned to die in one of his prettie mearie commedies";[3] of the young art agent Thomas Coke; of Sir Robert Drury, the future patron of John Donne; and of Robert Treswell, who accompanied Nottingham in his capacity as Somerset herald and as authorized chronicler.[4]

Thomas Coke, about to embark upon a career as art adviser to the earl of Shrewsbury and, after 1613, to the earl of Arundel, was well advised to join Nottingham's embassy, which promised to open up cultural sites hitherto inaccessible to the English. It was indeed part of Philip III's cultural strategy to impress the English courtiers with the arts as practiced and cultivated in Spain. The royal and aristocratic collections, rich in European paintings, in Italian and Flemish masterpieces, were all of a sudden within reach of Nottingham and his entourage. The Palacio Real in Valladolid and the suburban Palacio de la Ribera of the duke of Lerma treasured hundreds of paintings. Coke, I think, can claim to be the first art expert working for the English nobility who in 1605 must have seen some of those masterpieces by Titian, Veronese, and Correggio that, in 1623, whetted Prince Charles's desire in Madrid and Valladolid to add them to his own collection.[5] Coke is not known to have bought any pictures in Valladolid; nor has he left a record of a visit to a gallery in Astorga. Nottingham and his suite, on their strenuous overland journey from the Groyne to Valladolid, alighted at the castle of Don Pedro Alvarez Osorio, eighth marquis of Astorga, on Saturday, 11/21 May 1605. The marquis, providing a grandiose welcome to the English courtiers, showed them his "very faire gallery with many goodly pictures and pieces of painting both large and costly, and also a rich library with many fine rarities."[6] Unfortunately, Treswell does not specify what paintings the marquis called his own and took pride in displaying to his distinguished visitors from England. His may have been one of those traditional aristocratic collections that abounded in religious and mythological paintings.

Coke, however, is unlikely to have missed the prestigious collection of the count of Benavente, Juan Alonso Pimentel, viceroy of Valencia and of Naples, who accommodated Nottingham in his castle at Benavente on Sunday, 12/22 May. The anonymous chronicler of the embassy, "a better Souldier, then a Scholler," as he styled himself in the "Address to the Reader," compared the heavily fortified building to Windsor Castle. He recorded without much attention to chronology that "this house was of six hundred yeares standing, and that Hannibal and Scipio had layen in it." Obviously an officer in Nottingham's guard, he must have been admitted to the count's "Wunderkammer" and to his gallery containing mythological pictures, the standard portraits of famous men, and some Italian paintings, for he entered in his chronicle that he "did see the portratures" of Hannibal and Scipio, and "one of their thigh bones that was as big as any mans thigh, flesh and all, in anie part."[7]

The conciliatory force of portrait painting must first of all be seen in the context of the institutionalized rite of gift giving and gift exchange as prescribed by international court etiquette. The presentation of royal gifts and countergifts made during the ratification celebrations in London and Valladolid, the royal gifts for the departing English and Spanish ambassador and their retinues, the distribution of gifts made by the two ambassadors at their departure from London and Valladolid respectively, conformed to an ordered scheme. Each single item, from gold cups, gold and silver plate, jewels, pearls, chains, ewers, pendants, rings, cases, flagons, manufactured either in London, the Low Countries, or Valladolid, to hatbands, aigrettes, and crosses set with diamonds, dogs, horses, and firearms was meticulously inventoried and priced. The ostentatious display of jewelry was a traditional manifestation of wealth and power that used to be publicized. Thus the demand for spectacular court news in the Spanish Netherlands was catered for by a tract like the *Vray discours de l'arrivée de Monsier le Connestable de Castille en Angleterre, avec les cérémonies, pompes et grand triomphes, particularitez de joyaux, dons et présens donnez de part et d'autre* (Douai: Balthasar Bellère, 1604).[8]

Apart from the unbounded ostentation of wealth, gift giving had a symbolic value. The formal rite of gift exchange was seen as a public confirmation of the bond of amity concluded between the two countries. When the rite was officiated by the monarchs themselves, the ceremony used to assume an explicitly personal note. Thus King James opened the banquet, celebrated at Whitehall on the occasion of the ratification of the peace treaty, on 19/29 August 1604, by inviting Juan Fernández de Velasco, constable of Castile and duke of Frías, to share with him a melon and half a dozen oranges raised in the royal gardens, "diziéndole que era fruta de Hespaña transplantada en Inglaterra."[9] The fruit gift transcended the historic moment of the English/Spanish commensality in symbolizing equality of political partnership and prompting the prospective dynastic alliance between Prince Henry and the infanta Ana. The exchange of their portraits, discussed below, underlines the seriousness of the dynastic issue.

King James was to pursue the idea of a dynastic alliance with Spain until 1623. In 1604, he had to content himself with a political accommodation that he coded as a "marriage" between the two countries and in token of which he presented the constable with a diamond ring. The presentation is well documented in contemporary annals. On Monday, 20/30 August, at 4 p.m., King James, impatient to resume his summer progress and make the best of the interrupted hunting season, boarded a royal barge at Whitehall Stairs that took him to Somerset House. There in the intimacy of the bedroom he spent an hour in private conference with the constable, who was down with lumbago, and with the earl of Northampton, who served as interpreter.[10] On taking leave, King James "con mucho affecto de amor y cortesía, le dexó de su mano vna sortija con vn diamante rico, para memoria del 'mariage', que assí llamó a la paz"[11] (King James "with many protestations of love and courtesies took from his hand a finger-ring adorned with a rich diamond and gave it to the constable in memory of the 'mariage' as he used to call the peace in French.")

Memorial rings used to be given at crucial moments in human lives.[12] In the present case, it was a time of dramatic transformation, a peace treaty concluded between two former enemies. The donation of the ring was both a private and public act. Thus the Flemish contemporaries were informed that the ring offered in remembrance of the "mariage" was valued at "cincq mil escus."[13] In 1605,

Philip III, in accordance with court protocol, reciprocated the gift at the farewell audience he granted to the earl of Nottingham on 8/ 18 June. He gave Nottingham a "ring with a Diamond, said to be of the valew of 3000. pounds, which he put vpon his L. finger, and as he said, in token of wedding him in true loue perpetually."[14]

Queen Anna's attempt to personalize her public relationship with the constable of Castile deserves as much attention as the king's. As queen of England with overt Catholic leanings, she let the constable know that she fully subscribed to her husband's plans for a match between Prince Henry and the infanta Ana.[15] What convinced the constable that the queen was a Catholic was her support for the plans nurtured by Jane Dormer, duchess of Feria, to return to the English court as a maid of honor and as an ardent advocator of the English recusants.[16] During the peace celebrations the queen took an active part in the court entertainments, making up for her husband's physical incapacity to participate in the revels, particularly in the dances, and also for his seeming indifference to painting and drama. Unlike her husband, the queen took to articulating her personal view in favor of a political rapprochement between the two nations through the power of portraiture: she presented the constable with two miniatures and two portraits in large. The constable, gallant as he was with his royal hostess, allowed her to score some points in the cultural interchange as far as portraits were concerned, but in the final account of the competitive gift-giving rites he gained the upper hand.

Before entering upon a discussion of the queen's gift, it seems opportune to review the calculated generosity showered upon her and her ladies-in-waiting by the constable of Castile on behalf of the Spanish monarchs. The constable presented the queen with a dragon-shaped crystal cup, "vna serpiente de cristal guarnecida de oro con su tapador y vn Ercules encima de oro mazizo," which he had bought for 4,440 reales (£111) from "Euraldo Ciceron, platero," the bill of exchange dated from Brussels on 4 April 1604 (N.S.) and with which he was to drink to the queen the health of King James at the banquet held after the ratification of the peace treaty in Whitehall. He also presented her with a gold cross, "vna Joya Cruz de Oro quaxada de 260 Diamantes," which Don Blasco de Aragón had bought for 43,480 ½ reales (£1087) in Antwerp, the bill of exchange dated from Bruges on 25 July 1604 (N.S.). The queen moreover, received from him three pendants set with "Diamantes muy gruesos y con otros menores," which on 30 August 1604 (N.S.

he bought from "Pedro Gemens, joyelero jinglés" (sic) at a price of 130,000 reales, that is, £3,250. Finally, the queen was given two gold cases out of a set of twelve that had been ordered to be made by the three Brussels jewelers Pedro de Prado, Pedro de Quermens, and Jean Guiset. The price of 62,475 reales (£1561) for the twelve cases was paid by a bill of exchange dated from Brussels on 9 April 1604 (N.S.).[17]

The constable loaded or rather bribed Frances Howard, countess of Suffolk, with jewels worth 160,000 reales; with one of twelve gold cases made in Brussels (see above); and with 200,000 reales in cash, the total amounting to £9,130. He gave "Madama Belfort," Lucy Harington, countess of Bedford, an aigrette set with 106 diamonds "entre grandes y pequeños" (some big, some small) and valued "con el oro y hechura en 1800 escudos" (at 1800 ducats, gold and work included). It was one of six jewels the constable bought in Brussels from Jean Guiset by bill of exchange dated 17 May 1604 (N.S.). "Madama Riza," Penelope Devereux, Lady Rich, got another aigrette bought from "Adrian Rotini, joyelero" for 12,000 reales (£300) on 27 August 1604 (N.S.); so did "Madama Elfort," countess of Hertford, Lady Frances Howard, for 13,200 reales (£330). One of the six jewels made by Guiset in Brussels was an anchor, "vna Ancora con 39 Diamantes entre grandes y pequeños, tassada con el oro y hechura en 1328 escudos." The recipient of this symbol of hope was Anne Hay, the daughter of Francis Hay, earl of Erroll, one of the Catholic ladies of the queen's bedchamber. "Madama Verde," who can be identified as Lady Susan de Vere, the future countess of Montgomery, was rewarded with a cock, "Vn Gallo quaxado todo de Diamantes y rubíes, y seis Perlas, tassado en 160 escudos." It was one of eight jewels made in Brussels and paid by bill of exchange dated 11 February 1604 (N.S.). Another bill of exchange was issued on 27 August 1604 (N.S.) when 9,200 reales (£230) were paid to the London jeweler "Hernaldo Lux," Arnold Lulls, for a jewel set with diamonds which was to be handed out to "Madama de Erbi," countess of Derby, Lady Elizabeth de Vere.[18]

The recipients were chosen by the count of Villamediana, the Spanish ambassador to the English court. In June 1604 he drew up a list of recommendations to be approved of by the constable, who was still in the Low Countries. One of the ladies on the list was "Madama Cidne," the daughter of Sir Robert Sidney, the queen's great chamberlain. Although Sir Robert sympathized with the French party, Villamediana was of the opinion that a jewel ought to be given her for the sake of the queen. Thus Elizabeth Sidney was honored with a diamond set in a ring, which cost about 20,000 reales (£500) and was paid by bill of exchange dated 4 September 1604 (N.S.).[19] Villamediana likewise advised the constable to present Lady Arabella Stuart with "a jewel of some importance because of her position." Accordingly, the constable, on 30 August 1604 (N.S.), signed a warranty in London for seventy-two "botones de oro con tres Diamantes cada vno en 47520 reales" (£1,188) to be given to "Madama Arbela."[20]

Besides the countess of Suffolk, the most valuable collaborationist among the queen's ladies-in-waiting proved to be Lady Susannah Drummond. The principal lady of the queen's bedchamber, as Villamediana reported to the constable, was a Catholic and had given the Spaniards "Confidential advice." He therefore urged the constable that "she be kept under our protection, both to sustain the peace and because of our rivalry with the French." He found her "a prudent person, ready to give help at any time" and his "trust in her . . . always proved well-founded." It was through her intercession that Villamediana "exchanged letters with the Queen." She deserved to be rewarded, he argued, and would continue to further Spain's interests "as in every way she maintains the Queen firmly in our friendship." The constable's response to Villamediana's recommendation was favorable, but he could not help commenting in a marginal note added to Villamediana's report that it seemed "to be something new to go about in this fashion giving pensions to women." Accordingly, Lady Drummond was rewarded with an aigrette adorned with seventy-five "Diamantes entre grandes y pequeños, tassado con el oro y hechura en 920 escudos," which Jean Guiset had created and which were paid for by a bill of exchange dated 17 May 1604 (N.S.); and before the constable's departure from London she received a gratuity of 20,000 reales together with another jewel.[21]

Queen Anna's gift for the constable was partly made in response to Spanish munificence and was presented as a personal memorial of the "marriage" sealed in Whitehall. On the very day of the constable's departure from London, Saturday, 25 August/4 September, the queen's vice-chamberlain, Sir George Carew, rode to Somerset House and solemnly presented the constable with a necklace set with rich pearls for his wife, Doña María Girón, duchess of Frías, and with a so-called picture box, "vna caxa de retratos," as the Spanish chronicler put it, which contained the portraits of King James and Queen Anna as painted most likely by Isaac Oliver and set in lockets by John Spilman, the royal jeweler. The ornamental picture case was set with diamonds. The privacy and intimacy of the presentation was underscored by the fact that Sir George presented the miniatures as love tokens given to a cherished intimate.[22] Sir George declared on behalf of the queen—and we can take it for granted that he delivered the queen's personal message in Spanish[23]—that "se hallaua tan obligada a su Ex[cellenci]a, que le embiaua para sí aquellos retratos, en señal del reconocimiento y amor de sus dueños."[24] The constable responded to the gift giving by rewarding Sir George with "vna joya de Diamantes," which he bought from a French jeweler in London at the price of 12,000 reales. His bill of exchange was dated 3 September 1604 (N.S.).[25]

Within a year or two after the accession of King James to the English throne, Queen Anna established a separate court of her own and set up an independent patronage scheme. In the summer of 1603, she appointed Sir Robert Sidney as lord chamberlain and Sir George Carew as vice-chamberlain,[26] and in June 1605 she nominated Isaac Oliver as "painter for the art of Limning." Oliver, who had made a name for himself as a new-wave artist, appealed more to the queen's advanced aesthetic taste than had the traditionalist Nicholas Hilliard.[27] It is, therefore, legitimate to advance the view that the miniatures representing Queen Anna and King James must have been painted by Oliver and that their commissioner was the queen. The recipient of the gift, who had been governor of Milan, may also have had a say in the choice in so far as the queen is likely to have sensed that Oliver's continental style would be more consonant with the Italian taste of the Spanish grandee than would Hilliard's native style. Whether the portraits were originals made ad vivum or duplicates of standard portraits is a question that must be left unanswered.

The Spanish chronicle of 1604 provides some evidence to support the view that the constable had already obtained two portraits, most likely full-length, of Queen Anna and Prince Henry. On 20/30 August, as the Spanish author records, just before King James presented the constable with the memorial ring in his bedchamber in Somerset House, the king, the earl of Northampton, and the Spanish ambassador, Don Juan de Tassis, count of Villamediana, spent more than a quarter of an hour at his bedside, "hablando de differentes cosas de caça, y recreación, y de los Retratos de la Reyna, y del Príncipe, que tenía el Condestable en el mismo aposento; loándolos el Rey por bien hechos."[28] It would, I think, be wrong to conclude from this account that the portraits belonged to Somerset

House and were hung up in the bedchamber to grace the presence of the constable. The fact that the two portraits caught the king's eye a few minutes before he was to slip off his ring and hand it over to the constable goes to show that he must have been pleased to see the likenesses of his wife and son in the constable's bedroom.

Their presentation must have taken place on 18/28 August, when the queen, in the presence of some twenty ladies-in-waiting, received the constable "con mucho affecto de gusto, y demonstración de amor," refusing to sit down, contrary to the strict observance of court etiquette, before the constable took his seat. The audience lasted more than an hour, during which the queen asked Prince Henry to give a demonstration of his dancing talent. She also invited the constable to kiss all her ladies, as was the fashion in England, on their mouths. After the queen's audience, the prince, left on his own, impressed the constable by his horsemanship, and the constable, appreciating the young prince's manly prowess, ordered his master of the horse, Don Martín de Bañuelos, to let Prince Henry have a Spanish horse, "ricamente enjaezado, y vna casaca, y vna banda bordada de lo mismo muy curiosa"[29] (richly harnessed, and a tunic, and an embroidered waistband of the same material, very elegant).

There were, then, at least some four or five portraits in the constable's luggage crated for shipment to Valladolid: one state portrait of Queen Anna, another state portrait of Prince Henry, one miniature of King James, and the companion piece of Queen Anna.[30] In addition to these royal portraits, it is justifiable to speculate that most of the English commissioners who had sat with the constable at the negotiation table at Somerset House had given him their standard portraits as a memorial.[31] It is on record that one of them, Sir Robert Cecil, earl of Salisbury, gave him his type portrait as duplicated in the workshop of John de Critz the Elder.[32] The de Critz stock representation of Cecil in the constable's possession promises to help unlock the contested authorship of The Somerset House Conference and unravel the technique of portraying the commissioners in the Valladolid workshop of Juan Pantoja de la Cruz.

The mechanism of gift exchange did not operate between the queens of England and of Spain in 1604. Queen Anna, who was frequently beset with financial difficulties, let the constable know on the eve of his departure that although she felt so much obliged to Queen Margaret, she simply did not have the money, the "caudal para poderla corresponder."[33] These seem to be the very words in which Sir George Carew couched the queen's apology after presenting the two miniatures to the constable. It is not surprising to learn that the splendor and magnificence of the court festivities had drained Queen Anna's exchequer so that she could not even afford a second set of miniatures with which to respond to Queen Margaret's liberality.

* * *

The list of presents Queen Margaret prepared for Queen Anna in July 1605 can be taken as proof that in the meantime Queen Anna had complied with her promise to reciprocate the presents. In fact, on Friday, 24 May/3 June 1605, Thomas Knowles, King James's equerry, presented the Spanish monarchs with the royal gifts from England in the duke of Lerma's Palacio de la Ribera: "six Horses (three for the King, and three for the Queene) with saddles and clothes very richly imbroidered and costly; two Crosbowes with sheifs of Arrowes; foure Fowling-pieces, with their furnitures, all very richly garnished and inlayed with fine plate of golde; and one couple of Lime hounds of an extraordinary goodnesse." The following day, as Treswell records, the earl of Nottingham "visited the Queen and deliuered her a faire rich Iewell as a token from the Queen of England."[34]

Queen Margaret, in competitive response to Queen Anna, gave Nottingham the following gifts with the request to bestow them on the English queen. Among them were two portrait miniatures painted by Juan Pantoja de la Cruz:

> dos acaneas con sus sillones de plata, ygual drapas bordadas, de muy grande estima, tasadas en 5300 ducados. [two palfreys with their silver side-saddles, similar clasps embroidered and very highly esteemed, valued at 5300 ducats.]
> vna cajita del tamaño de vn vaipe con los retratos de sus Magestades,llena de diamantes, tasada en 6000 ducados." [a small case set with diamonds the size of a miniature with the portraits of their Majesties, valued at 6,000 ducats.]
> dos cadenas de diamantes tassadas en 5000 escudos." [two chains set with diamonds, valued at 5000 dollars.][35]

In Gascón de Torquemada's unpublished Discurso, "the two miniatures figure explicitly under the gifts made by "La Reina," yet they are listed by Pantoja in his register of works painted for Philip III. This seeming contradiction is cleared up by a statement made by the chamberlain to the queen, Doña Catalina de Zúñiga y Sandoval, daughter of the duke of Lerma. She certified on 20/30 December

1607 that all the paintings commissioned by the queen were actually paid by the king.[36] From this register the fact emerges that the king owed Pantoja 220 reales for the two miniatures of Their Majesties mounted on two copper plates. The price difference between Gascón de Torquemada's account and Pantoja's register is obviously due to the fact that the chronicler included the price charged by the jeweler for the case set with diamonds. On an average, Pantoja charged 110 to 150 reales apiece for what he styled an "original," a miniature painted from life.[37] Thus the two miniatures of the king and queen must have been originals, not replicas supplied by Pantoja's workshop, where miniatures were in stock ready to be delivered at short notice.[38] The presentation ceremony was conducted by Antonio Voto, keeper of the crown jewels, on Monday, 27 May/6 June 1605.[39] On that day the earl of Nottingham, according to Tomé Pinheiro da Veiga, a Portuguese professor of law on a lengthy visit to the Spanish court, had an important conference with the Council of Spain in the duke of Lerma's suburban Palacio de la Ribera.[40] The palace, renowned for its art collections and its picture gallery, provided the suitable environment for the gift-giving ceremony as it had done on 24 May/3 June, when Thomas Knowles delivered the presents on behalf of King James.[41]

For the English and Spanish courts the circulation of portraits and jewels as a means to strengthen their political and dynastic bonds was no innovation. A steady traffic of artifacts had flowed between the two countries when Henry VII and Ferdinand of Aragon entered into a political alliance that was sealed by the Treaty of Medina del Campo in 1489. Two years later the two kings settled the match between Prince Arthur and Princess Catherine of Aragon as a pledge of the treaty. The marriage settlement generated an interchange of portraits. The Spanish monarchs and the princess sent their portraits to the English court and Henry VII, Elizabeth of York, and Prince Arthur sent theirs to the Alcázar in Madrid, where portraits of Catherine as Princess of Wales were also on display.[42] Again portraits were exchanged when the marriage between Queen Mary and Prince Philip was being negotiated in 1554. Philip, moreover, took the distinguished Italian medallist and jeweller Jacopo Nizolla da Trezzo to London, where Trezzo carved his masterpiece, the full-length medallic portrait of Queen Mary, signed and dated 1555. In 1558 Philip left his sister-in-law, the newly crowned Queen Elizabeth, most of the precious stones and jewels he had given to the late Queen Mary. Among them was the marriage collar composed of the cipher of their initials P and M, evenly spaced and fringed with nine diamonds. Fifty years later this magnificent collar was worn by Queen Anna at the request of King James "agaynst the maske at twelfnyght 1607," that is Ben Jonson's *The Masque of Beauty*, which was performed at Whitehall on 10 January 1608, the Sunday after Twelfth Night. Beside the Queen as performer, there were also Lady Arabella Stuart and the Countesses of Derby and of Bedford, who may have worn the jewels given them by the Constable of Castile in 1604.[43]

Juan Pantoja de la Cruz, then, deserves to be acknowledged as ranking among those portraitists who from 1491 down to 1605 had been called upon to execute state portraits in support of the dynastic policies pursued by the courts of Spain and England, to wit, Michel Sittow, Titian, Antonis Mor, presumably Isaac Oliver, and some others. Very little is known of Pantoja's formative years as a painter. A follower of Alonso Sánchez Coello, he must have assisted his master in complying with his duties as *pintor de cámara* to Philip II, turning out a great number of state portraits.[44] After Sánchez Coello's death in 1588, Pantoja took over his workshop. He kept working for the court and the nobility, painting portraits of Prince Philip, the future Philip III, in 1592 and 1594.[45] By 1596 he had consolidated his position as court painter to Philip II, for in 1597 he received his first annual fee of 883 reales for 1596. On Philip II's death in 1598, his status as *pintor de cámara* was confirmed by Philip III, and when the court settled in Valladolid in 1601, Pantoja moved to the new capital.[46]

It is difficult to assess the quality of Pantoja's output because the body of his work that has come down to us is very fragmentary. His art has also come under the severe criticism of those historians who, like Carl Justi, were prejudiced against non-Italian portraiture and therefore dismissed Pantoja as an "uninspired, dull" though "painfully hard-working painter at the court of that feeble-minded Philip III," an "anachronism" in the development of Spanish court portraiture from Antonis Mor and Alonso Sánchez Coello to Diego Velázquez.[47] It has fallen to Maria Kusche to redress the balance in the first full-length study of Pantoja and to disclose the debt Velázquez owed to his predecessor. A fair assessment of Pantoja as an artist is bound to take into account that besides scoring a great success as the foremost portraitist of his time, he was a highly versatile painter at home in all the genres à la mode," the traditional as well as the latest modes. Thus he supplied the Spanish court and the aristocracy with religious paintings, mythological canvases, and historical compositions. He was held in high esteem as an animal painter who, as we will see, portrayed the lead dog presented to the Spanish king by Thomas Knowles. He was also known as a landscape and still-life painter who exploited the new secularized art forms that spread across Europe at the close of the sixteenth century.[48]

Disparaged though he was by modern art critics, Pantoja was acclaimed as a gifted artist by contemporary writers. None other than Lope de Vega and Francisco de Quevedo have left eloquent evidence of their admiration for Pantoja. In *La hermosura de Angélica* (1602), an imitation of Ariosto's *Orlando Furioso*, Lope de Vega couched his praise in the following couplet: "Juan de la Cruz que si criar no pudo / Dio casi vida y alma a un rostro mudo;"[49] and Quevedo extolled Pantoja's work as a miniaturist in the poem "El Pincel," written in 1615, seven years after Pantoja's death:

> Por ti Juan de la Cruz ha podido,
> docto, cuanto ingenioso,
> en el rostro de Lícida hermoso,
> con un naipe nacido,
> criar en sus cabellos
> oro, y estrellas en sus ojos bellos.[50]

The two miniature portraits painted by Pantoja and presented, on 27 May/6 June, to the earl of Nottingham, form part of a series of royal commissions fostered by a coincidence of historic events and religious festivals: the birth of Prince Philip, the future Philip IV (24 March/8 April); the entry of Nottingham's embassy into Valladolid (16/26 May); the christening of Prince Philip (19/29 May), delayed by royal order until after the arrival of the English embassy; the queen's churching (21/31 May); three processions during *semana santa*, the most important being the Procession of Corpus Christi (30 May/9 June); the ratification of the peace treaty between Spain and England (30 May/9 June); and the routine banquets, revels, masques, plays, barriers, bullfights, cavalry parade, and whatnot, all staged in honor of the heir to the crown and the peace treaty with England and conceived as a conspicuous self-representation of the Spanish monarchy and nobility.

Pantoja was virtually swamped with commissions of paintings to be completed for the festivities, and even with the combined forces of his studio, his attendants, apprentices, and collaborators, he could not cope with the orders of the queen and of the king. On the one hand, Pantoja was expected to meet the queen's demands obviously made in connection with the christening and the churching; on the other, he was expected to comply with the king's requests made in connection with the new alliance with England. He gave the religious paintings commissioned by the queen priority over the others. The state portraits commissioned by the king were still unfinished when Nottingham departed from Valladolid on 8/18 June.

On 27 May/6 June, the very day Pantoja delivered the two royal miniatures to Antonio Voto, the king's keeper of the jewels, he also delivered to Hernando de Rojas, the queen's keeper of the jewels, a painting, *The Virgin a Week before Her Confinement*, with many angels surrounding the Virgin and Joseph kneeling down. The queen ordered the painting for her oratory in lieu of a work that another painter had executed and that she disliked.[51] Three days later, on 30 May/9 June, Pantoja delivered two more paintings to Hernando de Rojas, one an original, the second a copy. The original, a huge canvas measuring 300 by 220 centimeters, had its place in the queen's oratory, enriching her well-known collection of religious paintings. It was a representation of *The Eleven Thousand Virgins*, the virgins clad in damask vestments. Pantoja called it a perfect painting, rich in ornament and studded with figures.[52] The copy, measuring 200 by 130 centimeters, was made from Hieronymus Bosch's *Temptation of St Anthony*.[53] Finally, on 29 June/9 July, Pantoja, then working in Lerma, gave the queen a portrait miniature of the three-month-old Prince Philip, the prince sitting on a velvet crimson cushion, dressed in white. This miniature, like so many of them, was sent to Germany to be added to the family gallery of the Habsburgs.[54]

It was only after the departure of the English embassy when the festivities had come to an end that Pantoja set to paint the three state portraits Philip III commissioned from him for the English court. Pantoja followed the court to Lerma and Burgos, and there during a period of thirty-five days, lasting from 30 June/10 July to 4/14 August 1605, he tried to complete the portraits of Philip III, Queen Margaret, and the infanta Ana, which he had begun in Valladolid, but he failed to do so.[55] He therefore delayed their delivery to Antonio Voto until 16 February 1606. The shipment of the portraits was entrusted to Don Juan de Mendoza, marquis of San Germán, governor of Galicia.[56] On their arrival in England, they were hung in the Cross Gallery in Somerset House,[57] but by 1613 they were moved to Whitehall where the duke of Saxe-Weimar saw them.[58]

The portrait of Philip III, now at Hampton Court (no. 406 in the 1898 catalog) is described in Pantoja's register as an original full-length portrait, the king, aged twenty-seven, wearing a suit of armor, his right hand holding a field marshal's baton, his left hand the pommel of a sword.[59] Its iconography is indebted to the representation of royalty, originating from Titian's portrait of Charles V, a copy of which, made by Pantoja, is at the Escorial.[60] The Titian legacy was handed down to Antonis Mor and from Mor to Alonso Sánchez Coello, who made a copy from Mor's portrait of Philip II.[61] These portraits share a number of iconographical features: identical pose, head and body turned to the right, legs astride, chest protected by suit of armor, right hand holding a baton, left hand the pommel of a sword.

In 1598, when he was called upon to commemorate Philip's accession to the throne, Pantoja adopted this formula for portraying Philip III as commander-in-chief. The portrait painted for the English court in 1605 and completed in 1606 is one of several pictures based on this iconographical paradigm.[62] But it has a variant that to me seems fraught with symbolic meaning. As the portrait was painted to commemorate the newly concluded bond of amity, King Philip, standing in front of a tent as commander-in-chief of the Spanish army, no longer points his left hand to a besieged fortress visible in the right-hand background, as he does in the 1598 portrait, but has now assumed the same peaceful posture of contained belligerence as depicted in the aforementioned portraits of Charles V and Philip II, his left hand holding the pommel of the sword and the background behind the tent commanding the view of a landscape. The portrait is a reflection of the king's spectacular change. The initially belligerent King Philip III is depicted as no longer seeking greatness in war but in peace with King James I.[63]

Compared to the portraits painted by his master and predecessors, Pantoja's do not strike a balance between the representation of the king as an individual and as an emblem of royalty. The predominance of symbolism over the delineation of character cannot, of course, be taken as proof of Pantoja's lack of creative sensibility; for in painting King Philip III, he was expected to respect the new concept of royalty as defined by the court of Philip III, then under the control of the duke of Lerma. His portraits of commoners are less reserved.

The portrait of Margaret of Austria, queen of Spain, now at Buckingham Palace, leaves no doubt that it was painted as a present to the queen of England in commemoration of the new alliance. The portrait, in my opinion, was less a manifestation of wealth and power than a personal memorial of the new bond of amity that, in the courtly parlance of the two kings, was styled a bond of wedlock. In token of this "marriage," King James, as noted above, presented a diamond ring to the constable of Castile, and so did King Philip III to the earl of Nottingham. In like manner the queen ordered from Pantoja a state portrait representing her in the full regalia of her wedding, celebrated in 1598, when she was fourteen years old. In none of the portraits discussed by Kusche does the queen wear her wedding robes except in the one she sent to England. The companion portrait in 1606, now in the Prado, conforms to the same formula. The composition and pose are the same, the headdress is alike, the shape and style of the gown identical, yet the queen does not wear her wedding robes.[64]

Pantoja has left a minute description of the queen's full-length portrait, which he priced at 4,000 reales, twice as much as he did the king's portrait sent to England. The queen, he recorded in his register, is wearing her white wedding robes made of spring fabric and bedecked with the coats of arms of Castile, Leon, and Austria, and bespangled with pearls. She has put on display the panoply of her jewelry, her pearl earrings, her belt studded with jewels, her diamond bracelets and diamond chain, the magnificent jewel on the breast of her robe, her headdress adorned with jeweled plumes. With her right hand she is taking a book of hours from a table, on its cover the illuminated portrait of the Virgin, and in her left hand she is holding a lace kerchief.[65] Pantoja does not mention the queen's face as if for him it were the least important part of the portrait. In fact, the small face of the twenty-year-old queen, placed at the vertex of the triangle formed by the head, the left and the right hand holding the book of hours, is sticking out of the voluminous folds of the ruff, and together with the heavy stiffness of the conical gown it imparts an air of aloofness and creates the expression of a royal doll.[66]

The state portrait of Princess Anne painted by Pantoja in 1605 and sent to England in 1606, together with the portraits of the king and queen, has been lost. It seems worthwhile, despite its loss, to look for the reasons that induced the infanta's parents to commission her portrait. Philip III, or rather the duke of Lerma, thought it advisable to secure the new political alliance with a matrimonial union that would guarantee the process of peacekeeping and improve the situation of the English Catholics. Thus the prospective match between Princess Anne and Henry, Prince of Wales, was being aired by the two countries in 1603 when Spain sent Don Juan de Tassis, count of Villamediana, as envoy to England. As already mentioned, King James made oblique allusions to a dynastic union at the state banquet held in August 1604. Yet right from the start the tentative matrimonial feelers were doomed to failure because the two courts used the bride and groom as ploys in their diplomatic struggle to settle the religious issue.[67] On his departure from London the constable left instructions with the new Spanish ambassador, Don Pedro ze Zúñiga, to inform King James that the marriage issue could be pursued only if he agreed to send Prince Henry to Spain to be educated as a Catholic.[68] In 1604/5 the most tangible evidence of the matrimonial game then afoot has to be sought in the ritual of gift giving, the reciprocal exchange of portraits representing the two royal houses. Queen Anna, left on her own by her husband, who had withdrawn to his hunting lodge, presented the constable of Castile, as we have seen, with the portrait of Prince Henry, and Queen Margaret, with her husband's consent, balanced the gift with the portrait of the infanta painted by Juan Pantoja de la Cruz.

Considering that the lost portrait of the infanta was an instrument of dynastic propaganda, a reconstruction of the portrait seems imperative. Pantoja's register offers plenty of information. Thus Pantoja recorded that he painted an original full-length portrait of the infanta in her stiff red gown she wore as godmother at the christening of her brother Philip, the butterfly sleeves slashed and trimmed with lace, its ornaments embroidered. The curtain (in the background) and the table (on the left covered with velvet) were crimson. On the table were some peaches, the infanta holding a fruit in her (right) hand, as she does in her 1602 portrait,[69] and a kerchief in her other (left) hand.[70]

All the contemporary chronicles I have consulted, in print and in manuscript, in Spanish and in English, contain eloquent accounts of the baptismal ceremony celebrated at Saint Paul's Church by the archbishop of Toledo on Sunday, 19/29 May 1605, in the presence of the whole court of Spain and of foreign dignatories and ambassadors, the prince of Morocco living in Spain included. The English guests of honor watched the procession in the morning from the windows of the residence of the count of Ribadavía and the baptism in the afternoon from a stand in the main chapel of St. Paul's. All the chronicles mention the infanta as godmother, who was borne "in a chaire," to quote from Treswell's eyewitness report, "by diuers Gentlemen of the Kings bed and Priuy chamber, on their shoulders, assisted by the yonger Prince of *Sauoy.*"[71] But only two of them refer to the gown the infanta wore. Pinheiro da Veiga's sartorial description unfortunately is of no use, for he mistook the infanta's gown for the white frock she put on two days later at the queen's churching. However, Gascón de Torquemada's *Discurso* discloses some more details. The gown, he tells us, was made of red satin, lined with silver brocade, and the infanta wore a satin golden headdress.[72]

Two conclusions can be drawn from these contemporary descriptions. First, the lost 1605 portrait of the infanta was no doubt a variant of the 1604 portrait. The alterations entitled Pantoja to call the 1605 portrait an original. Second, both the 1604 and 1605 portrait of the infanta conform, although in reduced scale, to the pattern of the queen's two portraits executed in 1605 and 1606.[73] The composition of the infanta's two portraits was the same: crimson curtain in the background, crimson table in the left middleground, princess dressed in stiff conical satin gown with slashed butterfly sleeves ending in laced cuffs, the satin lined with silver and gold brocade. There were some differences. The gown's color in the 1604 portrait is blue green, not red as in the 1605 portrait; the princess wears no headdress; on the table there is a monkey instead of peaches, and the princess is holding the monkey's chain in both hands in lieu of a peach in her right and a kerchief in her left hand.

The infanta's physiognomy in the 1604 portrait is that of a precocious girl, aged four, "very pretty and lively," as Tomé Pinheiro da Veiga noted when he saw her at the queen's churching.[74] The regal posture she has been forced to assume is not consonant with her natural endowments as a girl. It must, however, be borne in mind that Pantoja was called upon to execute a representational portrait destined to introduce the infanta to her Austrian relatives. For the same reason, the lost 1605 portrait was bound to conform to the formula for adult state portraits. It was, as mentioned, commissioned to introduce the infanta to the English court as the prospective wife of Prince Henry and hence as the prospective queen of England.

The immediate impact of the gift-giving ceremonies and their strict observance of reciprocity remains unknown. We do not know what reception Pantoja's three state portraits and two miniatures met with at the English court. In one case, however, in which Pantoja was implied, we do know the response to the gift. The Spanish king and queen took great pleasure in being presented with a pack of English dogs by Thomas Knowles on behalf of the English monarchs; and Philip III, developing a particular liking for the lead dog, commissioned a portrait of the *lebrel de Yngalatera* from Pantoja. The painting, unfortunately, has been lost, but Pantoja has left an account in his register.

The large canvas that Pantoja delivered about 1606/7 to Hernando de Espejo, keeper of the king's jewels and that he valued at 300 ducats or 3,300 reales, measured 200 by 150 centimeters. Taking up the iconographical stereotype of "dwarf" and "dog," which in Spain was known through Antonis Mor and which eventually was to climax in Velázquez's *Las Meninas*, Pantoja executed a full-length portrait of the court dwarf Bonami, who is keeping the English greyhound called Baylán on a leash. Bonami is booted and spurred, wearing hose and doubtlet of green velvet lined with silver and gold borders and a chain round his neck. In like manner Pantoja depicted a second dwarf, Don Antonio, who keeps two young hare hounds from Flanders on a leash. In the background of the painting there was a view of the Pardo and the countryside.[75]

The breed of the English dog portrayed is contested. According to Treswell, it was, as we have learned, a lyam-dog, a bloodhound; for Pantoja it was a greyhound; and to believe the anonymous English reporter, it was a beagle. Surprisingly, the unidentified English eyewitness provides much more accurate information on the English gifts presented by Thomas Knowles in "Valledeley" (Valladolid) than does the authorized chronicle written by the Somerset Herald. The unknown Englishman distinguished the presents given by King James from those given by Queen Anna and by Prince Henry. Thus he recorded that "Maister Knowles deliuered from his Maiestie to the King of Spaine, and to the Queene, six horses, three to the King, and three to the Queene, two with saddles and furniture to them, and foure with very rich cloaths, they being wrought with imbrodered workes: besides, hee deliuered a couple of very faire beagles, two Crossebowes, and two little peeces, the one beeing sent from Prince Henry, and the other beagle sent from the Queene with foure whelpes, which they didde receyue very gratiously and royally, making very much of the beagles: besides, he deliuered to the Queene, a very rich iewel, sent vnto her from our king."[76] Credit must be given to Pantoja's words rather than to the two English chroniclers. Renowned as an animal painter,[77] Pantoja certainly knew that Baylán, the king's favorite dog he was painting, was a greyhound.

To sum up, the English royal house, as a result of the political union and the bond of amity, called five Pantojas its own. A sixth was acquired by King Charles I for his collection: the portrait of Isabel Clara Eugenia, the archduchess of Austria, which Pantoja painted about 1597. It is now at Petworth House, Sussex.[78]

*   *   *

Before broaching the subject of Pantoja's authorship of *The Somerset House Conference*, let us bear in mind that he was the only court painter and court portraitist to be involved in the peace treaty and alliance with England. Both the Spanish king and queen, as we have seen, relied on the prestige of Pantoja's art in 1605 to buttress the new political union and to promote the prospective bond of wedlock between Princess Anne and Prince Henry. It is, therefore, logical to speculate that whoever ordered, in 1604, a pictorial memorial of the peace settlement must needs have known that Pantoja was designated by the Spanish royal house as the painter to commemorate the historic event. Pantoja, as shown above, had the honor to portray the royal peacemakers, and I am now going to argue that he had also the privilege to portray the commissioners who negotiated the treaty in London. In his capacity as court painter to Philip III, Pantoja, to put it in King James's metaphorical vein, was also called upon to portray the matchmakers most likely by the constable of Castile.

The art critics have cast doubt on the authenticity of what they consider an enigmatic painting. Their views, however, rest solely on impressionistic evidence. The vague statements, to my mind, do not carry enough weight to unsaddle Pantoja and father the work on another artist. The painting has generally been attributed to Marcus Gheeraerts the Younger. Feeling dissatisfied with this attribution, Roy Strong in his inventory of the National Portrait Gallery has hypothesized that the picture, to judge from its style of painting, is "directly connected with Frans Pourbus and his circle." Yet most biographers of King James and historians of his reign keep attributing the painting to Gheeraerts, who was living in London.[79] Kerr, on his part, has rejected the hypothesis of a Flemish artist in favor of an unidentified Spanish painter who accompanied the constable of Castile on his embassy to London.[80]

In order to authenticate the painting as Pantoja's I will have to clear up some misunderstandings about the occasion and the likely patron before entering upon a discussion of its signature, its date, its key to the commissioners, and of the likelihood of the painter's stay in London. The last point raises a number of technical problems that any painter would have faced while working in Somerset

House and then in his workshop, where his assistants under his supervision completed the painting. After authenticating the painting as Pantoja's, I will finally venture upon an analysis and reading. I admit that as a literary historian I am not armed with the tools of connoisseurship; nonetheless, I do hope to be up to the task I set myself of lifting the veil of mystery over *The Somerset House Conference* in the National Portrait Gallery (NPG).

At first sight *The Somerset House Conference* seems to be no more than the routine performance of a court painter who did his duty in executing a memorial painting commemorating the conclusion of a political alliance. We see the lower end of the conference chamber in which the commissioners used to meet in Somerset House. The upper half of the chamber, furnished with a state (throne) on a raised platform, lies outside the painted surface. It is the space in front of the conference table and the perspective of the composition that make it clear that the state, as we are going to see, is implied. The implied state, in fact, provides the key to a reading of the painting. The conference table is placed in the center of the painted space, and the commissioners are seated on high-backed chairs on either side of the table. The room is hung with two tapestries, whose borders bear the date 1560. In the background there are leaded windows; the lower pane of the window to the left is open, looking into one of the two courtyards and thereby underscoring the depth of the room.

The six members of the Hispano-Flemish delegation are seated to the left, the five English commissioners to the right. All of them are seated in order of precedence from the back to the foreground. Those highest in hierarchy are seated closest to the vanishing point placed in the left upper window. Consequently their faces are foreshortened in proportion to the faces of those delegates sitting in the foreground. Their names are given in two keys, one in the bottom left and the other in the right-hand corner. The spelling of the names, and seeming addition of a sixth figure, are crucial to the authentication of the painting.

Reading from the left the names are: Juan Fernández de Velasco, constable of Castile, duke of Frías; Juan de Tassis, count of Villamediana, ambassador; and Alessandro Rovida, senator of Milan, the constable's substitute. These three constitute the Spanish delegation. The next three colleagues are the delegates of Albert, archduke of Austria, governor of the Netherlands: Charles de Ligne, Count Arenberg; Jean Richardot, sire de Barly, president of the Privy Council; and Louis Verreycken, *audencier,* that is, privy councillor

and first secretary of state. Reading from the right, the English commissioners are: Thomas Sackville, earl of Dorset; Charles Howard,
earl of Nottingham; Charles Blount, earl of Devonshire; Henry Howard, earl of Northampton; and Robert Cecil, Viscount Cranborne.

The presence of the Constable in the painting is not "a contradiction in terms" as the catalog of the NPG makes us believe. In point
of fact, the constable summoned the delegates to attend the last
four meetings in Somerset House; and although he did not personally attend the first eighteen sessions, which took place between 20/
30 May and 6/16 July, he was masterminding the Hispano-Flemish
delegation, pulling the strings from the Low Countries, where, for
tactical reasons, he was biding his time and waiting for the final
instructions of Philip III concerning matters of trade and religion.[81]
He eventually landed at Dover on 5/15 August and got to London
on 10/20 August. In compliance with international diplomatic observance, he should have been given a solemn entry, as the earl of
Nottingham was going to be granted in 1605, but as King James
obviously repaid the constable's procrastination with his royal absence from London—the queen was present on the constable's arrival, as she was to be on his departure—the constable was not
granted the favor. However, he and his immediate entourage, among
them three nephews of his, together with the count of Villamediana
and Senator Rovida, enjoyed the privilege of residing in Somerset
House, which was furnished as if King Philip III had come in person.[82] A room had been converted into a chapel at the constable's request.[83]

Within five days the constable convened the nineteenth meeting,
on Wednesday, 25 August, at 2 p.m.; it lasted just over two hours.
The following day the delegates met for the twentieth, a morning
session, which lasted from 10 a.m. to 12 p.m. Then the constable
treated his colleagues to a princely working dinner in Somerset
House. The seating order at the table differed from the rigorous
order in the painting. The constable held the place of honor; the
earl of Dorset, the earl of Devonshire, the count of Villamediana,
the senator Rovida, and other gentlemen sat to the right. The earl
of Nottingham, Viscount Cranborne, the president Jean Richardot,
and other gentlemen, supposedly Count Arenberg and Louis Verreycken, sat to the left. During dinner, the constable, standing up
bareheaded, drank King James's health to the earl of Dorset. The
toast was passed around, each delegate in turn drinking amid the
applause and to the liking of all present. Next the constable drank
to the health of the queen and the toast again passed from delegate

to delegate. Thereupon the earl of Nottingham drank King Philip's health to the constable, and the same ritual was observed for the third time. There was a final bout of toasting and drinking when news arrived that King James had drunk to the health of the constable. After postprandial small talk, the delegates withdrew to the veranda, the constable to his apartment, to rest for half an hour. They met again for the twenty-first session, which lasted well into the afternoon. The last session took place on Saturday, 18/28 August, the day before the ratification ceremonies, between 2 and 4 p.m. The delegates with the constable in the chair went through the articles of the peace treaty, discussing the points the constable raised "para mayor firmeza y claridad de la paz."[84]

The scenario of the working dinner seems to have been outlined as a rehearsal of the banquet to be celebrated at the ratification. The announcement of King James's toast during the working dinner was most carefully timed. The king, feeling deeply committed to the practice of hospitality, had seen to it that a staff of qualified waiters, servants, and guardsmen was looking after the constable's well-being "dentro de casa como pages," as the Spanish chronicler Fermín López de Mendizórroz put it.[85] Among the English servants commissioned to wait upon the constable in Somerset House were the king's men.[86] Given the constable's consciousness of his exalted status, I think any personal contact between him and Shakespeare can be ruled out even though it is tempting to speculate that a grandee with literary pretensions and collector of medieval manuscripts who, during his governorship of Milan patronized dramatic court performances must have become acquainted with Shakespeare.[87]

The neglected report of the Spanish chronicler has provided evidence with which to rid *The Somerset House Conference* of one of the mysteries that has baffled English art critics. The portrait of the constable of Castile, far from being the dubious addition of an uninformed painter, has turned out to correspond to historical reality. Its inclusion raises the question of who commissioned the painting. If the patron has to be sought among the commissioners portrayed, he could only have been the constable; if the painting was made for the Spanish court, three men qualify for patronage: King Philip III, the duke of Lerma, and the constable. The three of them were collectors on a grand scale and renowned for their art patronage. The king, however, can be eliminated as patron, for in 1604 he commissioned no painting from Pantoja. Had he given the order, Pantoja would have listed it in his register. The duke of

Lerma can also be ruled out as patron. He did patronize Pantoja, but his principal painter was the Florentine Bartolemé Carducho. Had he patronized the painting, he would have exhibited it in one of his many picture galleries; yet the painting is listed in none of his inventories.[88] This leaves the constable as the likely patron.

The constable pursued a politics of patronage that was inspired by his rivalry with the duke of Lerma. A good case in point illustrating their cultural competition is the lavish entertainment they afforded the English embassy in Valladolid in 1605, each striving to outdo the other. Lerma spared no pains and money to triumph over the constable in patronizing two companies of actors, one run by Nicolás de los Ríos, the other by Diego López de Alcaraz, the first company playing Lope de Vega's *El Caballero de Illescas*, the second three *entremeses* as a double bill, to a multicultural audience made up of Englishmen, Scotsmen, and Spaniards gathered in the courtyard of the Palacio de la Ribera.[89] In Valladolid it was Lerma, the life and soul of the peace policy, who was in the limelight.

In London it had been the constable, the hesitant peacemaker, who showered enormous sums of money in the form of pensions, presents, jewels, and bribes on the English courtiers willing to support the alliance and the cause of the English Catholics. Queen Anna, hoping to secure his advocacy of a dynastic alliance, presented him, as already mentioned, with two portrait miniatures and two oil paintings, one being the likeness of Prince Henry, the prospective husband of Princess Anne, the four-year-old infanta, whose portrait was to be painted by Pantoja for her prospective parents-in-law.

The queen seems to have been au courant that the constable had assigned to himself two roles: one as peacemaker and the other as art patron. Besides coming to England to negotiate and sign the peace treaty, the constable in his capacity as lord of the House of Velasco and of the Seven Infants of Lara commissioned a painter in England to execute or copy a representation of the tragic legend of the "siete ynfantes de Lara," which was paid "con dinero de la jornada." The constable must have known through his mother, Ana de Guzmán y Aragón, who was born, brought up and educated in England, most likely in the household of Queen Catherine of Aragon, that such a painting existed in an English collection.[90] Thus when the constable left London, he took with him at least six paintings that he was to keep in his and his wife's collection.[91] In view of his spirit of cultural self-assertiveness—he also acquired, as appears from the 1613 inventory, ninety-eight "cuadros al temple . . . grandes y chicos . . . en Flandes en la jornada de las paces de Ynglaterra y de dinero della" (fol. 484)—it was quite in his nature to ask a Spanish artist to paint a picture commemorating his services rendered in concluding the alliance. In the eyes of the constable, the only eligible candidate to be entrusted with the task of executing the painting must have been Juan Pantoja de la Cruz, the official court painter to Philip III. In 1603, he had already patronized Pantoja, ordering from him two portraits, one each of his daughters Ana de Velasco y Girón, duchess of Braganza, and of Mariana de Velasco Ibarra.[92] It must also be borne in mind that the constable was wont to command group paintings glorifying his own political career. Thus as governor of Milan (1592–93) and 1593–1600) he saw to it that an Italian painter celebrated his martial qualities as a victorious general commanding a great army against the French troops or again that the Milanese poets praised, in panegyric sonnets, his portrait as commander-in-chief, which Giovan Ambrogio Figino had executed.[93]

The painting's signature confirms the foregoing argumentation. *The Somerset House Conference* bears the signature of Juan Pantoja de la Cruz. The painting is signed "Juan pantoja dela ✝." The signature is not a fake. Why should it be? Its authenticity was put to the test when the painting was cleaned in 1967 and it did not come off. It makes little sense to argue, as does the catalogue of the NPG, that the signature, having weathered the passage of time and the process of cleaning, could be an early addition.

The painting's wrong date is another mystery that has intrigued the critics. The Somerset House conferences took place in 1604. The painting, however, is dated 1594. The misdate is obviously due to a restorer. There are several Pantojas whose dates, having flaked off, have been misdated in the course of restoration. Thus the portrait of Queen Margaret in the collection of Prince Luis de Baviera y Borbón, Madrid, originally dated "Madriti 1602," was misdated "Madriti 1607."[94] The portrait of Philip III at the Kunsthistorisches Museum, Vienna, must originally have been signed "Juan Pantoja de la ✝ Regiae Mayestatis Philippi.3. Camerarius Pictor, faciebat Madriti 1598." What can be made out at present is just "Mayestatis."[95] The restorers of *The Somerset House Conference* obviously mistook a zero for a nine and a six for a five. A blurred 0 can easily be misread for a 9, and what may have been left of the lower half of the 6 probably looked like an S. In contemporary Spanish handwriting S and 5 were written alike. It is significant that the copy in the National Maritime Museum, Greenwich, has no date (see below).

The keys to the names of the two delegations, the key to the Hispano-Flemish delegation in the bottom left-hand corner and to the English delegation in the bottom right-hand corner, as well as the titles of the commissioners can also be adduced as indisputable evidence that the painter was Pantoja de la Cruz. The artist, as Xavier de Salas has pointed out, gives his identity away by adding two accurate keys, the Hispano-Flemish delegates being numbered and the English lettered. This was an idiosyncrasy of Pantoja's that was most manifest in the labored pedigrees of Philip II made by Pantoja in his 1599 copies of Pompeo Leoni's bronze figures of the royal tombs at the Escorial.[96] The keys are given in Spanish, the two delegations being introduced as the members "De Parte del Rey Despaña mi Sr" and "De parte del Rey de Ingalatierra." The painter has also taken some pains to give all the titles in Spanish. Thus the key of the English delegation reads: "A Thomas C[on]de de dorset Gran thess[ore]ro de Jng[alaterr]a / B Carlos C[on]de Nottingham Gran Almir[an]te / C Carlos C[on]de de Densier Virrey de Irlanda / D Henrico C[on]de de Northampton del Con[sej]o / F Roberto de Cecil Gran Secretario del rey." Surprisingly for a Spaniard, all the English titles are spelled correctly with the exception of Charles Blount's, earl of Devonshire. "Conde de Densier" is, in fact, the phonetic transcription of the earl's title in Spanish. No Flemish painter would ever have used it unless he were in Spanish service or had read the Spanish *Relación* (1604), which twice has "Conde de Densier" (pp. 29, 43). By way of comparison, the *Vray discours* (Douai, 1604) of the constable's embassy translated for French readers in Flanders and France has "Conte de Deuenshier" (sig. A4).[97]

Pantoja's authorship has also been disputed on the ground that he never traveled abroad. This view has never been substantiated for want of biographical data; neither will the contrary view, that he did make his way to London, unless we take *The Somerset House Conference* as visual evidence that he did. It seems all but logical to assume that the tide of events in 1604 set Pantoja on the road to England. The constable, wishing to be recorded for posterity in a memorial painting, no doubt summoned Pantoja to accompany him on his embassy. Kerr's objections that Pantoja's name cannot be traced among the accounts of the constable's expenses incurred in England and submitted to the Crown on his return to Valladolid in December 1604 are not convincing.[98] The majority of the 234 retainers of the constable, eight nobles, gentlemen, household officers, guards, heralds, servants, sailors, messengers, and carriers have likewise left no trace in the records. The only written document known to me that seems to corroborate Pantoja's absence from Valladolid is his register of the queen's commissions. From February 1603 until January 1604 Pantoja was busy working for Queen Margaret. On 1/11 February 1603, he delivered a portrait miniature of the seventeen-month-old Princess Anne dressed in blue, which was to be sent to Germany; on 27 February/9 March and 2/12 May, three portraits of the dead Princess María in her coffin, one to be sent to Germany, one to Flanders, one to be kept in the royal palace in Valladolid.[99] On 22 August/1 and 13/23 September, two more portraits of the dead infanta, obviously copies, were delivered; on 26 November/6 December, an original portrait of the queen five months pregnant; on 12/22 December, another original portrait of the queen dressed in black, which he had painted in the convent of the Discalced Nuns in Madrid; on 3/13 January 1604, an original portrait miniature of Princess Anne dressed in green and taking sweets from some small baskets, which he had also painted in the convent of the Discalced Nuns; and on 4/14 January, a portrait miniature of the king wearing a sable cape was delivered to the queen at the convent of the Discalced Nuns, Madrid.

Then follows a yawning gap of ten months in the chronological entries of the register until 24 October/3 November 1604, when Pantoja delivered the original portrait of Princess Anne dressed in blue that I have discussed above.[100] One would very much like to know why there was such a long break in the queen's commissions. A plausible explanation is that Pantoja was away from Valladolid on his journey to London.

When it came to executing the painting, Pantoja was confronted with a number of technical problems. How was it feasible for him to execute a group painting between 10/20 August and 24 August/3 September, not counting the days of arrival and departure, when the eleven delegates were taken up with last-minute negotiations, conferences, audiences, and the peace solemnities? Extra sittings for the painting would have upset the agenda of the delegates and would have caused additional transport problems, for the English delegates lodged in Whitehall and the archduke's in Durham House. One can take it for certain that there were no special group sittings for the painting. At best the delegates may have granted Pantoja individual sittings.

Pantoja responded to the situation he found in Somerset House by taking adequate measures. Other painters before and after him had to cope with the same problems. Holbein the Younger went to Brussels to portray Christina of Denmark on behalf of Henry VIII, but as she refused to sit longer than three hours to him, he was obliged to execute some drawings from which he worked up the portrait in his studio in England.[101] Rubens began the group portrait of Sir Balthasar Gerbier, his wife and nine children when he lodged with them in London and finished it in his Antwerp studio.[102] Pantoja, in like manner, was obliged to make a series of preliminary sketches and drawings which he then worked up in his Valladolid studio, copying the faces of the delegates either from miniatures or from standard portraits given to him and to the constable in London or sent to Valladolid.

Pantoja's portrait of Sir Robert Cecil, earl of Cranborne, unravels his method of working with portrait patterns. He obviously used a Cecil portrait as model for *The Somerset House Conference* which was Cecil's standard type of portrait attributed to John de Critz the Elder. Deformed as he was, Cecil was very sensitive about his appearance and obviously saw to it that Pantoja painted his likeness from his acknowledged standard portrait he presented to the constable in London or from another duplicate he may have given to Pantoja himself.[103] Again Pantoja's portrait of Charles Howard, earl of Nottingham, looks as if it had been duplicated from Nottingham's standard portrait.[104] Pantoja was highly experienced in working up sketched heads and in reproducing stereotyped portraits of his own making and of other artists.[105] He even went to the length of representing the faces of Queen Margeret's German relatives in his religious paintings. Thus two women in *The Birth of the Blessed Virgin* (1603) bear the features of the queen's sisters, whom Pantoja had never met.[106]

The achievement of Pantoja's art in the case of *The Somerset House Conference* is difficult to evaluate because this painting, perhaps more than any other of Pantoja's, is the product of his workshop. Pantoja obviously delegated to his assistants the task of working up the interior of the Conference Chamber in Somerset House and the portraits of the seated delegates from his sketches made in London. He reserved for himself the privilege, as he was wont to do, of setting in the heads of the eleven commissioners. The memorial painting strikes as being the symbiotic amalgam of the attendants' craftsmanship and the master's professional routine of duplicating the ready-made portrait patterns of the commissioners. It is less the artistic performance than the pictorial workman-ship that fascinates. After all Pantoja was expected to satisfy the international demand for the memorial painting rather than to exe-cute a masterpiece. We can take it for granted that the constable as patron, the courts in Valladolid, Whitehall, and Brussels, the En-glish embassy in Madrid, and many notables in the three countries involved required replicas of the painting commemorating their historic alliance. Clearly, a considerable number of copies must have been manufactured in Pantoja's workshop.

We do know that a copy was seen by Henry Coventry, secretary of state, in Sir Richard Fanshawe's Madrid residence, the Siete Chi-menaes, between 1664 and 1666. Fanshawe was then negotiating a peace treaty between England and Spain, which he signed on 17/27 December 1665 before informing his government. This new alli-ance, which cost Fanshawe his office, is likely to have renewed interest in Pantoja's painting. A copy, perhaps the same as in the English embassy in Madrid, is now in the National Maritime Mu-seum, Greenwich.[107] The version in the NPG was acquired by Rob-ert Spencer, earl of Sunderland, from Baron Belleville in 1681. It was first listed in a 1698 inventory of Hamilton House and re-mained there in the collection of the Dukes of Hamilton until 1882, when it was sold in an auction to the NPG.[108] The version in the NPG must be seen in the light of this international demand.

The key to the compositional formula of the painting is the dark spot in the left windowpane, a reflection of a top floor window on the opposite side of the courtyard. It marks the vertex of an equilat-eral triangle, the intersection of the sides a and b. The sides a and c intersect at the knob of Cecil's armrest, and the sides b and c at the knob of Verreycken's armrest. The side c marks off the near edge of the conference table; its far edge to the right corresponds to the middle of side a; its far edge to the left does not correspond to the middle of side b. As a result of this geometrical dispropor-tion, the table is shifted to the left. The right and the left line of the table converge to the vanishing point of the perspective placed in the second pane of the left upper window. The heads of the commissioners are systematically foreshortened as they recede into the distance toward the vanishing point of the perspective, Cecil's and Verreycken's being larger than the constable's and Dorset's. The receding lines bring out the commissioners' reclining position with the exception of Cecil's. He is leaning forward in his chair as if he were about to hand over to the implied viewer the articles of the peace treaty lying before him on the table.

The implied viewer provides the key to a reading of the painting. As the eye level of his fixed viewpoint corresponds to the level of the vanishing point, it follows that the implied viewer is looking down on the assembled delegates. He can be none other than James I and VI, king of England and Scotland. That the conference chamber in Somerset House was furnished with a state, is confirmed by the description of the Spanish chronicler. The presence chamber, he recorded, was furnished with a magnificent state, a canopy decorated with the royal coats of arms behind a chair of state and royal cushions. In another interior chamber there was a more modern dais and canopy, which had been made for one of the queen's recent masques. The Scottish coat of arms had been added, its ornamental border being embroidered with James's favorite motto: Beati Pacifici.[109] This then must have been the chamber Pantoja has represented in his painting, a conference chamber designed to propagate the Stuart myth of King James as *rex pacificus*, guarantor of peace in a divided Europe. The state from which the implied king presides over the delegates had been made for the first Jacobean court masque, to wit, Samuel Daniel's *The Vision of the Twelve Goddesses*, which was performed at Hampton Court on 8/18 January 1604, the count of Villamediana being one of the many guests. In this much criticized court masque, Queen Anna as Pallas, the goddess of wisdom, and her ladies-in-waiting bearing gifts to the Temple of Peace celebrated the cease-fire with Spain, which had been proclaimed by King James in March 1603 and which was requited by Philip III with his appointing the count of Villamediana ambassador to the English court.[110]

The subtle manipulation of the viewpoint enabled Pantoja to include King James without having to represent him physically. Thus the king has before him the principal makers of the peace alliance set in determinate space and time by Pantoja's art. From the implied throne the *rex pacificus* enjoys the view over the dignified delegates, who, after a pitched battle over political, religious, and commercial issues, exude order and harmony. Their rigorous seating order conforms, despite the lateral inversion, to the official diplomatic instructions. It was "thought fit to give the said commissioners" from Madrid and Brussels "the place of the right hand at the table, in respect of the great honor done to" King James "in sending the said commissioners to treat here within this realm."[111] The void surface of the conference table suggests that most of the difficulties dividing England and Spain have been overcome. The table, in fact, has been cleared of all objects save a pewter ink pot, a quill, a folded paper in Richardot's hands, and the articles of the peace treaty handwritten on vellum and lying in front of Cecil ready to be signed by King James. The evergreen indoor shrubbery in the background imparts the symbolic atmosphere of a perpetual spring to the new alliance concluded between the former enemies.

A major artistic challenge to Pantoja must have been to attune the painting to the iconographic traditions of the two countries. There was actually no necessity for him to respect English sensitiveness considering that the patron who commissioned *The Somerset House Conference* was undoubtedly the constable of Castile. The inclusion of the emblematic shrubbery, however, may testify to his respect for English iconography and for his country's new allies. To what extent he was committed to his patron and his sovereign can be seen from his ingenious experiment with the technique of perspective, its single vanishing point corresponding to the fixed viewpoint of the spectator. To represent King James in Somerset House without King Philip at his side would have been a political faux pas; and in terms of Spanish court etiquette, the representation of King Philip together with eleven commissioners would have been tantamount to a breach of the king's concept of invisibility and inaccessibility, which under the rule of the duke of Lerma had evolved into "a veritable religion of state that distinguished the Spanish monarchy from its European counterparts."[112] The Spanish King had become a figure, as the earl of Nottingham was to experience during his negotiations and the peace solemnities in Valladolid, "at once remote and yet the centre of universal attention."[113]

This reading of *The Somerset House Conference* brings home to us the meaning of the cryptic line in which Quevedo praises Pantoja as a learned and ingenious painter. Why should Pantoja have struck his contemporary as being erudite? Quevedo who, under the auspices of the duchess of Lerma, settled in Valladolid from 1601 to 1605 and wrote some forty works there, obviously ranked Pantoja among the most successful painters of his day because of his skillful manipulation of perspective. Perspective was regarded by Renaissance painters as a science that helped man understand the material world. Quevedo, committed to this tradition, came to value Pantoja as a painter who in *The Somerset House Conference* cultivated the science of perspective in order to convey a political message.

Maria Kusche has established beyond doubt that the compositional formula of Velázquez's state portraits derives from his Spanish predecessors, among them Pantoja de la Cruz. Liudmila L. Kagane holds the same view.[114] *The Somerset House Conference* confirms their findings. The painting shares with Velázquez's *Las Meninas* the ingenious use of the implied viewer. In both paintings, the most important focal point is the implied monarch (in Velázquez's king and queen), standing or sitting outside the painted space.[115] Yet for all the qualities of Pantoja's painting, it is quite beside the point to maintain, as does José Valverde Madrid, that *The Somerset House Conference* is "la perla de la pintura del siglo XVI en la Galería Nacional de Londres."[116]

Notes

1. Dates are mostly given in Old and New Style, for the English documents are invariably in OS, the Spanish in NS.

2. For the negotiations leading up to the peace treaty see Albert J. Loomie, "Toleration and Diplomacy: The Religious Issue in Anglo-Spanish Relations, 1603–1605," *Transactions of the American Philosophical Society* 53, pt. 6 (1963); for the earl of Nottingham's embassy to Valladolid see Robert W. Kenny, "Peace with Spain, 1605," *History Today* 20 (1970): 198–208; for the celebrations and cross-cultural experience, see W. R. de Villa-Urrutia, *Ocios diplomáticos* (Madrid, 1907); and John Walter Stoye, *English Travellers Abroad, 1604–1667: Their Influence in English Society and Politics* (London: Cape, 1962; reprint, New York: Octagon Books, 1968), 325–35; for the peacemaking policy in Brussels, London, and Madrid/Valladolid see Charles Howard Carter, *The Secret Diplomacy of the Habsburgs, 1598–1625* (New York: Columbia University Press, 1964).

3. British Library, MS Sloane 226, fol. 21r. The anecdote was omitted by Richard Hakluyt in *The Principal Navigations (1599–1600)*, ed. Ernest Rhys (London: J. M. Dent and Sons, 1928), ix, 249–75.

4. Treswell's chronicle is entitled: *A Relation of such Thinges as were observed to happen in the Journey of the right Honourable Charles Earle of Nottingham, L. High Admirall of England, His Highnesse Ambassadour to the King of Spaine* (London: Melchisedech Bradwood, 1605).

5. For Coke in Spain see David Howarth, *Lord Arundel and His Circle* (New Haven: Yale University Press, 1985), 20, 35; for Prince Charles's purchase of Italian masterpieces in Madrid, see Oliver Millar, *The Queen's Pictures* (London: Weidenfeld and Nicolson, 1977), 29–32: for the royal picture galleries in Valladolid see J. Rivera Blanco, *El Palacio Real de Valladolid.* Instituto Cultural Simancas, Diputación Provincial de Valladolid (Valladolid, 1981), 134; and Jesús Urrea, "La pintura en Valladolid en el siglo XVII," in *Valladolid en el siglo XVII: Historia de Valladolid*, vol 4, ed. Adriano Gutiérrez Alonso et al. (Valladolid: Ateneo, 1982), 155–92.

6. Treswell, *Relation*, 27.

7. *The Royal Entertainement of the Right Honorable the Earle of Nottingham, sent Ambassador from his Maiestie to the King of Spaine* (London: Valentine Sims, 1605; STC 13857.5), 5–6. For the impressive collection of the count of Benavente see J. Miguel Morán and Fernando Checa, *El coleccionismo en España: De la cámara de maravillas a la galería de pinturas* (Madrid: Cátedra, 1985), 170, 220–22, 233, 294–95; and Marcus Burke, "Private Collections of Italian Art in

Seventeenth-Century Spain," (Ph.D. dissertation, New York University, 1984, DA, 45 [1984–85], 1558-A.

8. The only known copy is in the Bibliothèque Municipale de Douai. For the gifts of the constable given to King James and Queen Anne, to the leading courtiers and the ladies-in-waiting, the total amounting to £104,500, see S. Parnell Kerr, "The Constable Kept an Account," *Notes and Queries*, 202 (1957): 167–70. Kerr, who does not disclose his source, is not a reliable scholar. The jewels, jewelers, recipients, and bankers were entered by the constable's treasurer in the "Partidas," the financial accounts, which are kept in the Archivo Histórico Nacional, Sección Nobleza, Hospital Tavera, Toledo, shelfmark Frías 617/20/1–18. A jewel bought by the constable from Johnson, a London jeweler, valued at £500, was lost and got into the hands of a third party. See PRO, SP 94/10/126. For the gifts of King James, some seventy pieces of silver and gold plate, among them the famous royal gold cup of the kings of France and England, "delivered to the Constable" by the Royal Jewel House, see PRO, SP 94/10/93, and the *Relación de la Iornada del Excmo Condestable de Castilla a las Pazes entre Hespaña y Inglaterra* (Antwerp, 1604), 38–39, 45–56. Its author can be identified as the constable's secretary and biographer, Fermín López de Mendizórroz. For the businesslike inventory of Spanish gifts donated in Valladolid and valued at 166,300 ducats see Gerónimo Gascón de Torquemada's *Discurso sobre las fiestas que se hicieron en Valladolid por el dichoso nacimiento del Rey nuestro señor Don Phelipe IV y todo lo que sucedió en los dos meses siguientes* (BL, Add. Ms. 10236, fol. 313v–315v). See also Antonio de Herrera, *Relación de lo sucedido en la ciudad de Valladolid* (Valladolid: Juan Godínez de Millis, 1605; BL shelfmark 811.d.4[1], cataloged under Philip IV), 45ff; and Treswell, *Relation*, 54. For the gifts presented by the constable see also Villa-Urrutia, *Ocios diplomáticos*.

9. *Relación*, 38. On 14/14 August 1604, the queen granted John Gerrard, herbarist, the lease of a garden plot adjoining Somerset House on condition of supplying her with herbs, flowers, and fruit according to the seasons. See Raymond Needham and Alexander Webster, *Somerset House: Past and Present* (London: T. Fisher Unwin, 1905), 68.

10. For Henry Howard, earl of Northampton, as an experienced hispanist see Gustav Ungerer, *Anglo-Spanish Relations in Tudor Literature*. Swiss Studies in English, 38 (Berne: Francke, 1956), 56–60; and *A Spaniard in Elizabethan England: The Correspondence of Antonio Pérez's Exile* (London: Tamesis, 1976), 2 : 268–69. For Northampton's position at the Jacobean court see Linda Levy Peck, "The Mentality of a Jacobean Grandee" in *The Mental World of the Jacobean Court*, ed. L. L. Peck (Cambridge: Cambridge University Press, 1991), 148–68.

11. *Relación*, 45. The event was also recorded at full length by Fermín López de Mendizórroz in his *Observaciones de la vida del condestable Juan Fernández de Velasco, y cifra de sus dictámenes* (Vigevano: Juan Baptista Malatesta, 1625), 175–76. In the late afternoon King James set out on his hunting progress. The constable stayed on in Somerset House until 4 September. King James's farewell visit paid to the constable allows us to date letter 108, which the king addressed to his "little beagle," Sir Robert Cecil, as being written on 20/30 August 1604. James complained to Cecil that "in earnest, I lose this year's progress if I begin not to hunt there upon Monday come eight days, for the season of the year will no more stay upon a king than a poor man, and I doubt if the Constable of Castile has any power in his commission to stay the course of the sun." Quoted from G. P. V. Akrigg, *Letters of James VI and I* (London: University of California Press, 1984), 232–33.

12. Patricia Fumerton, *Cultural Aesthetics: Renaissance Literature and the Practice of Social Ornament* (Chicago: Chicago University Press, 1991), 34; Peter Stallybrass, "Worn worlds: clothes and identity on the Renaissance Stage," in *Subject and Object in Renaissance Culture*, ed. Margreta de Grazia et al. (Cambridge: Cambridge University Press, 1996), 289–320, 312 resp.

13. *Discours*, sig. A6v. The relevant passage reads: ". . . le Roy print la main dudict Connestable, & luy mit au doigt vn diamant de la valeur de cincq mil escus, disant quil se marioit auec luy en amité auec ceste paix, & que de sa part, elle seroit à iamais inuiolable."

14. Treswell, *Relation*, 54–55. Both kings opted for a diamond solitaire instead of a more elaborate marriage ring. For the history of rings see Diana Scarisbrick's *Rings: Symbols of Wealth, Power, and Affection* (New York: Abrams, 1993).

15. Ethel Carleton Williams, *Anne of Denmark, Wife of James VI of Scotland, James I of England* (London: Longman, 1970), 93–94, 109–10.

16. Albert J. Loomie, *Spain and the Jacobean Catholics, vol. 1, 1603–1612.* Catholic Record Society Publications, 64 (London, 1974), 44; and *The Spanish Elizabethans. The English Exiles at the Court of Philip II* (New York: Fordham University Press, 1963; reprint Greenwood, 1983), chap. 4.

17. Archivo Histórico Nacional (henceforth AHN), Toledo, Frías 617/20/5–6, 9v, 10v; *Relación*, 32, 40; Kerr, "Constable Kept an Account," 168.

18. AHN, Toledo, Frías 617/20/1v, 2, 4, 6, 17v. Lulls, a Fleming from Antwerp, was one of Queen Elizabeth's jewellers. He is the author of a pictorial album of jewellery designs kept in the Victorian and Albert Museum. See Diana Scarisbrick, *Tudor and Jacobean Jewellery.* Tate Publishing (London, 1995), 35, plates 60 and 62.

19. AHN, Toledo, Frías 617/20/17. For Villamediana's list of recommendations see Loomie, "Toleration and Diplomacy," app. 1.

20. AHN, Toledo, Frías 617/20/14v; Loomie, "Toleration and Diplomacy," app. 1.

21. AHN, Toledo, Frías 617/20/3v, 17v. I have not been able to identify the "Condesa de Motinan" and "Madama Bisinjar" (617/20/17v).

22. On 6/16 September 1604, Spilman was paid £1,000 "for a tablet of diamonds with a great pendant pearl hanging at it, having in it the picture of the King and Queen's Majesties, given by the Queen to the Constable as also the sum of £260 for one other jewel with an A and R," sent by the queen to count Arenberg. See Frederick Devon, ed., *Issues of the Exchequer Being Payments made out of his Majesty's Revenue during the Rein of James I* (London: John Rodwell, 1836), 16. For a miniature as an expression of intimacy in Tudor and Stuart England, see Fumerton, *Cultural Aesthetics*, 70–71.

23. He was the translator of *The Historie of Araucana written in verse by Don Alonso de Ercilla translated out of the spanishe into Englishe prose*, ed. Frank Pierce (Manchester: 1964). He was also an assiduous reader of Spanish military treatises. See Ungerer, *Anglo-Spanish Relations*, 60–67.

24. *Relación*, 47. The high-flown rhetoric of the constable's biographer, Mendizórroz, reads: the Constable received "vna caxa con los retratos de sus Magestades, guarnecida de ricos diamantes, para que assí como le hauían entregado sus corazones, con el amor que le hauían cobrado, tuuiese cerca de sí sus retratos, ya que no les era posible gozar continuamente de su presencia" (*Observaciones*, 177). The text may be rendered as follows; he received "a locket with the portraits of Their Majesties set with rich diamonds so that he could keep their portraits close to his heart since it was not possible for them to be continually in his presence just as they had committed their hearts to him with the love they felt for him."

25. AHN, Toledo, Frías 617/20/14v.

26. Leeds Barroll, "The Court of the First Stuart Queen," in Peck, The Mental World, 191–208.

27. Roy Strong, Artists of the Tudor Court: The Portrait Miniature Rediscovered, 1520–1620 (London: Victoria and Albert Museum, 1983), 97, 105, 151.

28. Relación, 44.

29. Relación, 33–35. The bill of exchange for the horse amounted to 36,000 reales (£900) and was dated from Ghent on 31 September 1604 (N.S.). The entry in AHN, Toledo, Frías 617/20/18v, records that the harness was of embroidered velvet, "vn jaez rico de terciopelo bordado."

30. The portraits of Queen Anna and Prince Henry are listed in the inventory of the goods of Doña María Girón, duchess of Frías, which was made on 29 February 1608, after her death. The inventory lists some 380 paintings, most of them of religious subjects. The paintings were inventoried and assessed by the court painter, Diego de Cueva. See Archivo Histórico de Protocolos, vol. 24850, fol. 40–45, 70–71, 249–50v, 546–54v. The relevant item reads: "Mas el Retrato de la Reina de Inglat[er]ra y el Príncipe de Gales que se hicieron en Londres tassados ambos en doze ducados" (250).

31. The constable was a great art collector. He owned many Italian and Flemish paintings. In Flanders alone he acquired ninety-eight pictures. See Morán and Checa, El Coleccionismo en Espana, 237. See also entry in The Dictionary of Art, ed. Jane Turner (London: Macmillan, 1996), xx, 905–06.

32. Roy Strong, Tudor and Jacobean Portraits, National Portrait Gallery (London: HMSO, 1969), i, 275.

33. Relación, 47. Bruce P. Lenman has shown that the queen, a compulsive spender of jewels, was heavily indebted to her jeweler, George Heriot. See his essay "Jacobean Goldsmith-Jewellers as Credit-Creators: The Cases of James Mossman, James Cockie, and George Heriot," Scottish Historical Review 74 (1995): 159–77.

34. Treswell, Relation, 39–40. Sir Charles Cornwallis in his report to the Privy Council, dated from "Valíodalid," 10 June 1605, confirms that Nottingham "Deliuered vnto her a Jewell" (BL, Harleian MS 1875, fol. 19). However, Nottingham in his report to Sir Robert Cecil, dated from "Valdelith," 23 June, speaks of "Jewells" (PRO, SP 94/11/132–34, resp. fol. 134v). For a more accurate account of the English presents see below. Thomas Knowles was paid, on 21/31 July 1606, by royal writ signed by the earl of Worcester, master of the horse, on 10/20 March 1605, £82 and another £200 on 12/22 March 1607 for the provision of the horses and their transport from Dover to Valladolid as well as for "postages and carriages of trunks . . . from Portsmouth and back." See Devon, Issues of the Exchequer, 43, 61, 62.

35. Gascón de Torquemada, Discurso sobre las fiestas, 314r–314v.

36. "Quenta de las obras de pintura que Juan Pantoxa de la Cruz, Pintor de Cámara del Rey Nuestro Señor, a echo de su arte para el seruiçio de su Magestad desde el principio del año de 1603," published in Maria Kusche's Ph. D. thesis, Juan Pantoja de la Cruz (Madrid: Castalia, 1964), 243–48. For the chamberlain's certificate see Kusche, 241.

37. Kusche, "Pantoja de la Cruz," 47, 237–39.

38. The inventory of Pantoja's workshop and house made on 3 November 1608 registers seven miniatures of the queen found in a drawer. See ibid., 262.

39. Pantoja's entry reads as follows; "Deve más el Rey Nuestro Señor dos retratos chicos en dos chapas de cobre, vno de su Real Persona y otro de la Reyna Nuestra Señora, que se içieron para poner en una caxa de diamantes para dar al Almirante de Yngalatera; entreguelos Antonio Boto en 6 de junio de 605; balen

duçientos y beynte reales." The marginal note reads: "Entregáronse a Antonio Boto y él [los entregó] puestos en una caja de oro con diamantes al Enbajador de Yngalaterra; ay zédula de descargo de 24 de agosto de 1605." Quoted from Kusche, "Pantoja de la Cruz," 243–44.

40. Tomé Pinheiro da Veiga, *Fastiginia: Vida cotidiana en la corte de Valladolid*, trans. and with notes by Narcisco Alonso Cortés (Valladolid, 1916; reprint, Valladolid: Ambito 1989), 114.

41. For the rich holdings of Lerma's collections in Madrid, Valladolid, La Ventosilla, and Lerma see Sarah Schroth, *The Private Picture Collection of the Duke of Lerma* (Ph.D. thesis, Institute of Fine Arts, New York University, 1990), DA, 51 (1991), 2550–51A; also available in print.

42. Francisco Javier Sánchez Cantón, *Libros, tapices y cuadros que coleccionó Isabel la Cathólica*. CSIC. Institución Diego Velázquez (Madrid, 1950), 6, 155, 168.

43. For the portraits and medal of Queen Mary and for a memorial painting of the wedding in 1554, which Philip II kept at the Escorial, see F. J. Sánchez Cantón, "Inventarios reales muebles que pertenecieron a Felipe II," *Archivo Documental Español*, 10–11 (1956–59), ii, 174, 175, 229, 231, 251; for the Spanish jewellery inherited by Queen Elizabeth and Queen Anna see D. Scarisbrick, *Tudor and Jacobean Jewellery*, 14, 53, 75–76, and "Anne of Denmark's Jewellery Inventory," *Archaeologia*, 109 (1991), No. 406; for Trezzo see Stephen K. Scher's entry in *The Dictionary of Art*, ed. Jane Turner (London: Macmillan, 1996), vol. 31, pp. 318–19.

44. Stephanie Breuer does not specify the nature of collaboration in her Ph.D. thesis on Alonso Sánchez Coello (Munich: Uni Druck, 1984).

45. Kusche, "Pantoja de la Cruz," pl. 1 to 4.

46. Ibid., 25–46.

47. Justi's wording reads: "Pantoja de la Cruz war der geist-und leblose, peinlich fleissige Maler des Hofes jenes schwachköpfigen Philipps III; in seiner Zeit steht er wie ein Anachronismus." Quoted from Kusche, "Pantoja de la Cruz," 18.

48. See William B. Jordan, *Spanish Still Life in the Golden Age, 1600–1650: Kimbell Art Museum Exhibition* (Fort Worth, Texas, 1985), 4, 32.

49. Quoted from Kusche "Pantoja de la Cruz," 9. Here is my English prose rendering: Juan de la Cruz, though he could not create the world, almost breathed life and soul into a dumb face.

50. Quoted from Quevedo's *Obra poética*, ed. José Manuel Blecua (Madrid: Castalia, 1969), i. 401–6. A variant of line one has: "Por ti Richi ha podido," i.e., Antonio Ricci, an Italian painter working in the Escorial. My English prose translation reads: Thanks to your art, Juan de la Cruz, as learned a painter as ingenious, you generated in Licida's beautiful face, which has come to life in a miniature, gold in her hair and stars in her sweet eyes.

51. See Pantoja's Register in Kusche, "Pantoja de la Cruz," 239.

52. Ibid.

53. Ibid.

54. Ibid.

55. Ibid., 246–47.

56. Ibid., 244.

57. Millar, *The Queen's Pictures*, 29. The portrait of the infanta is not mentioned.

58. Oliver Millar, *The Tudor, Stuart and Early Georgian Pictures in the Collection of Her Majesty the Queen* (London: Phaidon Press, 1963), 14–15.

59. Pantoja's entry in his register reads "Deue más el Rey Nuestro Señor vn etrato entero suyo orijinal, con calças blancas bordadas y vn bastón en la mano,

armado con armas grabadas y una mano en la espada, debaxo de una tienda carmesí y en canpaña, con çielo y lexos y paises y un bufete carmesí y un memorial sobrel, todo muy bien acabado, que fue para ynbiar a Yngalatera; entreguele Antonio Boto en 16 de febrero de 606; bale dos mil reales." See Kusche, "Pantoja de la Cruz," 244.

60. For the copy see Kusche, "Pantoja de la Cruz," pl. 35.

61. For the copy see Fernando Checa, *Felipe II mecenas de las artes* (Madrid: Nerea, 1993), 168.

62. For the variants see Kusche, "Pantoja de la Cruz," 65–69.

63. For Philip III's exuberent belligerence see Patrick Williams, "Philip III and the Restoration of Spanish Government, 1598–1603," *English Historical Review,* 88 (1973); 751–69.

64. For the queen's portraits see Kusche, "Pantoja de la Cruz," pl. 17–22; for a discussion of the portraits, 76–81.

65. Pantoja's register reads as follows: "Deue más el Rey Nuestro Señor vn retrato entero de la Reyna Nuestra Señora, bestida de blanco con la misma saya que sacó el día que se casó, de tela de primabera, matiçada con las armas de Castilla y León y Austria, senbrada de perlas, y todas lax xoyas ricas, çintura, puntas, botones, braçeletes de diamantes, y la banda de diamantes y el joyel rico y vna gora adereçada de xoyas y plumas, y un bufete de brocado y dosel de lo mismo, y en la mano derecha vnas oras, en ellas pintada Nuestra Señora ymitando yluminaçión y un tapete en el suelo; está tasado por tres pintores en cuatro mil reales; fue para ynbiar a Yngalatera." Quoted from Kusche, "Pantoja de la Cruz," 244.

66. Queen Margaret was not a woman of great beauty, but she was an intelligent, independent, and critical observer of the court dominated by the duke of Lerma. See Ciriaco Pérez Bustamente, *La España de Felipe II.* Historia de España dirigida por Ramón Menéndez Pidal (Madrid: Espasa Calpe, 1983), 119. The queen did exercise a political voice at the Spanish court, as shown by Magdalena S Sánchez, who unfortunately remains silent upon the queen as patron of the arts See her paper "Pious and Political Images of a Habsburg Woman at the Court of Philip III, 1598–1621," in *Spanish Women in the Golden Age: Images and Real ism,* 91–107. (London: Greenwood, 1996).

67. For the matrimonial feelers see Loomie, "Toleration and Diplomacy," 25 27. The infanta, born on 22 September 1601, married Luis XIII in 1615. For an analysis of the desired dynastic alliance between the Habsburgs and the Stuart. see Per Palme, *Triumph of Peace: A Study of the Whitehall Banqueting House* (London: Thames and Hudson, 1957), 8–9.

68. Samuel R. Gardiner, *History of England from the Accession of James I to the Outbreak of the Civil War, 1603–1642.* Vol. 1, 1603–1607 (reprint, New York AMS Press, 1965), 220.

69. See Kusche, "Pantoja de la Cruz," pl. 28. For Pantoja's *bodegones* se Jordan, *Spanish Still Life,* 4, 32.

70. Pantoja's Register has the following entry; "Deue más el Rey Nuestro Señor vn retrato entero orijinal de la Sereníssima Ynfanta Doña Ana, bestida de encar nado con saya entera y manga de punta, con que fue madrina del Prínçipe Nuestro Señor, acuchillada y prensada; las guarniçiones bordadas y cortina y bufe carmesí y ençima unos alberchigos, tomando vno, y en la otra mano vn lienço fue tanbien para ynbiar a Yngalatera y está tassado por los dichos tres pintore en mil reales." Quoted from Kusche, "Pantoja de la Cruz," 244.

71. Treswell, *Relation,* 37.

72. The text of the Spanish chronicle reads: "quatro passos detrás de su Alteza [duke of Lerma] yua la S(ereníssi)ma Infanta su hermana y madrina en vna silla de manos descubierta sin cortinas ni cielo, con vn bestido de rasso encarnado acuchillado, forado en tela de plata, y vn capillo de rasso de oro del mismo color. Llevaban la silla quatro reposteros de camas de la Reina" (fol. 292).

73. For the infanta see pl. 29 and for the queen pl. 20 and 21 in Kusche, "Pantoja de la Cruz."

74. The princess was "muy bonita y avispada, y de todo va dando fe." Pinheiro de Veiga, *Fastiginia*, 100. The 1604 portrait is at the Kunsthistorisches Museum, Vienna.

75. Pantoja's accounts reads: "Más debe el Rey Nuestro Señor vn lienço de dos baras y media de ancho y siete cuartas de alto, retratando en él el lebrel de Yngalatera, que llaman Baylán, y otros dos galgillos que trujieron de Flandes y el enano Bonami que tenía a Baylán de traylla, retrato entero, con botas de camino y calçetas y espuelas, bestido de terçiopelo berde con passamanos de plata y oro y una cadena al cuello y asimismo Don Antonio, otro enano, y de traylla los galgillos de Flandes y un pays de retrato del Pardo; entreguelo Hernando Despexo, Guardaxoyas de Su Magestad; bale más de treçientos ducados." Quoted from Kusche, "Pantoja de la Cruz," 245–46.

76. *The Royal Entertainement*, 11.

77. See Kusche, "Pantoja de la Cruz," 11, 32, 38.

78. See ibid., pl. 11.

79. Strong, *Tudor and Jacobean Portraits*, i, 353, no. 665, pl. 680; the painting measures 205 by 268 centimeters. Maria Kusche has failed to take notice of this picture. Xavier de Salas, apart from José Valverde, is the only art critic known to me who has come up with a defense of Pantoja's authorship in "Un tableau de Pantoja de la Cruz à propos d'une monographie sur le peintre," *Gazette des Beaux Arts* (1966); 351–54. Surprisingly, ten years before Strong's attribution to Pourbus, the curators of the Fogg Museum, Cambridge, Massachusetts, erroneously attributed to Pourbus their portrait of Philip III painted by Pantoja. See George Kubler and Martin Soria, *Art and Architecture in Spain and Portugal and Their American Dominions, 1500 to 1800*, Pelican History of Art (Harmondsworth, 1959), 378–79, no. 28.

80. Kerr, "Constable Kept on Account," 167–70.

81. For the constable's stalling policy see Loomie, "Toleration and Diplomacy," 28ff.

82. Letter of Carleton to Chamberlain, dated 10/20 August 1605, in Maurice Lee, ed., *Dudley Carleton to John Chamberlain, 1603–1624* (New Brunswick, N.J.: Rutger University Press, 1972), 61. See also *Calendar State Papers Venice*, vol. 10, 1603–1607 (London, 1900), 153–55.

83. The "Plata para la Capilla," which Jean Gueldi, a Brussels jeweler, had provided, was entrusted to the care of the constable's Italian chaplain, Fabio de Maestri. The bill of the thirteen gold and silver plates, which amounted to 5,944 reales and 4 plazas, was settled on 9 April 1604 (N.S.). The items are inventoried in AHN, Toledo, Frías 617/20/6v–7.

84. *Relación*, 27, 29, 30, 33. For the political issues debated by the delegates see "A Journal of the Conference," ed. Robert Watson in the appendix to his study *The History of the Reign of Philip III, King of Spain* (Basle, 1792).

85. *Relación*, 23.

86. Ernest Law, *Shakespeare as a Groom of the Chamber* (London: G. Bell, 1910).

87. I intend to expand on this question in a forthcoming paper. The king's men are likely to have been remunerated by the constable. The only entry in his accounts that seems to imply the king's men reads: "A criados y casa del Rey 47656" reales "de la dicha Moneda de Inglaterra" and is dated 24 August/3 September 1604. See AHN, Toledo, Frías 617/20/14v. How much of the princely sum of £1191 was in fact allotted to the king's men is not possible to ascertain. Kerr, "Constable Kept on Account," p. 189, has made a mess of the issue. He quotes in English an entry from the accounts that actually refers to the gratuities given by the constable to "Violones, cornetas, chirimias, y atambores, y a algunos saldados, y limosnas a lugares pios y pobres" in Paris on 2 November 1604 (N.S.). See AHN, Toledo, Frías 617/20/12v. In addition to this error, he unscrupulously tampers with the original text, dishing up a manipulated version taken from another entry and adding the word *players:* "To boatmen, musicians, and players, gifts to King's Household, to the violins, flageolets, and drums, and to some soldiers, and alms to Holy Places and to poor . . . 4780 reales."

88. Sarah Schroth has investigated Lerma's picture collections and has edited nine previously unpublished inventories in her Ph.D. thesis (see n. 41). To be sure, the inventories never covered the complete holdings; but it is difficult to imagine that the large painting would have escaped the attention of the agents who drew up the inventories; most of them were household servants. It does not figure either in the "Inventario de los cuadros y otros objetos de arte en la quinta real llamada La Ribera en Valladolid," ed. José M. Florit, *Boletín de la Sociedad Española de Excursiones* 14 (1906): 153–60.

89. Pinheiro de Veiga, *Fastiginia,* 119; Gascón de Torquemada, *Discurso sobre las fiestas,* fol. 298.

90. See his letter addressed to King James from Bruges on 21 June/1 July 1604, in which he humors the impatient James with a piece of personal information, making him believe that with his mother's milk he imbibed her love for England. PRO, SP 94/10/65.

91. The painting is listed in the inventory of the constable's goods, which was drawn up in March 1613 after his death. The painters Antonio de Salazar and Juan de la Corte listed some 560 paintings. They also assessed them but did not bother to mention the artists with the exception of the pictures by Bassano. See Archivo Histórico de Protocolos, vol. 24851, fols. 195–204v, 418v–22, 473–84v. The relevant entry reads: "Vn quadro de los siete ynfantes de Lara hecho en Ynglaterra con dinero de la jornada el año de las pazes con marco blanco, tasaronle en mill y cien reales que balen treynta y siete mill y cuatro cientos maravedís" (fol. 475). Few pictures were offered for sale at the auction of his goods in March 1613. See Archivo Histórico de Protocolos, vol. 4719. On 25 August/3 September 1604, the constable had actually paid 911 reales (£23) for the painting "a vn pintor" in London. See AHN, Toledo, Frías 617/20/10v.

The "siete infantes de Lara" was a subject that was frequently represented by Spanish painters. The duke of Lerma owned up to fourteen *cuadros menores* of the princes. See Schroth, *Private Picture Collection,* 174, 200. The constable obviously asked a painter in London to copy the picture, a common practice. A parallel case is afforded by King Charles I, who in 1633 commissioned Michael Cross to copy the principal pictures in the royal collections at Madrid. See *DNB* under M. Cross; and R. Malcolm Smuts, "Art and the Material Culture of Majesty in Early Stuart England" in *The Stuart Court and Europe: Essays in Politics and Political Culture,* ed. R. M. Smuts (Cambridge: Cambridge University Press, 1996), 86–112, 104, n. 66, resp.

92. Kusche, "Pantoja de la Cruz," pls. 13 and 14.

93. For the martial painting see Willem Schrickx, *Foreign Envoys and Travelling Players in the Age of Shakespeare and Jonson* (1986), 81. Schrickx is also of the opinion that Pantoja painted *The Somerset House Conference* (87–88). The portrait of the constable is listed under "Collazione Ignota" in Roberto Paolo Ciardi's study, *Giovan Ambrogio Figino. Raccolta Pisana di saggi e studi diretta da Carlo L. Ragghianti*, no. 21 (Firenze: Marchi and Bertolli, 1968), 124. For Hercole Cimilotti's sonnet and the lines "Sopra il ritratto dell' illmo Contestabile di Castiglia" and "Principis armati effigiem, Figine, Velasco" see BL, King's MS 323, fols. 87, 33, 86. The portraits that graced the constable's residence in Milan can partly be recovered from oblivion. Among the goods sent to Madrid from Milan in 1613, the year of the constable's death, there figure "Vn Retrato entero del Condestable Juan de Valesco con arco de nogal que se hiço en Milán y lo trujo el Condestable consigo," twelve paintings in the twelve months; four "Payses grandes," eight "cuadros de pesca con otro menor," ten "cuadros perlongados largos y anchos sin figuras," eight "de cazas y montería con otro pequeño," twelve "Enperadores con doze Enperatrizes . . . grandes," "vn retrato del Condestable Bernardino en el caballo . . . en lienço grande," i.e., of the first duke of Frías, who died in 1512. See "Inventario de bienes de Juan Fernández de Velasco, marzo 1613." Archivo Histórico de Protocolos, tomo 24851, fol. 474v. It is reasonable to assume that many of his Italian paintings were shipped to Spain before the end of his second governorship in 1600. Thus his wife, Doña Mariá Girón, the duchess of Frías, owned a "Retablo del señor Condestable presente y es el que hizo el Boneuano en los barcos del Po en Lombardía." See "Inventario de Doña María Girón, duquesa de Frías, 29 de febrero de 1608." Archivo Histórico de Protocolos, tomo 24850, fol. 249.

94. Kusche, "Pantoja de la Cruz," pl. 18, comment, 152.

95. Ibid., pl. 6, comment 144.

96. De Salas, 353. Kusche, "Pantoja de la Cruz," pl. 37 and 38, comment, 101–3, description, 171–74.

97. Some additions and corrections were made in the handwritten copy of an extract taken from the *Relación* (1604), obviously with a view to preparing a second edition. Some of the names as copied from the printed text such as "Nortiñan," "Densier," and "Huester" (38) are crossed out and replaced by "Nortingham" for Nottingham, "Deuenshier" for Devonshire, and "Worcester." See "Relación de lo que ha passado vltimamente quando el Rey de Inglaterra juró la Paz" (Archives Générales du Royaume de Belgique, PEA, reg. 364, fols. 339–348, fols. 342, resp.).

98. Kerr, "Constable Kept on Account," 167–70.

99. Kusche, "Pantoja de la Cruz," pl. 25, comment 81–87, description, 162–63.

100. Register, ibid., 237–38.

101. Lorne Campbell, *Renaissance Portraits: European Portrait Painting in the 14th, 15th and 16th Centuries* (New Haven: Yale University Press, 1990), pp. ix, 12.

102. William Gaunt, *Court Painting in England from Tudor to Victorian Times* (London: Constable, 1980), 88.

103. For Cecil's presentation copy to the Constable see Strong, *Tudor and Jacobean Portraits*, i:275.

104. Millar, *The Tudor, Stuart Pictures*, no. 70.

105. His inventory of 1608 lists some dozen sketched heads. See Kusche, "Pantoja de la Cruz," 258–63.

106. Kusche, "Pantoja de la Cruz," pl. 43, comment 179.

107. L. Macfarlane, curator of the Picture Library at Greenwich, has been so kind as to let me know that their copy is signed by Pantoja but is not dated. It is reproduced in E. M. Tenison, *Elizabethan England: Being the History of This*

Country "In relation to all Foreign Princes" (Leamington Spa, 1958), 12:303. Fanshawe's copy is likely to have been acquired by his successor as ambassador, Edward Montagu, first earl of Sandwich. We have it on Lady Ann Fanshawe's authority that she was forced to sell all their "coaches and horses and lumber of the house" to Sandwich in order to pay the journey of her children and household back to London. She just managed to keep her jewels, the best of her plate, "and other precious rarities." Her husband had died on 26 June 1666, within five weeks after Sandwich had delivered the letters of revocation to Fanshawe on 29 May. See Ann Fanshawe, *The Memoirs of Ann Lady Fanshawe . . . Reprinted from the original manuscript in the possession of Mr. Evelyn John Fanshawe of Parsloes* (London: John Lane the Bodley Head, 1907), 198–99, 205.

108. Strong, *Tudor and Jacobean Portraits*, i:353.

109. The Spanish text of the *Relación* reads: the English "guardia assistía en la primera sala; y en la de presencia, que es la tercer pieça, hauía un dossel riquíssimo, con las armas de los Reyes de Inglaterra, y silla, y almohadas à lo Real. En la pieça más à dentro, hauía otro dossel más moderno, que se hauía hecho para vna mascarada de la Reyna, pocos meses antes, y tenía en el escudo añadidas las armas de Escocia, y en la orla esta letra: *Beati pacifici*" (23). Robert Watson in "A Journal of the Conference" is less informative. "A fair great chamber," he reports, "heretofore used for the council-chamber . . ., was expressly prepared by his majesty for the said meeting" (231).

110. Enid Welsford, *The Court Masque: A Study of the Relationship between Poetry and the Revels* (Cambridge, 1927; rpt. NY: Russell & Russell, 1962), 171–73. See also Roy Strong, *Art and Power: Renaissance Festivals, 1450–1650* (Woodbridge: Boydell Press, 1973 and 1984), 60.

111. Watson, "A Journal of the Conference," 231.

112. Antonio Feros, "Twin Souls: Monarchs and Favourites in Early 17th-Century Spain," in *Spain, Europe and the Atlantic World: Essays in Honour of John H. Elliott*, 27–47 (Cambridge: Cambridge University Press, 1995).

113. John H. Elliott "The Court of the Spanish Habsburgs: A Peculiar Instition?" *Spain and Its World, 1500–1700: Selected Essays* (New Haven and London: Yale University Press, 1989), 132–61.

114. I have read only a summary in English, which is prefixed to her study *Pantoja de la Cruz* (Leningrad: 1969). Like Kusche she seems to have overlooked Pantoja's *The Somerset House Conference*.

115. For an interpretation of *Las Meninas* see Jonathan Brown, *Images and Ideas in 17th-Century Spanish Painting* (Princeton: Princeton University Press, 1978), 92ff; and Sebastian Neumeister, *Mythos und Repräsentation: Die mythologischen Festspiele Calderons*. Theorie und Geschichte der Literatur und der schönen Künste, 41 (Munich: Fink, 1978), 283–87.

116. Valverde Madrid has made a botch of his paper "Dos cuadros de Pantoja de la Cruz," *Boletín del Museo e Instituto Camón Aznar* 18 (1984): 121–36. It does contain thirty-two valuable documents (124–34), which supplement the collection of documents in Kusche "Pantoja de la Cruz." However, the first three pages (121–23) are teeming with all sorts of mistakes. Thus the author, who apparently has never been to the NPG, states that the painting has "la fecha y la firma de Juan Pantoja de la Cruz en 1604."

Ganymedes and Kings: Staging Male Homosexual Desire in *The Winter's Tale*

Nora Johnson

Whitehall HISTORIANS discuss the relation between homosexual practice and homosexual identity in England before the eighteenth century, they often note that male same-sex behaviors coincided with
neither a set of psychosocial characteristics nor a clear sexual preference. Alan Bray, for instance, describes satirical portrayals of the
courtier who engaged in sodomy, arguing that these portrayals were
striking from a twentieth-century perspective because of their failure to represent a specifically homosexual identity: "on this point
[the satirists] are remarkably consistent: the sodomite is a young
man-about-town, with his mistress on one arm and his 'catamite'
on the other."[1] Following, as he says, "broadly" in the traditions of
Mary McIntosh, Jeffrey Weeks, and Michel Foucault, Bray argues
that representations of sodomy before the late-seventeenth century
reveal the historical contingency of the modern homosexual. He
cites Donne's first *Satire*, for example, which accuses one man-
about-town of enjoying the "nakedness and bareness" of a "plump
muddy whore or prostitute boy," and he notes that Jonson's Sir
Voluptuous Beast makes his wife listen to tales about his sexual
exploits, recounting to her "the motions of each petticoat / And
how his Ganymede moved and how his goat."[2]

The evidence that Bray culls from sources other than satire is
equally telling and equally resistant to identifying an exclusively
homosexual "type." He describes the reputation of Sir Anthony
Ashley, one of James I's courtiers known for his love of boys, who
was also known to be a married man and the father of a daughter.
He similarly reports Lucy Hutchinson's description of court life
under James:

> The face of the Court was much changed in the change of the king, for
> King Charles was temperate, chaste, and serious; so that the fools and

bawds, mimics and catamites of the former court grew out of fashion
and the nobility and courtiers, who did not quite abandon their de-
baucheries, yet so reverenced the king as to retire into corners to practice them.[3]

What emerges from Bray's study is more than simply the absence
of what twentieth-century historians would call "homosexuality."
These accounts suggest that homosexual practice was part of an
aristocratic sexual esthetic, a "fashion," in which the courtier sam-
pled at will from an array of erotic practices, none of which could
impose itself upon him as a rigid identity. Even Ashley's apparent
preference for boys seems to have been compatible with his role as
a husband and father. To reiterate the point that has become associated especially with the work of Foucault, sodomy in early modern
England is an act, not an identity.

Certainly homosexual desire as imagined by James himself seems
to have involved no sense of sexual nature. On the contrary, his
letters to his favorite George Villiers enact almost an escape from
identity, a sense that one of the pleasures of illicit sexuality was its
license to undo the categories of self-definition. James addresses
one such letter to "My only sweet and dear child," for instance,
and he prays

> That we may make at this Christmas a new marriage ever to be kept
> hereafter; for, God so love me, as I desire only to live in this world for
> your sake, and that I had rather live banished in any part of the earth
> with you than live a sorrowful widow's life without you. And so god
> bless you, my sweet child and wife, and grant that ye may ever be a
> comfort to your dear dad and husband.[4]

James thinks of this relationship as if it were a marriage in which
both partners are wives at the same time that James is father and
husband and Villiers is child and wife. Far from being identified
by his desire for another man, James imagines homoeroticism as an
undoing of identity itself. In fact, James's words to Villiers resonate
strongly with Bray's contention, developed further by Jonathan
Goldberg, that sodomy in this period belongs not so much to a
system of sexual taxonomy as to a system of unintelligibility, a
social order in which sexual contact between men signifies only
when it can be associated with chaos, anarchy, heresy, or sorcery.[5]
In this reading, the scandal James risks is not a revelation of personal identity so much as an unleashing of ideological forces that
could threaten to undo his own kingship.

Neither James nor the early modern courtier who employs a ganymede, then, is a homosexual in any modern sense of the word. But what are we to assume about the ganymede or catamite himself? The terms in which we are accustomed to explaining the invention of sexual identity—the molly house subcultures in Bray's account, the discursive subject in Foucault's analysis—are inadequate to explain the status of the passive "boy" whose presence guarantees homoerotic content in the accounts of debauchery mentioned above. The ganymede is emphatically not the homosexual subject Foucault teaches us to associate with modernity; among other disqualifying factors, his participation in the homoerotic is taken to be a function of his youth, rather than some expression of essence or nature. In some accounts the ganymede himself desires a woman, while an adult male desires him. But the early modern representations I will examine below suggest that the ganymede's role as an object of homosexual desire extends beyond mere passivity in important ways, that he is imagined as intrinsically fit to be such an object, even, at times, in spite of his own professed desires. Moreover, although we know little or nothing about the relation between actual boys and literary representations of ganymedes, the employment of boys as erotic objects in early modern theater makes the ganymede an integral part of a theater company's reputation. In this light, the eroticized boy is more than a literary strategy for representing aristocratic sexual license. Because The Winter's Tale is centrally concerned, in my reading, with legitimating theatrical practice, its meditations on boyhood similarly become more than nostalgia for the lost past of the two kings whose relationship dominates the play. Representing boyhood becomes instead a way of negotiating the homoerotic, both for Leontes and Polixenes and for the institution of theater itself. In both cases, the reputation for sodomy means more than "acts."

I will argue, then, that even in the absence of a totalizing rhetoric of homosexual identity, the ganymede's participation in the homoerotic identifies him powerfully, so much so that his presence onstage works to stigmatize the theatrical profession. Such an argument is offered not to counter the notion that homosexuality is a historically contingent construct; especially as formulated by Foucault, that insight has powerfully altered perceptions both of sexuality and of early modern Europe. Instead, I want to add this study to the growing body of work that moves beyond the potential reductiveness of a Foucaultian paradigm.[6] We can surely emphasize the radical newness of homosexuality "as we know it" without ignoring the multiple and complex ways that sodomy could interact with notions of self before the modern era. As Gregory Bredbeck argues,

> if [essentialist critics begin] with the assumption that we can trace an atemporal conception of homosexuality throughout history, the other alternative has been to say that because we *cannot* trace this particular concept through history, nothing can be traced. In each instance "the homosexual" is essentialized as the absolute standard of adjudication. "It" is what we must find if we are to find anything at all.[7]

This essay explores what might be traced, and examines the interactions between theatrical self-consciousness and illicit desire in The Winter's Tale.

II

Ganymedes were, of course, not the only group of individuals to be categorized by their participation in sexual acts. On the contrary, the typecasting of women is a familiar part of the early modern sexual terrain, and one that Foucault more or less ignores. One of the factors that makes women such fascinating additions to the sexual taxonomy of this period, though, and that makes them important for a discussion of ganymedes is their paradoxical relation to sexual subjectivity. Women could be characterized absolutely by their sexual acts, without really being imagined to possess agency, or even desire.

Early modern women were sometimes represented as a kind of sexual fixed point in an otherwise chaotic staging of eroticized identities. When Ben Jonson wants to portray debauchery at its worst, for instance, he has his master cozener Volpone engage in an elaborate fantasy of sexual license. "Inviting" the chaste and married Celia to be his mistress, Volpone promises her participation in an extended erotic stage play:

> my dwarfe shall dance,
> My eunuch sing, my foole make vp the antique.
> Whil'st, we, in changed shapes, act *Ovids* tales,
> Thou, like *Evropa* now, and I like *Iove*,
> Then I like *Mars*, and thou like *Erycine*.
> . . . .
> Then will I have thee in more moderne formes,
> . . . .
> And I will meet thee, in as many shapes:[8]

It is a mark of Celia's perfect adherence to the role of the virtuous woman that she refuses to participate in Volpone's theatrical production, that she maintains her personal integrity by declining to play the adulterous role that both her husband and her would-be lover have scripted for her. In spite of the bewildering transformations of the men around her (her husband reverses in minutes his initial decision to lock his wife up in a chastity belt, deciding instead to prostitute her in hopes of winning Volpone's money; Volpone himself leaps up from his pretended deathbed to inform her that he had appeared just the day before as a mountebank at her window), Celia remains constant to her own and her husband's honor. In fact, her character requires no development beyond the demonstration that she will never swerve from the course of chastity.

To repeat a point made often by feminist critics, a reputation for participating in or resisting participation in a particular sexual act had the power to characterize a woman absolutely—onstage, at least—in the English Renaissance.[9] For all that Jonson apparently delights in the possibilities of the ever-changing theatrical self, made manifest in the play's nearly endless recourse to disguise and deception, *Volpone* also exploits the notion of a woman's constancy, the possibility that a woman's sexual fidelity and, by extension, her infidelity, could stand for everything about her. Such a notion is possible, of course, only when women are considered as objects of greater or lesser use to the system of family and marriage, only in an essentially male erotic economy. To the Volpone who stages a theater of erotic pleasure, Celia matters because she either will or will not take up the adulterous part assigned her. Moreover, the conjunction of theatricality and sexuality in an endless exchange of erotic roles, so highly prized by Volpone, depends implicitly upon Celia's unwillingness to play those roles. Her absolute stillness and chastity make her appealing as a sexual object, after all, at the same time that her resistance to Volpone's role-playing provides him with a kind of foil for his sexual improvisations. The erotic fluidity of the self that characterizes Volpone's fantasy includes the deployment of a fixed sexual self, a feminine locus to which sexuality can attach as an identity, rather than a masculine escape from identity through sexual play. Celia inhabits this identity not so much because of her own desires as because of her perfect adherence to the desire of her husband.

I mention Celia here because I want to make the case that the ganymede, the effeminate boy who was stereotypically the object of male homosexual desire in early modern England, was similarly imagined to be defined by his sexual availability to mature men and similarly deployed as a locus of sexuality's power to stigmatize or characterize. When the dangerously powerful male favorite Gaveston plans to entertain his king in Marlowe's *Edward II*, for instance, he gives elaborate stage directions:

> Sometime a lovely boy in Dian's shape,
> With hair that gilds the water as it glides,
> Crownets of pearl about his naked arms,
> And in his sportful hands an olive-tree,
> To hide those parts which men delight to see,
> Shall bathe him in a spring.[10]

As many critics have noted, this passage is erotic in part because of the fantasy that the lovely boy is "in Dian's shape," that he impersonates a goddess.[11] Oddly, though, Gaveston expresses the fantasy that a boy wearing only bracelets and an olive branch could convincingly represent Diana. The erotic opportunity offered the viewer here is not in fact the deliberate impersonation of a goddess. The boy impersonates nothing. He simply has, always, "naturally," the body of a Dian; he entertains merely by displaying himself at opportune moments. In order, in other words, to do justice both to the passage's obvious homoerotic content and to its claims to represent a tale out of Ovid, an audience would have to imagine the boy's profound physical androgyny, a kind of ocular proof of his femininity that goes beyond the use of long gowns and chopines to emphasize the ambiguous "parts men love to see." This lovely boy is almost impossibly effeminate. In Gaveston's staging of erotic transformations, the boy's part is to register an ineluctable physical androgyny; what was free erotic play for James and Villiers becomes ontology for the lovely boy, his physical nature. The celebration of an eroticized fluidity of self relies implicitly upon the fixity of the boy as an androgynous erotic object, giving him a sexuality that has little or no relation to any desires he might be imagined to express. His body is, thus, paradoxically both fluid and fixed: fluid in its failure to adhere to any one gender and fixed in its permanent ambiguity.

Even when theatrical staging and physicality are not at issue, literary representations of the beloved boy tend to emphasize the inevitability of the boy's sexual objectification, the sense that this particular boy is made for this particular kind of love. When Richard Barnfield writes his *Affectionate Shepheard*, he imagines a ganymede whose appearance "intangled" the speaker Daphnis's will: "Cursing the Time, the Place, the sense, the sin; / I came, I saw, I viewed, I slipped in."[12] Even though Ganimede is in love with Queen Gwendolen and unlikely to respond to Daphnis's advances, Ganimede is imagined to be the cause of the older man's desires by virtue of his physical beauty. As the poem's second stanza indicates by its syntax, Ganimede's physical attributes insert themselves into the middle of Daphnis's (admittedly peremptory) self-examination, where they intrude upon the speaker's power to resist him:

> If it be sinne to loue a sweet-fac'd Boy,
>> (Whose amber locks trust vp in golden tramels
>> Dangle adowne his louely cheekes with ioy,
>> When pearle and flowers his faire haire enamels)
>>> If it be sinne to loue a louely Lad;
>>> Oh then sinne I, for whom my soule is sad.

Instead of penetrating the boy, this sentence structure suggests, Daphnis is physically penetrated by Ganimede's beauty. Into the middle of his meditation on sin is inserted a picture of Ganimede's amber locks and lovely cheeks. Daphnis's expressions move well beyond a statement of personal preference, here. Instead of noting simply that Ganimede's beauty pleases him, Daphnis implies that Ganimede's beauty acts upon him, virtually against the speaker's will. Even when the boy himself is imagined to love a woman, he is figured as the locus of homosexual desire; Ganimede's physical appeal is as absolute as the androgyny of Gaveston's boy. In each case, the speaker projects desire onto the body of the ganymede figure, making the boy a physical embodiment of homoeroticism.[13]

What the example of the ganymede suggests is that our current understanding of sodomy as lacking the power to inscribe early modern subjects is only a partial understanding. Representations of the subject who does the desiring, figured here as the courtly sodomite, do in fact imply that sodomy is merely one in a range of sexual behaviors with no particular signifying force. If we shift our focus to the object of desire, however, it becomes clear that the signifying force of sexuality has simply been deflected away from the sodomite. It registers instead in the body of the ganymede, the partner who, like a woman in a heterosexual coupling, might be said to lack power. The sodomite has the ability to change shapes at will; the ganymede, like the woman, is shaped by the sodomite's gaze into a static embodiment of that fluid will.

It is this imagined physical inevitability of the ganymede's participation in homosexual attraction that makes him, I think, an
important figure in discussions of the relation between theatrical
practice and homosexual identity. To the extent that "real-life" catamites were employed as boy actors, these boys would bring with
them a reputation for sodomy that included a larger cultural willingness to attribute homosexual desire to them as physical types.[14]
Thus the theater itself, as an institution, negotiates a complicated
set of attitudes about desire and the fixity of identity. Obviously
theatrical performance gave great pleasure to the majority of Londoners in the period, and certain players became well known and
much admired.[15] At the same time, players as a class remained
heavily stigmatized. Rather like the courtly sodomite, players were
imagined to shift identities at will and to partake of illicit sexuality.
On the other hand, resembling the literary figure of the ganymede
more than the aristocratic man-about-town, they were not well
shielded from the social consequences of their erotic performances.
In documents I will explore below, the Renaissance version of a
long antitheatrical tradition identified players as immoral and dangerous, not least because of their willingness to engage in sexualized display in general and to employ cross-dressed boys in
particular. Further complicating the player's status in this period,
city officials struggled to minimize or abolish professional playing
in London for reasons both economic and moral, while the court
officially acted as patrons of the theater companies, even asserting
that it was necessary to maintain professional players in town so
that Elizabeth could be properly entertained when she so desired.
As a result, players might be particularly familiar with the discrep-
ancies between aristocrats and citizens. Playing companies entertained most of London's population, but their official legitimacy
came from their ability to entertain the court, while a less exalted group of officials stigmatized playing for their own complex
reasons.

As an economic enterprise, then, the stage can be thought of as
trafficking in sexual identity, negotiating a form of exchange between its wealthy patrons—the courtiers (and sovereign) whose
sexual behaviors pointed toward no particular sexual identification—and the boys apparently desired by those courtiers, whose
sexual and economic employment inscribed homosexual desire
upon them. If free erotic play is the prerogative of the aristocratic
sodomite, it is the actor's profession and an important source of
his reputation. Like the ganymede, the player's body is given a

kind of heaviness that balances the weightless erotic play of the courtly sodomite.

III

I am drawn to this depiction of theater—as place in which sexual determinism negotiates with courtly erotic play—in part because it accords with my sense of late-Shakespearean romance. The romances seem to me preoccupied with two of the more prominent features of antitheatrical discourse: the suggestion that stage practice is inherently associated with illicit sexuality and the suggestion that play acting is an assault upon the stability of the individual self. Using the example of *The Winter's Tale*, I want to argue that the romances locate theatrical practice in close relation to illicit desire, acknowledging sodomy as a characteristic mode of being for the players and playwrights implicated in theatrical practice, incorporating both the erotic play of selfhood that typifies James's letters and the sense of sexual identity that characterizes the ganymede. While the ganymede and the courtier are not the only figures one can imagine participating in sodomy in the period—much of Bray's work, for instance, documents the prevalence of homosexual behaviors in households and villages, noting that there, as at court, the perpetrator of sodomy was in no way identified as "homosexual"—the ganymede and courtier represent two poles of sodomy's power to characterize. These two poles, moreover, figure prominently in the erotic imagination of *The Winter's Tale*, which juxtaposes questions of sexual stigma with questions of theatrical practice. What *The Winter's Tale* comes to associate with theater, finally, is not only the erotic indeterminancy that Valerie Traub has identified,[16] but also a dependance upon the notion of sexual fixity, a deployment of the ganymede as a figure for sodomy's power to characterize participants in theatrical practice. Furthermore, I will argue, the play uses these very stigmatized features of theatrical practice to legitimate playing. As a kind of defense of the institution, *The Winter's Tale* reinscribes theater as a force both sexual and moral.

The theater was, after all, the source of seemingly endless sexual allegations in early modern England. Anthony Munday notes the power of playgoing to corrupt women:

Some citizens wives, upon whom the Lord for ensample to others hath laide his hands, have even on their death beds with tears confessed, that they have received at those spectacles such filthie infections as have turned their minds from chast cogitations, and made them of honest women light huswives.[17]

Jonson himself, in *Poetaster*, has his stage version of the historical Ovid assume an automatic connection between playing and sodomy: "What? shall I have my son a stager now? an enghle for players?"[18] In "A Common Player" J. Cocke claims that an actor "If hee marries, hee mistakes the Woman for the Boy in Woman's attire, by not respecting a difference in the mischiefe."[19] Phillip Stubbes complains that after a stage play "every mate sorts to his mate, every one bringes another homeward of their way verye freendly, and in their secret conclaves (covertly) they play the *Sodomits*, or worse."[20] Cocke also notes that these sexually undiscriminating actors participate in an unacceptably protean selfhood because of the many roles they play and the costumes they wear: "Take him at the best, he is but a shifting companion; for he lives effectually by putting on, and putting off. . . . His own [profession] . . . is compounded of all Natures, all humours, all professions" (257). The net effect of this sexual and ontological impurity is for Thomas White a scandal of self-loss: "Wherefore if thou be a father, thou losest thy child: if thou be a maister, thou losest thy servaunt; and thou be what thou canst be, thou losest thy selfe that hauntest those scholes of vice, dennes of theeves, and Theaters of all lewdness."[21] The chaotic play of identity and desire that the aristocratic sodomite is imagined to enjoy freely becomes in these descriptions a sinister aspect of theatrical practice, a cause for the player's notoriety.

Moreover, as the title of one of these antitheatrical tracts, *A Very Fruitful Exposition of The Commandements*, suggests, those who protested theater's alleged sexual excess tended to position themselves on the side of fertility and nature, condemning plays for their failure to bear moral fruit.[22] John Northbrooke refers to plays as "unfruitfull and barren trees [that] shall be cut down" (75), while the author of the *Refutation of the Apology for Actors* refers to plays as "fruitless," and Henry Crosse says of the attraction to earthly pleasures that it "yeeld[s] no fruite at all."[23] Standing in opposition to the reaping of both orthodox spiritual profits and all-important economic profits, theater, with its alleged enticements to nonprocreative sexuality, seemed to fly in the face of God's great commandment to be fruitful and multiply. Ultimately, as *The Winter's Tale* figures and refigures theatrical practice, it will reappropriate this notion of fertility and claim it for the stage.

I begin my discussion of *The Winter's Tale*, however, by asking why the play's many descriptions of boyhood sound so like these early modern descriptions of theatrical practice. Like theater, it seems, boyhood is figured as a realm of sexual and ontological instability, as Leontes makes clear in a paranoid aside to Mamillius: "Go, play, boy, play: thy mother plays, and I / Play too; but so disgrac'd a part, whose issue / Will hiss me to my grave."²⁴ Child's play, sexual play, theatrical play—boyhood, illicit sexuality, theatrical stigma—are what come to mind when Leontes looks at his son. Childhood has become one repository for the scandal of the undifferentiated theatrical self. In a later passage, in fact, Polixenes describes youth in terms that again bring theater to mind. Leontes asks him, "Are you so fond of your young prince, as we / Do seem to be of ours?" and Polixenes describes his own son:

> Now my sworn friend, and then mine enemy;
> My parasite, my soldier, statesman, all.
> He makes a July's day short as December;
> And with his varying childness cures in me
> Thoughts that would thick my blood.
>
> (1.2.167–71)

To be free to cast off one's identity and assume another as boyhood does here is a pleasure—and a threat—associated with theatrical practice.²⁵ As the ganymede does for the sodomite, the child does for the institution of the theater in these passages. Talking about boys becomes an implicit way of talking about men.

Leontes also associated boyhood with an ambiguity of gender that is again a familiar component of attacks upon the theater:

> Looking on the lines
> Of my boy's face, methoughts I did recoil
> Twenty-three years, and saw myself unbreech'd,
> In my green velvet coat; my dagger muzzl'd
> Lest it should bite its master, and so prove,
> As ornaments oft do, too dangerous.
>
> (1.2.153–58)

To be "unbreech'd" is to be dressed in gender-neutral clothing; for a boy this implies a less than absolute separation from the female gender.²⁶ Mamillius (or, really, Leontes' fantasy of his own past, occasioned by Mamillius) wears his dagger muzzled, as if to indicate that he has not reached phallic manhood. There is, further-more, the implication that Mamillius's relative ambiguity of gender is imperiled by mature masculinity. Rather than imagine the harm that an unsheathed dagger might do to others, Leontes focuses upon the danger to the dagger's wearer. Sexual maturity, according to Leontes' fantasy, must mean an end to a fluidity of gender that has much in common with the fluidity of the theatrical self. At the heart of the play's anxious reminiscences about boyhood, then, is a larger cultural uneasiness about the theater.

At the same time, however, Polixenes sanitizes boyhood, idealiz-ing the instability of self that characterizes both boyhood and the stage:

> Herm.   Was not my lord
> The verier wag o' th' two?
> Pol.   We were as twinn'd lambs that did frisk i' th' sun,
> And bleat the one at th' other: what we chang'd
> Was innocence for innocence: we knew not
> The doctrine of ill-doing, nor dream'd
> That any did. Had we pursu'd that life,
> And our weak spirits ne'er been higher rear'd
> With stronger blood, we should have answer'd heaven
> Boldly "not guilty," the imposition clear'd
> Hereditary ours.
> Herm.   By this we gather
> You have tripp'd since.
> Pol.   O my most sacred lady,
> Temptations have since then been born to's: for
> In those unfledg'd days was my wife a girl;
> Your precious self had then not cross'd the eyes
> Of my young play-fellow.
>
> (1.2.65–80)

The absence of the individual self in this passage, the impossibility of distinguishing Leontes from Polixenes, has, ironically, become a sign of Edenic purity, a pastoral opposite to the ungodly crisis of self-definition provoked for tract writers by the scandal of theatrical role playing.[27] Polixenes has also managed in this passage to refig-ure fertility, the marital sexuality that culminates in Hermione's pregnancy, as the interruption of that Eden.[28] In much the same way that Polixenes makes the stigma of theatrical practice into an Eden, The Winter's Tale works to make that stigma into a more fertile pastoral, a realm that welcomes and ultimately makes use of heterosexual fertility as a way of legitimating the scandalous stage.[29] In its reflection upon the relationships between theatrical practice and illicit desire, moreover, the play negotiates a position for the theater that incorporates elements both of courtly erotic play and of the erotic fixity of the ganymede.

Polixenes' articulation of an all-male pastoral, and its interruption by Hermione, effects a double movement away from the realm of scandalous theatrical sexuality. First, the idealization of boyhood moves toward erasing any trace of the relation between youth and the stigmatized elements of theater embodied in the boy actor, a relation hinted at several times in the passages I have cited. Second, Polixenes posits Hermione's arrival as an absolute end to his union with Leontes, and as Camillo implies in the play's opening scene, that union is bound up both with theater and with homosexual desire. Camillo tells the courtier Archidamus:

> Sicilia cannot show himself over-kind to Bohemia. They were trained together in their childhoods, and there rooted betwixt them then such an affection which cannot choose but branch now. Since their more mature dignities and royal necessities made separation of their society, their encounters, though not personal, have been royally attorneyed with interchange of gifts, letters, loving embassies, that they have seemed to be together, though absent; shook hands, as over a vast; and embraced, as it were, from the ends of opposed winds. The heavens continue their loves! (1.1.21–32)

According to the logic of Camillo's narration, Leontes and Polixenes want to be together but must be separated. As Leontes and Polixenes abandon physical immediacy for "mature dignity," they begin to employ others as go-betweens, as expressions of their relationship. What is at stake here is the public representation of relationship between men, an interchange of loving embassies and letters that will ultimately come to seem at least partially defensive, an assurance that the contact between Leontes and Polixenes is "not personal."

Furthermore, their very identity as mature men, as kings, demands that they be kept apart. The literal import of these lines is that Leontes and Polixenes want to touch, but the lines also reveal that these men owe their mature dignities to the fact that they cannot embrace. As they move apart they grow in stature, so that by the end of this speech they seem larger than life, reaching out across a vast, from the opposite ends of the earth. The extent to which these men avoid touching one another, finally, is the extent to which they tower over other men. Their affection for one another, associated with boyhood, stands in opposition to their kingly stature. If boys could embody the homoerotic in the cultural imagination of early modern England, and if in doing so they allowed adult men to avoid the possible consequences of homosexual desire, that potential of boyhood, as Camillo's speech asserts, comes down to a more personal level; however wistfully, he narrates the all important distance here between men and sexualized, undifferentiated youth. It was a sign of the sodomite's power that he could play with desire and identity and not get caught, but players, outside the circle of privilege that supported courtly indiscretions, are much more likely to require a justification for their participation in sexual play. The Winter's Tale, concerned as it is with legitimating theatrical practice, voices at least initially an anxious desire to separate mature men from the scandal of the playing boy.

Camillo has implied that go-betweens and a narrative of maturation are the tools through which Leontes and Polixenes will be distanced from the sexual and ontological threats of boyhood. Important as boys are in this staging of kings, however, it is Hermione who symbolically continues their loves. If Hermione comes between Leontes and Polixenes, then she is also the most obvious of their intermediaries, the chief actor in the theater of their relationship. In act 1 Leontes calls her in to speak for him when he wants Polixenes to extend his visit ("Tongue-tied our queen? speak you" 1.2.27), an act she performs, to her peril, all too enthusiastically.[30] As she fulfills this function, Polixenes begins to cast her in the part I have described above: "O my most sacred lady, / Temptations have ... been born to's." Part sacred and part temptation, Hermione is placed by both men in the position of go-between, and imagined by both of them to be sexually compromised. Leontes and Polixenes collaborate in the staging of Hermione as a necessary expression of their relationship, as a means of imagining that their "affections" have been replaced by "mature dignities." At the same time, their shared willingness to imagine her sexual impurity hints at the instability of their erotic compromise with what the play at this point posits as maturity, as a kingly distance from the desire they associate with boyhood. For all the play's work to distance the king from the ganymede, it ultimately recuperates both figures, both in its representation of these men and in its exploration of theatrical practice.

Of course Hermione is not impure, in spite of Polixenes' fantasy that she has corrupted the men's youth and Leontes' mad conviction that she poisons their friendship in the present moment. Such an admission, moreover, creeps into the very language that Leontes uses to imagine her as an adulteress:

> Affection! thy intention stabs the centre:
> Thou dost make possible things not so held,
> Communicat'st with dreams;—how can this be?—
> With what's unreal thou coactive art,
> And fellow'st nothing: then 'tis very credent
> Thou may'st co-join with something; and thou dost,
> (And that beyond commission) and I find it,
> (And that to the infection of my brains
> And hard'ning of my brows).
>
> (1.2.138–46)

The speech is echoed at the moment Leontes sentences his wife, meant as a statement of confidence in his own suspicions, but expressed as a tacit admission that he has projected his own desires onto her: "Your actions are my dreams."[31] Leontes' own mind is engaging in the actions he attributes to Hermione. Affection—perhaps Leontes' own emotions and imaginings—"stabs the centre." For all the obscurity of the image, its sexual referent is clear, and the rest of the language used to describe Leontes' mental processes furthers the sexual implications. Moreover, Leontes' own thinking in this passage is fellowing, cojoining, coactive, both promiscuous and fertile, culminating in a kind of mental pregnancy, a swelling of horns upon Leontes' brow that parallels the swelling of Hermione's womb. Not only does his deranged creativity imply an admission that there is no reason to condemn his wife; it suggests further a strategy that the play as a whole takes up: the recuperation of sexual scandal as a fertile power. Leontes' individual use of Hermione as an expression of his imaginings is accompanied, ultimately, by the play's use of her as an expression and even a celebration of the imaginative power of a sexually stigmatized male theatrical community.

IV

The early scenes of *The Winter's Tale* enforce an anxious distinction between boys and men, letting boys stand in for the scandal of theatrical practice. Included in that effort is an attempt to use Hermione as a sign both of the distance between Leontes and Polixenes and of the loves they bear one another. The shared fantasy that she is impure suggests that the easy version of that story is inadequate, that desire and the implicit destabilization of identity cannot be dismissed or idealized as the province of boys. In addition, the language Leontes uses to describe that fantasy—as a promiscuous and fertile mental cojoining—resonates profoundly with what I believe to be a central part of the play's legitimation of theatrical playing.

Leontes' equation of his wife's fertility with his own mental processes—and his clear preference for the product of his own mind—recalls Plato's grounding of poetry in what Renaissance moralists would have regarded as a scandalous erotic context. In the *Symposium*, Socrates speaks of a lesson he has learned from the wise Diotima:

> Men whose bodies only are creative, betake themselves to women and beget children. . . . But creative souls—for there are men who are more creative in their souls than in their bodies—conceive that which is proper for the soul to conceive or retain. . . . And he who in youth has the seed of [virtue and wisdom] implanted in him and is himself inspired, when he comes to maturity desires to beget and generate. . . . and when he finds a fair and noble and well-nurtured soul, and there is union of the two in one person, he gladly embraces him, and to such an one he is full of fair speech about virtue and the nature and pursuits of a good man . . . and at the touch and presence of the beautiful he brings forth the beautiful which he conceived long before . . . and in company they tend that which he brings forth, and they are bound together by a far nearer tie and have a closer friendship than those who beget mortal children, for the children who are their common offspring are fairer and more immortal. Who when he thinks of Homer and Hesiod and other great poets, would not rather have their children than any ordinary human ones?[32]

These sentiments are, according to Diotima, among the lesser teachings of love, and although Socrates emphasizes that the love of one beautiful man should lead to an appreciation of the beautiful in general, many early modern readers identified the *Symposium* with homosexuality.[33]

The *Symposium* represents one way of legitimating the literary productions of an implicitly homosexual male culture, and it bears more than a passing resemblance to Polixenes' idealized male pastoral and Leontes' tormented and fertile imagination. Although the play will move to punish Leontes for his fantasy, and will reconfigure his attachment to Polixenes by way of the heterosexual marriage of their children, I emphasize Plato's idealization of a male homosexual poetics because a similar ideal is active throughout *The Winter's Tale.* The play works with considerable ardor to establish a convincing affiliation between the playwright's craft and "great creating nature," and while that affiliation can function as a heterosexual imperative—Hermione's pregnancy and the family bonds that guarantee an heir to the throne can be seen as the ultimate sources of truth, the play's ultimate wisdom—the affiliation between poetry and pregnancy can also serve as a platonic boast about the superiority of male poetic production. Indeed, *The Winter's Tale* and *The Symposium* employ women and fertility in ways that are, initially at least, remarkably similar. In "Why Is Diotima a Woman?" David Halperin analyzes Plato's adoption of Diotima as the mouthpiece for his erotic teachings, including, I would add, his eroticization of poetic production.[34] Referring to Diotima as "a version of pastoral," Halperin notes that her presence in *The Symposium* allows Plato simultaneously to "invest Diotima with an erotic and prophetic authority" and to evacuate that feminine authority, to use Diotima as a figure for "The male imaginary, the specular poetics of male identity and self-definition" (145). I will return to Halperin's reading of *The Symposium* in the final section of this essay, but I want first to trace the ways in which *The Winter's Tale*'s pastoral celebration and recuperation of Hermione lend themselves, like Diotima, to the preoccupations of an eroticized male poetic community. If the play's first half registers an anxious awareness of contemporary antitheatrical tracts and their complaints about the fruitlessness of the literary, its second half incorporates women and nature into a declaration of the procreative power of sexually stigmatized male theatrical production. In fact, the play goes to great lengths to emphasize the independence of women as part of a strategy, I will argue, that, like Plato's, will ultimately serve to highlight the powers and desires of men. Especially through the figures of Camillo and Hermione, *The Winter's Tale* legitimates its own erotic practice while simultaneously obeying the injunction to be fruitful and multiply.

In many ways, the sheep-shearing feast in act 4 is a clear vote for the kinds of fertility that are associated with spring and pregnancy and agriculture rather than with men and poetry. As in the Shepherd's reminiscences about his "old wife" and as in Perdita's preference for the flowers that nature makes, Perdita's frankly sexual remarks to Florizel indicate that this is a new pastoral to which women and heterosexual desire are most emphatically invited.[35]

Per.   O, these [flowers] I lack
         To make you garlands of; and my sweet friend,
         To strew him o'er and o'er!
Flo.   What, like a corpse?
Per.   No, like a bank, for love to lie and play on:
         Not like a corpse; or if—not to be buried,
         But quick, and in mine arms.

                                              (4.4.127–32)

Perdita's next remarks indicate as well that there is a new theater
in action here, charming even in its mild sexual scandal:

Per.   Methinks I play as I have seen them do
         In Whitsun pastorals: sure this robe of mine
         Does change my disposition.
Flo.   What you do,
         Still betters what is done.

                                              (4.4.133–36)

That Camillo and Polixenes should intrude upon this heterosexual
pastoral suggests that this "natural" sheep-shearing feast is in some
way anathema to the earlier male Eden in which twinned lambs
never had to face the shearer. Their intrusion says, I think, a great
deal about the uses of nature in a sexually stigmatized artistic
endeavor.

Camillo is established early on as an accessory to the erotic bond
between Leontes and Polixenes; he is the narrator of the opening
scene's story of the two kings' affections, and he keeps Leontes
from harming Polixenes. In addition, Leontes' exchange with him
in act 1 casts Camillo in a role that strongly recalls a well-known
icon of Renaissance homosexuality:

                                      . . . ay, and thou
         [Polixenes'] cupbearer,—whom I from meaner form
         Have bench'd and rear'd to worship, who may'st see
         Plainly as heaven sees earth and earth sees heaven,
         How I am gall'd,—might'st bespice a cup,
         To give mine enemy a lasting wink;
         Which draught to me were cordial.

                                              (1.2.312–18)

In his address to Camillo, Leontes reenacts the story of Jove's
Ganymede, the cup bearer to the god who raised him from earth
to heaven and who kept him as his lover. The language of raising
up an inferior, combined with the sense that Camilllo's vision now

spans the gap between heaven and earth, recalls both the erotic myth and its allegorical implications for the merging of the divine with the physical.[36]

Moreover, Leontes' chain of allusions implies that Camillo is, as Hermione has been imagined, somehow the favorite of both kings. Camillo is cup bearer to Polixenes, but his draught would nourish Leontes; he has been raised up by Leontes, but he attends Polixenes during his stay in Sicilia. The implied eroticism of Camillo's position is shared between the two kings, and the implication is that Camillo in some sense shares Hermione's role as erotic go-between and as actor in the theater of their affections. One of Leontes' most vivid declarations of certainty about Hermione's infidelity, after all, implies a symmetry between that infidelity and Camillo's promised poisoning of Bohemia: "I have drunk, and seen the spider" (2.1.45). As Leontes sees it, both Hermione and Camillo are objects of exchange between himself and Polixenes, and Camillo's associations with Ganymede make him a secondary player in the staging of the erotic bond between the two kings.

Camillo and Polixenes make their entrance in the play's second half negotiating once again the conflict between a man's duty to his homeland and his affection for another man. Although Polixenes stresses that he needs Camillo present for business reasons, his request that Camillo not leave is strongly reminiscent of the earlier exchange between Leontes and Polixenes: "I pray thee, good Camillo, be no more importunate: 'tis a sickness denying thee anything; a death to grant this" (4.2.1–3). That the business at hand should be Polixenes' interruption of a heterosexual pastoral (and that Florizel should apparently have no mother on hand, even in Bohemia), suggests that the concerns that shaped the earlier Edenic realm of twinned lambs have resurfaced in the relation between Camillo and Polixenes.

As mentioned above, Florizel claims that he is "heir" to his own "affections" as he makes plans to elope with Perdita. Camillo, however, who is more profoundly committed to the affections of his two masters, effects a reworking of Florizel's and Perdita's scheme for his own purposes:

> Now were I happy, if
> His going I could frame to serve my turn,
> Save him from danger, do him love and honour,
> Purchase the sight again of dear Sicilia

And that unhappy king, my master, whom
I so much thirst to see.

(4.4.509–14)

As Camillo puts it, he has "a woman's longing" to see his home
and his king, and his employment here as an assistant to the young
couple is a means toward the end of uniting himself and Polixenes
with the object of their affections. The implication is that Camillo's
participation in the staging of male affection stands in an opportu-
nistic relation to the spectacle of heterosexual affection and to the
natural pastoral upon which it intrudes. Perdita's comment upon
her own participation in the elopement ("I see the play so lies /
That I must bear a part," 4.4.655–66) is more apt than she realizes;
she is being made to play act not only her own marriage, but also
the reunion of the men whose desires are a powerful shaping force
in the play.[37]

If the play legitimates its own theatrical practice in part by staging a celebration of the "natural"—only to refigure that pastoral as
implicitly in the service of the homoerotic—it moves similarly toward legitimation in the staging of Hermione's return. The Winter's
Tale takes great pains to establish this source of moral veracity as
having come from outside the realm of male control and male fantasy. Paulina has disciplined Leontes thoroughly, calling his imaginings "Fancies too weak for boys, too green and idle / For girls of
nine," and speaking out of turn repeatedly to remind him of his
former tyrannies (3.2.181–82). Paulina speaks in direct opposition
to male authority, and her disclaimers as she reveals the statue to
be alive, protecting her from the possibility that she might be "assisted / by wicked powers" or that her "unlawful business" might
be "hooted at / Like an old tale," actually serve to emphasize the
power of her artistic deception, the fact that it transcends the laws
that govern acceptable stagecraft.

We learn too that backstage, as it were, during the sheep-shearing
celebration, Hermione and Paulina have quietly been staging their
own spectacle. While Paulina has engineered Leontes' sixteen years
of mourning, Hermione has "preserved / [Herself] to see the issue,"
with "issue" here meaning both the daughter she has lost and the
outcome of a play—in this case, a play partly of her making. Given
that Hermione began The Winter's Tale with the burden of representing Leontes' esteem for Polixenes, as a player in the theater of
male affection, it is remarkable that in the second half of the play
she and Paulina have taken control of the plot, have planned their

own theatrical strategy. Even though the ultimate result of this female theater is to reward Leontes for his conversion and to prove
Hermione's fidelity to her husband and his lineage, the play's ending looks like it is authorized by women, largely because of the
way that Paulina stages her power over Leontes and her power over
the "statue" of Hermione.[38] Like Diotima—in fact, much more emphatically than Diotima—Paulina speaks in a voice that insists
upon its own difference, its distance from the erotic preoccupations
of men.

The return of Hermione, then, looks like a kind of triumph for
the feminine, an artistic coup that, like the sheep-shearing feast,
seems to proclaim its independence from the all-male community
that produces sexually stigmatized theatrical spectacles. As meta-
theater, this apparent female power could be thought to represent
a final distancing from the stigmatized theatricality that marked
the play's opening scenes. Hermione's coming to life as a statue
seems, moreover, to be a final elision of the spectacle of the boy
actor, the figure who, more than any other, represents the sexual
dangers of the theater; the emphasis in the play's last scene is upon
the reality of Hermione's womanhood, after all, and not upon the
androgyny of the boy who represents her. Hermione appears to step
forward from out of the staged representation of "woman" and to
assert her living reality, a reality made more convincing by her
status throughout the play as the embodiment of truth. In this sense
she continues the motion begun by Polixenes in the "twinn'd lamb"
pastoral, the motion to erase the figure of the boy actor.

Furthermore, Paulina makes a brief remark that raises the question of lesbian desire, apparently marking an absolute distinction
between the erotic possibilities of her own stagecraft and that of
the two kings. In act 5, when Florizel and the unrecognized Perdita
arrive in Sicilia, a servant describes Perdita to Leontes and Paulina
with a sense of wonder:

> This is a creature,
> Would she begin a sect, might quench the zeal
> Of all professors else; make proselytes
> Of who she but bid follow
>
> (5.1.106–9)

Paulina responds with mock horror, "How! not women?" (5.1.109).
By underlining for us the sexual potential of this description of
Perdita, Paulina takes us into new erotic territory. She implies at
least an awareness of a desire that is outside male control, either

for the purposes of progeny or poetry. In fact, her joke seems to emphasize the hiddenness and unrepresentability of lesbian desire, and by extension its distance from traditional models of the literary.[39]

However, this heightened sense of the reality of the female at the end of The Winter's Tale also works paradoxically as a boast about the fecundity of the male community that produced the play. Like the gestures made in act 4 toward a heterosexual pastoral, the efforts that act 5 has made toward establishing the independence of women are simultaneously available as part of a male homosexual stagecraft. Paulina's passing joke about lesbian desire, for instance, is answered in a manner that suggests that the scandalous boy actor has not been as thoroughly removed from the play's erotic economy as my earlier argument implied: "Women will love her, that she is a woman / More worth than any man; men, that she is / The rarest of all women" (5.1.110–12). The servant's response highlights a different erotic possibility than Paulina's joke, emphasizing not the lesbian but the bisexual possibilities of Perdita's attractiveness. His rather elaborate explanation for her ubiquitous appeal sounds a bit like Sonnet 20 ("A man in hue all hues in his controlling, / Which steals men's eyes and women's souls amazeth," 7–8), or like the kinds of erotic play that characterize Twelfth Night; the play's response to the possibility of an independent lesbian desire is to return to the terrain of the boy actor, to reassert the fundamental androgyny of a Perdita who is played by a boy in women's clothes, and thus to remind its audience of the ganymede's participation in the broader range of theatrical eroticisms. Rather than figuring the ganymede as a sign of stigmatized sexual identity from which mature and powerful men can distance themselves, The Winter's Tale implicates the ganymede, finally, in every aspect of the stage's erotic practice. We are prepared by the play's boasts about the power and appeal of the ganymede to regard Hermione's return not so much as the elision of the boy actor but as his triumph. The boy who impersonates the "real" Hermione, along with the theatrical company that engineers his impersonation, asserts power so absolute that it dares to stage its own exclusion.

That exclusion goes beyond boasting that a boy can convincingly play a mature woman with miraculous powers, however. On a deeper level, the play uses this final moment to register in silent eloquence the cost of the effort to distance boys from men. Mamillius, identified repeatedly in the play's first half with his father's past, has died at the end of act 2 and is thus hauntingly absent in this scene of miraculous reunion. Leontes' family has in a sense acquired a son through Perdita's marriage to Florizel, but the effort to substitute Polixenes' son for Leontes' through the institution of marriage is, in light of the initial failure of Leontes' and Hermione's union to erase the past, a particularly hollow theatrical convenience. Paulina herself critiques it just before the newly wedded couple arrives in Sicilia:

> Had our prince,
> (Jewel of children) seen this hour, he had pair'd
> Well with this lord; there was not full a month
> Between their births.
>
> (5.1.115–18)

In her wonderful sadistic way, Paulina emphasizes the fatality of Leontes' former paranoia, keeping alive the memory of the past if not in this case the actual victim of it. In addition, she speaks uncharacteristically here for the union of men, subtly replacing the image of Perdita's marriage to Florizel with a different masculine pairing. Even the most independent voice of female power in this play speaks up to long for the past of the twinned lambs.

The play's final scene of miraculous heterosexual restoration, then, is claimed by the power of the sexually stigmatized boy in at least two ways. On the one hand, the very reality of the statue's femaleness is a boast about theater, about the power of a cross-dressed boy to fool an audience, even an onstage audience. On the other hand, the legitimate claim of Mamillius to be present at this family reunion ensures that the marriage of Florizel and Perdita and the miraculous rebirth of Hermione will on some level acquire their poignancy because they are compensation for another loss, for the jewel of children who cannot be replaced by stagings of even the most forgiving and fertile heterosexual embrace.

V

I return, finally, to Halperin's discussion of The Symposium in order to clarify the relation between The Winter's Tale's assumption of female procreativity and the problem with which I began this essay: the difference in signifying power between the participation of boys and the participation of men in homosexual and homoerotic acts. Halperin argues that Diotima functions as a mimetic device through which Plato appropriates a putatively "feminine" erotics as the cornerstone of his own teachings, his own articulation of what *The Symposium* calls "right pederasty." Concerned as she is with the erotics of pedagogy, Diotima aligns herself, in Halperin's account, with the symbolic appropriations of female procreativity that typify male rites of passage in ancient and modern patriarchal cultures. Like the couvade, like ritual scarrings that symbolize menstruation in men, like pederastic rites that initiate boys into manhood and employ procreative imagery, Diotima gives witness to "the determination of men to acquire the powers they ascribe (whether correctly or incorrectly) to women," which Halperin calls "a remarkably persistent and widespread feature of male culture."[40]

Importantly, according to Halperin, these appropriations of female procreativity inevitably depend upon the failure of men to represent women:

> Even in the midst of mimicking menstruation, pregnancy, giving birth, and breastfeeding, the male actors must share with their audience the understanding that their procreative performances are symbolic, not real—that nose-bleeding is *not* menstruating, that oral insemination is *not* breast-feeding. The point of all those rites, after all, is to turn boys into men, not into women: for the cultural construction of masculinity to succeed it is necessary that the process intended to turn boys into men be genuinely efficacious, no less "generative" than female procreativity itself, but it is also necessary that the men who do the initiating retain their identity as men—something they can only do if their assumption of "feminine" capacities and powers is understood to be an impersonation, a cultural fiction, or (at the very least) a mere analogy. (146)

Thus Halperin accounts for *The Symposium's* relative lack of concern for Diotima's authenticity, its willingness to let readers suspect that Socrates merely uses her as a voice through which to speak his own erotic doctrines.

The Symposium, then, lets the mask of female impersonation slip for the purposes of bolstering the power of men and bolstering the power of "masculine" and "feminine" as categories of definition. Its efforts to do so are, as Halperin points out, fully appropriate to a treatise on the pederastic initiation of Greek boys. *The Winter's Tale*, on the other hand, while similarly preoccupied with the transition from boyhood to "more mature dignities"—and with the erotic significance of that transition—performs its version of what Halperin calls "mimetic transvestism" to what is ultimately

a much more unsettling effect. Leontes and Polixenes portray themselves, and others portray them, as having outgrown their childish
proximity to one another and to the implicit homoeroticism of
boyhood. Because the ganymede repeatedly intrudes, however,
upon the terrain of heterosexual reconciliation and procreation, the
play finally dramatizes the difficulty of distancing men from boys,
of marking any absolute passage through time from one erotic mode
to another. As I have argued in the early portions of this essay, the
implied narrative of masculine development that relegates something like homosexual identity to boyhood (while allotting to mature men a literally insignificant or uninscriptive range of sexual
choices) is finally unsustainable in the erotic context of English
Renaissance theater. Because all players could share in the sexual
stigma of the ganymede, because everyone on the Shakespearean
stage was implicated in the boy actor's sexual display, no real rite
of passage is finally possible. When *The Winter's Tale* allows the
ganymede to peek out from behind its display of natural and female
fecundity, it reveals, finally, not the supreme confidence of Platonic
distinctions between male and female, but instead a peculiarly theatrical breakdown of the distinctions between ganymede and king.
In so doing, it claims for the theater not only the free play of sexual
desire, but also the power of that desire to adhere to subjects.

Notes

1. Alan Bray, *Homosexuality in Renaissance England* (London: Gay Men's
Press, 1982), 34.
2. John Donne, *Satire I* 1.39–40, *The Satires, Epigrams, and Verse Letters*, ed.
W. Milgate (Oxford: Clarendon, 1967), quoted in Bray, *Renaissance England*, 53;
Epigramme 25, "On Sir Voluptuous Beast," in *Ben Jonson*, ed. C. H. Herford and
Percy Simpson (Oxford: Clarendon, 1937), 8:34, quoted in Bray, *Renaissance England*, 16.
3. Bray, *Renaissance England*, 70; *Memoirs of the life of Colonel Hutchinson*,
ed. J. Hutchinson, rev. C. H. Firth, (London, 1906), 84, quoted in Bray, *Renaissance
England*, 55.
4. [December 1623?] Letter 218 in G. P. V. Akrigg, ed., *Letters of King James
VI and I* (Berkeley: University of California Press, 1984), 431.
5. See Jonathan Goldberg, *Sodometries: Renaissance Texts, Modern Sexualities* (Stanford, Calif. Stanford University Press 1992), 17 and throughout. In *James
I and the Politics of Literature: Jonson, Shakespeare, Donne, and Their Contemporaries*, Goldberg discusses at some length the difficult relationship between
James's kingship and his relations with his favorites (Stanford, Calif.: Stanford
University Press,1983), see esp. 143–46.
6. See for example Bredbeck's introduction, to *Sodomy and Interpretation:
Marlowe to Milton* (Ithaca: Cornell University Press, 1991), quoted in text. Gold-
berg argues that "the invocation of historical difference . . . cannot be used as a

way of cordoning off the past from the present' (*Sodometries*, 6). Louise O. Fraden-burg and Carla Freccero present a series of articles that complicate the "acts vs. identities" debate, including their own introduction, which asks whether "al-terism functions within current historicist practice precisely to *stabilize* the iden-tity of 'the modern'" ("Premodern Sexualities in Europe," *Gay and Lesbian Quarterly* 1 [1995]:378). See also Lorraine Daston and Katherine Park, who chal-lenge "the conventional binary periodization of sexuality into 'modern' and 'pre-modern'" ("The Hermaphrodite and the Orders of Nature: Sexual Ambiguity in Early Modern France" *Gay and Lesbian Quarterly* 1 [1995]:419). Alan Sinfield's speculations are particularly helpful in their readjustment of the notion of histori-cal difference:

> I have a suspicion that the quest for the moment at which the modern homosexual subject is constituted is misguided. I suspect that what we call gay identity has, for a long time, been always in the process of getting constituted— as the middle classes have been always rising, or, more pertinently, as the modern bourgeois subject has for a long time been in the process of getting constituted. Theorists of post-structuralism . . . sometimes write as if they were showing that Shakespeare and his contemporaries did not envisage full or even coherent subjectivities in anything like the modern way. But actually these scholars tend to discover ambivalent or partial signs of subjectivity; they catch not the absence of the modern subject, but its emergence. . . . Of course, the human subject is never full, and hence may, at any moment, appear unformed. And so with gay subjectivity, which because of its precarious social position is anyway more fragile and inconstant: it is on-going, we are still discovering it" (*Cultural Politics—Queer Reading* [Philadelphia: University of Pennsylvania Press, 1994] 14).

7. Bredbeck, *Sodomy and Interpretation*, xi.

8. Ben Jonson, *Volpone*, in *Ben Jonson*, 5, ed. C. H. Herford and Percy Simpson (Oxford: Clarendon Press, 1937) 3.7.219–33.

9. This observation is too widespread to be cataloged, but the following examples are instructive. Madelon (Sprengnether) Gohlke notes that "Once Othello is convinced of Desdemona's infidelity . . . he regards her not as a woman who has committed a single transgression but as a whore, one whose entire behavior may be explained in terms of lust" ("'I Wooed Thee with My Sword': Shakespeare's Tragic Paradigms," in *Representing Shakespeare: New Psychoanalytic Essays*, ed. Murray M. Schwartz and Coppelia Kahn, 174 [Balti-more: Johns Hopkins University Press,1980]). Similarly, Coppelia Kahn points out that "the cuckold may take revenge against either his wife or her lover, or against both. According to the double standard, however, she has become a whore, irrevocably degraded by even one sexual transgression" (*Man's Estate: Masculine Identity in Shakespeare* [Berkeley: University of California Press, 1981], 121). Janet Adelman's reading of, for instance, *Hamlet*, speaks power-fully of the importance of sexuality in the characterization of a Gertrude or an Ophelia, and the play becomes for her a paradigm for the anxieties about women's sexuality that resonate throughout the Shakespearean canon: "as they enter into sexuality, the virgins—Cressida, Desdemona, Imogen—will be trans-formed into whores, their whoredom acted out in the imaginations of their nearest and dearest; and the primary antidote to their power will be the exci-sion of their sexual bodies, the terrible revirginations that Othello performs on Desdemona, and Shakespeare on Cordelia" (*Suffocating Mothers: Fantasies of Maternal Origin in Shakespeare's Plays, "Hamlet" to "The Tempest"* [New York: Routledge, 1992], 36). Speaking not so much of adultery but simply of marriage, Carol Thomas Neely argues that the loss of virginity signals for Shake-speare's heroines the loss of "their position as idealized beloveds" (*Broken*

Nuptials in Shakespeare's Plays [New Haven: Yale University Press, 1985], 63).
Critics who focus more primarily upon the inscription of women's bodies also
locate sexuality—perhaps necessarily—at the center of the idea of woman.
Susan J. Wiseman, writing about *'Tis Pity She's a Whore*, notes that "it is . . .
Anabella's body rather than Giovanni's which comes to bear the meaning" of
the incest they commit together ("*'Tis Pity She's a Whore*: Representing the
Incestuous Body," in *Renaissance Bodies: The Human Figure in English Cul-
ture*, c. 1540–1660, ed. Lucy Grant and Nigel Llewellyn [London: Reaktion
Books, 1990] 188). Peter Stallybrass analyzes contradictory cultural assump-
tions about women's sexuality that are expressed as actual features of women's
bodies, be they figured as "grotesque" or "classical" ("Patriarchal Territories:
The Body Enclosed," in *Rewriting the Renaissance: The Discourses of Sexual
Difference in Early Modern Europe*, ed. Margaret W. Ferguson, Maureen Quilligan, and Nancy J. Vickers [Chicago: University of Chicago Press, 1986]).

10. H. B. Charlton and R. D. Waller, eds., *Works and Life of Christopher
Marlowe*, 2d. ed. (London: Methuen, 1933), 1.1.61–66.

11. For a variety of approaches to this scene and the play as a whole, see
Alan Bray, "Homosexuality and the Signs of Male Friendship in Elizabethan
England," in *Queering the Renaissance*, ed. Jonathan Goldberg 40–61 (Durham,
N.C.: Duke University Press, 1994); Bredbeck, *Sodomy and Interpretation*, 56–
86; Goldberg, *Sodometries*, 105–43; Lisa Jardine, *Still Harping on Daughters:
Women and Drama in the Age of Shakespeare* (New York: Columbia University
Press, 1983), 22–24; Bruce R. Smith, *Homosexual Desire in Shakespeare's En-
gland: A Cultural Poetics* (Chicago: University of Chicago Press, 1991), 209–23.
These critics all note the boy's androgyny, but stop short of emphasizing the
extent to which his appearance here really is not a cross-dressed performance.
The boy is more or less naked. His body, not his costume, is in Dian's shape.

12. *The Poems of Richard Barnfield*, ed. Montague Summers (London: Fortune Press, 1936), 1–24. See Bray, *Renaissance England*, 60–61, Bredbeck, *Sodomy and Interpretation*, 149–60, Goldberg, *Sodometries*, 68–9, and Smith,
Homosexual Desire, 99–115 for more extensive readings of Barfield.

13. There is the further suggestion that Ganimede is physically inscribed
even by heterosexual desire when Daphnis describes him as a beloved "Vpon
whose fore-head you may plainely reade / Loues Pleasure, grau'd in yuorie
Tables bright" (15.4). Again, it is not the desire of the boy himself that is at
stake here, so much as his susceptibility to being inscribed by pleasure.

14. Among the many critics who discuss the erotic significance of the boy
actor see especially Laura Levine, *Men in Women's Clothing: Anti-Theatricality
and Effeminization, 1579–1642* (Cambridge: Cambridge University Press,
1996); and Stephen Orgel, *Impersonations: The Performance of Gender in
Shakespeare's England* (Cambridge: Cambridge University Press, 1996). See
also Valerie Traub's challenge to the notion that pederasty and effeminacy
were primary modes of male homosexual expression in this period (*Desire
and Anxiety: Circulations of Sexuality in Shakespearean Drama* [New York:
Routledge, 1992], 94). My own intention is not to conflate pederasty with sodomy, so much as to explore the signifying power of this one form of sodomitical
desire. There is, of course, merit to Stephen Orgel's claim that early modern
England evinced no "morbid fear of homoeroticism as such" (36). While recognizing the culture's investment in homoerotic patronage and friendship, and
in transvestite theater, I want nevertheless to give antisodomical discourse its
due. As Louis Montrose has recently argued, to accept antitheatricalism as an
authentic cultural expression rather than a negligible pathology is "to respect

the intelligence and sincerity of contemporary opponents, and also to appreciate that the Elizabethan theater may have exercised a considerable but unauthorized and therefore deeply suspect affective power upon those Elizabethan subjects who experienced it" (*The Purpose of Playing: Shakespeare and the Cultural Politics of the Elizabethan Theatre* [Chicago: University of Chicago Press, 1996], 45). It seems unlikely to me, given the importance of Puritan belief in this period, that the pleasure of theater was unaccompanied by a genuine awareness of its controversial sexuality.

15. The two books that most powerfully influence my understanding of theater as an institution in this period are Andrew Gurr, *Playgoing in Shakespeare's London* (Cambridge: Cambridge University Press, 1987); and Leeds Barroll, *Politics, Plague, and Shakespeare's Theater* (Ithaca: Cornell University Press, 1991). Both stress the dangers of overstating the connections between the theaters and the aristocracy, Gurr by critiquing the notion that it was predominantly the wealthy and powerful who frequented the theaters, and Barroll by arguing persuasively that James I did not in fact regard the stage as an extension of his own monarchy, as some new historicists have implied. Nevertheless, their own works imply a complex interaction between patronage and regulation of the theaters, not because the court understood the greatness of art and the city officials were moralistic puritans, but because both governing bodies knew the stage could be defended or attacked for strategic reasons. See Montrose, *Purpose of Playing*, chapter 5, for a careful study of the relation between court patronage and city regulation in Elizabeth's reign. I am also grateful to A. R. Braunmuller and the members of his Folger Institute seminar, 1996, for many rich discussions of the position of the stage in early modern England, and to Susan Zimmerman's colloquium at the Folger, 1996–97, for very helpful feedback on this essay. This work and the larger project from which it was taken would have been impossible, moreover, without the help of Janet Adelman and Joel Altman.

16. Traub, *Desire and Anxiety*, 16.

17. *A second and third blast of retrait from plaies and Theaters* (London, 1580) 3–4.

18. Ben Jonson, *Poetaster*, in *Ben Jonson*, 4, ed. C. H. Herford and Percy Simpson (Oxford: Clarendon Press, 1932) 1.2.15–16.

19. "But so long as he lives unmarried, hee mistakes the Boy, or a Whore for the Woman; by courting the first on the stage, or visiting the second at her devotions" (E. K. Chambers, *The Elizabethan Stage* [Oxford: Clarendon Press, 1923], 257). *A Common Player* is attributed to Cocke by Chambers, who reproduces the text from two variant editions included among the essays of John Stephens (255).

20. *The Anatomie of Abuses: contayning a Discoverie, or briefe Summarie, of such Notable Vices and Imperfections, as now raigne in many Christian Countreyes of the Worlde, but (especiallie) in a verie famous Llande called Ailgna*, 1583. Ed. F. J. Furnivall (London: New Shakespeare Society, 1877–79) 144–45.

21. White argues that "the cause of plagues is sinne . . . and the cause of sinne are playes: therefore the cause of plagues are playes." For White, the devastation caused by the plague joins with the moral destructiveness of theater, making tangible the self-loss associated with theatrical practice (*A Sermon preached at Pawles Crosse on Sunday the thirde of November 1577 in the time of the Plague*, [London, 1578], 48).

22. Noted in Russell Fraser, *The War against Poetry* (Princeton: Princeton University Press, 1970), 26. Fraser outlines early modern objections to the poetic, noting that the attribution of sterility to poetry was related to a growing capitalist emphasis upon productivity. See especially 4–6.

23. John Northbrooke, *A Treatise Wherein Dicing, Dauncing, Vaine playes, or Enterluds . . . are Reproved*, London, 1577–75; Henry Crosse, *Vertues Common-wealth: Or the Highway to Honour* (London, 1603), V4. In *Refutation*, I.G. charges that "men have deuised many unlawful artificiall Pleasures, whereby they might passe away (as their name *Pastimes* signifie) the most precious time of their life . . . idlely and fruitlesse, without any profit to the Church, or Common-wealth wherein they liue, or to their owne soules . . . choking up the good Seed of the Word, which should dwell plentifully in their heartes, and in sted thereof, sowing the Tares reaped from ungodly and obscaene Stage-playes" (1615, introduction and bibliographical notes by Richard H. Perkinson [New York: Scholars' Facsimiles and Reprints, 1941] A3–4).

24. *A Winter's Tale*, ed. J. H. P. Pafford (London: Methuen, 1963) 1.2.187–89. All further references are to this edition.

25. Like the catamite who seems intrinsically homoerotic, boys seem here by their nature to be theatrical beings. Their "varying childness" makes them paradoxically static, full-time occupants of a state of undifferentiatedness that others visit only in memories of childhood, or onstage. The pleasure of changing identities was also associated with homosexual practice in early modern England. Discussing romance in chapter 4 and satire in chapter 5 of *Homosexual Desire*, Bruce Smith argues persuasively that homosexual behavior in this period, along with its literary representation, could include extensive play with gender identity. See also Smith's discussion of "boy" as a term that inscribes "a distinction in power vis-à-vis a social or moral superior" (195).

26. For a discussion of breeching, see Adelman, *Suffocating Mothers*, 7. Adelman discusses breeching in relation to the maternal in *The Winter's Tale* on 228.

27. Although Virgil's eclogues are the Renaissance's source for pastoral convention, early modern writers also knew a version of pastoral that downplayed the political import of Virgil's poetry in favor of a more sentimentalized nostalgia for the rustic life, figured as an Eden or a Golden Age. To the extent that Polixenes' description of childhood can be compared with the pastoral at all (admittedly, among more important differences, most pastoral poetry was not written from the perspective of the sheep), it must be as an echo of this latter nostalgic pastoral rather than as a Virgilian treatment of social problems. The play's later sheep-shearing scenes, however, are much more strongly Virgilian in their use of pastoral landscape and song to discuss what are clearly not utopian concerns. For extended treatments of both Polixenes' nostalgia and the sheep-shearing scene, see Peter Lindenbaum, *Changing Landscapes: Anti-Pastoral Sentiment in the English Renaissance* (Athens: University of Georgia Press, 1986), 111–27; and Paul Alpers, *What Is Pastoral?* (Chicago: University of Chicago Press, 1996), 204–22.

28. Bruce Smith discusses Polixenes' version of the pastoral in the context of the all-male educational institutions in which Elizabethan men spent their childhood and adolescence, noting the likelihood that these institutions fostered homosexual behavior (*Homosexual Desire*, 98–99).

29. Jonathan Dollimore explores the contradictions of the "natural" in relation to the perverse, meaning by *perverse* a category of oppositions to the dominant order (disguising itself as natural) that come increasingly to be iden-

tified with sexual difference. I see some such relation working itself out in *The Winter's Tale*, with Puritan assumptions about the natural order of heterosexual fertility and economic productivity standing in opposition to the imagined unnatural behaviors of theatrical practicers and patrons. Like Dollimore's work, *The Winter's Tale* explores the contradictions inherent in the category of the natural, and it further embarks upon a reappropriation of nature as a function of a homoeroticized artistic endeavor (*Sexual Dissidence: Augustine to Wilde, Freud to Foucault* [Oxford: Clarendon Press, 1991]).

30. Stanley Cavell writes compellingly of the necessity for Polixenes to leave Sicilia (*Disowning Knowledge in Six Plays of Shakespeare* [Cambridge: Cambridge University Press, 1987], 212–14. Charles Frey identifies with a particular poignancy Hermione's success at bridging the gap over which the two kings shake hands, noting that just after Leontes has described his initial sexual conquest of her as a sour and crabbed opening of her white hand, Hermione turns and offers that hand to Polixenes: "Why lo you now; I have spoke to th' purpose twice: / The one, for ever earn'd a royal husband; / Th'other, for some while a friend [*Giving her hand to Pol.*]" (1.2.106–8). (*Shakespeare's Vast Romance: A Study of "The Winter Tale"* [Columbia: University of Missouri Press 1980], 122).

31. The classic source for this observation is C. L. Barber ("'Thou That Beget'st Him That Did Thee Beget': Transformation in *Pericles* and *The Winter's Tale*," *Shakespeare Survey* 22 [1969], 59–67). For a reading of Shakespeare's sonnets that locates male-female relationships within an economy of male bonds, see Eve Sedgwick, *Between Men: English Literature and Male Homosocial Desire* (New York: Columbia University Press, 1983), 24–48.

32. Plato, *The Symposium*, in *The Republic and Other Works by Plato*, trans. B. Jowett (New York: Anchor Press, 1973) 352. All further references are to this edition.

33. Sidney, for instance, remarks that philosophers "do authorize abominable filthiness" more than poets do, and he offers the *Phaedrus* and *Symposium* as evidence (*The Defense of Poesie*, (1583), in *Literary Criticism: Plato to Dryden*, ed. Allan H. Gilbert, 406–61 [Detroit: Wayne State University Press, 1940]). See also Gilbert 444 n. 94, which cites Scaliger's condemnation of the *Symposium* "and other monsters." I am indebted to Heather Weidemann for her suggestion that the *Symposium* was central to my reading of *The Winter's Tale*. I am not, however, suggesting that the *Symposium* is a source for the play or that Shakespeare knew it. The parallels between these two texts seem to me attributable to the persistence of certain strategies for legitimating male writing.

34. David Halperin, "Why Is Diotima a Woman," in *One Hundred Years of Homosexuality and Other Essays on Greek Love* (New York: Routledge, 1990). I am grateful to Gregory Bredbeck for suggesting the parallels between Halperin's reading of Plato and my own work with this play, and for additional suggestions beyond the scope of individual citation.

35. A long line of critics associate the play's pastoral with the female; see especially Adelman's discussion: "Through its association with the female and its structural position in the play—outside Leontes's control, outside his knowledge—the pastoral can figure this [maternal] body, the unknown place outside the self where good things come from" (*Suffocating Mothers*, 231). Peter Erickson agrees that *The Winter's Tale* associates this pastoral with women, while he emphasizes the extent to which such a female power serves patriarchy (*Patriarchal Structures in Shakespeare's Drama* [Berkeley: University of California Press, 1985] 158–62).

36. Leonard Barkan discusses the importance of Ganymede as an image of homosexual desire in the Renaissance in *Transuming Passion: Ganymede and the Erotics of Humanism* (Stanford, Calif.: Stanford University Press, 1991).

37. Frey argues that one of the great purposes of *The Winter's Tale's* second half is to recuperate the notion of "play" that Leontes' jealousy had made suspect in the play's first half. He sees Perdita's and Florizel's use of costumes as an important motion toward the restoration of faith in drama (*Shakespeare's Vast Romance*, 143–47). I would argue, however, that an early modern audience's faith in drama would require awakening for cultural reasons that go beyond Leontes' personal expressions of mistrust, including the complex of sexual allegations made about theatrical practice in the period.

38. Many critics have noted that the play's resolution depends upon Leontes' ability to rely upon female powers. See, for example, Kahn, *Man's Estate*, 216–19, and Marianne L. Novy, *Love's Argument: Gender Relations in Shakespeare* (Chapel Hill: University of North Carolina Press, 1984), 176–77. Neely argues that the romances make possible an intertwining of "sexual/marital anxieties" with "political conflicts," in part because the frightening power of female sexuality has been displaced onto the father-daughter bond as a result of the mother's real or imagined death. She finds in *The Winter's Tale* the most powerful transformation of incestuous desire into an acceptance of heterosexual fertility, a transformation brought about through the agency of Hermione, Paulina, and Perdita (chap. 5). Although Adelman claims that the romances aim collectively to restore "the ideal parental couple lost at the beginning of *Hamlet*" (*Suffocating Mothers*, 193), in her reading paternal authority is the play's ultimate concern, and she would agree that paternal authority manages at best a momentary compromise with the sexual mother in *The Winter's Tale* (220–38). In Erickson's reading, Paulina is "less of an exception to the general rule of female obedience than she appears to be" (*Patriarchal Structures*, 162), since, like the play's other women, she exerts her efforts on behalf, ultimately, of male power (148–70).

39. In characterizing lesbian desire as an unrepresentable realm potentially outside of male control, I am building on the sense of its remoteness articulated in Donne's "Sapho to Philaenis":

> Men leave behinde them that which their sin showes
>   And are as theeves trac'd, which rob when it snows.
> But of our dallyance no more signes there are,
>   Then fishes leave in streames, or Birds in aire.
> And betweene us all sweetnesse may be had;
>   All, all that Nature yields, or Art can adde.
>
>   (39–44)

The poem itself belies the separateness of lesbian sex—which after all serves Donne's purposes, not Sappho's—but nevertheless invests in a fantasy of its utopian isolation. I am of course using the term "lesbian" here and throughout with a consciousness of its historical anachronism. See Valerie Traub, "The (In)Significance of 'Lesbian' Desire in Early Modern England," in Goldberg, *Queering the Renaissance*.

40. Halperin, "Why Is Diotima a Woman?" 143.

Pure Resistance: Queer(y)ing Virginity in William Shakespeare's *Measure for Measure* and Margaret Cavendish's *The Convent of Pleasure*

Theodora A. Jankowski

I

W E ALL KNOW that there were no early modern heterosexuals, homosexuals, lesbians, gays, or bisexuals. There were also no early modern queers.[1] Now that you know I know that, let me explain why I want to consider the position occupied by adult virgin women as a queer space within the early modern Protestant sex/gender system. I use the term "queer" to define not only varieties of nonheterosexual activity, but also to define nonreproductive heterosexual activity and nonsexual erotic activity. I agree with Alexander Doty's contention that "queerness should challenge and confuse our understanding and uses of sexual and gender categories."[2] I have chosen to use the term "queer" to define or categorize the position of the adult woman virgin primarily because of the inclusivity of the term. While there has developed a political agenda around the use of the term "queer," I want to detach my usage of it from this contested space and focus on the way in which the notion of "queer" or "queerness" allows a space for examining issues of sexuality that are not restricted to the binary axis of homo- versus heterosexuality.[3] This more inclusive use of "queer" perhaps began with the 1991 "Queer Theory" issue of *differences*. While in her introduction to the volume Teresa de Lauretis states that "the work of the conference [from which the issue's articles originated] was intended to articulate the terms in which lesbian and gay sexualities may be understood and imaged as forms of resistance to cultural homogenization, counteracting dominant discourses with other constructions of the subject in culture," she also indicates that "[i]n a sense, the term 'Queer Theory' was arrived at in the effort to avoid all of these fine distinctions in our discursive proto-cols, not to adhere to any of the given terms, not to assume their ideological liabilities, but instead to both transgress and transcend them—or at the very least problematize them."[4] While the volume seems to be grounded in the notion of lesbian and gay sexualities as the only forms of resistance to the heteronormal, de Lauretis does claim that queerness can "act as an agency of social change" and "construct another discursive horizon."[5] Her intrinsic equa-tion of queer with lesbian and gay is shared by Sue-Ellen Case. While stating that "queer theory . . . is not gender specific," Case simply means that "queer foregrounds same-sex desire without designating which sex is desiring."[6] From here she goes on to argue that queer theory challenges "the Platonic parameters of being—the borders of life and death," while "queer desire is constituted as a transgression of these boundaries."[7] This move allows her to set "queer" in opposition to the "rather polite categories of gay and lesbian" and view it as that which "revels in the discourse of the loathsome, the outcast, the idiomatically-proscribed position of same-sex desire. . . . The queer is the taboo-breaker, the monstrous, the uncanny."[8] Although Case's move opens up homosexual desire to *include* the realm of the taboo and the monstrous—not simply to *reflect* heteronormativity's denigration of *all* homosexual desire as taboo or monstrous—her theory still seems lodged within the binary opposition of hetero/homo.[9] Even the new forms of being, or "beings," discussed in her article are lesbian vampires, creatures that result from the inversion of two binaries, the hetero/homo and the dead/undead.

While de Lauretis's and Case's use of the term queer is certainly productive for exploring issues of lesbian and gay desire, I want to focus more on the kind of move made by Eve Sedgwick in her definition of *queer*:

> That's one of the things that "queer" can refer to: the open mesh of possibilities, gaps, overlaps, dissonances and resonances, lapses and excesses of meaning when the constituent elements of anyone's gender, of anyone's sexuality aren't made (or *can't* be made) to signify mono-lithically. The experimental linguistic, epistemological, representa-tional, political adventures attaching to the very many of us who may at times be moved to describe ourselves as (among many other possibili-ties) pushy femmes, radical faeries, fantasists, drags, clones, leatherfolk,

ladies in tuxedos, feminist women or feminist men, masturbators, bull-daggers, divas, Snap! queens, butch bottoms, storytellers, transsexuals, aunties, wanna-bes, lesbian-identified men or lesbians who sleep with men, or . . . [ellipses in original] people able to relish, learn from, or identify with such.[10]

In the list I have just quoted, as well Sedgwick's list, (cited in note 10), she presents a (possibly) random, certainly limited catalog of various sexual identities and positions. Some clearly concern only women, others clearly concern only men. Similarly, some are positions occupiable only by homosexuals, others are equally occupiable only by heterosexuals. But other positions—leatherfolk, masturbators, wanna-bes, for example—can be occupied by women, men, transgendered people, homo-, hetero-, bi-, or transsexuals, and probably anyone else I have left out. It is the inclusiveness of Sedgwick's definition—one shared by Doty—that appeals to me personally, but especially in terms of this particular project. The problem with generating such a huge list of queer behaviors/positions is that one inevitably leaves out some type of person or category. Interestingly, Sedgwick does not mention virginity, celibacy, or chastity as queer sexual practices.[11] This is not surprising. Especially in the twentieth century we are more apt to regard the refusal to engage in sexual activity with another person as a choice that *removes* the celibate from all categories of sexuality rather than as a specific choice of manifestation *of* sexuality.[12] "Chastity and virginity are moral categories denoting a relation between the will and the flesh," states Arnold Davidson, "they are not categories of sexuality."[13] But I want to use the notion of queer as a category that disrupts the regime of heterosexuality to understand just how the concept of the perpetually virgin woman acted as a threat to the sexual economy of early modern England. I want to do this by suggesting that virginity represented a queer space within the otherwise very restrictive and binary early modern sex/gender system.

Focusing exclusively on the adult woman virgin's consistent refusal to be integrated into the early modern sexual economy allows me to consider her in terms of Monique Wittig's "lesbian" and Marilyn Frye's "Virgin." In "The Straight Mind" (1980), Wittig claims that "lesbians are not women" and that, if the foundation of society is heterosexuality, women cannot exist other than in "the position of the dominated."[14] Wittig's subjects of inquiry are lesbians specifically because they resist the position of submission women are guaranteed within patriarchal straight society.[15] Marilyn Frye (1990) similarly sees women as inevitably occupying the position of the heterosexually dominated in patriarchal society, though she uses "Virgin" to define the female subject who is "sexually and hence socially her own person."[16] While using different terms to separate their subjects of inquiry from women, both theorists acknowledge the fact that patriarchal society is structured in a way that almost completely destroys female autonomy and uses women either as direct sexual slaves or as "objects" through which male homosocial bonds are secured.[17] The term "woman" is thus marked through its use as the descriptor of the nonautonomous, cipher, chattel, object, or wife whose presence is necessary to allow the continuance of male privilege/patriarchal society. As Wittig says, "'woman' has meaning only in heterosexual systems of thought and heterosexual economic systems."[18] Thus, female humans who resist such a positioning need to be defined in ways that acknowledge that resistance. Wittig and Frye construct "lesbians" or "Virgins" as subjects who consistently resist their culture's positioning of them as "dominated" and try to construct their lives in opposition to patriarchal social systems. Such an analysis not only tries to reclaim certain female subjects from a subordinate position, but also suggests that these same female subjects are *not* destined for the "acceptable" position within the patriarchal sexual economy as the property of men.

While both Wittig and Frye choose different terms to describe their subjects, the terms they choose are not necessarily as rigidly defined as the words themselves would suggest. For Wittig, "lesbian" is neither necessarily nor exclusively to be understood in its usual twentieth-century context as a woman whose primary or exclusive sexual/emotional activities occur only with other women. Similarly, for Frye, the use of "Virgin" indicates that the women she is writing of do not necessarily possess intact hymens. Both Frye and Wittig see their subjects as challenging the patriarchal construction of "woman" as subservient to men. While Frye's term "Virgin" appears to be closer to my own notion of "queer virgin" since it linguistically includes the possibility that some of its subjects *are* intact virgins, Wittig's "lesbian" helps to focus on the resistant nature, the real threat to the sex/gender system that I am claiming for my queer virgins. But the two words—lesbian and Virgin—in and of themselves in twentieth-century parlance do represent sexual positions that *do not include men*. Thus, whether virgins or lesbians are not sexually active at all or sexually active only with women, *neither* is sexually active with a man.[19] Since normative heterosexual activity is absent from both positions, they can be defined as "queer."

The kind of queerness I am considering reflects a multitude of sexual, gender, and/or erotic positioning. What I want to do in this essay is recover (specifically early modern) non-normative gender positions for women in order to disrupt the regime of heterosexuality. I intend to do this by opening up the restrictive male/female binary of the early modern Protestant sex/gender system to the possibility of multiple sexual/erotic combinations. Consequently, my essay will involve a necessary negotiation with several historical periods. The theoretical grounding of my argument in twentieth-century queer theory provides the base for contesting previous analyses of the sex/gender system of early modern England. Yet in order to make my points regarding the rigidity of the early modern sex/gender system, I need also to recollect that the sex/gender system of medieval England and Europe was not as restrictive as it would become under Protestantism. I want to recall the possibilities of a more fluid system that existed within Catholic Europe, but was closed down as a result of theological decisions that were essential to the Reformation. The Roman Catholic sex/gender system was based upon the writings of early Christian theologians such as Jerome (ca. 340–420), Ambrose (ca. 340–97), and Augustine (354–97) who consistently argued that virginity for both men and women was superior to marriage. Augustine's beliefs that consecrated virgins were "a greater blessing" than the married and that the desire for children "must not be thought capable of making up for the loss of virginity" became important components both of Christian monasticism and the Roman Catholic discourse of sexuality.[20] As a result, within Catholic Europe, gender was organized not only around the traditional man/woman binary, but around the theological virgin/not-virgin one as well. Such an organization makes gender more difficult to analyze, but also allows more options for exploring gender positions. The idea that women were considered as capable as men of maintaining their physical integrity allowed both genders a socially and culturally acceptable alternative to marriage. Like men, women could marry or they could become members of celibate religious orders. Marriage—or illegitimate sexual activity—did not prevent widows and widowers or unmarried persons of either gender from entering religious orders or taking annual, renewable vows of chastity. Communities of unmarried—but not necessarily never married—Beguines and married or single Third Order Franciscans also provide examples of quasi-religious/quasi-secular living and working arrangements that are not easy to define.[21] I would argue, then, that the plurality of sexual/erotic arrangements within Catholic medieval Europe had the potential to destabilize the categories of sex and gender, especially when contrasted to the more limited, and therefore restrictive, sex/gender arrangements of early modern Protestant England.

Protestant early modern England organized gender in terms of bodily differences[22] and an actively heterosexual gender paradigm. This organization derived specifically from both Martin Luther's and John Calvin's contention that virginity was not a more spiritual state than matrimony. Both theologians argued that marriage is the norm, and Luther even suggests that vowed virginity is unnatural: "who commanded you to vow and swear something which is contrary to God and his ordinance, namely, to swear that you are neither a man nor a woman, when it is certain that you are either a man or a woman, created by God."[23] Luther's insistence on the biological facts of gender and on sexual desire as what defines the humanness of both men and women serves to reinforce the traditional man/woman binary at the expense of the theological virgin/not-virgin one. Consequently, the Protestant organization of society reduces not only people's sexual options, but also their gender options.

Such a theoretical positioning becomes evident in early modern Protestant marriage manuals and sermons, like John Wing's (1620): "wherunto we adhaere according to duty, and perswade our selves, that virginity is good, but marriage is better. . . . For our parts, we will not take away, or extenuate, any due praise that God giveth to virginity; only, it may not pearch above marriage."[24] The only sexual continence that Protestants were willing to accept was that which occurred within marriage. Virginity became a transitory category for women, while the ideal wife was expected to remain chaste. As William Gouge (1622) indicates, "matrimoniall chastitie, . . . [is] that vertue whereby parties maried; observing the lawfull and honest use of mariage, keepe their bodies from being defiled with strange flesh: . . . so as they that keepe the lawes of wedlocke are as chaste as they that containe."[25] Since Protestant society conceived of marriage as the norm for both men and women, both were assumed to spend their adult lives as sexually active persons. The man/woman gender binary in early modern England, then, could also be rendered as husband/wife. Acceptable exceptions to this binary or paradigm were few, but the importance of marriage to the construction of the binary/paradigm assumes, of course, that the ultimate social destiny of *all* women was to become the sexual property of men. The premarital virgin woman was, thus, in a transitional stage—currently the property of one man (her father), she was "soon" to become the specifically sexual property of another man (her husband). What I am concerned with is the problem inherent within this gender arrangement for understanding those women who choose to resist incorporation into the sex/gender system as sexually active women by retaining their virginity beyond its "transitional phase" well into adulthood.

I am proposing to place these resistant virgins in the queer middle—or at the queer end—of the Protestant/patriarchal sex/gender system in an "officially" unnamed—and often untheorized—seemingly "empty" position that is fundamentally dissident. Valerie Traub has written of (mostly European) women who were tried and often executed for transgressing gender boundaries and acting like men—either by cross-dressing, employing dildos, or acting as tribades either with or without abnormally large clitorises. Traub contrasts these transgressive women, and the erotic practices that made them unavailable for reproduction, with "femmes," who "would be assumed available to give birth." Women's sexual relationships with other women "only *become* oppositional," Traub maintains, "when perceived as a threat to the reproductive designs of heterosexual marriage. . . . [And] the 'femme' women . . . challenged neither gender roles nor reproductive imperatives."[26] While I agree with Traub that cross-dressed women and tribades were remarkably transgressive, I disagree with her contention that women who engage in nonreproductive femme-femme sexual activity are to be read exclusively as nonthreatening. The queer virgins I am considering are those who confound the sex/gender system *not* by trying to be men, but by *not being* "women." In order to clarify just what I mean by a queer virgin, I would like briefly to compare two virgin characters—Helena of *All's Well That Ends Well* and Marina of *Pericles*—who seem to be "transitional virgins" who fit easily into the Protestant early modern sex/gender system with some queer virgin characters—Isabella of *Measure for Measure* and Lady Happy (and her companions) of *The Convent of Pleasure* who *cannot* fit into that system. That Helena and Marina are not as normative as they might initially seem to be points out the amazing potential for queerness of all virgin women characters.

The "traditional" young virgin character is easy to understand. She spends virtually all of her play searching for a husband and ends definitely married or definitely about to be. Yet she also knows that her inevitable marriage is dependent upon the preservation of her virginity until her quasi-ritual defloration by her husband on her wedding night. The necessity of a young woman's maintaining—and yet, at the proper time, readily losing—her virginity is at the basis of what might seem to be a truly bizarre "debate" between Helena and Parolles at the beginning of the play. The young woman asks the professional man-at-arms how best she might preserve her virginity, how best to "barracado" it against the assaults of men (1.1.114–15).[27] Parolles asks why Helena would want to preserve anything so unnatural, something that "breeds mites, much like a cheese, [and] consumes itself to the very paring" (1.1.143–44). He likens virginity to suicide and suggests that it is more important to *lose* virginity than to retain it, for "Loss of virginity is rational increase, and there was never virgin got till virginity was first lost. . . . Virginity by being once lost may be ten times found; by being ever kept it is ever lost" (1.1.129–31, 132–33).

While our tendency may be to write off Parolles' "outrageous" position—when, indeed, do we unqualifiedly believe *anything* this character says?—I do not think we are meant to do so in this case. Parolles is not speaking through his cap or simply manufacturing techniques for getting Helena into bed. At least not entirely. The character is, in fact, reiterating the standard Protestant attitude that a woman should remain virgin only until marriage, a position articulated by such tract and marriage-manual authors as Bullinger (1541), Niccholes (1615), Whately (1617), Wing (1620), Gouge (1622), Dod and Clever (1630), Brathwait (1641), Rogers (1642), and Taylor (1650).[28] Parolles' speech further reminds Helena of the economic necessity of women for the reproduction of capital and the waste that virginity represents in this economic model.

In abiding by this normative notion of virginity, Helena represents both Protestant society's ideal virgin, who sacrifices her virginity only to her husband, as well as its ideal wife, who not only follows her husband's instructions to the letter, but remains his chaste "companion" whether or not he is at her side. But *All's Well* is a problematic play because it challenges these "normative" virgin behaviors even as it reifies them. Under ordinary circumstances, few would expect a dowryless, middle-class physician's daughter to be able to obtain *any* sort of a husband, much less such a "prize" as the wealthy and aristocratic Bertram. Helena does so in a way that can only be considered "magical." She stakes her "maiden's name" (2.1.174), as well as her life, upon her father's remedy for the king's fistula. That this penniless and untrained women succeeds where all other medical practitioners have failed points out the "miraculousness" of her cure, which is intrinsically bound to her own virginity. The quasi-magical power associated with virginity can be seen in many early modern plays. In *Pericles*, for example, Marina is able not only to escape death and retain her virginity in a brothel but also to convince many of Mitylene's gallants that a chaste life is preferable to a profligate one. And, like Helena, she is magically able to effect a medicinal cure.

While *All's Well* presents us with a seemingly normative narrative of virginity in Helena's quest for Bertram, there is still something distinctly queer about Helena's character. She does not disintegrate after being repudiated by Bertram. She sets out to win him a second time and employs Diana to help her do so. It is very important to recognize that Helena is economically in control of her life during the second part of her play. Not only does she have her profession as healer to support her, but she has the financial wherewithal to buy Diana's help with bags of gold and the promise of a dowry. And the consummation of Helena's marriage does not remove a virginal presence, for Diana takes over as the play's queer virgin. Although the king tries to recuperate her into the sexual economy with the promise of marriage—"If thou be'st yet a fresh uncropped flower, / Choose thou thy husband, and I'll pay thy dower" (5.3.327–28)—like Isabella, Diana remains silent, never "verbally" agreeing to the proposal nor choosing a husband. Her behavior at the end is absolutely in line with her act 4 statement, "Marry that will, I live and die a maid" (4.2.74). The money she receives from Helena may be enough to make her financially able to remain queer and continue to resist marriage.

As you can see, my interest is in examining what happens to the gender arrangements of the early modern drama when the traditional narrative of virginity is violated, when women characters choose to be queer and use their virginity in ways that resist the Protestant early modern dependency narrative I have outlined above. Resistance to this narrative can take three forms. Militant resistance occurs primarily because women characters find ways to maintain (or regain) control of their physical bodies in such a way as to render them (and their bodies) incapable of traffic within the patriarchal sex/gender system. This resistance is usually accomplished by a woman's refusal to surrender her virginity to a man, by her determination to retain her virginity long beyond the time when socially mandated marriage would occur. Erotic resistance occurs when the virgin, while not necessarily sacrificing her strictly biological virginity, engages in sexual activity that is outside the bonds not only of Protestant marriage, but of the patriarchal sexual economy itself. Economic resistance occurs when the virgin discovers or creates a means of economic independence that insures she does not have to enter the sexual economy to survive. Virgins who devise a life that allows them to engage in any one or a combination of these three kinds of resistance are queer.

Queer virginal resistance is so threatening to the Protestant/patriarchal social order that it must be recuperated. We are not surprised when characters such as Beatrice or Hermia—who either refuse marriage outright or demand to choose the husband—are incorporated into the sexual economy at the play's end. Nor are we surprised when characters like Portia and Rosalind—who for a time break out of the strictures of patriarchal gender roles—are redirected into these roles, albeit after some modification of them. What really *does* surprise us are those characters who are *never* recuperated into the sexual economy: characters like Isabella, who never "verbally" agrees to marry the Duke, or the inhabitants of *The Convent of Pleasure*, who seem perpetually to refuse marriage. The threat to patriarchal society presented by all of the women characters I have named above is enormous, yet their resistance to marriage would not be threatening at all were they not clearly marked as virgins, subjects who can potentially exercise "magical" powers. And their being so marked serves to reinforce the fact that these virgins totally destabilize the Protestant early modern sex/gender system because they are queer.

II

As a novice nun in a cloistered order who refuses marriage, Isabella not only signals an incursion of Roman Catholic discourse into the play but represents a large group of women whose "profession"—and means of economic support—entails commitment to perpetual virginity. Isabella's consecrated virginity can remind audience members that English society once allowed women an option to their subservient position in marriage.[29] The novice's cloistered and virginal existence is sharply juxtaposed to the various kinds of sexual "slavery"—actual (prostitution) and symbolic (marriage)—that women are subjected to in patriarchal society. As a result, Isabella becomes a site of reader/viewer dissatisfaction because of her refusal to engage in any way with the sexual economy, whether by trading a few illicit hours with Angelo for her brother's life or accepting the licit proposals of the Duke.[30] But truly to understand the nature and extent of Isabella's queerness, it is necessary to understand the dissident nature of her relationship to these two most powerful men in the play. Angelo seems to be unsure of how to respond to Isabella after their first meeting. Even though she bears specific "marks" of her virginity—her position as a novice and her habit—marks even the lecherous Lucio can "read," the deputy remains unclear about whether or not she is chaste:

> From thee, even from thy virtue!
> What's this, what's this? Is this her fault or mine?
> The tempter or the tempted, who sins most, ha?
> Not she, nor doth she tempt; . . .
> Can it be
> That modesty may more betray our sense
> Than woman's lightness.
>
> (2.2.169–72; 175–77)

Angelo's inability to "read" Isabella correctly derives not from her failure to present herself as a virgin but from his own failure to accept her social positioning and self-definition. His illicit sexual desire for the novice prompts him to redefine her as woman in accordance with his desire; his social/political power to mandate this redefinition reinforces the parameters of the sexual economy and any woman's relationship to it. The Duke similarly exercises power over Isabella through his ability to redefine her. Having controlled her as a deus ex machina friar, he contemplates the similar, though different, control he will exercise once he has defined her as his wife.[31] As each man tries to exercise his patriarchal power over Isabella, this control necessarily involves recategorizing the adult virgin as either "whore" or "wife," unchaste or chaste woman. Neither Angelo nor the Duke is content for Isabella to remain virgin.

But how does Isabella, a woman whose *profession* demands perpetual virginity, respond to being incorporated into the Protestant early modern discourse of chastity? When offered Angelo's ultimatum, she responds:

> were I under the terms of death,
> Th'impression of keen whips I'd wear as rubies,
> And strip myself to death as to a bed

That longing have been sick for, ere I'd yield
My body up to shame.

(2.4.100–104)

Critics have always acknowledged the thrilling undertones of a "deviant" sort of pleasure within these lines—either Isabella's desire to couple with death or simply to engage in some form of Catholic flagellation.[32] I would argue otherwise. While I acknowledge the sense of pleasure implicit in these lines, I see it as lying in Isabella's almost militant *resistance* to Angelo's attempts to redefine her. This resistance derives not simply from her refusal to acquiesce to his wishes, but from the realization that *she herself* is responsible—through the exercise of *her own* free choice—for the preservation of her virginity.[33] The fact that we are generally unused to encountering women in the early modern drama making such important and unaided decisions can explain why we may be unprepared to see this choice as being both remarkable and very power-full for Isabella.[34] The type and extent of the power that her choice grants her is revealed in the lines in which Angelo assumes that Isabella *will* comply with his proposition because *all* women are "frail" and she is a woman:

I do arrest your words. Be that you are,
That is, a woman; if you be more, you're none.
If you be one, as you are well expressed
By all external warrants, show it now
By putting on the destined livery.

(2.4.135–39)

The deputy denies Isabella's claims to a virtue greater than the majority of her gender by explaining that if she claims to be "more"—that is, "better than"—a woman, she is "none", that is, "not a woman." This line is the key to my reading of Isabella.

Probably intended as an insult, these lines—which echo Luther's contention that a virgin was "neither a man nor a woman"—really *do* serve to define what Isabella is, which is, in fact, *not* a woman.[35] Isabella is a virgin, but one who has *professed* virginity, has accepted it as the defining characteristic of her life. As an "adult" virgin *not* destined for marriage, she represents that which is queer both within the society of Vienna and within the sexual economy of early modern England. In a society that has a place for a woman only as a powerless (sexual) servant of men—wife or whore—the virgin with her intact hymen and unpenetrated body is most definitely *not* a woman, for she challenges her society's most basic notion of "woman." Angelo recognizes this by presenting Isabella with the option of "acting" as a woman for his pleasure, or being defined as a "deviant"[36] "not-woman." But his ultimatum backfires. Women, in Angelo's society, are represented as being powerless to choose to refuse the pleasures of highly placed, powerful men. Isabella, however, in accepting the name of one type of not-women—queer virgin—has wrested both the power of choice and the power of defining, or categorizing, herself away from men. Only by being a queer virgin can she challenge the sexual economy by creating a category of autonomous female who has the power to resist both Angelo's illegal—and the Duke's legal—proposals of sexual servitude.

But if a society divides gender into man/woman, the acceptable social opposition to woman is man, *not* not-woman. If man/woman is the operative binary, not-woman exists outside the accepted terms and can be read as "deviant." Thus, even though Isabella's choice of a queer virgin life is validated by her society's institution of the virginal life of the professed nun—which, of course, was not necessarily the case in Protestant early modern England[37]—her identification as not-woman can be read in secular terms as deviant. I want to expand this idea of the queer virgin as not-woman into a broader definition that includes various "women" who resist incorporation into the patriarchal sexual economy and/or who attempt to redefine themselves and their pleasures against that economy or against masculinist notions of pleasure/female subservience. Included in this definition are all queer women who choose to live as celibates, whether or not they are physically virgin: those "religious" celibates who see the source of their life/pleasure in "god," as well as those "secular" celibates whose pleasures reside somewhere other than in sexual activity. I also view as queer virgins those who do not simply resist the patriarchal sexual economy but who actively create an alternative sexual economy with other queer virgins through the exclusion of both men and women.

The character Isabella, while threatening and queer in terms of Protestant discourse, is clearly a virgin in the biological sense. But she is also a lesbian in Wittig's sense and a Virgin in Frye's sense. While I am not necessarily arguing that Isabella is a lesbian in the sense of being a female homosexual—though I would also not like to rule out that possibility—she is more easily regarded as one of Frye's Virgins because her queerness positions her in opposition to patriarchal society, as are the "unspeakable" females Frye describes.[38] While the nun Isabella's vowed virginity marks her as queer, it also demonstrates that for *some* early modern women, there *was* an alternative to being in the position of the dominated. Queer virgins did have the potential to carve out and occupy a space of autonomy that resisted the man/woman binary. Because of their profession, nuns can easily be seen as resisting the position of the dominated both militantly and economically. Yet their vows of virginity problematize just how they might or can resist erotically. Being a nun implies that a virgin needs to choose a life of asceticism removed from sexual contact with men or women.

Or must she? Isabella is a difficult character to "read" since she is a Roman Catholic nun in a play written in a Protestant country for a Protestant audience. Thus she is the locus both of Protestant "fears" of Catholicism and Protestant animosity toward the religion of Mary Tudor, Mary Stuart, the pope, the Jesuits, and the Guise and toward the home of the Armada. Not surprisingly, the "oddness" of cloistered nuns particularly signaled them out for anti-Catholic scapegoating. Yet even for members of Catholic religious communities, the close ties between cloistered women suggested the potential for deviant or unnatural behavior. Most orders forbade what were often known as "particular friendships"—"exclusive intimacy with another sister," which could draw the participants "away from total dedication to God and community" and were seen as a "prelude to Lesbian relationship."[39] If Catholics feared the homoerotic potential of women's communities, it is not surprising that Protestants would seize upon such possibilities to discredit Roman practices, as Andrew Marvell does when he has the experienced nun in "Upon Appelton House" promise Isabel Thwaites she could "each night [from] among us to your side / Appoint a fresh and virgin bride" (185–86).[40] Indeed, "the Nun's smooth tongue has suckt her in" (200)—in more ways than one, Marvell implies. While I do not wish to argue that Isabella and Francisca—the only other nun we see—share a "particular friendship," I do want to suggest that the suspicion/belief that such "practices" occurred in Catholic convents could easily have colored an early modern response to Isabella.

But in Isabella's act 2, scene 4 response to Angelo, *Measure For Measure*, suggests even queerer sexuality than that implied by particular friendships: "Th'impression of keen whips I'd wear as rubies / And strip myself to death" (101–2) rather than yield. I have already talked about these lines in one way; I would now like to look at them in a very different way. Carolyn Brown argues that these lines refer to the Catholic practice of religious flagellation, which she defines as "erotic." Although I disagree with Brown's overall analysis of the play, her valid points about flagellation bear closer examination. While the use of the "discipline"[41] usually occurred in private, Brown suggests that flagellation also took place in the public spaces of the convent, where superiors administered punishments for violation of church rules to naked members of the community. The erotic and orgiastic aspects of this discipline, Brown claims, led to its restriction: "The sects [of flagellants] became so prevalent and powerful and the performances so unmistakably promiscuous that Pope Clement VI issued a bull against them."[42] While, again, I do not want to pursue the question of whether or not Isabella enjoys flagellation, or whether members of her house engage in sadomasochistic practices, I do want to suggest that the knowledge that flagellation *did* occur in Roman Catholic convents/monasteries *could* influence how Protestants perceived the inmates.[43]

I have not raised the issues of (homoerotic) friendship and (erotic) flagellation simply to drop them as the figments of overactive Protestant imaginations. I think the fact of their existence—to *whatever* degree—does reinforce not only the *potential*, but the *range* of queer sexual practices open to virgins. Nuns spent years living cloistered with other nuns. What was more natural than that they should develop deep and caring friendships for each other that may (or may not) have been expressed erotically. Since superiors were more likely to work hard to guard against hetero- rather than homoeroticism—the results of it (pregnancy/childbirth) being easier to detect—it is not surprising that this type of sexuality would achieve more recognition.[44] Flagellation could, of course, also provide homoerotic pleasure to both the giver and the receiver, whether engaged in as a couple or group.[45] And I do not wish to ignore the possibilities of autoeroticism, whether resulting from fantasy or administered digitally or with the discipline. The virgin Isabella represents one sort of threat because she can resist male power and male sexuality, as represented by Angelo and the Duke, to live a queer life. But the possibility that she maintains an erotic life *without* male contact—and outside the patriarchal sexual economy—makes her doubly threatening by suggesting that queer virgins *could* live with sexual pleasure and without men.

III

Although *Measure for Measure* and *The Convent of Pleasure* were both produced within Protestant England and both depend upon the institution of the Roman Catholic convent for their analyses of gender, they cannot be said to exist precisely within the same historical moment. The early-seventeenth-century *Measure for Measure* (ca. 1603–4) resuscitates the "medieval" Catholic religious site as trace memory within the gender history of women, while the later *Convent of Pleasure* (ca. 1645–68) uses the site more playfully for the purposes of satire. By the mid-seventeenth century, the gender system of Protestant England had become more fixed. My purpose in examining Cavendish's play in light of Shakespeare's is to demonstrate that the potential for queerness among virgins still existed—though in a slightly different form—despite an increasing gender rigidity and the personal circumstances of the Duchess of Newcastle's own life.

Like *Measure for Measure*, *The Convent of Pleasure* is a text that imagines ways in which queer virgins can resist patriarchal society militantly, economically, and/or erotically. The queer community of this play is created as a playful, though perhaps also deliberate, alternative to a patriarchal society that is marked by the objectification and subjugation of women.[46] The play-within-the-play (act 3) visualizes this society of rigid gender roles where women are either wives or whores. Here husbands physically abuse their wives or children (3.2), steal their wives' portions and jointures, and/or spend their money on whores (3.4). Women suffer not only these social effects of marriage, but "biological" ones as well. Pregnancy is a time of continuous illness (3.3) leading to such painful labor (3.7) and difficult delivery that the woman or her child may die (3.9). Successful delivery does not reduce a woman's care, for her child may ruin her own life through "illegitimate" pregnancy or be executed for a crime (3.8). Nor are unmarried women safe, for they may be raped into a life of whoredom if they refuse to enter it willingly (3.10). Given this hideous view of male-dominated society, it is not surprising that Lady Happy, the play's economically independent protagonist, wishes to create an alternative world where women can live with each other—but apart from men—and exercise their autonomy. While this choice to retire to a convent *can* be viewed as distinctly queer in a society that sees *all* women as ultimately "marriageable" (that is, destined for sexual servitude to men), Cavendish initially represents the impulse as "natural" in the sense of being extremely logical. Lady Happy demands for women what marriage, as shown in act 3, can never provide: personal autonomy, economic independence, and erotic pleasure. Since men are "the only troubles of Women . . . [those who] cause their pains, but not their pleasures . . . [and] make the Female sex their slaves" (1.2),[47] the only thing women relinquish by encloistering themselves is the source of all their pain—men.

Lady Happy's intention "to live incloister'd and retired from the World . . . but not from pleasures" (1.2, p. 7) does raise the question of how and in what context sexuality/sexual activity is included among the "pleasures" this secular convent has to offer. Cavendish's text is mightily unclear on this matter, though Lady Happy provides the beginnings of a context for understanding queer virginal pleasure. The character claims that she is

> resolv'd to live a single life, and vow Virginity; with these I mean to live incloister'd with all the delights and pleasures that are allowable and lawfull; My Cloister shall not be a Cloister of restraint, but a place for freedom, not to vex the Senses but to please them. (1.2, p. 7)

Within a patriarchal context, virginity means not only lack of penile vaginal penetration resulting in the perforation of the hymen, but implies an overall, often religiously determined, ascetic behavior. If men are forbidden the convent, Lady Happy's companions presumably remain virgin in the "biological" sense. But the restrictions inherent in the ascetic connotations of "virginity" do not easily coordinate with Lady Happy's claims that her cloister is a place of "freedom," not "restraint," where the "Senses" are to be teased with "pleasures that are allowable and lawfull." Obviously there are pleasures that women can indulge in without compromising their biological virginity, but few that would similarly not compromise their "ascetic" virginity. The convent's elaborate food, clothing, gardens, and furnishings (2.2, pp. 13–16) are both sensual and pleasurable. Though clearly nonsexual, they are also nonascetic. Cavendish's use of "pleasure" thus negotiates uneasily with patriarchal definitions of virginity. Yet "pleasure" does have a sexual connotation, and the word's use raises the question of whether the virgins in this convent are allowed to be sexual with each other and, if so, to what degree. We are again confronted with the question of how women who isolate themselves from the patriarchal sexual economy are to be categorized. Cavendish's juxtaposition of "pleasure" with a clearly nonascetic "virginity" suggests that her virgins are to be considered queer. Since they also resist being placed in "the position of the dominated," they must be defined not only in terms of their resistance to masculinist notions of pleasure, but to masculinist notions of female subservience and economic dependence. We can view their pleasure, then, as being created as a form of resistance to the sexual economy. While Cavendish may not be as clear as we might wish in her explication of just what pleasure between queer virgins encompasses, some interesting possibilities are raised within the context of Lady Happy's relationship with the Princess.

Upon entering the convent, the Princess agrees to exchange her crown and power for Lady Happy's friendship, "the greatest pleasure" (3.1, p. 22). In a pair of couplets—

> *Lady Happy.* More innocent Lovers never can there be,
> Then my most Princely Lover, that's a She.
> *Princess.* Nor never Convent did such pleasure give,
> When Lovers with their Mistresses may live
>
> (3.1, p. 23)

—Cavendish begins her redirection of the male-female rhetoric of courtly love to the service of queer virginal desire and thus focuses attention on the conventual "particular friendship." The queer aspects of such a relationship are foregrounded in act 4, scene 1, where a very unhappy Lady Happy ponders the "unnatural" aspects of her affection for the Princess:

> why may not I love a Woman with the same affection I could a Man? . . . our Goddess Nature, . . . I fear will punish me, for loving [the Princess] more than I ought to. (4.1, p. 32)

The Princess, in contrast, argues first, that lovers cannot love too much especially if their love is "virtuous, innocent, and harmless," and second, that they should please themselves as "harmless Lovers use to do" (4.1, p. 32). I will quote the rest of the dialogue:

> *Lady Happy.* How can harmless Lovers please themselves?
> *Princess.* Why very well, as, to discourse, imbrace and kiss, so mingle souls together.
> *Lady Happy.* But innocent Lovers do not use to kiss.
> *Princess.* Not any act more frequent amongst us Women-kind; nay, it were a sin in friendship, should not we kiss: then let us not prove our selves Reprobates.

> [*They imbrace and kiss, and hold each other in their Arms.*]
> Princess. These my Imbraces though of Femal kind,
> May be as fervent as a Masculine mind.
>
> (4.1, p. 33)

Obviously the attitudes of the lovers differ as to what lawful, allowable, and "natural" pleasures between virgins can be. Lady Happy, fixated on the unnaturalness of her affection—presumably not articulated physically—seems to consider any action "guilty." The Princess considers discourse, embracing, and kissing—all of which contribute to mingling of souls—legitimate pleasures.

But discourse, embracing, and kissing in such a way as to cause souls to mingle is open to various interpretations. One is that the "mingling" of souls implies platonic, nonerotic bonding.[48] Cavendish presents such a spiritual connection between the Empress and the Duchess (her own persona) in *The Blazing World* (1668):

> and truly their meeting did produce such an intimate friendship between them, that they became *Platonick Lovers*, although they were both Femal. . . . [T]he Empress's Soul embrac'd and kiss'd the Duchess's Soul with an Immaterial Kiss, and shed Immaterial Tears.[49]

Marilyn Williamson suggests that Cavendish insisted on the "platonic friendship of souls" because souls "do not raise all kinds of sexual innuendos that bodies might."[50] This is true, of course, and a platonic reading of the relationship between Lady Happy and the Princess would maintain the allowable, lawful, and "natural" aspect(s) of their affection.

Another possibility is raised through Cavendish's use of a blazon of the female body in her poem "A Bisk [Bisque] for Nature's Table" (1653):

> A large great Eye, that's black and very quick; . . .
> Two Cherry Lips, whereon the Dew lies wet, . . .
> A sharp and quick, and ready pleasing Tongue;
> A Breath of Musk and Amber, Breasts which Silk
> In Softness do resembl', in whiteness Milk;
> A Body plump, white, of an even growth,
> That's active, lively, quick, and void of sloth; . . .
> A Hand, that's fat and smooth, and very white,
> Whose Inside moist and red, like Rubies bright;
> And Fingers long, . . .[51]

The body described is "active, lively, quick" with a "quick" eye. "Cherry Lips" are either active or warm, since the "Dew lies wet" upon them. This wetness calls attention to the tactile quality of the body, as does the "Silk . . . Softness" of the breasts and the smoothness of the hand. The body's visually erotic beauty is evident in the darkness of the eye, the redness of the lips, and the whiteness of the body, breasts, and hand. The author is not specific about the kinds of pleasures "A sharp and quick and ready pleasing Tongue" grants, though the line suggests the tongue of Marvell's experienced nun. The hand—a particular site of queer female erotic interest—has long fingers and its "Inside [is] moist and red," from what cause(s) the poet does not indicate. Even though Cavendish explored the non-erotic possibilities of a platonic affection between women in *The Blazing World*, this poem is evidence that she may also have considered the specifically erotic aspects of queer female attraction, a possibility also present in those lines from act 4, scene 1 I have been considering. The Princess could be using "discourse" (4.1, p. 33) as synonymous with "marital conversation," a euphemism for "sexual intercourse within marriage."[52] The notion of erotic, passionate, or even lewd discourse then becomes possible. Kisses and embraces, which *can* be nonerotically platonic, can also be just as remarkably erotic. Within a context of queer virginal eroticism, the Princess's remark that it is a "sin" for women friends *not* to kiss (4.1, p. 33) distinctly suggests erotic communication between sexually intimate "particular friends." The fact that Cavendish's text raises so many possibilities of erotic and nonerotic content/practice totally destabilizes the field of virgin-virgin sexuality. We are never sure how far affection between queer virgins does (or can) go.

A further example of this destabilization occurs in terms of the Princess's dress. Shortly after her appearance in act 3, scene 1, she asks to be allowed to "accoustre" herself in "Masculine-Habit" to "act the part of [Lady Happy's] loving Servant" (3.1, p. 22). As precedent she indicates that some of the inhabitants of the Convent so dress themselves to "act Lovers-parts." If this indeed occurs— and the stage directions tell us it does for the Princess, at least[53]— then what we would see onstage for virtually the entire play is *not* a number of virgins exploring natural or unnatural pleasures, but groups of lovers who *look* like traditional, "heterosexual" lovers, namely, men and women. What we see, though, are *not* men and women but *virgins* who *look like* men and women, prototypes of what would come to be called "butches" and "femmes." Cavendish seems to have presented the earliest literary example of (proto-)butch-femme role-playing. I want to use the term "(proto-)

butch-femme"—which alludes to the twentieth-century practice of role-playing for erotic purposes[54]—to distinguish this activity from the kind of cross-dressing (as disguise for safety or technique of audience titillation) that occurs in *Twelfth Night* or *As You Like It*. Viola does not cross-dress to obtain Olivia's love, nor does Rosalind do so to obtain Celia's (or Phebe's). Despite some gender confusion, Viola and Rosalind (almost) always seem focused on a male love-object. Like butches who dress as "men" to attract/court "women" (femmes), Cavendish's virgins wear "Masculine-Habit" to "act Lovers-parts"—take the (act)ive role within a queer virgin couple.

I have (perhaps perversely) refrained until now from mentioning the major "challenge" to my argument in favor of overt virgin-virgin eroticism in this play. That is, of course, the circumstance that the Princess is "really" a man, and the recuperative gesture of "heterosexuality" is the reincorporation of Lady Happy into the patriarchal sexual economy. While some might argue that this revelation serves to dequeer, or stabilize, the play, to channel it inexorably into the heterosexual mainstream, I would like to suggest that what it really does is destabilize the play even more. The easy answer to Lady Happy's emotional dilemma is that her affection is completely "natural," for the "virgin" she loves "with the same affection [she would] a Man" (4.1., p. 32) is, in fact, a man. But if this is the case, as apparently it is, why does Cavendish wait until act 5, scene 1 to reveal the Prince(ss)'s real gender? Or, to rephrase the question more provocatively, why does she insert the dialogue between Lady Happy and the Prince(ss) regarding the (un)naturalness of affection between virgins (4.1) if this kind of affection is to be ultimately repudiated? The "heterosexual" impulse of recuperation is clearly lessened by the Prince(ss)'s urgent argument in favor of the "sinlessness" of kisses and discourse between virgin friends. I suggest that uneasy dialogue is there because it concerned an issue Cavendish was interested in and which she considered in *The Blazing World* and a number of her poems.

Even though this text strives to present instances of queer virginal eroticism, the staging of (proto-)butch-femme couples would counteract that impulse and show us "men" and "women" being erotic with each other. But Cavendish's text is remarkably unstable, and this seeming solidification of gender roles into the traditional is yet again destabilized by the circumstance that she most likely wrote her play with women actors in mind.[55] In thus reversing the material practices of the Elizabethan/Jacobean theater, Cavendish allows for the staging of an erotic potential between *women* actors (whether or not they are cross-dressed)[56] that reinforces the queer erotic impulses between the characters. The casting of the Prince(ss) would further complicate matters. *The Convent of Pleasure* presents a male actor playing a Prince who, before the play begins, is disguised as a woman (Princess), who then dresses as a man and is later revealed to be one. In its original staging, *all* of *Twelfth Night*'s characters were played by men. Olivia would presumably not look more (or less) "feminine" than Viola. In Cavendish's play, however, presumably all the "real women's" parts—including the (proto-)butches—are played by women. Would Lady Happy, then, look more or less "feminine" than the Prince(ss) in her woman's clothes? Would the (proto-)butch virgins look more or less "masculine" than the Prince(ss) in his man's attire? In other words, would the overwhelming number of woman actors effectually render the Prince(ss) queer, somehow genderly "unreadable" in a way that Viola and Rosalind never were/are? Although these questions are virtually impossible to answer, I raise them to reinforce the fact that any reading of this play must necessarily be both highly speculative and willing to entertain multiple possibilities.

If the play were to be staged only in Cavendish's mind (see n. 55), presumably no one but the author would be concerned with any resistant elements it might contain. But even if it was not staged, the play was printed. Cavendish may have felt it was too queer to exist without being straightened out in some way(s). It does, after all, condemn the patriarchal sexual economy and reveal women's position as sexual slaves (act 3). Cavendish seemingly also tries to defuse this difficult section by having the Prince(ss) state

> My sweet Mistress, I cannot in conscience approve of it [the play-within-the-play]; for though some few be unhappy in Marriage, yet there are many more that are so happy as they would not change their condition. (3.10, p. 31)

This response attempts to reify that same patriarchal social ideology already condemned by denying the universal suffering of women and suggesting that it is only experienced by "some few."[57] If Cavendish felt the need to "recant" on her remarks regarding her society, she may have felt equally needy regarding her exploration of virgin-virgin erotic affection. *The Convent of Pleasure* is best described as a volatile play. It raises many possibilities of spiritual, and erotic unions between virgins, yet refuses to commit itself as to which connections are acceptable. While the play's secular location provides for the development of more kinds of pleasure than might be found in a religious convent, its recuperative gestures struggle to contain the radical issues of queer pleasure and social critique raised. Ultimately, though, I would argue that the text's instability allows more potential for queer virginal eroticism than it forecloses. After all, even though we may "see" (onstage) only "men"-women couples,[58] we "hear" (or read) a distinct language of queer eroticism expressed within the context of a virtually all-woman cast.

Measure for Measure and The Convent of Pleasure concern women who are uncategorizable—and who therefore can be considered queer—within the Protestant society of early modern England. Both plays are threatening because they allow their virgin characters to escape existence as pariahs by accepting their queerness and militantly resisting women's traditional "position of the dominated." Their resistance extends to the economic sphere, for none of the virgins is dependent upon any man for financial support. Their existence in a space physically "removed" from patriarchal society—the convent—reflects this economic independence and separation and allows these virgins to resist erotically by defining their pleasure in terms of each other. Whether what they create is erotic or nonerotic is not as important as the fact that they do create worlds and pleasure systems that are queer. Yet no matter how "removed" these convents may be from the centers of patriarchal power, they are still actually located within the patriarchal society they challenge. Thus the new societies they create can, in one sense, be considered illusory. How, indeed, can one completely separate oneself from one's own society? But even given the fact that an actual separation cannot occur, the physical removal of the convent—symbolized by its walls—does invoke the attempt at ideological separation its inmates undergo. So, if patriarchal society depends upon various sorts of female sexual slavery and pain, the queer resistance represented in these plays imagines a recategorization of virgins as their own subjects within their own economies of pleasure.

I have been arguing that the really queer threat Isabella and Lady Happy's companions represent derives from the fact that they resist marriage, something the femmes Traub examines do not. I would also point out, as I have argued elsewhere,[59] that even some virgins who accept marriage reveal their (or the queer virgin's) potential for resisting it. Almost no one views our favorite "saint in the brothel," Marina, as threatening, yet while a resident of that brothel, this virgin creates a "profession" for herself by selling her abilities to weave, sew, dance, and sing that is so financially successful that she is able to support not only herself but her owners. Marina does marry, but this virgin demonstrates the economic potential of the marketplace for survival that is available to queer virgins who wish to resist the sexual economy of marriage.

There is no early modern name for the queer position occupied by such virgins as Isabella and Lady Happy's (proto-)butches and (proto-)femmes. I would speculate that there is no named position because the concept of naming it was too terrifying—not in the nineteenth-century sense that telling women about lesbians might make them all run off to join up—but in a more profound sense that to name that position would indicate that early modern society possessed a "third gender" that was *neither* man/husband *nor* woman/wife. This inability to theorize a place for adult virgin women is obvious in the "problems" that arise when trying to make sense of characters like Beatrice and Hermia, Rosalind and Portia, but especially characters like Isabella and Lady Happy's companions, whose desires are fulfilled by *not* having to marry, engage in sexual activity with men, and accept the "position of the dominated." These characters are most threatening because they militantly maintain their personal autonomy and resist control by men, actively choose virginity as an erotic stance, and are economically able to resist incorporation into the sexual economy. That such behavior is not only resistant but also severely threatening is obvious from the "unreadability" of queer virgins, from the fact that so few plays of the early modern period provide us with examples of adult virgins who remain alone, unmarried, unpunished, and unrecuperated at the end.

Notes

I would like to thank Jean Howard, Dympna Callaghan, and Greg Bredbeck, who generously read earlier drafts of this essay and gave me extremely valuable critiques.

1. By now it is well known that "homosexual" as a term was coined in 1892 and "heterosexual" was a back-formation from it. Similarly, "lesbian," "gay," and "bisexual" are terms that either originated or were first applied to nonheterosexual persons only in the twentieth century. While few early modern terms were available to describe male homosexuals, fewer still described female homosexuals. The category of "sodomy" in its early definitions could be used to refer to acts between sexual partners of the same biological sex. "Sodomite," then, was a general term usable to define any person of either biological sex who engaged in any of the acts considered to be sodomy. While female homosexuals could be referred to as

"sodomitesses," this term was also used to define women who engaged in hetero-sexual prostitution. The term "tribade" referred specifically to the woman who rubbed her (perhaps larger) clitoris against her partner's, penetrated her partner with her clitoris, or used a dildo or other "instrument" to penetrate her.

Early modern terms that referred to female and male homosexuals referred to sexual behavior and practices, not to groups of people or "sexual identities," as twentieth-century terms often do. This is one of the major problems of writing about nonheterosexual, especially lesbian, behavior in the early modern period. Consequently, like many of my colleagues, I will be forced to employ some twentieth-century terms "anachronistically" in an early modern context. I will use the term "queer virgin" to refer to a sexual category that is *both* "virgin and lesbian" *and* "virgin or lesbian." I will use "lesbian" alone to refer specifically to a desire by female humans for other female humans and "(proto-)femme" and "(proto-)butch" to refer to the twentieth-century sexual practices they define anachronistically projected back to an earlier incarnation in the early modern period. "Queer" will be defined in greater detail below.

2. Alexander Doty, *Making Things Perfectly Queer* (Minneapolis and London: University of Minnesota Press, 1993), xvii. Doty also indicates that

> After all, in any of its uses so far, queerness has been set up to challenge and break apart conventional categories, not to become one itself.... Therefore, when I use the term "queer" or "queerness" ... I do so to suggest a range of nonstraight expression in, or in response to, mass culture. This range includes specifically gay, lesbian, and bisexual expressions: but it also includes all other potential (and potentially unclassifiable) non-straight positions.... I want to construct "queer" as something other than "lesbian," "gay," or "bisexual"; but I can't say that "lesbian," "gay," or "bisexual" *aren't* also "queer." ... As such, this cultural "queer space" recognizes the possibility that various fluctuating queer positions might be occupied whenever *anyone* produces or responds to culture. (xv, xvi, xvii, 3)

3. Doty further points out that

> Queer Nation's use of the term often sets up queerness as something different from gay, lesbian, and bisexual assimilationism. In this case, to identify as a queer means to be politically radical and "in-your-face": to paradoxically demand recognition by straight culture while at the same time rejecting this culture. Part of what is being rejected here are attempts to contain people through labeling, so "queer" is touted as an inclusive, but not exclusive, category, unlike "straight," "gay," "lesbian," or "bisexual." (xiv)

While the practice of using "queer"—as opposed to "gay and lesbian"—is currently highly contested, I do not want to enter that discussion. In the course of this section, I will make clear why I want/need to employ the term "queer" to define the category of virginity in the early modern period. However, since I do not want to seem to foreclose discussion on definitions of "queer," I present the following as variations on the positions I examine in the body of my text. Paula Blank, in "Comparing Sappho to Philaenis: John Donne's 'Homopoet-ics,'" *PMLA* 110 (1995): 358–68, "agree[s] with those who have argued that 'queering' is a universalizing approach to the study of sexuality ... , one that challenges the idea of a unitary or essential sexual identity (which may be gay or lesbian identity)" (366 n. 3).

Lisa Duggan, in "The Discipline Problem: Queer Theory Meets Lesbian and Gay History," *Gay and Lesbian Quarterly* 2 (1995): 179–91, indicates that

> [q]ueer theorists are engaged in at least three areas of critique: (a) the critique of humanist narratives that posit the progress of the self and history, and thus tell the

story of the heroic progress of gay liberationists against forces of repression; (b) the critique of empiricist methods that claim directly to represent the transparent "reality" of "experience," and claim to relate, simply and objectively, what happened, when, and why; and (c) the critique of identity categories represented as stable, unitary, or "authentic." (181)

Louise O. Fradenburg and Carla Freccero, in "The Pleasures of History," *Gay and Lesbian Quarterly* 1 (1995): 371–84, "take queer theory to be a pleasure-positive discourse . . . and one of the most important analytical challenges offered today by queer positionalities is their reconsideration of the very stances of epistemological certitude that have played so large a role in the definition and proscription of dangerous pleasures, indeed of pleasure *as* dangerous" (378).

Scott Bravmann, in "Queer Historical Subjects," *Socialist Review* 25, no. 1 (1995): 47–68, feels that,

[a]s a heuristic device, "queer" has helped us to refocus our attention on how culturally sanctioned versions of the normal and the natural have been constructed and sustained. Queer criticism, then, reveals the normal and the natural themselves to be cultural fictions enabled only through their dependent relationship with the abnormal and the unnatural. . . . [T]his transition . . . to the term *queer* has significantly altered the scope of inquiry to include a larger range of deviant sexualities and has focused its inquiry on the problem of heteronormativity. (49)

Penelope J. Englebrecht, in "Strange Company: Uncovering the Queer Anthology," *National Women's Studies Association Journal* 7, no. 1 (1995): 72–90, argues that "Queer nation and like-minded individuals have adopted the term 'queer' to indicate not only its 'traditional' homosexual referents . . . [but also others including] 'friendly' straights. . . . In this new currency 'queer' has come to signify anyone 'other,' different, marginal, or (especially sexually) perverse, identifying the 'abnormal' as positive element via a (perverse) binaristic relation to 'normal' society" (74–75). And Lauren Berlant and Michael Warner, in "What Does Queer Theory Teach Us about X?" *PMLA* 110 (1995): 343–49, believe that

[i]t is no accident that queer commentary—. . . —has emerged at a time when United States culture increasingly fetishizes the normal. . . . [Q]ueer work wants to address the full range of power-ridden normativities of sex. This endeavor has animated a rethinking of both the perverse and the normal: . . . Queer commentary shows that much of what passes for general culture is riddled with heteronormativity (345–49).

4. Teresa de Lauretis, "Queer Theory: Lesbian and Gay Sexualities: An Introduction," *differences* 3, no. 2 (1991): iii–xviii, iii, v.

5. Ibid., xi.

6. Sue-Ellen Case, "Tracking the Vampire," *differences* 3, no. 2 (1991): 1–20, 2.

7. Ibid., 3.

8. Ibid.

9. Working to theorize homosexuality against, or in contrast to, heterosexuality (inevitably?) results in binary thinking. However, part of this problem, as Rosemary Hennessy, in *Materialist Feminism and the Politics of Discourse* (New York and London: Routledge, 1993), articulates, has to do with how heterosexuality itself is constructed: "Heterosexuality depends upon the assumption that sex differences are binary opposites and the simultaneous equation

of this binary sex difference with gender" (88). Even when some critics, like Gayle Rubin in her interview with Judith Butler, "Sexual Traffic: Interview," *differences* 6, nos. 2–3 (1994): 62–99, consider binaries useful, their restrictions do become obvious: "I think these binary models seemed to work better for gender, because our usual understandings posit gender as in some ways binary, . . . But as soon as you get away from the presumptions of heterosexuality, or a simple hetero-homo opposition, differences in sexual conduct are not very intelligible in terms of binary models. Even the notion of a continuum is not a good model for sexual variations" (70–71).

10. Eve Kosofsky Sedgwick, "Queer and Now," in *Tendencies* (Durham, N.C.: Duke University Press, 1993), 1–20, 8. See also Sedgwick, *Epistemology of the Closet* (Berkeley and Los Angeles: University of California Press, 1990), 25–26 for a more detailed list.

11. While she also does not specifically mention celibacy or chastity in her longer list, Sedgwick does list two categories that could include the celibate: "Some people like to have lots of sex, others little or none" and "[s]ome people's sexual orientation is intensely marked by autoerotic pleasures and histories—sometimes more so than by any aspect of alloerotic object choice. For others the autoerotic possibility seems secondary or fragile, if it exists at all" (*Epistemology*, 25–26).

12. During the early modern period, sexual abstinence was definitely considered a sexual position, as Donald N. Mager in "John Bale and Early Tudor Sodomy Discourse," in *Queering the Renaissance*, ed. Jonathan Goldberg (Durham, N.C. and London: Duke University Press, 1994), 141–61 indicates. He states that, according to John Bale (ca. 1550), "abstinence and celibacy are just as perverse as are onanism, bestiality, and pederasty" (151). Further, Bale's citation—"Their sodomytycal chastyte agaynst Gods fre instytucyon"—not only links chastity—(refraining from sexual activity) with sodomy (the ultimate sexual perversity) but with ungodliness (cited in Mager, *John Bale*, 160 n. 6). For an unusual examination of celibacy as a category of twentieth-century sexuality, see Sally Cline, *Women, Passion, and Celibacy* (New York: Carol Southern, 1993). I thank Dympna Callaghan for this reference.

13. Arnold Davidson, "Sex and the Emergence of Sexuality," in *Forms of Desire: Sexual Orientation and the Social Constructionist Controversy*, ed. Edward Stein (Garland, 1990; reprint, New York and London: Routledge, 1992), 89–132, 117.

14. Monique Wittig, "The Straight Mind," in *The Straight Mind and Other Essays* (Boston: Beacon Press, 1992), 21–32, 32, 29.

15. Wittig also indicates that

> Lesbian is the only concept I know of which is beyond the categories of sex (women and men), because the designated subject (lesbian) is *not* a woman, either economically, or politically, or ideologically. For what makes a woman is a specific social relation to a man, a relation that we have previously called servitude, a relation which implies personal and physical obligation as well as economic obligation . . . a relation which lesbians escape by refusing to become or stay heterosexual. . . . [Lesbians' survival] can be accomplished only by the destruction of heterosexuality as a social system which is based on the oppression of women by men and which produces the doctrine of the difference between the sexes to justify this oppression. (20)

Whether they agree with Wittig or not, most late-twentieth-century theorists of sexuality see the position of the "lesbian" as one that exists in direct opposition to patriarchal notions of "woman" as nonautonomous, nonsubjects within the

patriarchal sexual economy. Barbara Creed, in "Lesbian Bodies: Tribades, Tom-
boys, and Tarts," in *Sexy Bodies: The Strange Carnalities of Feminism*, ed.
Elizabeth Grosz and Elspeth Probyn (London and New York: Routledge, 1995),
86–103, recognizes how easy it is for virgins—or any other "women" perceived
as threatening because of their failure to accept patriarchal definitions—to collapse into the category of "lesbian":

> Regardless of her sexual preferences, woman in whatever form—whether heterosexual
> or lesbian—has been variously depicted as narcissist, sex-fiend, creature, tomboy, vam-
> pire, maneater, child, nun, virgin. One does not need a specific kind of body to be-
> come—or to be seen as—a lesbian. All female bodies represent the threat or
> potential—depending on how you see it—of lesbianism. Within homophobic cultural
> practices, the lesbian body is constructed as monstrous in relation to male fanta-
> sies. . . . The woman who refuses to see her sexual organs as mere wood chips, designed
> to make the man's life more comfortable, is in danger of becoming a lesbian—an active,
> phallic woman, an intellectual virago with a fire of her own. . . . The lesbian body is
> a particularly pernicious and depraved version of the female body in general; it is
> susceptible to auto-eroticism, clitoral pleasure and self-actualization. (87, 95)

The resistant nature of the lesbian is also recognized by Bat-Ami Bar On in
"The Feminist 'Sexuality Debates' and the Transformation of the Political,"
Hypatia 7, no. 4 (1992): 45–58:

> A lesbian is the rage of all woman condensed to the point of explosion. . . . The lesbian
> rejects male sexual political domination; she defies his world, his social organization,
> his ideology, and his definition of her as inferior. . . . Woman-identified Lesbianism is
> . . . more than sexual preference; it is a political choice. . . . Our rejection of heterosex-
> ual sex challenges male domination in its most individual and common form. (48)

That the concept of the lesbian is a totally threatening one is further revealed by
Judith Butler's examination of its "unthinkableness" in "Imitation and Gender
Insubordination," in *Inside/Out: Lesbian Theories, Gay Theories*, ed. Diana
Fuss, 13–31 (New York and London: Routledge, 1991)

> Lesbianism is not explicitly prohibited in part because it has not even made its way
> into the thinkable, the imaginable, that grid of cultural intelligibility that regulates the
> real and the nameable. How, then, to "be" a lesbian in a political context in which the
> lesbian does not exist? That is, in a political discourse that wages its violence against
> lesbianism in part by excluding lesbianism from discourse itself? . . . Part of what
> constitutes sexuality is precisely that which does not appear and that which, to some
> degree, can never appear. (20, 25)

This "unthinkableness" occurs in part because, as de Lauretis contends, the
"lesbian is not 'an individual with a sexual preference' but a 'rewriting of self',
a subject constituted 'in a process of interpretation and struggle' . . . , the lesbian is also, as the eccentric metaphor implies, a position outside or in excess
of the discursive-conceptual horizon of heterosexuality" (cited in Hennessy,
Materialist Feminism, 85).

16. Marilyn Frye, "Willful Virgin or Do you Have to be a Lesbian to be a
Feminist?" in *Willful Virgin: Essays in Feminism, 1976–1991* (Freedom, Calif.:
Crossing Press, 1992), 124–37, 133. "The word 'virgin' did not originally mean
a woman whose vagina was untouched by any penis, but a free woman, one
not betrothed, not married, not bound to, not possessed by any man. It meant
a female who is sexually and hence socially her own person. In any universe
of patriarchy, there are no Virgins in this sense. . . . Hence Virgins must be

unspeakable, thinkable only as negations, their existence impossible. . . . Such Virgins are no more possible in patriarchy than are lesbians, and if they impossibly bring themselves into existence, they will be living lives as sexually, socially and politically outlandish and unnatural as the lives undertaken by radically feminist lesbians" (133–34). See also Judith Butler, Gender Trouble: Feminism and the Subversion of Identity (New York and London: Routledge, 1990), 112–28; and Jonathan Dollimore, Sexual Dissidence: Augustine to Wilde, Freud to Foucault (Oxford: Clarendon Press, 1991), 58–60, on Wittig. See also how similar Frye's definition of "Virgin" is to the definitions of "lesbian," in n. 15.

17. Claude Lévi-Strauss in The Elementary Structures of Kinship (Boston: Beacon Press, 1969) defines culture, like marriage, as a "total relationship of exchange . . . not established between a man and a woman, but between two groups of men, [in which] the woman figures only as one of the partners" (115). His idea is the basis of Eve Sedgwick's explications of male "homosocial" relations in Between Men: English Literature and Homosocial Desire (New York: Columbia University Press, 1985); and Epistemology of the Closet. She also calls attention to Heidi Hartmann's similarly focused definition of patriarchy in "The Unhappy Marriage of Marxism and Feminism: Toward a More Progressive Union," in Women and Revolution: A Discussion of the Unhappy Marriage of Marxism and Feminism, ed. Lydia Sargent (Boston: South End Press, 1981), 2–41, as "a set of social relations between men [emphasis added], which have a material base, and which, though hierarchical, establish or create interdependence and solidarity among men that enable them to dominate women" (14; also cited in Sedgwick, Epistemology, 184). The following also provide compelling analyses of how women figure in the patriarchal sexual economy: Veronica Beechey, "On Patriarchy," Feminist Review, no. 3 (1979): 66–82; Gail Omvedt, "'Patriarchy': The Analysis of Women's Oppression," Insurgent Sociologist 13 (spring 1986): 30–50; Gayle Rubin, "The Traffic in Women: Notes on the 'Political Economy' of Sex," in Toward an Anthropology of Women, ed. Rayna R. Reiter (New York: Monthly Review Press, 1975), 157–210.

18. Wittig, "Straight Mind," 32. Butler, in Gender Trouble, points out that

In The Lesbian Body and elsewhere, however, Wittig appears to take issue with genitally organized sexuality per se and to call for an alternative economy of pleasures which would both contest the construction of female subjectivity marked by women's supposedly distinctive reproductive function. . . . Indeed, a lesbian, she maintains, transcends the binary opposition between woman and man; a lesbian is neither a woman nor a man. But further, a lesbian has no sex; she is beyond the categories of sex. Through the lesbian refusal of those categories, the lesbian exposes (pronouns are a problem here) the contingent cultural constitution of those categories and the tacit yet abiding presumption of the heterosexual matrix. . . . Indeed, the lesbian appears to be a third gender or, as I shall show, a category that radically problematizes both sex and gender as stable political categories of description. (26, 113).

19. Butler, in Gender Trouble, says that

we can understand this conclusion to be the necessary result of a heterosexualized and masculine observational point of view that takes lesbian sexuality to be a refusal of sexuality per se only because sexuality is presumed to be heterosexual, and the observer, here constructed as the heterosexual male, is clearly being refused. . . . As in Lacan, the lesbian is here signified as an asexual position, as indeed, a position that refuses sexuality. . . . Significantly, Lacan's discussion of the lesbian is contiguous within the text to his discussion of frigidity, as if to suggest metonymically that lesbianism constitutes the denial of sexuality. . . . This is the predicament produced by a matrix that accounts for all desire for women by subjects of whatever sex or gender as originating in a masculine, heterosexual position. The libido-as-masculine is the source from which all possible sexuality is presumed to come. Here the typology of gender and sexuality needs to give way to a discursive account of the cultural production of gender. (49, 52, 160 n. 20, 53)

Guy Hocquenghem, in *Homosexual Desire* (Editions Universitaires, 1972; reprint, Durham, N.C., and London: Duke University Press, 1993), adds that "[o]ur society is so phallic that the sexual act without ejaculation is felt to be a failure. After all, what do men care if—as is often the case—the woman remains frigid and feels no pleasure? Phallic pleasure is the raison d'etre of heterosexuality, whichever sex is involved" (96).

20. Augustine, *De sanctu virginitate*, trans. John McQuade, S.J.; *Saint Augustine: Treatises on Marriage and Other Subjects*, ed. Roy J. Deferrari (New York: Fathers of the Church, 1955), 133–212, 143, 153, 151. For a more detailed analysis of the differences between the Roman Catholic and Protestant discourses of virginity, see Theodora A. Jankowski, "'The scorne of Savage people': Virginity as 'Forbidden Sexuality' in John Lyly's *Love's Metamorphosis*," *Renaissance Drama* 24 (1993): 123–53, especially 128–37.

I am referring to Foucault's use of the term "discourse," specifically in terms of his contention that categories of discourse create our experience(s) and regulate our world. Foucault discusses "discourse" in "The History of Sexuality," in *Power/Knowledge: Selected Interviews and Other Writings*, ed. Colin Gordon, trans. Gordon et al. (New York: Pantheon, 1980), 183–93; *The History of Sexuality*, vol. 1, *An Introduction*, trans. Robert Hurley (New York: Vintage, 1990); and *The Archaeology of Knowledge and the Discourse on Language*, trans. A. M. Sheridan Smith (New York: Pantheon, 1972), esp. pt. 2.

21. We can also consider, in this context, Foucault's contention that "homosexuality" has the potential to overthrow the category of sex, especially in terms of how "gender transgressions"—like that of the hermaphrodite Herculine Barbin—"challenge the very distinction" between hetero- and homosexual "erotic exchange" (Butler, *Gender Trouble*, 100–101).

22. I want to refer specifically to Thomas Laqueur's analysis in *Making Sex: Body and Gender from the Greeks to Freud* (Cambridge and London: Harvard University Press, 1990), of the prevalence of Galenic notions of gender in the early modern period. This belief held that the sexes were "biologically" the same: "women were essentially men in whom a lack of vital heat—of perfection—had resulted in the retention, inside, of structures that in the male are visible without" (4). Yet even though Galenic medicine would seem to argue for male/female similarity, Laqueur maintains that "sex, or the body, must be understood as the epiphenomenon, while gender, what we take to be a cultural category, was primary or 'real'" (8). Talking about "biological sex" in the early modern period, then, really means talking about "the social order that it both represents and legitimates" (11); even though the "biological" understanding of sex maintained "sameness," the social concept reinforced the magnitude of gender difference.

23. Martin Luther, "Sermon on Marriage at Merseburg (1545)," cited in *Not in God's Image: Women in History from the Greeks to the Victorians*, ed. Julia O'Faolain and Lauro Martines (New York, San Francisco, London: Harper and Row, 1973), 198.

24. [J]ohn Wing, *The crowne Coniugall or, the Spouse Royall*. . . . , STC25844 (Middleburgh: [J]ohn Hellenius, 1620), Sig. Qv, Sig. Q2.

For all sixteenth-and seventeen-century texts, spelling is modernized as regards v/u, vv/w, i/j, long s, and tildes. Sporadic or excessive italics are also eliminated.

25. William Gouge, *Of Domesticall Duties. Eight Treatises.* STC12119 (London: [J]ohn Haviland, 1622), Sig. P4v.

26. Valerie Traub, "The (In)significance of Lesbian Desire in Early Modern England," in *Erotic Politics: Desire on the Renaissance Stage*, ed. Susan Zimmerman (New York and London: Routledge, 1992), 150–69, 164.

27. William Shakespeare, *All's Well That Ends Well*, in *The Complete Works of William Shakespeare*, 4th ed., ed. David Bevington, 367 (New York: HarperCollins, 1992). All further references to Shakespeare's plays will be to this edition and will appear in the text.

28. [Heinrich Bullinger], *The Christen State of Matrimony*, trans. Miles Coverdale, English Experience #646 (1541; reprint, Amsterdam and Norwood, N.J.: Walter J. Johnson and Theatrum Orbis Terrarum, 1974); Alex[ander] Niccholes, *A Discourse, or Marriage and Wiving: and of* . . . , STC18514 (London: Leonard Becket, 1615); W[illiam] W[hately], *A Bride-Bush or a Wedding Sermon:* . . . , English Experience #769 (London: William [J]aggard, 1617; reprint, Amsterdam and Norwood, N.J.: Walter J. Johnson and Theatrum Orbis Terrarum, 1975); [J]ohn Wing, *Crown Coniugull;* William Gouge, *Of Domesticall Duties;* [J]ohn Dod and Robert Clever, *A Godly Forme of Household Governement,* . . . , STC5388 (London: Thomas Man, 1630); Rich[ard] Brathwait, *The English Gentleman and English Gentlewoman* . . . , Wing B4262 (London: John Dawson, 1641); D[aniel] R[ogers], *Matrimoniall Honour: or The mutuall Crowne* . . . , Wing R1797 (London: Th[omas] Harper, 1642; Jeremy Taylor, *The Rule and Exercise of Holy Living* in vol. 3, *The Whole Works of the Right Rev. Jeremy Taylor, D.D.,* 10 vols., ed. Reginald Heber and Charles Page Eden (London: Longmans, 1883).

29. See Eamon Duffy, *The Stripping of the Altars: Traditional Religion in England, 1400–1580* (New Haven and London: Yale University Press, 1992), for an analysis of the extent of Catholic practice—"traditional religion"—in England during the reigns of Henry VIII, Edward VI, and Elizabeth I. I would like to thank Jim Shapiro for bringing this book to my attention.

30. Antipathy toward Isabella's virginity—or rather toward the character's consistency in maintaining her sexual "purity"—has formed an important subdivision of criticism for some time. George Geckle, in "Shakespeare's Isabella," *Shakespeare Quarterly* 22 (1971): 163–68, names Isabella the play's "greatest critical 'problem'" and also gives a brief summary of (mostly condemnatory) attitudes toward the novice going back to the eighteenth century (163–66). Marcia Riefer, in "'Instruments of Some More Mightier Member': The Constriction of Female Power in *Measure for Measure*," *Shakespeare Quarterly* 35 (1984): 157–69; Harriet Hawkins, in *Measure for Measure* (Boston: Twayne, 1987), 106–8; and Jonathan Dollimore, in "Transgression and Surveillance in *Measure for Measure*," in *Political Shakespeare: New Essays in Cultural Materialism*, ed. Jonathan Dollimore and Alan Sinfield, 72, 82, 86 (Ithaca and London: Cornell University Press, 1985), also provide histories of Isabella-criticism. The following critics have problems with Isabella's virginity: Ernst Schanzer, *The Problem Plays of Shakespeare: A Study of "Julius Caesar," "Measure for Measure," and "Antony and Cleopatra"* (London: Routledge and Kegan Paul, 1963), 98–99; W. L. Godshalk, *"Measure for Measure:* Freedom and Restraint," *Shake-*

speare Studies 6 (1970): 137–50; Rosalind Miles, The Problem of "Measure for Measure": A Historical Investigation (New York: Barnes and Noble, 1976), 215, 221, 225–26; Harriet Hawkins, "The Devil's Party: Virtues and Vices in Measure for Measure," Shakespeare Survey 30 (1978): 105–13; Harry V. Jaffa, "Chastity as a Political Principle: An Interpretation of Shakespeare's Measure for Measure," in Shakespeare as Political Thinker, ed. John Alvis and Thomas G. West, 182, 208 (Durham, N.C.: Carolina Academic Press, 1981); Susan Moore, "Virtue and Power in Measure for Measure," English Studies 63 (1982): 308–17; Ronald R. Macdonald, "Measure for Measure: The Flesh Made Word," Huntington Library Quarterly 53 (1990): 265–82; Carolyn E. Brown, "Erotic Religious Flagellation and Shakespeare's Measure for Measure," English Literary Renaissance 16 (1986): 139–65.

Critical opinion is divided as to whether Isabella (ever) accepts the Duke's proposal of marriage. My own opinion is that the character does not accept. Vincentino's "But fitter time for that" (5.1.504)—as well as Isabella's textual silence—would indicate her inability to "hear" his first proposal. That a second proposal (5.1.545–48) is necessary would reinforce this fact. Isabella's textual silence regarding the second proposal reinforces my belief that she never agrees. Some critics, like Riefer, see Isabella's silence as emblematic of her tragedy, while others, like David N. Beauregard, in "Isabella as a Novice: Shakespeare's Use of Whetstone's Heptameron," English Language Notes 25, no. 4 (1988): 20–23, read it as acceptance of the proposal (21). Steven Mullaney, in The Place of the Stage: License, Play and Power in Renaissance England (Chicago and London: University of Chicago Press, 1988) thinks interpretation of the silence as resistance is "questionable" and that the proposal "has become inevitable" (110). I would argue, however, that this particular silence emblematizes strength. (See also Asp, cited at 116 n. 51). The Duke cannot marry Isabella without her consent; she does not give it. Her silence, therefore, represents her choice to resist the Duke. Unlike Hermia and Helena, who are silenced as a result of marriage, Isabella uses silence to prevent marriage. My overall reactions to this play have been profoundly influenced by Dollimore's eye-opening analysis in "Transgression and Surveillance."

31. John Halkett, Milton and the Idea of Matrimony (New Haven and London: Yale University Press, 1970), 72, 83, 86–87; Kathleen M. Davies, "'The sacred condition of equality': How Original Were Puritan Doctrines of Marriage?" Social History 1–2 (1976–77): 563–80; Theodora A. Jankowski, Women in Power in the Early Modern Drama (Urbana and Chicago: University of Illinois Press, 1992), 31–36.

32. Schanzer, Problem Plays, 98; Miles, "Problem of Measure for Measure," 226; Hawkins, "The Devil's Party," 107, 109. Brown has much to say on the subject of religious flagellation. I will return to some of her points later in this section.

33. The New Catholic Encyclopedia (New York: McGraw-Hill, 1967) indicates that an individual Catholic can/must make a specific choice to retain virginity. Consequently, "accidental and involuntary loss of physical integrity (e.g., by accident, surgical operation, rape) leaves virginity, which is most essentially in the will, intact" (703). This position derives from Augustine, in St. Augustine: The City of God, Books 1–4, trans. Demetrius B. Zema, S.J., and Gerald G. Walsh, S.J. (New York: Fathers of the Church, 1950) who "affirm[s], therefore, that in case of violent rape of an unshaken intention not to yield unchaste content, the crime is attributable only to the ravisher and not at all to the ravished" (bk. 1, chap. 19, 49). Thus the essence of Isabella's vow of

virginity—and indeed her religious and personal integrity—resides in her abil-
ity to choose how, if, and to whom to bestow her physical body. This position
casts light on the critical opinions that Isabella is either emotionally cold or
blameworthy for refusing to sacrifice her virginity for Claudio's life: Moore,
"Virtue and Power," 313; Godshalk, "Freedom and Restraint," 141, 145–46;
Hawkins, "The Devil's Party," 106; Macdonald, "Flesh Made Word," 275–78;
Jaffa "Chastity," 211, 213, Barbara J. Baines, "Assaying the Power of Chastity in
Measure for Measure," *SEL* 30 (1990): 283–301. There are critics who see Isa-
bella's decision as justified: Geckle, "Shakespeare's Isabella," 163, 167, 168;
Schanzer, *Problem Plays*, 99–100; Bernice W. Kliman, "Isabella in *Measure for
Measure,*" *Shakespeare Studies* 15 (1982): 137–48, Riefer, "Instruments,"
163–64.

34. Although Baines and I agree that virginity/chastity allows Isabella the
means to claim autonomy, we differ as to how that occurs. Baines maintains that

> Isabella's values . . . are representative, not eccentric; and they are grounded more
> firmly in the secular than in the religious. Society, not scripture, defines chastity as
> the definitive virtue that gives identity and place to women and to men. . . . Thus
> chastity becomes for women a form of power; through it the woman legitimizes the
> power of the man and preserves the patriarchal social structure. (284, 286)

What I am arguing, however, is that Isabella's claiming Roman Catholic consecrated *virginity* as the source of her power *is* "eccentric" and results in her
being perceived as queer in Protestant society: an adult female virgin uncontrolled by any man. Thus her "power" serves not to support the social/cultural
status quo—as Baines argues—but to challenge the very notion of woman's
dependency upon men and men's control of women's bodies. In this, the character can be seen as belonging to the (Catholic) humanist tradition that validated a woman's right to the free choice of a husband, as demonstrated in
Henry Medwall's *Fulgens and Lucres* (ca. 1497). See the following in this context: Catherine Belsey, *The Subject of Tragedy: Identity and Difference in Renaissance Drama* (London: Methuen, 1985), 194–200; Jankowski, *Women in
Power*, 170–71.

35. See section 1, above. The "none/nun" pun reinforces this point.

36. "Deviant," in the sense of sexuality or psychologically "not normal," is
a modern usage. Medieval and early modern usage was synonymous with "de-
viate" in the sense of "deviating," "divergent," or "that [which] diverts or causes
to turn aside" *(OED)*. However, the notion of "not-woman"—also not an early
modern term—is implicit in some of the early modern derogatory terms used
to refer to women: "witch," "succubus," "wanton" (def. 2), etc. Even "sodomy"
or "buggery" could be said to define the "not-woman." Jonathan Goldberg reminds us, in *Sodometries: Renaissance Texts, Modern Sexualities* (Stanford:
Stanford University Press, 1992), that the first English sodomy law (25 Henry
VIII c.6) does not precisely define the acts that constituted "buggery" or the
genders of those performing them (3, 11). Other usages were often as unspecific.
Thomas Cooper's 1552 *Biblioteca Eliotae* simply indicates that "sodomy" is
"afaynste naturae," though never states what acts by which gender performers
are "unnatural" (cited in Gregory W. Bredbeck, *Sodomy and Interpretation:
Marlowe to Milton* [Ithaca and London: Cornell University Press, 1991], 10).
The *OED* cites Tomson's 1579 translation of one of Calvin's sermons as an
instance where "sodomite" can refer to women: "whores as they are, yea . . .
vile and shameful Sodomites, committing suche heinous and abhominable
actes, that it is horrible to thinke of." (This reference could also imply that men

are "whores.") In addition, "sodomitess" is defined as "a woman sodomite" in the Authorized Bible (Deut. 23:17), where "whore" is glossed as "sodomitess." Thomas Blount, in *Glossographia* (1670), defines "Buggerie ... [as] *carnalis copula contra naturam*," which could occur between "a man or a woman with a bruit beast, ... a man with a man, or a woman with a woman" (cited in Bredbeck, *Sodomy and Interpretation*, 17). The *OED* defines "bugger" simply as "one who commits buggery; a sodomite" (def. 2). though offers "buggeress" as "a female bugger."

37. In England, the final Act of Dissolution (of monasteries) was passed in 1539. It is important to realize that the character Isabella is represented as a Catholic novice within a Protestant, at times very anti-Catholic, social structure. Darryl F. Gless, in *"Measure for Measure," the Law, and the Convent* (Princeton: Princeton University Press, 1970), discusses the implications of this situation at length and Miles *The Problem of Measure for Measure* in less detail (216–18).

38. Frye, "Willful Virgin," 133.

39. Rosemary Curb and Nancy Manahan, eds, *Lesbian Nuns: Breaking Silence* (Tallahassee, Fla.: Naiad Press, 1985), xxvii, 369. The twentieth-century conflation of nun/virgin with lesbian is easily seen in the publication history of Curb and Manahan's book. Originally brought out by the feminist Naiad Press, the book quickly became a cause célèbre in the heterosexual mainstream. That the excitement the book generated had to do with the linking of nun and lesbian—and the male heterosexual fascination with the erotic possibilities of such a linkage—is evident from *Penthouse*'s purchase of the rights to reprint several of the book's stories. The mainstream house Warner subsequently reprinted the book at $5.95—$4.00 below the Naiad Press' price. Interestingly, Judith C. Brown's *Immodest Acts: The Life of a Lesbian Nun in Renaissance Italy* (New York and Oxford: Oxford University Press, 1986), hailed as a historical study of a previously hidden conventual "lesbian" episode, is more about ecclesiastical power struggles than the sexuality of nuns. See also Traub "(In)significance," 165–66 n. 3.

40. Andrew Marvell, *The Complete Works of Andrew Marvell*, vol. I, ed. Alexander B. Grosart (1872; reprint, New York: AMS Press, 1966), 20. All references to Marvell's poem will be to this edition and will appear in the text. The nun who forbade Thwaites access to Fairfax is identified as Lady Anna Langton (41 n).

41. The "discipline" is a "whip made of leather straps tipped in metal, small chains, or strands of knotted rope used to flagellate one's bared shoulders, thighs, or buttocks as a penance while reciting penitential psalms; begun in 13th century [or perhaps earlier] and continuing, in moderation, until recently" (Curb and Manahan, *Lesbian Nuns*, 365). The "upper discipline" involved whipping the bare back and shoulders, the "lower discipline" the bare thighs and buttocks (Brown, "Erotic Religious Flagellation" 141).

42. Brown, "Erotic Religious Flagellation" ... 141, 144, 147.

43. As Brown indicates, "The accounts [of flagellation] that did appear, and these many years after the practice's heyday, must be regarded with considerable circumspection since religious biases could easily slant a report, an adversary discrediting an opposing religion by disesteeming one of its tenets" (ibid., 45).

44. Rabelais's "Abbey of Thélèma" episode in *Gargantua and Pantagruel* (1532–52) showed how easily monks and nuns could heterosexually violate their vows of chastity in the dual monasteries. Boccaccio's *Decameron* (1471)

and [Robinson's] *The Anatomie of the English Nunnery at Lisbon in Portugal* (1623) both demonstrate how nuns arranged, against great odds, to get men into their convents.

Penelope D. Johnson's study of religious houses in France, *Equal in Monastic Profession: Religious Women in Medieval France* (Chicago and London: University of Chicago Press, 1991), examines the myth that *all* nuns were/are unchaste. Studying a number of men's and women's houses in thirteenth-century Normandy, she discovered that nuns were *not* more apt than monks to break their vows of chastity. Only a small percentage of religious did break this vow and, of those who did, both men and women offended at the same rate. Louis Crompton, in "The Myth of Lesbian Impunity: Capital Laws from 1270–1791," in *Historical Perspectives on Homosexuality*, ed. Salvatore J. Licata and Robert P. Petersen, 89–132 (New York: Haworth Press/Stein and Day, 1992), does cite one case of two sixteenth-century Spanish nuns who were burned for using "material instruments" to pleasure each other (117). This is the only case he cites that concerns nuns. Obviously I do not mean to imply that male homoeroticism did not occur between monks. That situation is not the subject of this essay.

45. Brown does not specifically consider the homoerotic possibilities of religious flagellation, but does indicate that, predictably, abbesses and abbots punished the same-gender members of their own houses ("Erotic Religious Flagellation" 144), who might then discipline each other (141). Only in double monasteries could opposite-gender flagellation easily occur. The current lesbian S/M debates have produced a large body of work that raises interesting questions/issues that can be applied to my argument. A good place to begin exploring the issues raised on both sides of the question is Carole S. Vance's collection, *Pleasure and Danger: Exploring Female Sexuality* (Routledge and Kegan Paul, 1984; reprint, London: Pandora, 1992), especially the articles by Gayle Rubin, "Thinking Sex: Notes for a Radical Theory of the Politics of Sexuality," 267–319; Kaja Silverman, "Histoire d'O: The Construction of a Female Subject," 320–49; Esther Newton and Shirley Walton, "The Misunderstanding: Toward a More Precise Sexual Vocabulary," 242–50; Paula Webster, "The Forbidden: Eroticism and Taboo," 385–98; Amber Hollibaugh, "Desire for the Future: Radical Hope in Passion and Pleasure," 401–10; and Vance's "Introduction: More Danger, More Pleasure," xvi–xxxix. See also Julia Creet, "Daughter of the Movement: The Psychodynamics of Lesbian S/M Fantasy," *differences* 3, no. 2 (1991): 135–39. As an interesting aside, "Roger Scruton [in *Sexual Desire*] subdivides perversion into bestiality, necrophilia, paedophilia, sado-masochism, homosexuality, incest, fetishism, masturbation, and *chastity*" (emphasis mine; cited in Dollimore, *Sexual Dissidence*, 175 n. 7).

46. A lack of stage directions or textual clues has made it difficult to pinpoint the social/historical location of Cavendish's play. Given her utopian propensities, she may have intended a fantasy setting. However, she may also have masked the location to destabilize the "social critique" in the play. For the sake of my argument, I have "located" the convent (and its surrounding "world") in late-seventeenth-century England.

47. Margaret Cavendish, *The Convent of Pleasure* in *Plays. Never Before Printed* (London: A. Maxwell, 1668), 7. All further references to this play will be to this edition and will appear in the text. Note: no line references appear in this edition, so each quote is identified by act, scene, and page number. The plays in this edition are individually paginated.

48. Sophie Tomlinson, "'My brain the stage': Margaret Cavendish and the Fantasy of Female Performance," in *Women, Texts and Histories, 1575–1760*, ed. Clare Brant and Diana Purkiss (London and New York: Routledge, 1992), 134–63, 154, 156.

49. Margaret Cavendish, *The Description of a New World Called the Blazing World* in *The Description of a New World Called the Blazing World and Other Writings*, ed. Kate Lilley (New York: New York University Press, 1992), 119–225, 183, 202.

50. Marilyn Williamson, *Raising Their Voices: British Women Writers, 1650–1750* (Detroit: Wayne State University Press, 1990), 62.

51. Margaret Cavendish, *Poems and Phancies, written by the Thrice Noble, Illustrious, and Excellent Princess the Lady Marchioness of Newcastle*, the Second Impression, Much Altered and Corrected (London: William Wilson, 1664), 159. I have quoted selected lines from this poem and the ones below. The "blazon" is, of course, a figure often used by male poets to enable their male speakers to reflect upon the erotic possibilities of women's bodies. In addition to using the figure as a female poet, Cavendish makes the described bodies the visual focus of qualities personified as female. The "bisk" is for Nature's—gendered female—table. She creates similar erotic female blazons in "A Tart":

> Then did she [Life] take some Lips like Cherries Red,
> And Sloe-black Eyes from fair Virgin's Head,
> And Strawb'ry Teats from th' Banks of each white Breast,
> And Fingers ends like Juice from Raspers prest; . . .
> . . . This Meat did Nature much commend,
>
> (161)

and "Nature's Landskip":

> Then I a Garden did of Beauty view,
> Where sweet Complexion's Rose and Lilly grew;
> And on the Banks of Breasts most perfect there
> Did violets of Azure-Veins appear;
> Lips of fresh Gilly-flowers grew up high,
> Which oft the Sun did Kiss as he pass'd by;
> Hands of Narcissus shew'd most perfect white,
> Whose Palms fine Tulips were streak'd with Delight.
>
> (177–78)

52. Halkett, *Milton and Matrimony*, 52.

53. The Prince(ss) is clearly described in several stage directions as appearing in male clothing. Stage directions specify only male clothing for virgins during two of the plays-within-the-play (3.1, p. 23; 4.1, pp. 34, 38–39).

54. For analyses of butch-femme roles/relations and gender roles in general as "performance," see Case, "Tracking the Vampire"; Joan Nestle, "The Femme Question," in *Pleasure and Danger: Exploring Female Sexuality*, ed. Carole S. Vance (Routledge and Kegan Paul, 1984; reprint, London: Pandora, 1992), 232–41, Butler, *Gender Trouble*, 17, 21–29 and "Imitation"; and Rubin, "Thinking Sex."

55. Since it appeared in the 1668 edition of Cavendish's plays, *The Convent of Pleasure* could have been written after the 1662 appearance of the first woman actor on the Reformation stage. Most critics, however, believe that all of Cavendish's plays were written during the Interregnum: Douglas Grant, *Mar-*

garet the First: A Biography of Margaret Cavendish, Duchess of Newcastle, 1623–1673 (London: Rupert Hart-Davis, 1957), 161; Jean Elisabeth Gagen, The New Woman: Her Emergence in the English Drama, 1600–1730 (New York: Twayne, 1954), 32; Linda R. Payne, "Dramatic Dreamscape: Women's Dreams and Utopian Vision in the Works of Margaret Cavendish, Duchess of Newcastle," in Curtain Calls: British and American Women and the Theater, 1660–1820, ed. Mary Anne Schofield and Cecilia Macheski, 18–33, 30 (Athens: Ohio University Press, 1991); Kathleen Jones, A Glorious Fame: The Life of Margaret Cavendish, Duchess of Newcastle, 1623–1673 (London: Bloomsbury, 1988), 130; Tomlinson "My brain the Stage,'" 137. But even if they were, the circumstances of Cavendish's own life would indicate that she probably had women actors in mind.

In 1643, she became a maid of honor to Charles I's queen Henrietta Maria, a woman who performed in masques and court dramas and "turned female acting into a fashionable and controversial issue . . . and inspired a growth in women's participation in private theatricals which continued into the Interregnum years" (Tomlinson, "'My brain the Stage,'" 138, 137). Cavendish then followed the court to Paris, where she had the opportunity to see professional women actors there and, later, in Antwerp (ibid., 139, 134–35, 140; Henry Ten Eyck Perry, The First Duchess of Newcastle and Her Husband as Figures in Literary History [Boston and London: Ginn, 1918; reprint, London and New York: Johnson Reprint, 1968], 50, 54, 52.) Yet despite such compelling evidence of her own compiling, Tomlinson claims "it is not my intention to suggest that Cavendish's plays were written for women actors" (140).

It is doubtful, however, that Cavendish's plays were ever acted, and many critics claim they are basically "unactable" (Perry, First Duchess, 214; Grant, Margaret the First, 161; Gagen, New Woman, 32–34; Jones, Glorious Fame, 130; Payne, "Dramatic Dreamscape," 30). Although Cavendish occasionally explains why her plays are not produced, it is generally accepted that their primary staging was to be internal.

> for I did take
> Much pleasure and delight these Playes to make;
> For all the time my Playes a making were,
> My brain the Stage, my thoughts were acting there
> (Cavendish, Playes (1662), cited in Tomlinson, "My brain the Stage," 136; Perry, First Duchess, 213)

56. See the following on the erotic possibilities and gender-destabilizing effects of cross-dressing on the male-only Elizabethan/Jacobean stage: Lisa Jardine, "As boys and women are for the most part cattle of this colour': Female Role and Elizabethan Eroticism," in Still Harping on Daughters: Women and Drama in the Age of Shakespeare (New York: Columbia University Press, 1989), 9–36; Stephen Orgel, "Nobody's Perfect: Or Why Did the English Stage Take Boys for Women?" South Atlantic Quarterly 88, no. 1 (1989): 7–29; Laura Levine, "Men in Women's Clothing: Anti-Theatricality and Effeminization from 1579–1642," Criticism 28 (1986): 121–43; and Steve Brown, "The Boyhood of Shakespeare's Heroines: Notes on Gender Ambiguity in the Sixteenth Century," Studies in English Literature 30 (1990): 243–63.

57. The "softening" of act 3's condemnation of marriage could also have resulted from Cavendish's own unusually happy union. Hilda Smith, in Reason's Disciples: Seventeenth-Century English Feminists (Urbana, Chicago, London: University of Illinois Press, 1982), points out that her husband "en-

couraged her in all her intellectual pursuits and spent great sums on books for her to read and the costs of her publications" (91, 85–86). Cavendish's own inability to have children also spared her many of the health problems married women had to suffer (89–90).

A number of Cavendish's other works similarly reify marriage. The heroine of "Assaulted and Pursued Chastity" (1656), in *The Description of a New World Called the Blazing World and Other Writings*, ed. Kate Lilley (New York: New York University Press, 1992), 45–118, spends virtually the entire text escaping from a Prince who "was a grand monopolizer of young virgins" (50). Despite various adventures and near-death experiences, she ultimately marries the Prince—once he is free to do so—and lives happily ever after. The act of marriage clearly erases whatever animosity the heroine may have justifiably felt toward her Prince. Similarly, in *The Blazing World*, the Empress is willing to forget the trials of her abduction by the merchant to marry the Emperor. And despite the "platonic" affection between the Empress and the Duchess (Cavendish's persona), both women are presented as happily married to their respective spouses.

58. We would "see" *only* "men"-women couples if there were an equal number of (proto-)butches and (proto-)femmes. A small number of (proto-)butches would allow the possibility of (proto-)femme-femme couples in the background, further destabilizing the "heterosexual" impulses of the (proto-)butch-femme and Prince(ss)–Lady Happy pairings.

59. In "The scorne of Savage people."

Puritanism in Comic History: Exposing Royalty in the Henry Plays

GRACE TIFFANY

SINCE THE publication of Jonas Barish's seminal *The Anti-theatrical Prejudice* in 1981, it has become a truism in Renaissance studies that English Puritans despised English theater.[1] However, though it is undeniable that many Puritan moralists condemned the "chappel of Satan," as Anthony Munday called the London playhouse,[2] the relationship of many "precise" Protestants, or Puritans, to late-sixteenth- and early seventeenth-century theatrical entertainment was complex and ambivalent. Although Puritan ministers like John Rainholds opposed all theater, branding "all stage-players generally with infamie,"[3] others were more tolerant. As both Paul White and David Bevington have shown, many early radical Protestants and first- and second-generation Puritans, such as John Bale and Munday, fought hard not to destroy but to transform London theatrical entertainment.[4] These men feared the naturalistic stage representation of vice, which, in Munday's words, made "both the actors and the beholders giltie alike," since while audience members "saie[d] nought, but gladlie looke[d] on, they al by sight and assent [were] actors."[5] Therefore some Puritans sought to replace dramatizations of evil with stagings of virtuous behavior. For example, despite his round condemnations in the 1590s and early 1600s of the licentiousness of playhouses, Anthony Munday was himself a playwright who sought, with the Admiral's Men, to produce moral drama that expressed and supported the growing Puritan temper of Renaissance London. Plays like *Sir John Oldcastle* and the Earl of Huntingdon series, written primarily by Munday and produced close to 1600, glorified Puritan martyrs like Oldcastle—an early-fifteenth-century Lollard burned at the stake for his allegedly heretical views—and expressed a low-church anticlericalism.

We cannot logically assume that sympathetic audiences were lacking for these successful plays, for Puritan influence was spreading through England in the 1580s and 1590s, during which time many of the godly migrated "from provincial villages to towns and cities, London especially," as the historian Douglas Tallack notes.[6] It is difficult to categorize the Puritans of this time according to the sectarian divisions that became distinct in the seventeenth century, when Puritans gradually gave up hope for achieving the reforms they wanted within the national Church. In the sixteenth century, Puritan impulses toward Anabaptism, Congregationalism, and Presbyterianism were variously experienced and championed by a variety of churchgoing English people and their pastors who still, in the words of Arthur J. Klein, "regarded themselves as part of the Anglican establishment."[7] Patrick Collinson writes of the popularity of the low-church movement among members of Elizabeth's court as well as the general public, due not only to eloquent Puritan preaching but to "the sustained influence of puritan masters, tutors, and lecturers" in the university towns from the 1560s on.[8] Members of the resultant Puritan "church within a church," as Collinson calls it,[9] were widely dispersed in the London population, and many of these had not yet abandoned the playhouses, despite the pamphlets and sermons that reformers and divines were beginning to direct against the stage.[10]

Perceiving the Puritans as diverse constituents of the London Renaissance theater audience rather than as a uniform, self-marginalized antitheatrical group is essential to our appreciation of the Puritan as represented by Shakespeare. Shakespearean Puritans were sometimes reprehensible and often extremists, but were never unsympathetically rendered or wholly unattractive. That they were not was probably not only the result of Shakespeare's large-mindedness, but of the hard economic fact that increasing numbers of Londoners were coming to think and behave the Puritan way, and that the Puritan segment of the public had a measure of box office clout.

Nowhere is this fact more evident than in the recorded circumstances of Shakespeare's change of the *Henriad's* Sir John Oldcastle's name to Sir John Falstaff. In his flouting of various types of authority, Shakespeare's "Oldcastle" bears some resemblance to the historical John Oldcastle, Lord Cobham, a proto-Puritan who was martyred during Henry V's reign for his resistance to episcopal authority.[11] But soon after the play's earliest staging Shakespeare changed the character's name. As Kristen Poole has shown, though

Shakespeare scholars "have almost universally claimed that the name-change was the direct result of protests by William Brooke, Lord Cobham," Oldcastle's powerful descendant, "we have only circumstantial, secondhand evidence of [Brooke's] opposition."[12] As Poole also notes, Thomas Pendleton more persuasively argues that "The change from 'Oldcastle' to 'Falstaff' seems to have been motivated ... much more ... by the displeasure of a significant part of Shakespeare's audience at his treatment of a hero of their religion."[13] Thus Shakespeare's epilogue's claim in 2 Henry IV that "Oldcastle died a martyr, and this [Falstaff] is not the man" (line 32) seeks to pacify those playgoers who venerated the memory of a radical Protestant "saint."

Presumably such playgoers were offended by the representation of a rollicking, drunken Oldcastle (based partly on the Oldcastle of the anonymous Famous Victories of Henry V, produced some years before Shakespeare's Henry plays). And presumably their opinions were powerful enough to occasion Shakespeare's diplomatic retraction of Oldcastle's name. However, here I will argue not only that Shakespeare did intend Falstaff to be an exaggerated representation of both Oldcastle and contemporary Puritans, but that this representation embodied some of the tremendous affective power of Puritan ideas and practices. This is not to say that through the amusing figure of Falstaff, Shakespeare was urging popular acceptance of a carnivalesque Puritanism. To the contrary, Henry IV concludes with the clear suggestion that Falstaffian influence, whatever its attractions, is politically and morally dangerous, and will be rejected by a sane commonwealth. However, Falstaff's skill at undermining the theatrical fictions on which England's governing systems depended leaves even contemporary audiences uneasy at his dismissal. Perhaps Falstaff's attractive subversiveness left late-sixteenth-century audiences more generously disposed to the Puritans' leveling project than Shakespeare consciously intended.

A similar argument has recently been advanced by Kristen Poole, who links Falstaff with the anti-Puritan caricatures of satires penned in the 1580s by John Lyly, Robert Greene, and Thomas Nashe. These satires were commissioned by an anxious prelacy in response to the Puritan-authored "Martin Marprelate" tracts, anonymous pamphlets that had begun appearing on the London streets in 1589. The Martin Marprelate pamphlets mocked the Anglican hierarchs and even questioned the queen's headship of the church. In Poole's words, the Marprelate pamphlets "confronted the bishops with a new breed of ecclesiastical enemy: the puritan wit."[14] The bishops' and the queen's remedy, the satirical rebuttals of hired guns Lyly, Greene, and Nashe known as the anti-Marprelate tracts, lampooned the Marprelate authors and marked "the entrance of the puritan figure into popular literature."[15] To the amusement of Londoners, satires flew back and forth between the anonymous "Martinists" and their conservative enemies Nashe, Lyly, and Greene from 1589 through early 1590. Targeting the bishops and occasionally the queen, the Martinists protested against the corrupt and invasive hierarchy that imposed increasingly unpopular religious practices on the English people. The anti-Martinists retaliated by ridiculing "Martin" and Puritans in general, depicting them as anarchic, self-aggrandizing, hypocritical windbags. Quoting extensively from Nashe's, Lyly's, and Greene's anti-Martin Marprelate tracts, Kristin Poole shows that the view of the Puritan they promoted was not one of "the lean, mean Malvolio . . . that post-Restoration readers and audiences . . . would exclusively associate with the term *puritan*." Instead, these satires presented "puritans as grotesque individuals living in carnivalesque communities"—an image to which Falstaff clearly conforms.[16] Like the anti-Marprelate tracts' disorderly caricatures of Puritan Martin, a gluttonous clown who distorts law and would topple the state's institutionalized hierarchies, Shakespeare's Falstaff embodies chaos in his "Bakhtinian grotesque body," wherein "death, birth, sex, and bodily functions are often simultaneous and inextricable"[17] (Falstaff appears to die in 1 *Henry IV* but does not, and was "born . . . with a white head" [1.2.187–88]).[18] While Poole acknowledges that the Elizabethans probably disapproved of a Puritan outlaw who "respect[ed] neither rank nor hierarchy,"[19] she observes that Lyly's, Greene's, and Nashe's carnivalesque caricatures of Martin gained attractiveness when, transformed into Falstaff, they migrated from page to stage. On stage "the legacy of Martin's popular appeal overwhelms the pressures of satire, and the audience finds itself . . . laughing with the target of the attack."[20]

This is undeniably so. It is impossible for playgoers to watch Falstaff's tricks without engaging, to a degree, in the imaginative participation in vice that Puritans like Munday feared "made both the actors and the beholders giltie alike." Thus late-Elizabethan audiences may not only have been seduced into approving Falstaff's vices by the theatrical dazzlement deplored by Puritan antitheatricalists. Ironically, these audiences may also have been encouraged to identify Falstaff's vices with Puritanism.

Such a representation of Puritanism was not, in itself, likely to take the low-church cause anywhere its serious proponents wanted to go. But Falstaff performs a compensatory function that even ardent low churchmen and churchwomen might well have appreciated, for he exposes the theatrical unreality of the dignities of office that Elizabethan Puritans were beginning to condemn. Mocking the lord chief justiceship and, ultimately, the monarchy (though, interestingly, not the chief target of Puritan attacks, the prelacy—a point that I will ultimately address), Falstaff demonstrates the illusoriness of claims to hereditary authority and to authority bestowed by hereditary monarchs. His subversion operates on two levels. In obvious ways, Falstaff embodies the danger of both Oldcastle and the sixteenth-century German religious reformer Thomas Munzer, both of whom led disenfranchised peasants and townsmen in famous rebellions. As did Oldcastle and Munzer, Falstaff leads a troop of ragged "slaves" and "ostlers trade-fall'n" to battle (1 Henry IV 4.2.25, 29), and so evokes, despite the ostensibly royalist cause for which he fights, a vision of the kind of "Munzer's commonwealth" that conservative sixteenth-century English people feared.[21] But Falstaff's true antihierarchical subversiveness lies deeper than these superficial images of popular revolt, and is bound to his language and behavior even in the plays' peaceful scenes. In those, against the Henriad's rhetoric of divine right—articulated by Bishop Carlisle in Richard II (4.1.121–49) and ultimately embraced by Henry V (2 Henry IV 5.2.129–33)—Falstaff acts out the powerful suggestion that the king is not the man born for the task, but the man who currently plays the role. Thus the theory underlying the nonparliamentary apparatus of state power, including justices and prelates appointed by the monarch, is destabilized through Falstaff's festive play.[22] And this destabilization, despite the regard Elizabethan Puritans cautiously expressed for Elizabeth, was one of Puritanism's ultimate goals.[23] Thus Falstaff does something to advance Elizabethan Puritans' interests. Staging a version of Puritan antitheatricalism, he turns comedy against itself, using theatrical rhetoric and behavior to expose the histrionics of monarchs and magistrates. Falstaff's moral hollowness, in other words, is balanced by his exposure to the hollowness of royal claims to authority.

Falstaff's theatrical exposure of royal theatrics depends crucially on a technique that was becoming increasingly associated with Puritanism in the 1580s and 1590s: sophistical argument. Patrick Collinson writes of how in the late 1580s, Puritan lawyers "were able to parade a useful array of legal quibbles to confuse the processes of ecclesiastical discipline" and defend low-church practices (such as Sabbatarianism).[24] Falstaff, as I will show, is a past master of such legal casuistry, which he performs in a rhetorical style redolent of Puritanical argumentation and preaching. Yet this sophistical brilliance does not damn his character as the play's pious hypocrite (an identity that the anti-Marprelate tracts strove to fashion for the Puritan Martin). While Falstaff's obvious sophistry calls his "truth" into question, his slippery argumentative skills become part of his comic charm. Further, we see Falstaffian sophistry, a kind of verbal histrionicism, borrowed and perfected by Prince Hal. Hal ultimately enfolds sophistry into his repertoire of royal stage tricks, performing the role of repentant crown prince in *2 Henry IV* and king in *2 Henry IV* and *Henry V* with consummate verbal skill. Thus even Falstaff's morally suspect "Puritan" features contribute to the plays' overall destabilization of monarchy's claims to intrinsic authority: that is, to authority that is inborn rather than theatrically performed.

There was, then, something for everyone in the *Henriad*. The plays support skepticism toward both radical and conservative theories of governance alike. Despite their ostensible rejection of the Puritan leveling impulse embodied by Falstaff, whose theatrics and familiarity with the prince reduce (in audience imagination at least) ranked hierarchical structures to rubble, the plays' political moral is ambiguous. The *Henriad* leaves audiences with a choice: smug disapproval of Puritan chaos or skepticism regarding a state hierarchy that depends from a sophistical, playacting monarch, no matter how skillful and even virtuous one such monarch may be.

I

The carnivalesque Puritan is, as Kristen Poole notes, unfamiliar to readers used to the image of the dour Puritan spoilsport, despite "the fact that the official [American] holiday celebrating puritans is one of nationwide gluttony."[25] And it is, indeed, difficult to replace the sober Malvolio—called "a kind of puritan" by Maria, though she then retracts the charge (*Twelfth Night* 2.3.140, 147)—with the Falstaffian Toby Belch as our vision of the Shakespearean Puritan. After all, Malvolio, who condemns festive celebration, is a stereotype justified (if any are justified) by radical Elizabethan and Jacobean Puritans' published diatribes against "cursed mirth,"[26] "New-yeares-gifts," "Christmas-keeping," and "May-games."[27]

Yet the carnivalesque or "Bahktinian" Puritan was a caricature naturally attractive to the conservative anti-Marprelate authors, who feared that reforms called for in the Marprelate and other Puritan tracts, as well as by famous preachers such as John Field, Thomas Wilcox, and Edward Dering, would wreak a different kind of mayhem by leveling the institutions that ordered England. "The *Martinists*," wrote a disapproving Thomas Nashe, "seeke to drawe every place in this Campe royall [England] to an equalitie with themselves."[28] While no such radical project was explicitly articulated by Martin, Martin's attacks on the bishops yet implied a disregard for social and political rank that suggested his general hostility to the unelected elements of English government. In *Theses Martinianae*, for example, Martin radically proposes "That the places of lord bishops are neither warranted by the word of God, nor by anie lawfull humane constitutions"; "That the governement of the church of England, by lord archbishops and bishops, is not a church governement set downe in the worde, or which can be defended to be Gods ordinance"; and "That the gouvernement of lord archbishops and bishops is unlawefull, notwithstanding it bee mainteined, and in force by humane lawes and ordinances."[29] These pseudonymously expressed Puritan views reiterated those earlier set forth in Field and Wilcox's 1572 *Admonition to the Parliament*, which complained of any appointment to clerical office that depended on the authority of queen or bishop rather than "the common consent of the whole church"[30] (remarks for which Field was ultimately jailed).[31] As John Lyly wrote in one anti-Marprelate tract, *Pappe with an Hatchet*, such attacks on the Anglican hierarchy and championings of the masses amounted to putting "Religion into a fooles coate."[32] Similarly, Nashe likened these projected social levelings to holiday foolery, calling them "the May-game of Martinisme."[33] Thus, though Puritans focused their attacks on Church rather than secular government, their antiestablishmentarianism was easily associated with the threat of a permanent "May-game," or national carnival: the chaotic obliteration of all class rank, as well as of government offices not designed and filled by communal consensus.

With its characteristic ambivalence, Shakespeare's *Henriad* registers both Anglican dismay at the prospect of such chaotic leveling and Puritan skepticism regarding the institutionalized alternatives. Prince Hal's observation that "If all the year were playing holidays, /

To sport would be as tedious as to work" (*1 Henry IV* 1.2.204–5) is from one perspective deeply conservative. Delivered in a speech predicting his eventual rejection of Falstaff, the speech seems to express disapproval of the permanent Puritan heyday implied by Falstaff's scanting of rank: the Levelers' chaos represented by the fat knight's disrespect toward all royally authorized persons, from the lord chief justice to the "rascal" Prince of Wales (2.2.18) to the king himself (whom Falstaff rudely interrupts in part 1, act 5 [5.1.28]). However, Hal's speech, when closely attended to, actually *encourages* a Falstaffian irreverence for royal authority, for Hal's reference to the tedium of a yearlong holiday finally points not to Falstaff's tiresomeness, but to the tiresomeness of displaying his own royal character for sustained periods of time. In this way the prince justifies his immersion in Falstaff's holiday world. The references to holiday, which superficially discredit the Boar's Head revelers, are thus deeply connected to Hal's anticipation of his own future royal performances. This early use of an image proper to the tavern world to describe the arena of royal theater begins to merge the worlds in audience imagination. That is, Falstaffian play begins, in Hal's own language, to describe royal play as well, and hence to undermine the seriousness of images of monarchical authority. The endless May Day, it would seem, is threatened by the performances of the monarch, no less than by the "Munzer's Commonwealth" threatened by Falstaff.

The identification of the ranked establishment with carnival chaos was not (as I will show) a Shakespearean innovation, but one made a decade earlier by Martin Marprelate. For the most part, however, English fears of chaotic political innovations focused on the Puritans no less than on the Catholic threat, from the 1570s on. The Puritan push toward what seemed, to staunch Anglicans, an indiscriminate authorization of all voices on issues of moral import was described in a letter from George Carleton, a Northamptonshire Puritan gentleman, to Lord Burghley, the queen's secretary, in 1572. Carleton speaks of "a great people, daily increasing," who "consist of all degrees from the nobility to the lowest. . . . This people, as they do not like the course of our Church, so they do and will practise assemblies of brethren in all parts of this realm."[34]

This dangerous subversion of hierarchy by united "brethren" included the influence of outspoken women like Jane Minors of Barking, who left her churching rite complaining that it "was a ceremony."[35] The early-seventeenth-century Puritan minister Thomas Carew, of St. Margaret's parish in Essex, reputedly preached that "it was not lawfull for princes nor magistrates to have any government in the discipline of the church," but that church government should involve "widows, elders and deacons."[36] In London, at St. Anne's Blackfriars, the popular Puritan preacher Stephen Egerton led a congregation composed "mostly of merchant's wives . . . drawn from all parts of the city."[37] In Anthony Munday's Huntingdon plays, which championed Robin Hood as an egalitarian Puritan hero, Robin's equal relationship with Maid Marian reflected and encouraged the increased stature of women in Puritan assemblies.[38] (Fond of the figure of "Robin Hood" of Huntingdon,[39] Munday in his 1600 *Sir John Oldcastle, Part 1*, presented Oldcastle as another Robin Hood type, stressing Oldcastle's alignment with the poor and his partnership with his wife in championing peasant causes.)[40] In fact, as Collinson notes, the Martin Marprelate operation was largely financed by women, such as Elizabeth Crane of East Molesey, whose home for some time housed Martin's printing press.[41]

The key role women played in the Puritan movement is surprising given the simultaneous Puritan attacks on "feminizing" corrosiveness of certain kinds of social entertainments and practices, like "lascivious effeminate Musicke" and men's wearing of "Periwigs"[42] (attacks delivered by Munday himself, along with later Puritan authors like William Prynne).[43] But however resistant some Puritans were to such "feminizations," the Puritan movement as a whole was generous to females themselves—a fact usually overlooked by critics of Renaissance literature, if not by historians.

Certainly sixteenth-century Puritans were mocked by their enemies for the place and privilege they gave to women in their churches. Thomas Nashe goes so far as to charge Puritan Martin with androgyny, in a sentence that mocks the Maid Marian of Puritan legend: in Martin's "May-game," "Martin himselfe is the Maydmarian, trimly drest uppe in a cast Gowne, and a kercher of Dame Lawsons, his face handsomlie muffled with a Diaper-napkin to cover his beard."[44] Shakespeare released this image's comic potential by staging something much like it in *The Merry Wives of Windsor*, when Falstaff dons a woman's gown to escape the jealous inquiries of Master Ford, but fails to hide his beard: "I spy a great peard [beard] under his muffler," one onlooker observes (4.2.194). (Falstaff of the Henry plays has androgynous aspects as well: of his girth, he complains, "My womb, my womb, my womb undoes me" [*2 Henry IV* 4.3.22].) The gender-inclusive constituency of Puritan assemblies is also mockingly alluded to in *2 Henry IV*, when Prince

Hal's page likens the Boar's Head tavern, where Falstaff resides, to the meeting place of "Ephesians . . . of the old church" (2.2.150): that is, to the primitive church that Puritan congregations strove to emulate.[45] "Sup any women with him?" the prince asks, and is told, "None, my lord, but old Mistress Quickly and Mistress Doll Tearsheet" (lines 151–53). Like Hal's speech on "playing holiday," this dialogue cuts two ways. From one perspective, the page's lines grant a mock moral dignity to Falstaff and his heterogeneous crew by likening them to the primitive Christians; from another, they degrade Puritan meeting places by comparing them to ale shops and brothels, and impugning the characters of the women who frequent them (as well as those of the men). Yet, as Poole has suggested, the transfer of the anti-Puritan satire from page to Shakespearean stage unleashes its comedy and encourages audiences to join in Puritan "carnival revelries," despite these revelries' moral suspiciousness.

In his anti-Marprelate tracts, Thomas Nashe mocks both the female presumption encouraged by Puritan congregations and the involvement of lowly artisans at Puritan meetings. He recounts that at "an assemblie of the brotherhood at Ashford in Kent" which he visited,

> The roome was full of Artificers, men and women, that sat rounde about uppon stooles and benches to harken to [the Scripture reading]. The Chapter was, the I. Cor. 3, which being read, the reader began first to utter his conceit upon the Text, in short notes; then it came to his next neighbours course, and so in order Glosses went a begging, and Expositions ranne a pace through the Table.

Asked to give his own gloss of Scripture when his turn came, Nashe reports, he at first refused but then "spake among them," and the result of the experience was that he "needed no Minstrill to make me merrie, my hart tickled of it selfe."[46] Thus the proceedings of the godly assembly, comically (from Nashe's perspective) involving the participation of lower-class craftsmen and women in the high pursuit of scriptural interpretation, are likened by Nashe to a festive minstrel show. Such mockery of the carnivalesque empowerment of the lower classes in Puritan assemblies is, in fact, pervasive in Nashe's anti-Marprelate texts. "Where had this [Martinesque] brable his first beginning but in some obscure corner . . . in the land, in shoppes, in stalles, in the Tynker's budget, the Taylors sheares, and the Shepheardes Tarboxe?" Nashe sneers in *The Returne of Pasquill*.[47] In *A Countercuffe Given to Martin Junior*, he jokes, "I can bring you a Free-mason out of Kent, that gave over his occupation twentie yeeres agoe. He will make a good Deacon for your purpose: I have taken some tryall of his gifts; he preecheth very pretilie over a Joynd-stoole."[48]

Again, the Puritan-like social leveling Nashe mocks is dramatized in the Henriad's Boar's Head scenes, especially in the sustained saturnalia in 1 Henry IV 2.4 and 2 Henry IV 2.4. In the former scene Hal declares himself "sworn brother to a leash of drawers" (tapsters) and Falstaff ("false staff") plays king from a "join'd-stool" throne (lines 6–7, 380). In the latter scene a disguised Hal waits on Falstaff at dinner ("From a prince to a prentice?" Hal exults beforehand, "a low transformation!" [2 Henry IV 2.2.175–76]). And again, the anti-Puritan mockery loses its edge in Shakespeare, as the audience shares Hal's delight in the carnivalesque subversion of rank and power.

These Shakespearean subversions, it might be argued, take place in a comic tavern world separate from the field of hard human striving: the court and the battlegrounds to which Hal is continually pulled, and to which he finally submits as he accepts his role as king. Thus the audience sympathy generated for Falstaff might be thought carefully limited by Falstaff's own restricted power within the play. When Hal finally accepts his authority over Falstaff, this argument runs, the audience accepts it as well: when, as Henry V, Hal rejects the knight ("I know ye not, old man" [2 Henry IV 5.5.47]), we reject him too, along with the Puritan social revolution he has embodied. Such a containment of Puritan subversiveness, to adapt Stephen Greenblatt's term,[49] might be said to be accomplished by As You Like It as well. In that play—in some ways analogous to Munday's Huntingdon plays, that featured Robin Hood as proto-Puritan champion[50]—Shakespeare displaces a duke and his court to the Arden forest, where they live in an egalitarian community "like the old Robin Hood of England" (1.1.116). The Arden Green World dignifies workers like Corin, a "true laborer" who "earn[s] that [he] eat[s]" (3.2.73–74). This world also empowers women, like the cross-dressed Rosalind, who buys property near the forest (2.4.88–100). But though social positions and even gender roles are enjoyably suspended in this wilderness, the suspension is necessarily temporary. Rosalind must resume her submissive femininity to marry Orlando, and the comedy ends with the old duke preparing to return to his lands and to the old gradations of power (5.4.163–65). Thus, historical-comic and comic representations of female and lower-class self-governance are, in Shakespeare, holiday diversions from normal life: short-lived, as all holidays should be. According to this argument, espoused by Louis Montrose,[51] these plays could not have inspired sympathy for the Puritan communities that their comic communities invoked, since these "leveled" communities were desirable only insofar as they were temporary. "If all the year were playing holidays, / To sport would be as tedious as to work."

But this argument does not take into account the growing criticism of traditional systems of rank that increasingly characterized the left-leaning Elizabethan public and a large portion of the theater audience as well. To approve the restored power of kings and dukes, audiences must approve of royal and ducal power in the first place. As I have begun to show, increasingly, Puritans in the audience no longer did—or at least disapproved of the extent of powers invested in such manmade offices. Specifically, from the 1570s on Puritans expressed resistance to the queen's authority in religious matters—matters that pertained to crucial aspects of her subjects' lives, including tithing, church attendance, and, as noted, the rights of common men and women to speak in assemblies. George Carleton wrote that the growing Puritan congregations, "as they hate[d] all heresies and popery, so they [could not] be persuaded to bear liking of the queen's proceedings in religion."[52] Martin Marprelate himself directly (though pseudonymously) questioned the queen's authority in these crucial matters, asking his opponents, "doe you thinke our Churche governement to be good and lawfull because hir Maiestie and the state who maintaineth the reformed religion alloweth the fame? Why, the Lorde doth not allow it; therefore it cannot be lawfull."[53]

Nashe satirized the Martinists' alleged designs against monarchical power in *The Returne of Pasquill*, warning that "at the next pushe, Martin and his companions might overthrow the state and make the Emperiall crowne of her Maiestie kisse the ground."[54] Perhaps Nashe was right: the 1601 rebellion of the earl of Essex, whose connection to Martin Marprelate was rumored, was reputedly tied to "the Calvinist doctrine that the lesser magistrates had a right to restrain princes." The revival of Shakespeare's *Richard II* is famously associated with Essex's Puritanically minded revolt, and, as Patrick Collinson notes, on the Sunday after the rebellion "not only [the Puritan pastor Stephen] Egerton but two other leading puritans, Anthony Wotton of Tower Hill, Essex's chaplain, and Edward Phillips, preacher at St. Saviour's, Southwark, failed to deliver from their pulpits the official account and condemnation of the rebellion."[55] These acts of defiance reflected the progressive disillusionment with the queen that many Puritans felt after the 1584 Parliament, during which she had failed to honor their interests.[56] Though Lyly and Nashe (whose anti-Marprelate tracts were state-subsidized) condemned all such slightings of monarchical authority, even the conservative bishop John Jewel preached of the monarchy's conditional legitimacy and the queen's consequent responsibility to her subjects:

> The people of Babylon built themselves a Tower as high as the heavens, to shew forth their pryde, and get themselves a name. Hereof David sayth, the kinges of the earth band themselves, and the Princes are assembled together against the Lord, and against his Christ. He sayeth not, the vulgar people, or a sort of Raskals onely, but Kinges and Princes, and they which beare authoritye in the worlde, assemble themselves against the Lord, and in this power they think they are invincible.[57]

In short, the Elizabethan population was familiar with suggestions from various quarters of the precariousness of royal claims to authority, and thus of the claims to authority of all prelates and courtiers installed by monarchical fiat. Hence, it is logical to suppose Shakespeare's audience's openness to—if not outright approval of—the staged leveling of such structures, which was the carnivalesque achievement of the comic history plays. Further, it is likely that *Henry IV* and *Henry V* supported the more radical members of their audiences in their skepticism regarding the privileges of rank, by presenting royalty not as a divinely bestowed quality, but as a special kind of stage show: one that depended on rhetorical skill of the very kind displayed by John Falstaff.

II

John Bale's 1544 account of the martyrdom of Sir John Oldcastle—next to Foxe's *Acts and Monuments*, the most popular sixteenth-century source of the story—presents a hero who is superficially as different from the anti-Marprelate caricatures of Puritans and from Shakespeare's licentious Falstaff as he could be. Though, as Bale recounts, Oldcastle was *accused* in the early-fifteenth century of having condemned "the order of priesthood," he was no such enemy of hierarchies or leader of rebellious masses. Instead, says Bale, though Oldcastle condemned the pope, he stressed that it was the duty of the "common people" to "bear their good minds and true obedience to the . . . ministers of God, their kings, civil governors, and priests." Thus, according to Bale, the bishops who tried Oldcastle distorted his words to convict him of blasphemy and treason, using not truth, but "their wits and sophistry."[58] Bale thus lays sophistry, the self-serving manipulation of words, to the charge of the tyrannical bishops serving King Henry V. A similar complaint was lodged by John Foxe, whose account of Oldcastle's martyrdom refers to the inquisitorial prelates as "subtle sorcerers" whose "common practice" was "to blear the eyes of the unlearned multitude with one false craft or other."[59]

Following the Protestant martyrologists Foxe and Bale,[60] The Martin Marprelate tracts accused not only bishops but their defenders of sophistry, writing in one tract that an anti-Marprelate author has given invalid "reasons for the defence of [his] hierarchie" and has ignored crucial points of Martin's antibishop argument in an attempt to rebut it:

> he [Martin's antagonist, presumably Greene and Lyly or Nashe] might (if he had any learning in him or had read anything) know that every . . . logician giveth this for an inviolable precept that the conclusion is not to be denied. For that must needs be true if the major and minor be true. He in omitting the major and minor because he was not able to answer thereby granteth the conclusion [that bishops have no lawful standing] to be true.[61]

In a reversal that would become characteristic of the Marprelate controversy, however, the anti-Marprelate authors turned the charge of sophistry back on Martin in particular and on Puritans in general. In their "I'm rubber, you're glue" style of argument, the anti-Marprelate tracts responded to Puritan criticism of English May games by attacking the "May-game of Martinisme." Similarly, they responded to Puritan charges of Anglican sophistry by criticizing the Puritans' own style of argument and by incorporating a tendency for casuistical quibbling into the Martin caricatures on which Shakespeare would partly base Falstaff.[62] Lyly disclaims all logic in his attack on Martin in *Pappe with an Hatchet* since (as he claims) the Martinists themselves abandon logical disputation. Thus,

> [s]eeing that either [Puritans] expect no grave replie, or that they are settled with railing to replie; I thought it more convenient, to give them a whisk with their owne wand, than to have them spurd with deeper learning. . . . if here I have used bad tearmes, it is because they are not

to bee answered with good tearmes: for whatsoever shall seeme lavish in this Pamphlet, let it be thought borrowed of Martins language.[63]

Similarly, Nashe likens the controversy between him and Martin, as well as Puritan Bible studies like the one he claims to have attended in Kent, to the ancient "contention in the Schooles of Philosophers and Rhethoritians," when "Every one that had a whirlegig in his braine, would have his own conceit to go currant for as good paiment as any infallible grounde of Arte." The parodic association between Puritans and sophists appealed to the Puritans' enemies well into the seventeenth century (Thomas Hobbes, for example, likened Puritan preachers to the ancient Sophists, accusing them of spreading "apparent" rather than "genuine" truths).[64] Like Socrates—unfairly stigmatized as an arch-Sophist by Erasmus[65]—Puritan pastors relied on an inner spiritual call for their persuasive powers. Socrates attributed his philosophical insights to a *daimon*; similarly, Puritan pastors claimed to be filled with the Holy Spirit when they preached.[66] Mocking the Puritans' attribution of their exegetical skills to divine promptings, Nashe scoffs that Martin Marprelate

> would have that to be the meaning of the holy Ghost, that his mastership imagines. . . . They that believe what soever they lust in holy Scriptures, are a generation that give more credit to themselves than to the Scriptures. . . . They take the word by the nose with a paire of Pinchers, and leade it whether soever it pleaseth them. . . . So now we must either burne all the Bookes and famous Libraries in the worlde, and take Martins assertions for undoubted Maximes, or else fetch up the Apostles by conjuration, to demand of them whether we be right or no?[67]

Ending by again appropriating and redirecting the Puritan critiques of carnival activities, Nashe charges that "It is the propertie of Martin and his followers, to measure Gods mouth, by theyre own mouth, as you shall see in the May-game that I have promised you" (what follows is the mocking description of the gospelers' discussion of Scripture, described in part I, above).[68] That this boomeranging or circular disputational style could go on indefinitely is suggested by Martin's own seizure of the insulting carnival reference. In *Hay any worke for Cooper*—a treatise that mocked the verbose Bishop Cooper of Winchester with a title taken from the street cry, "Ha'ye any worke for the Cooper"[69]—Martin compares the episcopal prelates to lords playing "Maie game[s]"—and, ironically, to Robin Hood's merry men.[70]

The mockery of carnival, play, and sophistry in Shakespeare's Henry plays has this same circular character. Shakespeare's Falstaff contains all the vices of which Martin's enemies accused Martin (though in Falstaff, as noted, these vices are at least partially converted to charismatic qualities). In "A Whip for an Ape," John Lyly calls Martin a "Scoggins," or court jester (line 56);[71] in 2 *Henry IV* Justice Shallow likewise calls Falstaff a "Scoggins" (3.2.30). Falstaff and his Boar's Head henchmen are, in a Robin Hood allusion, merry "foresters" (1 *Henry IV* 1.2.26), robbing rich travelers to fill their own empty purses.[72] As noted, Falstaff's presumptuous familiarity with the prince and his mockery of the kingly office (1 *Henry IV* 2.4.398–432) suggest his carnivalesque embodiment of the dismantling of hierarchy. And central to Falstaff's carnivalesque features and to his mockery, as I will show, is his sophistic ability to appear to win arguments. Yet just as the anti-Marprelate authors played Martin's own game to defeat him, Prince Hal imitates Falstaff even as he prepares to reject him. In his close association and continuous interaction with Falstaff, Hal demonstrates—or absorbs—a Falstaffian talent for the carnival disruption of hierarchy and for sophistic play. But Hal's carnival and sophistry, realized in his play with Falstaff, are part of his design ultimately to emerge as Falstaff's clear superior, and to banish Falstaffian/Puritan community revelry ("I do, I will," he warns [1 *Henry IV* 2.4.481]). We are privy to this plot from the start, when Hal, in soliloquy, discloses the speciousness of the communitarian image he will project, and his ultimate goal publicly to manifest his power over the revelers:

> I know you all, and will a while uphold
> The unyok'd humor of your idleness,
> Yet herein will I imitate the sun,
> Who doth permit the base contagious clouds
> To smother up his beauty from the world,
> That when he please again to be himself,
> Being wanted, he may be more wond'red at. . . .
>   (1 *Henry IV* 1.2.195–201)

Thus, the *Henriad's* final incarnation of the trickster sophist is not the mock Puritan Falstaff, but the monarch himself.

To demonstrate the "migration" of sophistry from Falstaff to Hal, I will begin by identifying the sophistic tendencies, themselves evocative of the anti-Marprelate Puritan caricatures, at which Falstaff excels. As noted, Falstaff wins disputes by sleight-of-tongue, as when he defends his cowardice at the Gad's Hill robbery by claiming to have recognized his opponent as the prince ("was it for me to kill the heir-apparent? Should I turn upon the true prince?" [1 *Henry IV* 2.4.268–70]). Falstaff is sophistic again later in this scene when, playfully impersonating Hal, he verbally translates his own gluttony and dissoluteness to virtue: "If sack and sugar be a fault, God help the wicked! . . . If to be fat be to be hated, then Pharaoh's [lean] kine are to be lov'd" (lines 470–74). In part 2, Falstaff repudiates Mistress Quickly's claim that she and he are affianced with a glib ad hominem rebuttal: Quickly "is a poor [mad] soul. . . . poverty hath distracted her" (2.1.104, 107). And near the end of part 1, Falstaff justifies his battlefield cowardice by a false proof discounting the existence of honor, since honor has no tangible effects: "Can honor set to a leg? No. Or an arm? No. . . . What is honor? a word" (5.1.131–34). Such mock Socratic argument— again, associated by Erasmus and other sixteenth-century authors with sophistry—is basic to the character of Falstaff, who is adept at "wrenching the true cause the false way," as the Lord Chief Justice charges (2 *Henry IV* 2.1.110–11).[73] And, as we have seen, such parodic uses of philosophical debate had become associated, via the Marprelate controversy, with Puritan rhetoric: recall Nashe's likening of Puritan disputation to ancient "contention in the Schooles of Philosophers and Rhethoritians."

Indeed, like the satirically realized Puritan zealots and like the Aristophanic and Erasmian Socrates, Falstaff is inspired by a kind of "whirlegig in his braine" (to recall Nashe's phrase), brought on by the operation of sack. Sack "ascends me into the brain," Falstaff tells us, "dries me there all the foolish and dull and crudy vapors which environ it, makes it apprehensive, quick, forgetive, full of nimble, fiery, and delectable shapes, which deliver'd o'er to the voice, the tongue, which is the birth, becomes excellent wit" (2 *Henry IV* 4.3.97–102). This "indwelling" of spirit(s) parodies the Puritans' divine inspiration, mocked by Nashe: in Nashe's account of the meeting of the Kent godly, he describes the "breathing time" given to each participant "to whisper with the holy Ghost, to know what should be put into his head to utter" when it came time for him to speak.[74] As Harold Bloom has suggested,[75] Falstaff himself parodies Puritan sermonizing with his inspired "excellent wit," as when, exhorting Poins to involve Hal in the Gad's Hill robbery, Falstaff intones, "God give thee the spirit of persuasion and him the ears of profiting, that what thou speakest may move and what he hears may be believ'd" (1 *Henry IV* 1.2.152–54). For the Elizabethans, Falstaff's argumentative "I deny your major" (1 *Henry IV*

2.4.495) also would have evoked Martin Marprelate's logical proofs, with their heavy reliance on "major" and "minor" syllogistic points. (This rhetorical style continued to characterize Puritan pamphlets for decades. Lambasting London vices in *Histrio-Mastix*, William Prynne writes of how his "Minor therefore must be granted" and his "Major is unquestionable."[76] Such writers, joked John Lyly, "hath sillogismes in pike sauce."[77]) Like Martin Marprelate, the Falstaff of both the Henry plays and *The Merry Wives of Windsor* tends to control arguments by summarily declaring questions "answered" or concluded: in response to Justice Shallow's charge that Falstaff has "beaten my men, kill'd my deer, and broke open my lodge" in *Merry Wives*, Falstaff belligerently retorts, "I have done all this. That is now answer'd" (1.1.111–16). Falstaff's summary dismissal of his opponents' arguments echoes Martin Marprelate, who in *Hay any Worke for Cooper* declares that his enemies' "reasons for the defence of [their] hierarchie . . . are already answered."[78] But rather than just "an overweight, ungodly knight making barroom jokes" about zealous pastors and Puritan pamphleteers, Falstaff represents those pastors and pamphleteers, as Kristen Poole notes.[79] And never is Shakespeare's satire of Puritans more pointed than when, as above, Puritan "persuasion" is lampooned as drunken, self-serving blather.

"Puritan" sophistry as performed by Falstaff is always directed toward winning the argument by verbal dazzle, if necessary at the expense of truth: hence the Lord Chief Justice's accusation that Falstaff "wrench[es] the true cause the false way." Falstaff's persuasiveness, like that of Socrates (at least according to Socrates' Elizabethan reputation), derives partly from his strategically posed rhetorical questions, whose emotive impact (though not whose logic) orients the listener toward his position, or at least melts the listener's opposition into laughter. Thus Falstaff characteristically "answers" questions with his own witty questions, displacing original interrogatives with others to which the answers, he suggests, should be obvious:

> *Poins.* Come, your reason, Jack, your reason.
> *Fal.* What, upon compulsion? . . . Give you a reason on compulsion?
>
> (1 *Henry IV* 2.4.235–39)

> *Poins.* Come, let's hear, Jack, what trick hast thou now?

Fal.	. . . Why, hear you, my masters, was it for me to kill the heir-apparent? Should I turn upon the true prince?

(1 Henry IV 2.4.265–70)

Ch. Just.	Go pluck him by the elbow, I must speak with him.
Serv.	Sir John!
Fal.	What? a young knave, and begging? is there not wars? is there not employment?

(2 Henry IV 1.2.69–73)

Host.	You'll pay me all together?
Fal.	Will I live?

(2 Henry IV 2.2.159–61)

At times Falstaff poses as both interrogator and respondent, structuring both question and reply, as in "What is honor? a word" (1 Henry IV 5.1.133–35). But whatever the form of his disputation, Falstaff's discourse becomes a proof of whatever he *wants* to be true: that he is brave, that he is not subject to law, that he will pay his debts.

That Falstaff manages to win every argument, or at least to escape the consequences of losing, testifies to the excellence of his verbal *showmanship*. His sophistry, in other words, is like that of Martin Marprelate, whose captivating "straunge phrases" and railings are like the actions of a "stage player," as Lyly writes.[80] The Elizabethan view of the Puritan speaker as dazzling player was not, however, due solely to the Marprelate controversy. The showmanship of popular Puritan pastors was widely acknowledged,[81] and Falstaff's rhetorical tricks—when joined with his other Puritan associations—must have reminded even audiences unfamiliar with the Marprelate controversy of the aural "spectacle" such pastors presented. Bryan Crockett speaks, for example, of the "moving . . . performance" of a 1595 sermon by Thomas Playfere, the "showiness" of the general Puritan "style of preaching," and the "verbal pyrotechnics" of pastors Playfere, Ralph Browning, and Thomas Adams.[82] In Elizabethan England, as Crockett notes, Puritan preaching was frequently regarded as a kind of auditory "spectacle," distinct from the "visual display" of the licentious playhouse entertainments many Puritans decried.[83]

Of course Falstaff, as stage Puritan, *unites* the visual and auditory realms in his self-promotional theatrics (as will the reformed Prince Hal). Significantly, Falstaff's most famous act of casuistic self-defense is also his most obvious act of theatrical self-presentation. In the central tavern scene of part 1, Falstaff diverts inquiries into his cowardly departure from Gad's Hill with the question "What, shall we be merry, shall we have a play extempore?" (2.4.279–80). In the ensuing playlet, Falstaff mockingly portrays King Henry IV and, speaking as Henry, creates a deceptively excellent "character" for himself: "And yet," he tells Hal, "there is a virtuous man whom I have often noted in thy company. . . . A goodly portly man, i'faith . . . of a cheerful look, a pleasing eye, and a most noble carriage, and as I think, his age some fifty. . . . I see virtue in his looks" (lines 417–28). A few lines later, switching to the role of Prince Hal, Falstaff continues to construct the appealing character of "sweet Jack Falstaff, kind Jack Falstaff, true Jack Falstaff" (lines 475–76) in a staged rhetorical defense against charges of his iniquity.

What prevents this self-serving sophistic theater from being merely an ironic mock at subversive antihierarchs like Falstaff (and, by extension, the Puritans) is the active participation of Prince Hal in Falstaff's performances; for Hal's delighted acceptance of the roles of prince to Falstaff's king (lines 420–21) and, later, servant at Falstaff's table (2 *Henry IV* 2.4) helps merrily destabilize the hierarchical distinctions on which his royal authority will ultimately depend. Further, and more insidiously, through Hal's verbal interaction with Falstaff we see Hal's absorption of the same sophistic tricks Falstaff uses to win arguments and to construct a virtuous image. These tricks Hal "studies . . . / Like a strange tongue" in Warwick's words (2 *Henry IV* 4.4.68–69), and ultimately deploys—ironically—to legitimate his own authority over Falstaff, Falstaff's comrades, and the entire realm of England. Shakespeare's disclosure of the theatrical means by which Hal finally exercises his authority thus tempers the *Henriad's* critique of Puritan "leveling" projects, however ridiculously those projects have been presented onstage—for if the king himself is a sophist, awing his subjects into submission by dazzling theatrical rhetoric, then the hierarchical system of power that depends from his throne has no intrinsic justification.

Hal's reliance on theater's capacity to awe is, as noted, a key aspect of his character from his first soliloquy, wherein he announces his intention to dazzle future audiences by a showman's strategy: by first hiding behind and then casting off his licentious companions (the "base contagious clouds"). With its visual metaphor of light banishing darkness, however, this speech diverts us from the rhetoricity that is the essence of Hal's skillful performances. Hal's rhetorical virtuosity takes various forms, most of which owe something to Falstaff's sophistic practices. Hal imitates Falstaff's technique of evading a question by substituting a different question:[84]

> Fall.   What a plague have I to do with a buff jerkin?
> Prince.   Why, what a pox have I to do with my hostess of the tavern?
>
> (1 Henry IV 1.2.45–48)

In addition, Hal proves able to "wrench the true cause the false way" on several important occasions, on all of which he uses verbal strategy to bolster an image of his own honor or authority. In part 1, Hal deflects his father's anger with an improvised self-defense: one that relies on theatrical imagery to construct a vision of a future, virtuous son. Countering Henry IV's accusation that Hal is alienating his audience of future subjects—itself a charge that supports the image of kingship as performance—Hal responds that he will redeem lost reputation by performing nobly in battle, donning a "garment all of blood" and a "bloody mask" (3.2.135–36). In another interview with his father in part 2, Hal uses Falstaffian rhetorical skill to excuse his mistaken theft of the sleeping king's crown, and to convert his father's wrath to appreciation.

> Coming to look on you, thinking you dead,
> And dead almost, my liege, to think you were,
> I spake unto this crown as having sense,
> And thus upbraided it: "The care on thee depending
> hath fed upon the body of my father. . . .
> .   .   .   .
> Accusing it, I put it on my head,
> To try with it, as with an enemy. . . .
>
> (4.5.155–66)

The sophistic qualities of this speech are reinforced by Henry IV's answering remark: "God put [it] in thy mind to take it hence, / that thou mightst win the more thy father's love, / Pleading so wisely in excuse of it!" (lines 178–80, my emphasis). The approving comment suggests that Hal is beginning to meet Henry IV's own standards for performative verbal skill, essential for the maintenance of royal power.

Hal's greatest rhetorical victories are, of course, reserved for his actual performances as king, chiefly in Henry V. "[W]hen he speaks" as king, says the Archbishop of Canterbury in Henry V,

"The air, a charter'd libertine, is still, / And the mute wonder lurketh in men's ears / To steal his sweet and honeyed sentences" (1.1.47–50). We hear the young king's power verbally to enchant in his inspiring St. Crispian's Day speech, his wooing of the French princess, and, most centrally, his dialogue with soldiers Bates, Williams, and Court on the eve of Agincourt, a dialogue that again combines the tropes of theater with the tricks of rhetorical persuasion. On this occasion Henry costumes himself as a common soldier to argue the king's right to lead men to their deaths in battle. Henry's proof that "every subject's duty is the King's, but every subject's soul is his own" (4.1.176–77) substitutes sophistic style for genuine logic—his example of a son who dies while conveying his father's merchandise (lines 147–48) is an unfit analogy for soldiers deployed in war, which *always* kills men. But the analogy persuades his hearers. Williams agrees, "'Tis certain, every man that dies ill, the ill upon his own head, the King is not to answer for it" (lines 86–87). Thus, again, the king's authority is shown to rest not on intrinsic ability or even on the judgments of reason, but on a persuasive verbal performance.

We know, of course, that Hal's claim to the throne, like his usurping father's, must rest on this verbal mastery: chiefly, on his ability to persuade his public of his legitimacy, since the throne does not descend to him by unquestionable hereditary right. It is to learn persuasive skill, including an ability verbally to project a symbolic image of fraternity with even the lowest of his subjects, that Hal initially involves himself with the Boar's Head tavern crew, down to the tapsters who tell him that when he is king he will "command all the good lads in Eastcheap" (1 *Henry IV* 2.4.13–15). Of course, as king, Henry V immediately distances himself from his lower-class following, stressing in speeches only the symbolic character of his brotherhood with all subjects. As Stephen Greenblatt notes, Henry's communitarian promise that soldiers who bleed with him shall achieve royalty—"shall be [his] brother[s] (*Henry V* 4.3.61–62)—is undone by the Chorus's and Henry's own styling of the king as supraroyal, or divine.[85] The fraternal vow is also undercut by the conspicuously ranked list of the dead Henry reads after Agincourt, which emphasizes the "blood" and "quality" of the slaughtered (4.8.90).

But since the Henry IV plays, beginning with Hal's first soliloquy, have presented royal identity itself as a theatrical effect, Hal's ultimate spectacular revelation of the distance between himself and the lower classes seems no more than a performance when it finally occurs. Thus, even when Hal claims his royal birthright and repudiates Falstaff at the close of part 2, both the claim and the rejection—the last delivered in regal costume and both made in public, before approving audiences—are undermined by their contrived, theatrical character. Before the barons and the Lord Chief Justice, Hal claims to embody majesty, to contain the "tide" of royal blood (5.2.129–33)—a rhetorically fitting espousal of the divine right theory, but one that, if considered deeply, would invalidate his father's (and thus his own) claim to the throne. Similarly, in the London street, when the newly crowned Henry V forbids Falstaff "to come near our person by ten mile" (5.5.65), the public, theatrically impressive nature of this command tempts us to agree with Falstaff's conclusion that the rejection is a rhetorical performative ploy: "he must seem thus to the world," Falstaff asserts. "I shall be sent for soon at night" (lines 78, 89–90). We cannot entirely sympathize with Falstaff here: the antihierarchical chaos he embodies, conceived according to the satiric anti-Puritan model, has rendered him too dangerous a voice for inclusion in the serious business of governance. The moral and political problem—at least for Elizabethan audiences—arises from the fact that, given the sophistic, performative character of Hal's strategies of rule, we cannot fully support the monarchy either.

III

Various New Historicist critics of the past decade and a half, as well as earlier critics, have hypothesized Shakespearean history theater's power to desacralize English kings by presenting kings as humans playing royal roles. Jonathan Dollimore, for example, speaks of a "demystification of political and power relations" in Renaissance tragedy which fostered "a radical social and political realism.[86] The "rude handling of sacred totems" like the crown "is what [Renaissance] drama is all about" notes Russell Fraser.[87] Stephen Greenblatt Leonard Tennenhouse, and David Scott Kastan have all written extensively of the way the staged presentation of royalty affected audiences' reverence toward the monarchy (though their conclusions differ).[88] And Franco Moretti boldly links Shakespeare's role-playing kings to the mid-seventeenth-century Puritan revolution, saying that tragedies and history plays "[h]aving deconsecrated the king," it became "possible to decapitate him.[89]

While I would not support Moretti's direct line of causality between Shakespearean drama and the English revolution of a half-century later (if only to keep Shakespeare from spinning in his grave), I hope I have cast additional light on the process of monarchical desacralization so integral to the political event to which Moretti alludes: the lawful execution of Charles I by the English community of saints. The Henry plays helped demystify monarchy by demonstrating its association with sophistic theatrical tricks such as those used by Falstaff. Paradoxically, the *Henriad* achieves this effect despite its satire of the Puritans in Falstaff, for Prince Hal's bond with Falstaff and likeness to him, chiefly in the area of casuistic skill, tars royalty with the same satirical brush. (Thus Hal's friendship with Falstaff has, in a way unanticipated by the disapproving Henry IV, "carded," or adulterated, "his state" [1 *Henry IV* 3.2.62].) The anti-Marprelate satires used Martin's own style against him, rendering their anti-Puritan pamphlets rhetorically similar to the pamphets of their target. Similarly, Hal uses Falstaffian sophistic skill to reject Falstaffian subversion and to structure and defend his own royal image. But in stooping to Falstaff's level, he compromises the whole show. Thus, though the Henry plays mock Puritans, they also slight the sophistic royal authority of which Puritans were beginning to complain.

These theatrical dynamics prevent the *Henriad* from being a successful attack on Puritanism through the Falstaff caricature. First, as Poole has argued, non-Puritan audience members probably experienced a festive emotional response to the carnivalesque Puritan onstage, though they might have intellectually disapproved of his hypocrisy; thus the Falstaff image probably softened the anti-Puritan attitudes of mainstream playgoers who recognized the caricature. Second, Puritans in the audience were not likely to accept Falstaff as an embodiment of Puritan values, evidenced by their apparent protest against the use of Oldcastle's revered name. And finally, these same Puritan audience members, whatever they thought of Falstaff, would have found their antihierarchical prejudices confirmed by the theatrical sophistries of Prince Hal/Henry V. For the intellectual, legal, and theological casuistry of which conservatives accused Puritans was a charge radical Protestants (like John Bale) brought against their government as well.[90] Thus, Shakespeare's *Henriad* encouraged the skepticism of a people already beginning to doubt the sacred origins of monarchy and to lobby for power at the lower levels of their society.

In "Invisible Bullets: Renaissance Authority and Its Subversion,"
Stephen Greenblatt argues that Hal's participation in festive demol-
ishings of rank constituted, for Elizabethans, a deceptive promise of
lower-class empowerment. After all, Greenblatt reasons, Hal betrays
Falstaff and the Boar's Head brethren once he is crowned king;
moreover, the playhouse itself contains whatever subversive energies have been released in the audience by the staged release from
ranked social structures. Greenblatt insists, "[W]e are, after all, in
the theatre": the arena of acknowledged make-believe.[91] We (or the
Elizabethans) therefore do not expect to see the comic stage carnival reproduced in the outside world. If Greenblatt is correct, then
the sympathy the Henry plays generate for the grotesque Puritan
Falstaff was harmless sympathy—that is, a tolerance that stopped
at the playhouse exit, and did not extend to real London Puritans
or their social and religious reforms. The charismatic subversiveness that urged audiences to celebrate Falstaff, and hence the Puritan communities he represented, must simply have evaporated in
the London air.

But the logic of this argument is flawed in two ways. The first is
the argument's failure to acknowledge that imaginative transformations acquired in the playhouse, or anywhere, cannot be easily dis-
carded. If comic catharsis is deeply experienced, then, as Gene
Fendt writes, "the audience of the comedy"—or the comic history—"can go forth into its world, carrying the green world's heart
within them." Thus drama transforms "the community's moral
imagination":[92] in the words of former West German chancellor
Willy Brandt, the "so-called illusions" of theater "are an integral
part of our reality."[93]

The second flaw is the argument's neglect of another question.
What influence do sympathetic stage characters exert on audience
members *already disposed* toward the ideas these characters
represent? When Puritanical audience members, disdainful of
absolutism, confronted a comic hero who playfully revealed the
monarchy's dependence on sophistical theater, were their antimonarchical prejudices not reinforced?

This question's answer depended, no doubt, on the individual
audience member: on what his or her strongest prejudices were,
on what notions he or she was most willing to hear supported.
The histories, with their heteroglossic accommodation of multiple
voices and viewpoints, must have functioned to support a variety
of political leanings. The Henry plays, like most Shakespearean
histories and tragedies, are finally politically ambivalent. They mix
a Puritanical awareness of the questionable legitimacy of kings and

a Puritanical scorn for corrupt hierarchs with a recalcitrant reverence for the royal mystique. At times Shakespeare seems intent on theatrically appropriating the antiprelatical feeling of the Elizabethan Puritans—which was gradually becoming a disaffection with monarchy as well—for the monarchy or royal family itself: we see this appropriation when pious Prince John of Lancaster chastises the Archbishop of York, "th' [imagin'd] voice of God himself," for "misus[ing] the reverence of [his] place" (*2 Henry IV* 4.2.19, 23), and when the crooked bishops of *Henry V* are seen complaining of the king's Robin Hood-like redistribution of their wealth "to relief of lazars, and weak age / Of indigent faint souls past corporal toil" (1.1.15–16). This flattering portrayal of the younger Lancastrians' social conscience must have strengthened some audience members' reverence for the monarchy, even as it fed Puritan contempt for the bishops. In portraying the royal family's support of the people *against* evil prelatical designs, Shakespeare appeals to a Puritan royalism, despite the comically degrading presentation of Puritanism his plays have also provided through the character of Falstaff.

But by the close of the 1590s, "Puritan royalism" was fast becoming an oxymoron. The gradual Puritan disaffection with monarchy was due partly to the queen's refusal to support wished-for Puritan reforms aiming at increased congregational power. But it stemmed also—and more deeply—from the public's dawning realization of the theatrical character of the entire hierarchical apparatus of her government, and the loss of faith that realization entailed. Thus the Henry plays' disclosure of its kings' theatrical strategies assisted the process of Puritan disenchantment with monarchy and with the dissemination of power from above, despite these plays' often reverent treatment of Hal/Henry V himself. If kingship—as the Henry plays implied—was a theatrical tour de force, then inborn regality was a contradiction in terms. A public who believed that their monarch ruled not by divine right but by performative skill might suffer him, or her, when that monarch showed not only theatrical virtuosity but concern for and responsiveness to public will (as, for the most part, does Shakespeare's Henry V). But the presentation of the king as performer sets the stage for his dismissal if and when he does not.

Notes

I would like to thank Western Michigan University for a Faculty Research and Creative Activities Support Fund grant, which helped me to do research for this article.

1. Jonas Barish, *The Anti-theatrical Prejudice* (Berkeley: University of California Press, 1981). The capitalization of "puritan" should not mislead readers into the assumption that the "godly" were a unified sect.

2. Salvian and "Anglophile-Eutheo" (Anthony Munday), *A Second and Third Blast of Retrait from Plaies and Theaters* (London, 1580; reprint, New York, Johnson Reprint Co., 1972), 89.

3. John Rainolds, *The Overthrow of Stage-Plays: By the Way of Controversie between D. Gages and J. Rainolds* (London, 1599; reprint, New York, Johnson Reprint Co., 1972), 9.

4. See David Bevington, *Tudor Drama and Politics* (Cambridge: Harvard University Press, 1968), 256–57 and 293–99; and Paul White, *Theatre and Reformation: Protestantism, Patronage, and Playing in Tudor England* (Cambridge: Cambridge University Press, 1993), for discussions of Puritan involvement in Tudor theater. A session at the 1996 Medieval Congress in Kalamazoo, Michigan, included papers that also stressed the interrelationships between early Puritan reform and theater, notably Alexandra Johnston's "Parish Drama and Parish Crisis in England: 1535–65"; William R. Streitberger's "New Models for Court Drama: 1535–62"; and Peggy Knapp's "Traces of the Medieval in Early Protestant Polemical Drama."

5. Munday, *A Second and Third Blast of Retrait*, 3.

6. Douglas Tallack, *Twentieth-Century America: The Intellectual and Cultural Context* (New York: Longman, 1991), 324.

7. Arthur J. Klein, *Intolerance in the Reign of Elizabeth, Queen of England* (Port Washington, N.Y.: Kennikat Press, 1917; reprint, 1968), 134. Although J. Sears McGee has more recently argued that Anglicanism and Puritanism were mutually exclusive religious categories in Renaissance England (*The Godly Man in Stuart England: Anglicans, Puritans, and the Two Tables, 1620–1670* [New Haven: Yale University Press, 1976]), the evidence compiled by Klein and the later author Patrick Collinson demonstrates that in the Elizabethan period, no such clear distinction obtained. See Patrick Collinson, *The Elizabethan Puritan Movement* (Berkeley and Los Angeles: University of California Press, 1967), esp. 28; and also Collinson, *Godly People: Essays on English Protestantism and Puritanism* (London: Hambledon Press, 1983), 98.

8. Collinson, *The Elizabethan Puritan Movement*, 51–52, 125–29. I am indebted to Collinson not only for providing a detailed and impeccably researched history of Elizabethan Puritanism but for making available passages from difficult-to-obtain Puritan documents.

9. Ibid., 51.

10. As Bevington writes, as late as 1603, "The great London public"—a significant portion of which was Puritan—"was reluctant to abandon the theater as a forum in which to express its political and religious aspirations" (*Tudor Drama and Politics*, 294). Bryan Crockett also maintains that "there can be little doubt that the audiences at the sermons and plays of the [Elizabethan] period overlapped considerably." See Crockett's "'Holy Cozenage' and the Renaissance Cult of the Ear," *Sixteenth-Century Journal* 24, no. 1 (spring 1993): 63, as well as Crockett's book, *The Play of Paradox: Stage and Sermon in Renaissance England* (Philadelphia: University of Pennsylvania Press, 1995). Martha Tuck Rozett makes a similar argument in *The Doctrine of Election and the Emergence of Elizabethan Tragedy* (Princeton: Princeton University Press), 15–25.

11. Alice Lyle-Scoufos provides an extensive exploration of the links between Falstaff and Oldcastle in *Shakespeare's Typological Satire: A Study of the Falstaff-Oldcastle Problem* (Athens: Ohio University Press, 1979). Among other things,

she finds much joking about Oldcastle's martyrdom—he was burned at the stake—in the Henry plays' characters' references to Falstaff's roasting, burning, and melting (76–77). Other studies that note Falstaff's resemblance to the image of the Puritan martyr or contemporary Puritan reformer are John Dover Wilson, *The Fortunes of Falstaff* (Cambridge and New York: Cambridge University Press, 1944), chap. 2; and David Bevington, *Tudor Drama and Politics*, 257. John Dover Wilson also investigates the possibility that *Henry V*'s Fluellen was based on Roger Williams, suspected author of the Marprelate tracts, in *Martin Marprelate and Shakespeare's Fluellen* (1912; reprint, Folcroft, Pennsylvania: Folcroft Press, 1969).

12. Kristen Poole, "Saints Alive! Falstaff, Martin Marprelate, and the Staging of Puritanism," *Shakespeare Quarterly* 46, no.1 (spring 1995), 49, 8 n.

13. Thomas Pendleton, "'This Is Not the Man': On Calling Falstaff Falstaff," *Analytical and Enumerative Bibliography*, n.s. 4 (1990): 59–71, esp. 68–69.

14. Poole, "Saints Alive!" 58.

15. Ibid., 54.

16. Ibid.

17. Ibid., 59.

18. All quotations from William Shakespeare are from *The Riverside Shakespeare*, ed. G. Blakemore Evans (Boston: Houghton Mifflin, 1974).

19. Poole, "Saints Alive!" 70.

20. Ibid., 75.

21. See Collinson's account of the Munzer rebellion and its reputation, *The Elizabethan Puritan Movement*, 480 n.

In regard to the image of popular military revolt presented by Falstaff's unfortunate soldiers, I disagree with Kristen Poole's statement that "[i]n Shakespeare's account Oldcastle's qualities as traitor and militant religious leader are dispersed among other characters in the plays" (i.e., that Falstaff does not embody these qualities). See Poole, "Saints Alive!" 69.

22. As Munday wrote, "Nothing entereth in more effectualie into the memorie, than that which commeth by seeing. . . . the tokens of that which wee have seen, saith Petrarch, sticke fast in us whether we will or no" (*A Second and Third Blast*, 95–96).

23. While sixteenth-century Puritan writings such as the Marprelate tracts and John Field and Thomas Wilcox's 1572 *An Admonition to the Parliament* cautiously avoided direct criticism of the monarch, arguments regarding the legitimacy of rebellion were already brewing in the 1580s and 1590s, as is evidenced by the great energy devoted to refuting such arguments. For example, Richard Bancroft's 1593 *Daungerous Positions and Proceedings, Published and Practised within this Island of Brytaine* makes reference to seditious books which claim that "The authoritie, which Princes have, is given them from the people: Kings, Princes, and governours, have their authoritie of the people; and (upon occasion) the people may take it away again" (London: J. Windet and J. Wolfe, 1593).

24. Collinson, *The Elizabethan Puritan Movement*, 399, 435. See also Lawrence Stone, *The Causes of the English Revolution* (London: Routledge and Kegan Paul, 1972), 62–75, 97–98, 103–5, and 114, for a similar argument; and Walter Cohen, "*The Merchant of Venice* and the Possibilities of Historical Criticism," in *Materialist Shakespeare: A History*, ed. Ivo Kamps, (New York, Verso, 1995), 71–92.

25. Poole, Saints Alive! 54.

26. Munday, *A Blast of Retrait from Plaies and Theaters*, 88.

27. William Prynne, *Histrio-Mastix: The Player's Scourge or, Actor's Tragedy* (London, 1633; reprint, New York: Johnson Reprint, 1972), introduction.

28. Thomas Nashe, *The Returne of Pasquill*, vol. 1 of *The Works of Thomas Nashe*, 5 vols., ed. Ronald B. McKerrow (Oxford: Basil Blackwell, 1966), 91.

29. Martin Marprelate, *Theses Martinianae*, in *The Marprelate Tracts* reprint, (Leeds, Scolar Press, 1967).

Christopher Hill also notes that Martin's chief intent was to subvert hierarchy (i.e., not to moralize against social decadence). See *The Collected Essays of Christopher Hill*; vol. 1, *Writing and Revolution in Seventeenth-Century England* (Amherst: University of Massachusetts Press, 1985), 77.

30. John Field and Thomas Wilcox, *An Admonition to the Parliament* in W. H. Frere and C. E. Douglas, *Puritan Manifestoes: A Study of the Origin of the Puritan Revolt* (1572; reprint, London, Church Historical Society, 1954), 10.

31. Collinson, *The Elizabethan Puritan Movement*, 120, 148, 150.

32. John Lyly, *Pappe with an Hatchet*, 412 in *The Complete Works of John Lyly*, 3 vols., 3:388–422 (Oxford, Clarendon Press, 1967), 412. (Robert Greene was a possible collaborator in this work.)

33. Nashe, *The Return of Pasquill*, 83.

34. Quoted in Collinson, *The Elizabethan Puritan Movement*, 144.

35. Quoted in Patricia Crawford, *Women and Religion in England, 1500–1720* (New York, Routledge, 1993), 55.

36. From the Norwich Diocesan Archives and quoted in Collinson, *The Elizabethan Puritan Movement*, 34–41.

37. Ibid., 341.

38. See Anthony Munday, *The Downfall of Robert Earl of Huntington* (London, 1598; reprint Oxford: Malone Society Reprints, Oxford University Press, 1965), and *The Death of Robert Earl of Huntingdon* (London, 1601; reprint, Oxford: Malone Society Reprints, Oxford University Press, 1967).

39. "Like that of Cromwell, the name of Huntingdon had compelling topical associations for the English elect: the third Earl of Huntingdon had been, as a candidate for succession to the throne during the 1560's, the hope of many ardent Protestants fearful of Elizabeth's untimely death, and his brothers had served the Puritan cause in Parliament throughout the reign" (Bevington, *Tudor Drama and Politics*, 295.)

40. See Michael Drayton, Richard Hathway, Anthony Munday, and Robert Wilson, *Sir John Oldcastle, Part 1* (1600), in *The Oldcastle Controversy*, ed. Peter Corbin and Douglas Sedge, 36–144 (New York: Manchester University Press, 1991).

41. Collinson, *The Elizabethan Puritan Movement*, 391.

42. William Prynne, introduction to *Histrio-Mastix* (London, 1633).

43. See Jonas Barish's chapter on Puritanism in *The Anti-Theatrical Prejudice* for the seminal discussion of Puritan resistance to "feminization." I briefly discuss Puritan misogyny in Grace Tiffany, *Erotic Beasts and Social Monsters: Shakespeare, Jonson, and Comic Androgyny* (Newark: University of Delaware Press, 1995), 58–61.

44. Nashe, *The Returne of Pasquill*, 83.

45. Field and Wilcox's *Admonition* is an appeal for the Anglicans' return to "olde church" practices (9).

46. Nashe, *The Returne of Pasquill*, 89.

47. Ibid., 77.

48. Thomas Nashe, *A Countercuffe Given to Martin Junior*, in vol. 1, *The Works of Thomas Nashe*, 5 vols., ed. Ronald B. McKerrow, 1:62 (Oxford: Basil Blackwell, 1966).

49. Stephen Greenblatt, "Invisible Bullets: Renaissance Authority and Its Subversion, *Henry IV* and *Henry V*," in ed. Jonathan Dollimore and Alan Sinfield,

Political Shakespeare: New Essays in Cultural Materialism 34–43 (Manchester: Manchester University Press, 1985).

50. David Bevington notes that "Shakespeare's awareness of and concern with the widening split between the private theater and the Puritan-leaning citizenry are tactfully evident in such plays as *Twelfth Night* (1600–1601) and *As You Like It* (1599–1600)," although he argues against any close thematic connection between *As You Like It* and Munday's Huntingdon plays (*Tudor Drama and Politics*, 297).

51. Louis Montrose, "The Place of a Brother in *As You Like It*: Social Process and Comic Form," in *Materialist Shakespeare*, ed. Ivo Kamps, 39–70 (New York: Verso, 1995). (Montrose does not discuss the likeness of comic communities to the anti-Marprelate caricatures of Puritan communities, though he notes, as do numerous critics, the social leveling by which the former are characterized.)

52. A letter to Lord Burghley, the queen's secretary, written in 1572, quoted in Collinson, 144.

53. Martin Marprelate, *Hay Any Worke for Cooper?* (London, 1588; reprint, Leeds, The Scolar Press, 1967), 4–5.

54. Nashe, *The Returne of Pasquill*, 77.

55. Collinson, *The Elizabethan Puritan Movement*, 447.

56. Ibid., 292.

57. John Jewel, *Certaine Sermons Preached before the Queenes Majestie, and at Paules Crosse. Whereunto is Added a Short Treatise of the Sacraments* (London: C. Barker, 1583).

58. John Bale, *Select Works* (London, 1544), ed. Henry Christmas (Cambridge: Cambridge University Press, 1849; reprint, New York, Johnson Reprint Co., 1968), 19, 21, 37.

59. John Foxe, *Actes and Monuments* (London, 1559–96; New York: AMS Press, 1965), 3:321.

60. As Collinson writes, Martin's "distinctive polemical methods" owed much to a "martyrological technique" originating with John Foxe and others (*The Elizabethan Puritan Movement*, 394).

61. Martin Marprelate, *Hay any worke for Cooper*, 21.

62. In calling Falstaff a late incarnation of the anti-Marprelate caricatures of Puritans, I do not mean to deny that numerous other literary and dramatic traditions are involved in the design of his character. For what is still the best discussion of these, see John Dover Wilson's *The Fortunes of Falstaff* (New York: Macmillan, 1944), 15–35. Finally, of course, Falstaff is himself greater than the sum of his parts.

63. Lyly, *Pappe with an Hatchet*, 396.

64. See Gary Remer, *Humanism and the Rhetoric of Toleration* (University Park: Pennsylvania State University Press, 1996), 181.

65. Alice Goodman has shown that Socrates' Renaissance reputation derived from the image of him as sly Sophist, which originated with Aristophanes and which was popularized by Erasmus (see Alice Goodman, "Falstaff and Socrates," *English* 34, no. 149 [summer 1985]: 97–112). Despite the fact that Plato's Socrates protested vehemently against Sophists and their rhetorical manipulations, numerous Renaissance authors chose to portray him as sophistical himself. For example, Philibert de Vienne's 1547 *The Philosopher of the Court*, translated in 1575 by George North, calls Socrates "the greatest dissembler in the world" (97–98).

66. Collinson discusses the importance of the Puritan sense of the inward call to ministry (336).

67. Nashe, *The Returne of Pasquill*, 86–88.

68. Ibid., 88.

69. Collinson, The Elizabethan Puritan Movement, 392.

70. Martin Marprelate, Hay any worke for Cooper, 3–4.

71. Lyly, "A Whip for an Ape," in The Complete Works of John Lyly, 418–22.

72. Falstaff plans to rob the "pilgrims going to Canterbury with rich offerings" (1 Henry IV 1.2.126) (though he ends up robbing the king instead). The plot owes something to Bale's account of Oldcastle's condemnation of pilgrimages (see Bale, Select Works, 38). Henry IV as a whole thwarts the upper classes' interest in holy pilgrimages; the highest such thwarted design is, of course, Henry IV's plan to invade Jerusalem, which he finally gives over near the close of part 2 (4.5.234–35).

73. Michael Platt also notes Falstaff's Socratic sophistry in "Falstaff in the Valley of the Shadow of Death," 171–202 in Falstaff, ed. Harold Bloom, 180 (New York: Chelsea House Publishers, 1992). Among the numerous other critics who have noted the likeness between Falstaff and Socrates are Alice Goodman (cited in n. 64 above); John Robert Moore in "Shakespeare's Henry V," Explicator 1 (1942): item 61; Monroe M. Stearns, "Shakespeare's Henry V," Explicator 2 (1943): item 19; and John Dover Wilson, ed., Henry V (Cambridge: Cambridge University Press, 1947), 147.

74. Nashe, The Returne of Pasquill, 90.

75. Harold Bloom, Ruin the Sacred Truths: Poetry and Belief from the Bible to the Present (Cambridge and London: Harvard University Press, 1989), 84.

76. Prynne, Histrio-Mastix, 263.

77. Lyly, Pappe with an Hatchet, 411.

78. Martin Marprelate, Hay any Worke for Cooper, 21.

79. Poole, "Saints Alive!" 54.

80. Lyly, Pappe with an Hatchet, 402, 409.

81. See Joan Webber, "Celebration of Word and World in Lancelot Andrewes' Style," in Seventeenth-Century Prose, ed. Stanley E. Fish (Oxford: Oxford University Press, 1971), 337.

82. Bryan Crockett, "'Holy Cozenage,'" 46, 49, 46.

83. Ibid., passim.

84. It might, of course, be argued that Falstaff learns his evasive speaking from Hal, and in fact Falstaff himself accuses Hal of corrupting him in various ways (1 Henry IV 1.2.90–95; 2 Henry IV 1.2.145). Yet with whomever the "damnable" argumentative style (1 Henry IV 1.2.90) originates, Hal's and Falstaff's credibility is mutually undermined by it.

85. Stephen Greenblatt, "Invisible Bullets," 43–44.

86. Jonathan Dollimore, Radical Tragedy: Religion, Ideology and Power in the Drama of Shakespeare and His Contemporaries (Chicago: University of Chicago Press, 1984), 5.

87. Russell Fraser, introduction to Russell Fraser and Norman Rabkin, eds., Drama of the English Renaissance New York: Macmillan Publishing Co., 1976), 3.

88. See especially Greenblatt, "Invisible Bullets"; Leonard Tennenhouse, "Strategies of State and Political Plays: A Midsummer Night's Dream, Henry IV, Henry V, Henry VIII," in Political Shakespeare: New Essays in Cultural Materialism, Jonathan Dollimore and Alan Sinfield (Manchester: Manchester University Press, 1985); and David Scott Kastan, "Proud Majesty Made a Subject: Shakespeare and the Spectacle of Rule," Shakespeare Quarterly 37, no. 4 (winter, 1986): 459–75.

89. Franco Moretti, "'A Huge Eclipse': Tragic Form and the Deconsecration of Sovereignty," Genre 15 (spring and summer, 1981): 8.

90. Peggy Knapp's "Traces of the Medieval in Early Protestant Drama," a conference paper cited above, discussed Bale's critiques of Anglican sophistries.

91. Greenblatt, "Invisible Bullets," 34–43.

92. Gene Fendt, "Resolution, Catharsis, Culture: *As You Like It*," *Philosophy and Literature* 19 (1995): 251. In this article Fendt also acknowledges the Greenblattian view of comic release, which (in Fendt's words) likens catharsis to "circling a track for an hour . . . it's hypnotic, we forget our problems; but then the hypnotic or incantatory effect ends and we wake to the world going on apace. This is the explanation of comic catharsis of all those who think of art as mere entertainment," Fendt notes, but he adds that if the explanation is true, "there is no reason to study the humanities rather than watch football." A staged fiction of lower-class empowerment would be more likely to "face" audiences "with the complete inadequacy of their own daylight world, and such comedy is likely to be as socially upsetting as Plato is said to have feared" (251).

93. Willy Brandt, speaking at the municipal theater in Dusseldorf, Germany, 17 September 1972.

RESPONSES:
FORUM: A FUNERAL
ELEGY *BY W.S.*

Shakespeare and the Peters in History

Donald W. Foster

Editor's Note

Scholars participating in the *Forum* on *A Funeral Elegy* (*Shakespeare Studies* 25) were invited to respond to any points raised in that general discussion. The responses of those who accepted this invitation are presented below.

With a freedom that is hardly warranted by the fullness of the available evidence, a few scholars have indulged in fantasy about William Peter. Leah Marcus considers the Elegy in its cultural context and, rising above hysteria to history, rightly endorses a Shakespearean attribution; yet even Marcus's welcome "Plea for Literary History" has its lapses. At one point Marcus determines that William Peter was "considerably more prosperous" than his killer, Edward Drew.[1] She bases her inference on my observation in *Elegy by W.S.* that while Peter carried a fashionable rapier, the Drews had only swords. Had I foreseen that so much would be inferred from so little, I would have couched the remark. By the standards of the better-heeled Devon gentry, Will Peter was hard-pressed. Though he was the first descendant of Mayor John Peter to graduate from university, he attended on a fellowship. When Otho Peter died in 1607, William as the younger son inherited £100 outright, plus poor land in Marldon and Ipplepen having an annual income of just £5. Peter's financial situation improved by his marriage to Margaret Brewton in 1609, but barely.[2] Shortly after his funeral, his widow was ordered to confer with the Orphans' Court of Exeter to answer for her husband's desperate debts.[3] Those debts were paid through her subsequent marriage to Edward Cotton—but Cotton received Peter's property. The two daughters, Rose and Margaret, married poor.[4]

By way of comparison, Peter's killer, Edward Drew, inherited in 1598 the chief messuage, mansion house, barton, and demesne lands of Combe Rawlegh, Devon. His three sisters received £1,800 just for their wedding gifts (cf. Will Peter's £5 income). John and George Drew, younger sons, received annuities for life (John, £30, and George, £40); and the eldest son, Thomas, received everything else—a sizable fortune in real estate.[5] Their mother, Bridget, even in her widowhood received a pension of £20 granted by Queen Elizabeth to her husband (the error was discovered in 1603 by the Privy Council and the pension halted).

Marcus was drawn into a discussion of A Funeral Elegy by circumstance. Her own ongoing work demands—as does every scholar's—her best attention. She could not have gleaned the above information from published sources, nor should she be expected, upon being enlisted to review claims for the Elegy, to book a flight to London and then motor down to Devon, where such evidence can be mined. Still, there is something substandard in the assumption that William Peter's and Edward Drew's relative wealth can be weighed by consulting a trivial fact such as the weapons they carried on a particular day. This judgment is so far beneath Marcus's usual shrewdness that it can only be ascribed, I think, to a notion generated by the media that the attribution of A Funeral Elegy was achieved by computer. That the media would take this approach is inevitable. The World Wide Web is swarming, and as I write in the summer of 1997, technology stocks drive the market higher. Academics, encountering crass dreams of a computer-appointed rosy future, may seek a rational foothold outside the madness. Hence, I imagine, Marcus—assuming that the computer has presumed to speak oracularly—makes her stand for "old-fashioned literary history." But to rely on Wallace Macaffrey's 1958 text on Exeter for information on the Devon gentry is too old-fashioned, as Marcus herself knows: at the end of her essay she cites the perfectly reliable 1963 text of Mark Eccles, but even there displays scruples, noting that everything found in Eccles "needs to be checked against the manuscript sources."[6]

Those original sources have already been consulted. I have said before and may need to say again that it is not the computer but scholarship that has established W.S.'s identity. Archival sources—in seven English counties—have played a larger role in that determination than the press has given out. Though I have not yet found a convenient moment to publish a history of William Peter and his circle, I must add enough here to what is already in print to over-throw wrongful assumptions evident in the 1997 forum.

The use of *predestinated* in the first line of the Elegy, and once again in a later line, has caused Leah Marcus and Katherine Duncan-Jones to assume that W.S. is a Calvinist. Duncan-Jones mentions further that *predestin-* occurs only once in canonical Shakespeare, from which she infers—quite apart from generic considerations—that the word was not to his liking (though "free will" occurs just once, too, in *Antony and Cleopatra*).[7] As it happens, *predestinated* was available vocabulary even to Anglo-Catholics and Anglicans, as is attested by five instances in the Rheims New Testament, against two instances in the Authorized New Testament. Unlike most Calvinists, the elegist blames "fate" for his own failure to sustain a full hope in bodily resurrection; he equates predestination with personal death and universal doom, not with eternal salvation; and it is "fate" and even time, not God, that is blamed for Peter's death (FE 1–2, 490–98, 561–68).[8] But there are stronger, historical, reasons to doubt the slipshod attempts by Duncan-Jones to figure W.S. as a Puritan, and by Marcus to link William Peter with Puritanism.

Far from being stridently or even moderately Puritan, the Peters of Exminster, Bowhay, and Whipton were vigorously anti-Puritan from the Anglican Reformation through the Civil War and beyond. Nor did the quarrel between Edward Drew and William Peter spring from religious difference. (The Drews were high church or Catholic as well.) The quarrel originated rather in a loan for a horse purchased by Edward Drew. When Drew defaulted on the loan, the seller asked Peter to intervene with an appeal to Drew's mother. Peter willingly complied—and died for it.[9]

Marcus is right to follow MacCaffrey in noting that there were many Puritans among Exeter's merchant elite. There were even a few devout Calvinists among Peter's own extended kin, such as the Southcotts of Mohuns Ottery and the Peters of Cornwall. Peter's eldest first cousin, Sir Thomas Ridgway (1565–1631), secretary of wars in Ireland, was famed for his severity toward Irish Catholics—but Ridgway may be glanced at in the disdainful remark about "some in nothing famous but defame," such as lurk in "the *Ridgway . . .* / That leades to ruine" (FE 41–42, original italics). William Peter and his father and brother and sister and wife and children were all, like their ancestors, Roman Catholic, or at least high church, and they bore no sympathy with Puritan zealots.

The Peter family monument, built probably by John, for father Otho's tomb in 1607, comes close in its sepulchral inscription to a papist reading of Christ's words to Simon Peter as the rock of the Church. A year after Otho died, Peter's mother married Sir Christopher Harris of Plymouth, whose brother was "specially favored of the earl of Northumberland" and had been suspected in 1605–6 of complicity in the Gunpowder Plot.[10] William and Margaret Peter's eldest daughter Rose in 1630 named her only child Philip (a daughter), a popular name among Devon Catholics. William, of course, perished in 1612, but his elder brother fought the Puritans to his death. During the Civil War, John Peter gave his only daughter in marriage to Allen Apsley, governor of the Fort of Exeter during the Puritan siege. The Peter family manor at Bowhay was burned, possibly in 1646 by parliamentary forces. John Peter and his fifteen-year-old son and Margaret Cotton (William Peter's widow) were buried in 1642–43 during the hostilities, their cause of death unrecorded.

William Peter's wife and in-laws, the Brewtons, were anti-Puritan as well. A year after the murder, Margaret Brewton Peter preferred her dead husband's boyhood friend, William Ford, a high churchman, to the living of East Coker; in 1647, a Puritan Parliament sequestered his rectory. On 2 February 1612/13, Margaret married Edward Cotton, son of William Cotton, the fiercely anti-Puritan bishop of Exeter. Edward shared his father's convictions, and he, too, paid for his beliefs in 1647, at which time the Puritans sequestered from him the rectories of Duloe (Cornwall), Shobrooke, and Bridestow (Devon).

Confronted with spotty documentary records, it is tempting for historians and literary scholars to generalize from the few historical facts already at hand. In 1891, for example, in excavations near the Rougemont Castle, workers unearthed a human skeleton of unusually large proportions. Because the skull was caved in, a local historian—who knew nothing of the Peter elegy but who knew of Peter's death from the Martin inquest in the Devon Record Office—concluded that the skeleton must be that of William Peter of Whipton, who had lived and died nearby, and perished from a blow to the head. The local press, pleased to assign "the giant" a local habitation and a name, renamed him "Will Peter."[11] Similarly wishful thinking has moved Katherine Duncan-Jones to rename Peter's elegist "William Sclater." But the historical William Peter (whose body was laid to rest in the Exminster church on 1 February 1611/ 12), and the real W.S., invite better history.

Notes

1. Leah S. Marcus, "Who Was Will Peter? Or, A Plea for Literary History," *Shakespeare Studies* 25 (1997): 219.

2. Otho Peter, P.C.C. 69 Huddleston (prob. 4 July 1607); Elizabeth Brewton, P.C.C. 26 Wood (prob. 19 Nov. 1624).

3. Book Proceedings of the Orphans' Court (1611), Devonshire Record Office, Exeter, Minute n.d., [February or March] 1611/12.

4. Edward Cotton, P.C.C. 2 Essex (prob. 31 Jan. 1647/8). Rose (d. 1630) married John Kittey of Plymouth, and Margaret, Edward Gould of Heavitree.

5. Edward Drew [Sr.], P.C.C. 44 Lewyn (prob. 16 May 1598).

6. Marcus, "Who was Will Peter?" 228, n. 12, n. 21.

7. Katherine Duncan-Jones, "Who Wrote *A Funerall Elegie?*," *Shakespeare Studies* 25 (1997), 195; Marcus, "Who was Will Peter?" 219.

8. William Shakespeare, attrib. *A Funerall Elegye. By W.S.* (London: G. Eld [for T. Thorpe], 1612).

9. Margery Waldron, [Deposition, 8 April 1612], Exeter City Chamber. Act Books, 7 (1611–12), art. 29, Devonshire Record Office, Exeter.

10. M. S. Giuseppi, ed., *Historical Manuscripts Commission Calendar of the Manuscripts . . . at Hatfield House*, pt. 17 (London: P.R.O., 1938), 489–90.

11. Mr. and Mrs. Frank Drew of Duncan, B.C. (Letter to the author, 2 January 1996). I thank the Drews for alerting me to their family's tattered clipping of this story, evidently from Exeter's *Western Morning News* (1891).

Paradigms of Authorship

Ian Lancashire

Dᴇᴄɪᴅɪɴɢ ᴛʜᴇ authorship of A Funeral Elegy seems to me to depend on confirming Donald Foster's finding that Shakespeare shares with A Funeral Elegy "dozens of words that occur nowhere in . . . other corpora" (1997: 120), and on an electronic library that includes works by many candidate authors, not just the small pool bearing the initials "W.S." Yet instead of testing Foster's application of this method, both opinions in the current debate over the attribution, pro and con, sidestep it.[1] They look elsewhere for confirmation of their views. Stephen Booth, like me, agrees that W. S. is Shakespeare, but Booth says Foster's "computer-generated evidence" is "altogether vulnerable" (1997:234), characterizes all statistics as arbitrary and obscure, and remarks "As to the tests themselves, I don't pretend to understand them" (237). Because there are no statistics in simple counts of all "rare" words (those with a frequency up to twelve), Booth's skepticism may not be quite so damning a factor: statistical tests are normally only used on a sample, a part of a much larger body of data that cannot be studied directly, to determine the probability that the characteristics of the sample hold true for the whole group. What persuades Booth that Foster and Abrams are right is an incident in contemporary history, Foster's success in attributing Primary Colors to its (now admitted) author. Yet if Foster used the same method for these two attributions, how can the results in one case be "vulnerable," and not the results in the other?

Katherine Duncan-Jones shares Booth's doubts about the method but not his belief in the attribution. She disputes Shakespeare as author of the Elegy "no matter what Professor Foster's database may reveal" (1997: 192). In proposing instead a candidate whose style she does not analyze but claims does not make her "feel . . . that he definitely composed the Elegie" (206), Duncan-Jones expresses disbelief in the viability of stylometry itself as method.

Leah S. Marcus walks the same line. She objects to "limiting our-selves to stylistic analysis when there are other promising avenues to explore" (1997: 211); and she also proposes a rival candidate without analyzing his style in detail, although she is sympathetic to the Shakespeare attribution. However, she does cite the absence of stylistic traits of Shakespeare in *Elegy* as evidence against Fos-ter's attribution. Marcus says that *Elegy* is "curiously lacking in distinctive [Shakespearean] markers," by which she means, not the grammatical mannerisms that Foster points out ("who" or "whom" as "an impersonal relative pronoun," and hendiadys, 1997: 121–22), but instead "metaphoric density and vividness of language" (212). *Elegy* favors abstract and plain language, which she concedes may be "stylistically appropriate" for the subject (219). She believes this concession may strengthen the case for Shakespearean author-ship, but in referring to metaphor and vivid language as matters of appropriate style, Marcus implicitly characterizes them as markers over which a writer has conscious control. Any competent author could empty his verse of both for some reason. If so, neither trait can be counted on to distinguish any author's handiwork from any other's. Another reason for wariness is the ambiguity in such features. English plain speech is built on a graveyard of dead meta-phors. What counts as a metaphor? Foster uses unambiguous mark-ers: a word, a phrase, or a collocation either exists in someone's writings or does not.

Stanley Wells accepts style as a valid criterion for deciding au-thorship. Nonetheless a skeptic, he points out stylistic "contraindi-cations" in the *Elegy*, features that he does not find in Shakespeare's works, particularly several uses of *of* including "of deserving praise" and "nine of years" (1997: 188). Depending on a function word everyone uses (*of*), and being unambiguously countable, Wells's negative markers warrant careful scrutiny. When I searched a TACT database of the New Oxford Shakespeare, some collocations closely resembling his examples turned up[2]; and Wells's negative findings are consistent with a generally accepted observation that Shakespeare's style changes over time. Not every feature in *Elegy* need be traced in Shakespeare's other works.

There are reasons why researchers greet a word/phrase-frequency method, based on the overlap of lexical or phrasal items in the writings of two authors, with puzzlement and skepticism. The trou-ble is not quantities or criteria based on numbers ("statistics"). Most of us now accept that Shakespeare's metrics change over his career and that counts of simple features like caesural pause, enjambment, and unstressed endings reliably chart this variation. It can be seen easily by comparing a short passage from *Titus Andronicus* with another from *The Tempest*. Unlike prosodic repetition, which belongs to a consciously applied poetic craft, frequencies of words seem to depend not on the author's skill, but on us, the readers, juxtaposing widely separated points of text in the works, dissociated items that only our bulky printed concordances and the more trim returns of our text-analysis searches can knit together. Who can resist a groundswell of suspicion when the lines making up a frequency group lack all continuity? Doubts about the database can also occur. Are texts by all candidate authors part of it? Has a line or phrase from a key text gone missing, so that not every stitch is being accounted for? Ill informed often as to which editions have been used or on how the character set has been interpreted for the sorting algorithm, anyone looking at results of a search request on a sea of data may well feel a lack of confidence. Yet this skepticism arises from a conflict of two paradigms, not from these worrying factors.

Wells expresses the paradigmatic nature of this disagreement indirectly in the subtitle of his commentary, "Obstacles to Belief." Shakespeareans are as interested as anyone in learning the truth about the authorship of *The Funeral Elegy*, but they work within a literary paradigm. They prefer readable text, especially primary historical sources—known editions of the works, originals listed in the STC, facsimiles, and historical manuscripts—over frequency distributions. Frequencies cannot be read as text; they depend for intelligibility on a belief in a paradigm that treats words and word combinations as fundamental particles created by someone considered merely as a biological entity capable of speech. Those who trust in "primary sources" locate conditions for truth in authorship questions within the intellectual coherence of the texts in question, not in the neural structures that leave their signatures in those texts. The literary paradigm regards frequencies as accidental characteristics of text, of no more significance than white noise in an art gallery.

It is instructive how Wells, Duncan-Jones, and Marcus frame their commentaries by drawing on beliefs about Shakespeare's abilities, mind, and life to question his authorship of the *Elegy*, on beliefs that arise from a paradigm that defines a human being by reference to appropriate or inappropriate ideas in the texts he writes. Wells cannot believe that, at forty-seven, Shakespeare would refer to himself "as young" (1997: 187), assuming that the passage

"Yet time . . . / May one day lay open malice which hath cross'd it [the poet's reputation], / And right the hopes of my endangered youth" (*Elegy*, lines 145–48), does so. Duncan-Jones cannot believe that Shakespeare, the playwright who created play-loving Hamlet, would slight the acting profession in the phrase "some loose Mimicks" (193; *Elegy*, line 275), or that someone who had attacked Puritans in the character of Malvolio would commit himself to a "Calvinist" notion of "predestinated" time (lines 1, 497). Marcus is unconvinced that W. S. borrowed from Shakespeare or others when "common cultural inheritance" might explain the parallels (1997: 214–25). Almost everyone, Foster included, believes the poem to be mediocre, hardly up to the high standard we have come to expect of Shakespeare at his best.[3] Yet any person can deliberately throw over private or public text-based ideas, beliefs, knowledge, and even values in a matter of days, let alone years. In everything over which individuals have conscious control, from bookish tastes to religious conversion, change can happen overnight by a simple act of will or emotion. A person's views in a text are a by-product of current personal decisions and are neither a consequence of known past actions nor a sufficient determinant of future behavior.

Attribution is possible only when we can identify reliable markers of authoring. To be reliable, markers must be habitual, difficult for the author to observe, to edit in, and to cut, and unambiguous. They must be ones of which the author is not conscious. Word, phrase, and collocation frequencies often meet these requirements. These features, collectively, can be signatures of authorship because of the way the writer's brain stores and creates speech. Even the author cannot imitate these features, simply because they are normally beyond recognition, unless the author has the same tools and expertise as stylometrists undertaking attribution research. Reliable markers arise from the unique, hidden clusters within the author's long-term associative memory. Frequency-based attribution methodology recognizes these and depends on a biological, not a conceptual, paradigm of authorship.

These two paradigms diverge over one belief: that in the possibility of (partly) unconscious authoring. In distinguishing the work of Fletcher from that of Beaumont, Cyrus Hoy (1956: 130) refers to "linguistic preferences" and argues that, when only one author (A) uses a feature (x), among a large body of other authors (who do not use it), (x) reliably marks A's work. Hoy does not insist that (x) be impossible for A to avoid using, or that it be unconsciously invoked; as a result, he implies that A can choose (prefer) to use or not to use (x). If so, then other authors can also choose (prefer) to use and not use (x); and thus the method fails in principle. David J. Lake (1975: 7) may share Hoy's views. Thomas B. Horton insists (rightly, in my opinion) that a unique marker in A, clearly not found in any other author, is insufficient: that marker must be accompanied by evidence that it is substylistic and unconscious.

> Unfortunately the textual features that stand out to a literary scholar usually reflect a writer's conscious stylistic decisions and are thus open to imitation, deliberate or otherwise. Tests of authorship that are founded on subconscious habits are a desirable goal in most (if not all) applications. (1987: 9)

In my opinion, frequency data will warrant the critic's belief only if the data are supported by a theoretical paradigm resting on experimental scientific research. Current evidence shows that the mental process of creating an utterance is a parallel (not a serial) one: it involves many areas of the brain simultaneously (Ojemann: 1991). This process appears to call for a sudden collapsing of many actions (and potentials) in diverse parts of the brain into one action, which is the utterance (Kosslyn and Koenig 1992: 48, 268–69). This distributed process explains why the memory of how to make an utterance is a procedural memory, something that we cannot observe directly but can only recall in doing. Authors cannot clearly know in detail the linguistic shape of what they are going to write before it is written. Before the realizing of utterance in text, much of the detail in authoring is unconscious or un-self-conscious. Afterward, only linguistic patterns that cannot be perceived in reading—particularly combinations of function words and other collocations—resist conscious editorial alteration. It is these markers, not stylistic choices, that we must have before we turn to external evidence for confirmation.

Notes

1. My analysis of a passage from the *Elegy* in the context of Shakespeare's works (180–181) does not repeat Foster's procedures but provides corroborating evidence of a general kind. Hieatt and Hieatt, however, question Foster's method of calculating rare-word percentages and so represent a typically scientific reaction to a new empirical discovery (which is to attack details of the procedure rather than the results).

2. Wells cites five phrases from *Elegy* but only one does not occur, in a variant form, in Shakespeare's works: "The good endeavors of deserving praise" (cf. the

collocation of "deserved" and "praise" in Sonnet 29, line 9; *H5* 3.7.33; and *Cym* 4.5.50); "his best of time" (cf. "the best of our times," *Lr* 1.2.47), "his spring of days" (cf. "spring of day," *2H4* 4.4.35); "in the waste of many idle words" (cf. "idle words," *Luc* 1016; and *Shr* Induction 2.83); "the vain of boast" (cf. "vain boast," *Oth* 5.2.264); and "nine of years" (a collocation not found in Shakespeare, although "of year/years" occurs ten times).

3. Yet is someone's death not a commonplace, and do not the grieving need comforting that expresses itself the same for us all? Was the author of the *Elegy* thinking of the wife and children of William Peter when he sacrificed vivid poetry for consolation? Would we not think poorly of that author if he had used the occasion to show off his poetic arsenal?

Works Cited

Booth, Stephen. "A Long, Dull Poem by William Shakespeare." *Shakespeare Studies* 25 (1997): 229–37.

Duncan-Jones, Katherine. "Who Wrote *A Funerall Elegie?*" *Shakespeare Studies* 25 (1997): 192–210.

Foster, Donald W, "A Funeral Elegy: W[illiam] S[hakespeare]'s 'Best-Speaking Witnesses'." *Shakespeare Studies* 25 (1997): 115–40.

Hieatt, Charles W., and A. Kent Hieatt, "Attributing *A Funeral Elegy*." *PMLA*, 112 no. 3 (May 1977): 429–31.

Horton, Thomas Bolton. *The Effectiveness of the Stylometry of Function Words in Discriminating between Shakespeare and Fletcher* (Ph.D. dissertation; Department of Computer Science, University of Edinburgh, December 1987).

Hoy, Cyrus. "The Shares of Fletcher and His Collaborators in the Beaumont and Fletcher Canon (I)." *Studies in Bibliography* 8 (1956): 129–46.

Kosslyn, Stephen M., and Olivier Koenig. *Wet Mind: The New Cognitive Neuroscience.* New York: Free Press, 1992.

Lake, David J. *The Canon of Thomas Middleton's Plays: Internal Evidence for the Major Problems of Authorship.* Cambridge: Cambridge University Press, 1975.

Lancashire, Ian. "Empirically Determining Shakespeare's Idiolect." *Shakespeare Studies* 25 (1997): 171–85.

Marcus, Leah S. "Who Was Will Peter? Or, A Plea for Literary History." *Shakespeare Studies* 25 (1997): 211–28.

Ojemann, George A. "Cortical Organization of Language." *Journal of Neuroscience* 11, no. 8 (August 1991): 2281–87.

Wells, Stanley. "'A Funeral Elegy': Obstacles to Belief." *Shakespeare Studies* 25 (1997): 186–91.

Exit Sclater

RICHARD ABRAMS

KATHERINE Duncan-Jones's ascription of the Peter elegy to the Puritan minister William Sclater represents the most detailed attempt so far to locate an author other than Shakespeare. In her conclusion, though, Duncan-Jones announces that her case for Sclater is only tentative ("my mind is not quite made up on this subject").[1] Her belated irresolution, whose better part may well be honest doubt, serves also a rhetorical function. Broached at a juncture when her argument runs into serious trouble, Duncan-Jones's irresolution implies that finally it does not matter much who wrote the Elegy—if not Sclater, then some other nonentity—so long as we're agreed it wasn't Shakespeare. In view of Duncan-Jones's hesitation, and in the light of Donald Foster's newly presented evidence of the Peter family's anti-Puritan (and probably Catholic) convictions, my systematic effort in this essay to refute the Puritan Sclater's claim may smack of overkill. But a detailed argument deserves a detailed response, in the course of which I shall take the opportunity to correct several misassumptions about the Elegy that Duncan-Jones's essay puts in circulation.

Clearing ground for her attribution, Duncan-Jones offers aesthetic impressions that would "rule out any possibility of Shakespeare's authorship" (192). For her, Shakespeare is a known quantity, "our Shakespeare," and this is not the man. But Duncan-Jones's totalizing attempts to capture Shakespeare's essence are, for all their appeal to common sense, dated, reductive, and ideologically partial; they produce a Bard who would be unrecognizable to many readers. Observing that Shakespeare "had just celebrated theatrical illusion brilliantly" in *The Tempest* (194), Duncan-Jones cannot imagine him admiring the reserved, untheatrical Peter. She forgets Prospero's weary disengagement with his own theatrical artifice as "rough magic." Similarly, as a playwright to the king, Duncan-Jones's snobbish Shakespeare would not get mixed up in some "dingy project" involving a "fairly modest Devon gentry family." But Shakespeare was other things besides a court poet; he befriended publicans and sinners—witness his involvement in the Bellott-Mountjoy trial the very year of the Peter elegy. Nor would Duncan-Jones's Shakespeare become pious or "preachy" even in a funeral poem. But do we really know the conscience of the man who retired early from the stage, cut his adulterous son-in-law out of his will, and perhaps "dyed a papist"? Most incredibly, despite his celebrated powers of imaginative identification, Shakespeare, as "a nongraduate," cannot "have cared about the fact that William Peter was "'double honor'd in degree'" (195). This last assertion betrays a blindness that is pervasive in Duncan-Jones's argument. Just as she overlooks the possibility that certain features of the Elegy, such as its praise of Peter's achievements—which happen to have been scholastic—may be mandated by genre, so she fails to consider that W. S.'s disclaimer of "Exercise in this kind" may refer to the genre ("kind") of elegy, not broadly to poetic composition.

In proposing an alternative candidate to Shakespeare, Duncan-Jones constructs a profile of W. S. based on speculatively interpreted internal evidence, then locates a historical figure matching her profile. She begins with a strained demonstration that, as she maintained in a letter to the *Times Literary Supplement* (29 March 1996, p. 17), "the world of the author and subject of the *Elegy* [are] almost wholly Devonian." Foster had demonstrated that W. S. favors standard London English, and Duncan-Jones fails to challenge this finding; nor does she herself argue that W. S. possessed an insider knowledge of Devon. Instead, her whole argument rests on the contention that the poem salutes four luminaries associated with the region. The Elegy's "strongest poetic echoes" are John Ford and Samuel Daniel, both West Country natives, who composed elegies on the death of a third West Country man, Sir Charles Blount, Lord Mountjoy. Duncan-Jones's fourth West Country figure turns out to be, surprisingly, Sir Philip Sidney, whom she indirectly connects with Mountjoy. After Sidney's death, Mountjoy became the lover of Penelope Rich, Sidney's Stella, whom he eventually married. In Duncan-Jones's view, this triangulation qualifies Sidney for inclusion as an honorary West Country man.

Much is wrong with Duncan-Jones's argument. Nowhere in his canonical writings does Sclater display an interest in contemporary secular authors, much less in West Country authors. Moreover, by the time he moved to Somerset (around 1606), Daniel and Ford had already moved away to London, which became the center of their literary activities (Duncan-Jones adduces no evidence of their attracting favorite-son followings in the West Country).[2] Mountjoy possesses a stronger claim; after subduing Ireland he was created earl of Devonshire in 1604. But Mountjoy never returned to Devon; he lived out his brief life at his London estate of Wanstead, dying in 1606. In short, not one of Duncan-Jones's three principal West Country figures would spontaneously have thrust himself upon a local consciousness; all would require cultivation. But from the time of Sclater's arrival in Somerset he was embattled; his life of complaint and vexation in his adoptive region hardly seems conducive to the formation of chauvinistic reading tastes.

Four names on Duncan-Jones's list quickly boil down to two, and then just one. If W. S. associated Peter with Mountjoy (not only because of the Devon connection but for reasons I'll mention in a moment), then Ford and Daniel may be implicated only incidentally, not as West Country poets but as protobiographers whose elegies constituted the readiest sources for Mountjoy's life and death. As for Sidney, though Mountjoy indeed married Stella, the marriage gave rise to scandal. Mountjoy died three months later, prompting the court gossip John Chamberlain to write:

> The Earl of Devonshire left this life on Thursday night last, soon and early for his years, but late enough for himself; and happy had be been if he had gone two or three years since, before the world was weary of him or that he had left that scandal behind him.[3]

W. S. models his grieving account of Peter's death on Ford's treatment of Mountjoy's fall, which in turn follows popular representations of Essex's fall. Accordingly, W. S. often writes as though Peter died the victim of an envious faction rather than a single hand, and he fears that Peter's bad end will, like Mountjoy's, destroy his reputation. Such sympathies are plausible in Shakespeare, the apparent admirer of Essex, who can also be linked with Mountjoy via Southampton; when Southampton incurred the Queen's wrath for his unauthorized marriage to Elizabeth Vernon, Mountjoy courageously proclaimed him his best friend.[4] But the same sympathies are unlikely in Sclater, who would have balked at taking up the scandalous Mountjoy and would have frowned at Penelope's loud contempt for her Puritan husband and her long flirtation with Catholicism (rumored to have ended in a deathbed conversion).[5] For Sidney to enter "Sclater's" poem under such auspices was to be tarnished by association.

In sum, of the four names on Duncan-Jones's list, only Mountjoy, who was more a Londoner and a habitué of the court than a West Country man, seems relevant. But a fifth name is strangely absent from Duncan-Jones's list: Shakespeare's. Even scholars skeptical of Shakespeare's authorship concede that the Elegy contains many echoes of his work. Duncan-Jones fails to explain why a Somerset-based Puritan minister scornful of "loose mimics" should have phrases from Shakespeare rattling around his head.

Jacobean literary and aristocratic society was close-knit, degrees of separation minimal. For this reason, any number of lines can be drawn connecting Duncan-Jones's Elegy-related figures. To illustrate, one way to link Mountjoy, Ford, Daniel, Sidney, and Shakespeare, while emphatically excluding Sclater, is through the countess of Pembroke's Wilton. Shakespeare performed and visited there, Sidney was the countess's brother, Daniel enjoyed her patronage, Ford dedicated texts to both her sons, and Mountjoy took over as Daniel's patron after Daniel left her service. What is more, Otho Peter, Will's father, seems to have had land dealings with the countess.[6] Still, I do not deceive myself that Wilton holds a lost key to the Elegy any more than I believe in Duncan-Jones's West Country network. Wilton's viability as an alternative common denominator highlights the flaw in Duncan-Jones's method.

Returning later in her essay to W. S.'s alleged West Country orientation, Duncan-Jones observes that "every single one" of Sclater's five books published between 1610 and 1612 "had a West Country dedication" (201). The coincidence would be significant *only if* the books were dedicated to acquaintances living elsewhere—for example, in Sclater's former residence of Staffordshire—*and if* the Elegy were also dedicated, unaccountably, to a Staffordshire resident. Taken by itself without support from Duncan-Jones's bogus West Country "echoes," the Elegy's dedication to Peter's brother who lived in Devon is unremarkable.

Duncan-Jones argues that W. S. was not just a West Country resident but a Puritan. Besides noting the Elegy's contratheatrical motif (discussed in my previous essay), she submits only two pieces of evidence: (a) the word *predestinated*, for which see Foster's present discussion, and (b) W. S.'s citations from the Bible, "especially those books most drawn on by Puritans, the Old Testament Prophets and Revelation" (196). One passage she traces to Rev. 20:12. But Revelation was a favorite Shakespeare text, adapted, by Naseeb Shaheen's count, no fewer than ninety-one times (including six adaptations of Rev. 20:12) in thirty-three plays.[7] Neither were the

Prophets a Puritan monopoly, but the point is moot since Duncan-Jones's two examples are questionable. The more plausible is W. S.'s very free adaptation of Dan. 9:27 (FE, 171–4);[8] the other, his phrase, "the path / Which guides to doing well" (FE, 503–04), to which Duncan-Jones compares Joel 2.8:

> Neither shall one thrust one another, they shall walke euery one in his path: and when they fall upon the sword, they shall not be wounded.

Duncan-Jones concedes that "the verbal link is a bit tenuous." Is there anything that links the two passages besides the word path, which, with its plural, occurs seventy-six times in the King James Bible?

Arriving at this plateau Duncan-Jones surveys the ground she has traversed: "Putting all these things together I believe that the Elegie's tone, preoccupations, imagery, and literary allusions point to its being the work of someone of strong Puritan faith, most probably a clergyman, living in the West Country" (197). I have faithfully recorded all of Duncan-Jones's evidence. From what then does she deduce not only a West Country Puritan but "someone of strong Puritan faith," and why a clergyman, unless "preachy" has been silently promoted from an aesthetic judgment to a historical datum? Duncan-Jones immediately builds on her inference: "If such a man were in holy orders he would probably be a university graduate." That lets out Shakespeare. But unless I nodded, no evidence for a formally educated Puritan clergyman ever emerges. Instead, turning to Sclater, Duncan-Jones demonstrates his possession of all the traits she herself conjures by innuendo.

Duncan-Jones saves for last her discussion of W. S.'s personal travails. During his Somerset ministry, Sclater suffered traducement and "hazard of life," possibly from a knife wound such as Peter received.[9] Duncan-Jones connects this with W. S.'s enigmatic allusion to his loss of "credit"—credit he hopes to regain in the place he lost it, "Even in which place the subject of the verse / . . . / Had education and new being" (149–52). The apparent reference is to Oxford, where Peter was "double honor'd in degree." But Sclater was a Cambridge man, whose troubles occurred in the West Country. Duncan-Jones positions herself with two arguments. First, she conflates the "place" where W. S. was traduced (148) with the "soil / Where [Peter] enjoy'd his birth, life, death and seat" (130–31), although eighteen lines separate the two words. "It is just about conceivable—" she condescends, "this writer not being distinguished for lucidity—that the 'soile' of line 130 is different from the 'place' of lines 148–49 . . . but to me this seems rather unlikely" (197). Why unlikely? When in her *TLS* letter Duncan-Jones admitted that "Exercise in this kind" might refer to elegiac composition, she similarly opted for a conversation-closing "But I find this unlikely." In neither instance does she give reasons for her privileged impression; and with respect to "place" she buoys up her reading with a citation that should have sunk it.

W. S. claims to have lost credit in the place where Peter "had education and new being" (152). Duncan-Jones interprets:

> In conjunction with "new beeing" [Q1], which presumably refers to birth, baptism, or both, I think the poet is using "education" in *OED*'s sense 1, current until the Restoration: "The process of rearing a child or young person." The phrase "education and new beeing" is a cumbersome expansion of the very familiar expression "bred and born"

For Duncan-Jones the poet is "forging a connection between the location" of his own loss of credit and the region where Peter was born and bred. Perhaps; but she further opines that in order "to make any real sense," this connection must be a "geographical coincidence" and not just an analogy between two hostile environments. Standard scholarly procedure to determine what W. S. had in mind when he wrote "education" is to compare the word's use elsewhere in the Elegy. Duncan-Jones ignores its occurrence in line 54 in context with "Learning" and "Teaching" (56, 61)—a train that leads W. S. to the conclusion that Peter "spen[t] his spring of days in sacred schools" (74), that is, at Oxford. As for "new being," though Duncan-Jones glosses the phrase as "birth, baptism, or both," baptism instantly drops away. Her argument requires her to read simply, "birth"; otherwise she could not generate her variant of the set phrase, "born and bred." (To read "birth" for "new being" additionally creates a unique redundancy with the phrase, "birth, life, death and seat.")

Determining that W. S. lost credit in the West Country, Duncan-Jones inquires into the cause of his loss. Her earlier hunch of a clergyman now gives rise to the inference that W. S. got into "trouble within some close-knit provincial community," where he was maligned by "his parishioners, perhaps." To enable this unfounded inference, she is obliged to disregard the word *sin* (W. S.'s enemies "sifted to imbane / [his] reputation, with a witless sin"). Thus convenienced, Duncan-Jones speculates that W. S. "may have been altogether too independent minded for some people's liking" (199).

The conjecture turns out to fit Sclater, who matches Duncan-Jones's profile in every particular:

> We are looking . . . for a man of education and ability who had got into some sort of serious trouble, perhaps for his religious convictions. These troubles were strongly linked with the same "place" where William Peter was born and died. This individual did not normally write poetry. (200)

Besides "ability," not one point here can be sustained by direct argument from the evidence. At such moments one may be excused for wondering whether Duncan-Jones's profile was not created to fit the suspect.

Even when Duncan-Jones's frame is in place, Sclater requires considerable grooming. In initially explaining her method of profiling the elegist, Duncan-Jones announced that her arguments "rule out any possibility of Shakespeare's authorship, no matter what Professor Foster's database may reveal." But Duncan-Jones discards more than just the evidence from Shaxicon. She ignores stylistic and linguistic indicators, ignores evidence of borrowings from a manuscript to which few writers besides Shakespeare could have had access, ignores similarities with nearly contemporaneous Shakespeare plays, and much more. At one point, acknowledging Sclater's stylistic differences from W. S. (this is the problem she sidesteps by abruptly declaring that her case for Sclater is only tentative), Duncan-Jones appeals to circumstances: W. S. composed in haste, in shock, and in an unfamiliar genre. The same argument could be used to support a claim for Shakespeare or just about anyone.

By way of positive lexical evidence, Duncan-Jones observes that "Sclater was an adventurous writer . . . capable of such a coinage as 'possibilited.' The *OED* includes several hundred citations from Sclater's works" (206). Over five hundred, by my count, and many strange indeed, but few that overlap W. S. The rarest matching word is *overgo*, which W. S. uses differently from the *OED* citation for Sclater, though in a sense corresponding to two out of three Shakespeare uses. The next rarest is *unrest*, which Duncan-Jones cites hopefully. But *unrest* is common enough in Shakespeare; indeed, according to Chadwyck-Healey, the language's earliest analogue to the Elegy's exact locution of "deep'st unrest" is "deep unrest" in *The Rape of Lucrece* (line 1275).[10] Most damaging, Sclater's coinages follow different principles of word-formation than those linking Shakespeare and W. S. "[T]his may not be significant," Duncan-

Jones explains, because of the Elegy's "complete difference, both in genre and subject matter, from [Sclater's] prose works" (206). But the Elegy also differs generically and in subject matter from Shakespeare's plays, narrative poems and sonnets, yet the principles of coinage never vary.

Especially misleading is Duncan-Jones's dogmatic assertion that W. S. "makes much of his lack of expertise in poetry" (209). On this point as elsewhere Duncan-Jones divides her evidence, filling the gap with bountiful hypothesis. Thus, Duncan-Jones's "much" turns out to consist of only two passages in the Elegy, one that she cites at the beginning of her essay, the other at the end. Both she misreads. In her final paragraph Duncan-Jones finds damning testimony in W. S.'s utterly conventional downplaying of "The value of my talent" (242). Were we to eliminate Shakespeare on this basis, we would need to discard every text in which he speaks of his own writing, including the dedications to Southampton, the sonnets, and the dramatic prologues and epilogues both early and late, for all allude in one way or another to the poet's "all-unable pen." (The same passage contains another obvious modesty topos; W. S. remarks that "no merit strong enough of mine" can fuel poetic praise [237]).

The second passage in which W. S. supposedly confesses poetic inadequacy is the dedication—and here I must dwell on textual particulars, not only to refute Duncan-Jones's reading but to refine my own. W. S. begins by asserting that in honoring Peter, he performs the "last duty of a friend," serving therein as "but a second to the privilege of Truth." The final four-word phrase derives verbatim from Ford's dedication of *Fames Memoriall* (1606), in which Ford affirms that Truth will out—Truth's privilege is to make itself known—so that in correcting the record about a slandered Mountjoy, he himself becomes Truth's humble mouthpiece. Similar logic governs W. S.'s opening. Because his friend's goodness speaks for itself, Peter's reputation will thrive with or without the poet's intervention; W. S. is merely Truth's "second," its backer-up (*OED*, sb, II.8.a; *Tmp* 3.3.103).[11] More than a courtesy is involved here; the hairsplitting distinction between primary and secondary witnesses recurs throughout the Elegy. Notably, the figure of self-revealing Truth caps the poem's opening meditation: "Truth doth leave / Sufficient proof" (26). And what Truth leaves proof of is not quite Peter's "good endeavors"—dying young, he left unperformed many noble deeds—but his "worth" or "deserts" (4, 7, 12). The idea is clearly important, for "deserts" occurs also as the last word of the

dedication, in which the Elegy is inscribed to Peter's brother and
to those who loved Will Peter "for his deserts."

The antithesis of deeds and deserts is bound up with the dedication's next sentence, in which W. S. disclaims "Exercise in this
kind." Duncan-Jones reads a non sequitur: I am new at writing
poetry—not an impossible reading. But for two reasons "Exercise
in this kind" reads better as "exercise in the elegiac mode that I
just labelled the 'last duty of a friend.'" That duty, of course, is to
bury and commemorate the dead—an act that W. S. *incidentally*
performs in verse. But the unaccustomed part lies not in the choice
of poetry as a medium but in the exercise of commemoration itself.
This is clear because the key notion of "warrant[ing]"—that is,
witness[ing]—"in [Peter's] behalf" recurs immediately in the second part of the sentence: "Exercise in this kind I will little affect
. . . but there must be miracle in that labor which, to *witness* my
remembrance to this departed gentleman, I would not willingly
undergo." Duncan-Jones wants to read here a greenhorn admission:
"divine intervention—indeed, a 'miracle'—will be required to sustain [W. S.'s] literary labor of love." But the words cannot support
that meaning without emendation.[12] More correctly, W. S. explains
that "in memorializing William Peter, I would undertake any labor
short of the miraculous" (Foster's gloss). In other words, he sheep-
ishly avers that he lacks practise in the art of humbly seconding
the truth (I am reminded of Donne: "You know my uttermost when
it was best, and even then I did best when I had least truth for my
subjects"[13]). But he accepts that only through such unassuming
service can he discharge "Such duties as [are] owe[d] to thy de-
sert" (226).

Further refuting Duncan-Jones's misreading of "Exercise in this
kind" is W. S.'s boast of artistic prowess the moment he enters the
poem in the first person:

> But that I not intend in full discourse
> To progress out his life, I could display
> A good man in each part exact and force
> The common voice to warrant what I say

(79–82)

As I noted in my earlier essay, W. S. trusts in his own power to
move an audience; by telling Peter's story he can compel broad
assent. Systematic allusions further indicate that W. S.'s wonted
narrative mode is theatrical—though my argument to this effect
drew fire from Stanley Wells and Leah Marcus (and a custard pie

from Stephen Booth). In denying that "progress [out]" is dramatur-gical, Wells misses my point, which is simply that the transitive infinitive means to narratize—the dramaturgical connotations rest on other elements in the passage. Marcus, too, errs in narrowly relating W. S.'s vaunt "to the language of the ecclesiastical courts": "Although Will Peter himself cannot prosecute for slander in the usual way—by bringing in six or more citizens to swear to his good name—W. S. can posthumously restore that name by serving himself as witness of the 'common voice.'" Certainly, the act of witness is relevant, but Marcus needs to make room for "force."[14] W. S. places himself in a dynamic relation to public opinion. Boast-ing ability to force the common voice, he cannot simultaneously embody it.

Clearly, W. S. boasts of his power to retrace Peter's life, but as I have come to realize, *progress out* also means something else. It means to come forward in time from Peter's death, projecting what he would have been had he lived. This more truly "progressive" meaning is guaranteed by the next quatrain with its explanatory "For":

> For if his fate and heaven had decreed
> That full of days he might have lived to see
> The grave in peace, the times that should succeed
> Had been best-speaking witnesses with me
>
> (83–86)

Though Peter's brief life exhibited only deserts, that same life, con-tinuing along the path it was following, would have produced "good endeavors" such as times future would have applauded. While affirming his ability to supplement Peter's deserts with fabri-cated deeds possessing verisimilitude, however, W. S. renews his commitment to seconding literal Truth, which already witnesses in Peter's behalf. Twice he echoes the dedication, declining to force an audience to "*warrant* what I say" (82), to turn contemporaries into "*witnesses* with me" (86). He refrains from intervening hero-ically because, by a fiction, Peter's deserts already guarantee lasting fame. "[S]hould [Peter] lie obscur'd without a tomb"—should W. S. fail in his act of poetic commemoration—"Time would to time his honesty commend" (159–60), Truth continue to exercise its privilege of speaking. No less fervently would "the times that should succeed" have applauded Peter's deeds had he lived than the present time will bear unprompted witness to his deserts.

W. S.'s ethical commitment entails an aesthetic loss. In this poem, fit service often means little more than to repeat flatly, with imperceptible variations, "He was good" (532; cf. 17, 346). But if W. S. high-mindedly performs an aesthetically disappointing act of witness, he keeps in focus the conditions by which he is able to stir the common voice. Because Peter exhibited perfect consistency of character, because "He was good," W. S. can conjure predictively his friend's unacted deeds, "display[ing] / A good man in each part exact"; he can present Peter (in Sidneian terms) not as he was but as he should have been. In thus claiming ability to complete the life-as-text that "Time . . . / Abridg'd" (1–2), W. S. takes as his province a vatic realm off-limits both to Duncan-Jones's preacher and Marcus's ecclesiastical court-witness. His power lies in his command of the poet's immemorial stock-in-trade of probable fictions. And though he declines the option of stirring an audience, he never doubts "The value of my talent" to achieve this end. He simply refuses, for once, to "range beyond [himself], courting opinion with unfit disguise."

One respondent suggests that I have tried to pass the Elegy off as "a good poem." I don't accept these as the terms of the debate. Granted, I derive more pleasure from a sonnet, but I find the Elegy interesting, and my experience in staging it (for four voices) has convinced me that several passages can be compelling. It's regrettable that authorship politics prevents some readers from hearing a syllable of the elegist's grief! Deferring critical appraisals, we need to be discussing the circumstances of the Elegy's composition. The suspicion, aired frequently at an earlier stage of discussion, that W. S.'s initials are falsified, seems to have died away, and a similar demise seems to be overtaking the misperception of W. S. as a paid hack ("Not hir'd").[15] Patently, a debate looms over the question of the elegist's acquaintance with Peter (for me, the issue is decided by W. S.'s divulgence of having sealed with his friend a "constant and irrefragable vow" [235]). These are matters to thrash out in the normal give-and-take of evidence. A harder question is how to break the vicious circle in which a nuanced reading of the Elegy becomes immediately suspect because readers assume that a Sclater-caliber author cannot have meant much of anything. I conclude with a crux that again engages both the poem and its dedication.

A stranger to "Exercise in this kind," W. S. in his dedication proclaims that he "little affect[s], and [is] less addicted to" elegiac composition. The verbs echo a passage (echo, in the sense that the poem gives evidence of anterior composition) in which W. S. praises Peter as one who neither *"Affect[ed]* fashions, nor [was] *addicted* wholly / To unbeseeming blushless vanities" (93–94). Is the repetition an unconscious reminiscence, or does W. S. exert strong artistic control over harmonies and minute variations of phrase? A fair amount hinges on the question. W. S. implicates himself in the degeneracy of Peter's murderer(s) through such devices as his climactic appropriation of the epithet "courting opinion" earlier applied to Drew and his kind. A similar irony may operate in W. S.'s understatement that he is not addicted to elegy; by using words elsewhere connoting theatrical excess, he may imply his own discomfort with pious exercises. But that is a debate we're not yet ready to engage, for we've yet to agree on the subtleties of which W. S. is capable. Right now, good poem or bad, the Elegy needs some better readers.

Notes

1. Katherine Duncan-Jones, "Who Wrote *A Funerall Elegie?*" *Shakespeare Studies*, 25 (1997): 192–210, 208.
2. Though a small matter, it is worth noting that Daniel probably came from the Bath area in the northeast tip of Somerset rather than from Taunton (where Duncan-Jones places him), in the extreme southwest, near Sclater's Pitminster; similarly, Beckington, to which Daniel retired, is in the northeast; cf. Joan Rees, *Samuel Daniel* (Liverpool: Liverpool Univ. Press, 1964), 2. Lisa Hopkins, *John Ford's Political Theatre* (Manchester: Manchester University Press, 1994), tentatively places Ford within a Catholic coterie. If she is right, Ford would be even less likely to be included in Sclater's reading list.
3. Cited in Cyril Falls, *Mountjoy: Elizabethan General* (London: Odhams Press, 1955), 235.
4. Mountjoy to Cecil, 8 June 1600, *CSP Ireland*, 9: 223. After Mountjoy's death, Southampton served as his chief mourner and took financial responsibility for his illegitimate children.
5. For Penelope's Catholic associations, cf. Hopkins, *Ford's Political Theatre*, 9–13. To be sure, Mountjoy and Sidney can be linked in other ways than through Penelope. But when all is said, one must question whether Sidney was regarded as an honorary West Country man, even in the "tangential" way Duncan-Jones suggests. Sidney's death met with an outpouring of memorial verse; anyone who could capitalize on an association did so. If Sidney truly functioned as a source of West Country pride, Duncan-Jones should be able to adduce evidence to that effect.
6. PRO, London: Inq. p.m. C142/296/106 (8 Oct. 1607); copy, Court of Wards, WARD 7/33/251.
7. Donald W. Foster, "Shakespeare and the Peters in History," *Shakespeare Studies*, 26 (1998): 293; Naseeb Shaheen, *Biblical References in Shakespeare's Tragedies* (Newark: University of Delaware Press, 1987); *Biblical References in Shakespeare's Histories* (Newark: University of Delaware Press, 1989); *Biblical*

References in Shakespeare's Comedies (Newark: University of Delaware Press, 1993).

8. "The Text of *A Funeral Elegy* by W. S.," ed. Donald W. Foster, *Shakespeare Studies*, 25 (1997), 95–114.

9. Inferring that Sclater may have been the victim of a knife attack, Duncan-Jones argues that his emotional identification with Peter inspired the poem. But W. S. never mentions a knife injury, and he alludes only obliquely to Peter's mode of death. If W. S. sustained such a wound, the coincidence with Peter would have been uncanny and he might be expected to make more of it. So if Sclater did suffer a knife attack, it can be argued that the circumstance *weakens* his chance of being the elegist.

10. Chadwyck-Healey, *Literature Online* (LION), online, available at http://www.chadwyck.co.uk/lion/index.html.

11. With regard to W. S.'s fiction of the universal self-revealing truth of Peter's goodness, Duncan-Jones's contention that W. S. "claims to be uniquely qualified to perform the task of creating a poetic monument to [Peter's] good name" is seriously misleading.

12. In the first version of my previous essay I myself misread along Duncan-Jones's lines, supplying a "but" before "to witness," "W[illiam] S[hakespeare's] 'Funeral Elegy' and the Turn from the Theatrical," *Studies in English Literature* 36 no. 2 (spring 1996): 435–460, 437.

13. John Donne, "An hymne to the Saints," in *Poems*, ed. H. Grierson (reprint, Oxford: Oxford University Press, 1966), 1: 288.

14. Stanley Wells, "'A Funeral Elegy': Obstacles to Belief," *Shakespeare Studies*, 25 (1997): 186–91; Leah S. Marcus, "Who Was Will Peter? Or, A Plea for Literary History," *Shakespeare Studies*, 25 (1997): 211–28, 218.

15. In a related view, Marcus conjectures that Shakespeare wrote the Elegy on retiring to Stratford to ingratiate himself with the "local magnate" Edward Greville, who was Peter's kinsman, or with members of Greville's family. But Stratford town historians such as Fripp make clear that Greville's fortunes had waned by 1612 (Greville had already surrendered the Manor of Stratford to the Crown by 4 March 1610, when it was sold to William Whitmore), that the Stratford Corporation despised Greville, and that his family regarded him as a loose cannon. For Shakespeare to cultivate such an alliance would have been bad town politics. Furthermore, Edward was rumored to be an accidental fratricide, and his mad-dog father (later executed for a different murder) supposedly aggravated the scandal by laughingly condoning the killing. To lament Peter as an Abel to Drew's Cain (*FE*, 383–90) in such company would not result in popularity. Equally unhistorical is Marcus's account of the departure of Shakespeare's cousin Thomas Greene from Stratford after "repeated shaming rituals" (Marcus, 226). Greene left Stratford because of strained relations not with Greville, apparently, but with William Combe. Greene's brother meanwhile remained on solid enough terms with Greville's ally George Carew for Carew to recommend him for town clerk on Thomas's departure. For Edward Greville and Thomas Greene, cf. Edgar I. Fripp. *Shakespeare: Man and Artist* (reprint: London: Oxford University Press, 1964), 2: 542–48, 833–36, *et passim*. A more recent and detailed account of Greville's decline may be found in Menna Prestwich, *Cranfield: Politics and Profits under the Early Stuarts* (Oxford: Clarendon Press, 1966), 70, 78, 86, 401ff.

REVIEWS

Broken English: Dialects and the Politics of
Language in Renaissance Writings.
By Paula Blank.
London and New York: Routledge, 1996.

Reviewer: David Lee Miller

Paula Blank's Broken English is not related to the recent film of the
same name, for which ads in the Lexington Herald Leader during
summer 1997 proclaim "The sex is wild!" The only copulation in
this Broken English is the sort that joins subjects with predicates,
and as far as I noticed it got wild only once, when a singular noun
in a subject clause near the top of page 41 took a plural pronoun
in the predicate. Despite this lapse in its otherwise chaste syntax,
Broken English should prove a very useful book. It combines a
survey of the controversies over standardizing English in the sixteenth and early-seventeenth centuries with persuasive rereadings
of literary works that directly or obliquely engage these issues. In
the first instance it adds significantly to our understanding of an
important historical context for reading the literature of the English
Renaissance; in the second, it shows how and why this context
matters. The result is a book worth the attention of anyone teaching
or writing about Renaissance literary texts in which the "difference
of English" figures.

As the phrase "difference of English" suggests, Blank is concerned not only with regional distinctions in form and pronunciation, but with a whole range of verbal traits that were cultivated
and castigated by turns (sometimes by the same writer) as English
culture in the formative stages of national self-awareness began to
seek an authoritative version of the vernacular. The "dialects" of
the book's subtitle include poetic diction, thieves' cant, neologism,
archaism, and class as well as regional differences in speech. Blank
gives sustained attention to the way literary authors imitate and
appropriate such differences in the effort to enhance the status of

Reviews

their own highly artificial dialects: among the more prominent works discussed are Spenser's *The Shepheardes Calender*; Shakespeare's *Love's Labor's Lost*, *Henry IV* (both parts), *Henry V*, *The Merry Wives of Windsor*, and *King Lear*; and Jonson's *Bartholomew Fair*, *A Tale of a Tub*, *A Masque of the Gypsies Metamorphosed*, and *Pleasure Reconciled to Virtue* (revised as *For the Honor of Wales*). The lesser works are too numerous to list; in style and genre they range from Udall's *Respublica* to Dekker and Middleton's *The Roaring Girl*; from Drayton's *Poly-Olbion* to Deloney's *Thomas of Reading*.

Chapter 1 briefly contrasts the nascent prescriptivism of England with the *questione della lingua* in Italy and France, turning from Bakhtin to Bourdieu for a theory better able to situate the "social discrimination of competing 'Englishes'" within a broader "struggle for dominance" and prestige in a period of rapid social and cultural change (16, 15). This chapter also shows how persistently discussion of the modern vernaculars in Renaissance Europe was linked to questions about specifically literary language. Subsequent chapters focus on the figurative economics of language (the coining, counterfeiting, importing, exporting, and stealing of words), on southern and northern regional differences, and on the imperial model of linguistic dominance offered by Roman precedent.

Broken English does make good on the *politics of* rubric announced in its subtitle and the title of the series in which it appears. Its politics are liberal in the sense of presuming sympathy for marginalized dialects while steering clear of self-congratulatory partisanship; the argument is valuable for its judiciousness. There are minor lapses. On page 39, for instance, the discussion slides too easily from "learned minority" to "upper classes" by way of "the elite," losing sight momentarily of the social and ideological distance between Renaissance authors and their patrons. And whatever one may wish to say about Shakespeare's use of dialect forms, it probably should not include the assertion that he "spoke his mind about the languages of the expanding British empire" (135) in works written for the stage. It would be unfair, though, to cite peccadilloes as representative. The care of Blank's discriminations is better illustrated by the conclusion to the chapter on southern dialect:

> The contingencies of Renaissance literary politics may have ensured the centrist loyalties of Renaissance authors, and their dependence on the aristocracy, if nothing else, biased their works against the interests

of commoners. But the new, literary interest of southern English, the *vox populi* of early modern literary dialects, sometimes speaks to the alienation of Renaissance English authors from the audiences—often, aristocratic audiences—that they, inevitably, served. The Renaissance appropriation of popular language, however, has nothing, finally, to do with "people" at all; like Edgar, these authors borrow accents, briefly, to serve their turn. Because Renaissance authors had a stake in the license to voice opposition or resistance, they continually found themselves in company with people for whom, otherwise, they had little to say. (99)

The value of such a flexible, relatively nuanced cultural history of the language for literary study in the period is nicely demonstrated in significant contributions to our understanding of works like *Henry V* and *The Shepheardes Calender.*

The approach does also have its limits. Blank remarks at one point on Shakespeare's serious use in other contexts of diction for which he mocks Armado and Holofernes in *Love's Labor's Lost.* "Shakespeare's satire," she concludes, "is not directed at particular words, but at particular people—namely, those who practiced neologism . . . solely to be 'counted wise' by others. Yet it is difficult, in practice, to dissociate Shakespeare entirely from those characters who concern themselves with barring others from the new trade in words" (51). It would be more accurate, I suspect, to say that Shakespeare directs his satire not at words or people but at habits of usage, for which he has a keen and subtle ear. To follow Shakespeare's implicit criticism of verbal behavior as dimension of ethos takes a critical practice as patient and lucid as Empson's analysis of the word *honest* in *Othello.* Blank's formulation may be only slightly reductive, but the reduction makes it difficult, in practice, to dissociate Shakespeare from Prince Hal mocking Francis the tapster for his damnable iteration of the word *anon.* In effect Blank reads Shakespeare as a type of the prince, using authorial privilege to set characters up for a mockery that reflexively enhances his own authority. But who is Shakespeare really mocking in the tavern scene—the harried apprentice or the Harry who sets him up? Surely we ought to recognize in such scenes a reflection on the motives of stage-managing inarticulateness.

The tendency to *normalize* literary texts—to read Shakespeare as if he were Robert Greene or Alexander Gill—seems to me a chief pitfall of cultural criticism. Blank is very good on the cultural politics Renaissance authors are practicing when they imitate usages marked as "uncommon," but she has little to say about the politics of more subtle or more radical textual innovation. She will, for example, list the specific phonological features that mark literary imitations of regional dialects, but she will not consider the less colloquial features (what Harry Berger, Jr., calls the "rhizomes") of literary textuality. For readers with a primarily sociological interest in language this will not present a problem. But it may explain why *Broken English*, for all it contributes to the study of Renaissance literature, has almost nothing to say about the period's most radical and sustained experiment in poetic diction, Spenser's *Faerie Queene*. Blank's interests end, it seems to me, where the reading of such a text needs to begin.

Subject and Object in Renaissance Culture.
Edited by Margreta de Grazia, Maureen Quilligan,
and Peter Stallybrass.
Cambridge: Cambridge University Press, 1996.

Reviewer: Joel B. Altman

This distinguished collection of essays was originally presented at the conference on Renaissance Subject/Early Modern Object at the University of Pennsylvania in 1992. The essays collectively attempt to redress what seemed by the early 1990s to be an unbalanced—and embattled—emphasis upon what had become known as the Early Modern subject, to the neglect of the world of objects to which that subject inevitably found itself related. It was not the case that the subject was any longer treated as transcendent in the Burckhardtian sense—far from it; nor was the nonsubject underrepresented. Rather we beheld, in the words of Louis Montrose, "on the one hand, the implacable code, and on the other, the slippery signifier—the contemporary equivalents of Predestination and Fortune"—contending for dominance.[1] Both persons and objects were often abstracted and commodified in a criticism grown increasingly aware of the disunities of the self and of the reproductive capacity of something we might call power, or ideology, or the symbolic.

These essays, though deeply informed by contemporary theory, are largely concerned with concrete persons and things. Their aim, as the editors explain in a brief introduction, is to revise the familiar Renaissance narrative of subjectivity by asking the question, "in the period that has from its inception been identified with the emergence of the subject, *where is the object?*" (2). One way of resisting the narrative is seen in the title: to describe the culture not as Early Modern but as Renaissance is to bracket its versions of selfhood from the Cartesian trajectory on which they were placed by nineteenth-century historians, and to discourage us from seeing in them only earlier instances of modernity. More broadly, the essays "urge an exploration of the intricacies of subject/object relations, so as to undo the narrative we have been telling ourselves over and over again: the rise of subjectivity, the complexity of subjectivity, the instability of subjectivity. What we have to gain from interrelating the object and the subject in the Renaissance is a sense of how objects have a hold on subjects as well as subjects on objects" (11).

The project gets off to a strong start in part 1, "Priorities," with essays by Margreta de Grazia, Patricia Parker, and Louis A. Montrose. As the rubric indicates, these essays focus in different ways on the need to reverse the instrumentalist concept of the subject working upon the world and to regard subject formation as (literally) dependent upon object relations. In "The Ideology of Superfluous Things: *King Lear* as Period Piece," de Grazia directly addresses the habit of mind that since Burckhardt and Marx has tended to sever subjects from objects and objects from subjects, thereby enabling that account of the Renaissance that stresses mobility of persons and goods—the one a category of freestanding subject, the other of freely circulating commodity—thus providing a model made in our image and likeness. Her object is not to challenge the fact of increasing mobility in the late-sixteenth and early-seventeenth centuries but rather to question the Cartesian/capitalist analytic that links it so smoothly to the modern. In its place, she offers a reading of *Lear*, so often regarded as a touchstone of the transition from feudal to capitalist sensibility, that stresses the role of things in the formation and maintenance of personal identity: "the play dramatizes the relation of being and having," she observes, "removing what a person *has* simultaneously takes away what a person *is*" (21). And she argues that in the end these things return to their places in the traditional hierarchy. Both in its emphasis on the informing power of things—not commodities—and its insistence that they be returned to their rightful owners, *King Lear* is a conservative, not a forward-looking, play. It is not just that Lear loses his social identity when he divests himself of his kingdom—clothing figuring both property and self—or that Edgar feels "I nothing am" when disinherited and proclaimed a traitor, and that both become better clothed, retrieve their property, and resume (Lear only briefly) the shapes they were. More critically at stake is the meaning of Lear's outcry, "O, reason not the need! our basest beggars / Are in the poorest thing superfluous" (2.4.264–65).[2] The cry offers a distinction between human subsistence and the overplus that makes someone feel who he or she is. But that distinction, de Grazia points out, while appropriate enough in an aristocrat, is hardly axiomatic, for the superfluous was a perquisite only of the well-to-do. When Lear counsels pomp to "take physic" and "shake the superflux" to poor, naked wretches, he comes closer to seventeenth-century reality. It is, in fact, his own perverse self-deprivation of superflux that appears to provoke other, more dangerous superfluities that threaten to obscure established social and gender hierarchies: his overflowing tears, the storm that might spill nature's germens, Edmund's vow to top the legitimate, Kent's conflict with Oswald, that "unnecessary letter." It is in this sense that the play reproduces a conservative ideology of superfluous things. To historicize superfluity in this way is, I think, a healthful corrective to our instinctive acceptance of Lear's heart-wrenching lament as universally applicable. Yet, "Allow not nature more than nature needs, / Man's life is cheap as beast's" (2.3.266–67) also bespeaks an awareness of the way in which even pins, wooden pricks, and nails are superfluities that tell the Poor Toms of *Lear*'s world who they are. What is necessary and what is superfluous, de Grazia finally demonstrates, become very hard to separate.

Patricia Parker's "Rude Mechanicals" takes its title from Puck's description of the Athenian workmen and would-be players in *A Midsummer Night's Dream*. Parker is concerned here to reveal the material basis of the aesthetic and spiritual sublimations represented in the play. Both "rude" and "mechanical" are terms of class distinction that also have low ontological claims—"rude" associated with the unformed, "mechanical" with processes of shaping "disordered matter." Players, too, were often classified among mechanical artisans, and when they succeeded to the gentry, theirs was an artificial or constructed genealogy compared to the natural genealogies of gentlemen born, and a potential reminder of the cobbled origin of many a natural genealogy—a matter that Shakespeare savors in the fifth act of *The Winter's Tale*. But as "rude mechanicals" are involved in the "shaping fantasies" of *Dream*— Bottom in his own and Titania's, all of them in assembling a play to be presented at Theseus's wedding that phantasmagorically represents the experience of the courtly lovers—it becomes a matter of more than routine interest to see how material "joining" and "joinery" function within the spiritual and intellectual spheres of Elizabethan culture. Shakespeareans will remember how Jacques tells Touchstone that Sir Oliver Martext will marry him to Audry "as they join wainscot; then one of you will prove a shrunk panel, and like green timber warp, warp" (*AYLI* 3.3.86–89); and how Claudius informs his court, in a painstakingly articulated period, how Gertrude has become "th'imperial jointress to this warlike state" *Ham* 1.2.9). It is not surprising, then, that the language of joinery is also found in textbooks on rhetoric, such as Richard Sherry's *Treatise of Schemes and Tropes*, where readers are counseled that "the myghte and power of eloquucion consisteth in words considered by them selves, and when they are joyned together," and learn that the natural order is that which places "men" before "women" (50). Rhetoric is one of the means by which gender takes its place in the social formation. The domains of logic and marriage are joined by Thomas Wilson in *The Rule of Reason* when he provides guidelines concerning "what wordes maie be truely joined together," echoing the language of the Ceremony of Matrimony in the *Book of Common Prayer*. Indeed, this carpenter's language is ubiquitous. "We cannot be *joynted* to Christ our Head, except we be glued with concord and charitie to one another," states a homily of 1547. Notes Parker: "In all of the senses of 'joinery' in this contemporary semantic network, the figure of the artisan joiner brings together the joining of pieces of wood into an object, the union of marriage and body politic, and the 'right writing' of order in discourse" (51).

So what? In the play, Parker argues, the rude mechanicals foreground the activity of making and ordering, thus continuously denaturalizing what would otherwise appear to be given. It is Bottom, after all, an unlikely St. Paul, who is granted "a most rare vision" that exceeds Theseus's reach, and whose dramaturgic solutions produce a materialist parody of the lovers' flight that physically desublimates the erotic longings of the previous night. But the language of making is contagious: Theseus uses it patriarchically when he likens Hermia to wax that must be shaped by the stamp of her father, and Helena uses it homoerotically when she asks

Hermia if she will "rent our ancient love asunder / To join with men in scorning your poor friend?" (3.2.215–16). Behind, within *Dream*, Parker implies, is a joiner's imagination that understands human culture as an activity of making, as she draws upon Theodore Leinwand's observation that actor-playwrights were coming to be counted among the "middling sort"—neither aristocratic nor basely artisanal—to suggest that this social liminality may have provided Shakespeare with precisely the perspective on craftsmanship that we find both comically exaggerated and ironically denied in his comedy.

Although Louis A. Montrose's essay, "Spenser's Domestic Domain: Poetry, Property, and the Early Modern Subject," reintroduces the contested terminology, he describes a subjectivity that is distinctly Elizabethan. He does so by both utilizing and rejecting Foucault's concept of author-function. He rejects as inappropriate for Early Modern England Foucault's view of the author as an ideological construct produced to restrict the proliferation of meaning and, following Robert Weimann, argues that because of the limited censorship apparatus available to the Tudors and the increasingly varied opportunities for textual production, "the author-function may have helped to *disseminate* discursive authority more than it worked to contain it" (93). Indeed, Spenser seems to have exploited the author-function with skill and self-awareness, expanding his share of discursive possibilities by positioning himself *per occasionem* as poetic heir, humanist scholar, humble client, and lord of a poetic realm in which he himself was figured and whose discourse he controlled.

Adapting the concept of "demesne," or domain, from Paul Alpers's work on the lyric, Montrose shows how Spenser, in the years between the 1590 and 1596 publications of *The Faerie Queene*, fashioned a poetic domain of increasing public authority, directing the encomiastic energies he had expended on the epic to the smaller lyric and narrative forms of *Colin Clouts Come Home Again*, *Amoretti*, and *Epithalamion*. Emblematic of this gain in authority is the change in the dedication of the 1596 *Faerie Queene*, where Spenser's name, formerly reduced in size and relegated to the bottom right-hand corner of the page, is now printed as prominently as the queen's. Yet this access of power has accrued to him through subjection to the queen. The phenomenon is glossed by Spenser himself in *Colin Clouts Come Home Again*: "By wondering at thy *Cynthiaes* praise, / *Colin*, thy selfe thou mak'st us more to wonder, / And her upraising, doest thy selfe upraise" (*CCCHA*,

353–55, cit. 90). By subjecting himself he has enhanced himself—
and not only in reputation. Beginning in 1590, his £50 royal pension and his position as colonial administrator permitted him to
acquire real estate in Ireland that contributed to the fashioning of
his poetic self-representation. In much of the poetry written during
these years, Montrose argues,"a rhetoric that affirms the poet's literary authority coincides with a thematics of property, marriage, and
lineage that enhances his social authority. In short, the construction
of a *poetic domain* here coincides with the foundation of a *domestic domain*" (95). And he demonstrates how the material basis of
Spenser's establishment in Ireland grounds the exploration of cos-
mic issues in *The Mutabilitie Cantos,* enables not only the anticourtly sentiments of *Colin Clouts Come Home Again* but also its
erotic mythopoeia, informs the eschatological aspirations of *Epithalamion,* and underlies the subtle displacement of the queen by
Elizabeth Boyle in canto 10 of book 6 of *The Faerie Queene* and
in the *Amoretti.* What the poems reveal, Montrose suggests, is the
construction of an "authorial persona as both a public and a domestic subject by means of profession, property, and marriage" (118).
This persona occupies an ambiguous psychological space because,
as an instrument of the monarch and her policies, he has been able
to create a place for himself that is not merely instrumental, within
which he speaks from several subject positions not necessarily consonant with one another. Montrose's Spenser emerges not as the
queen's man fashioning his subjectivity by violently defending Englishness against erotic and outlandish otherness, as Stephen
Greenblatt has argued, but as something of an other himself, fashioned by queen, land, and the books he wrote.

Books and pictures are the objects examined in part 2, "Material-
izations," by Stephen Orgel, Nancy J. Vickers, and Ann Rosalind
Jones. In "Gendering the Crown," Orgel studies several emblems
and portraits that have immediate and distant relations to Elizabeth
I, and shows how an analytic and syncretic habit of mind enabled
public construction of the ambiguously gendered self deliberately
promulgated by the queen. He begins by pointing out the polysemy
of such popular emblems as the pelican feeding her young with her
blood. As a common emblem of the *caritas* of Christ, the sacrificing
pelican crosses gender lines with ease, female imaging male. But
the pelican and its brood can also figure Lear's "pelican daughters,"
matricides feeding upon their father, and those chicks become
avangers when Laertes promises, "like the kind life-rend'ring pelican," to repast his supporters with *his* blood if they help him kill

the murderer of *his* father. A similar lability of signification informs the myth of Daphne's transformation into a laurel: it is a caveat against passion for Bernini, the reward of chastity for George Sandys.

Orgel remarks wryly that Renaissance iconographies and mythographies, which often assign the task of determining meaning to the interpretive capacity of the reader, are "the most postmodern of texts." It is an important observation and deserves emphasis, for iconographic polysemy is a function of that topical habit of mind that considers qualities in relation to their adjacents, contraries, causes, effects, passives, actives, antecedents, consequents, and the like, in such a way that apparent positivities display themselves in a network of cognates that both distinguish themselves from and suggest one another. His theme, however, is not just that images are convertible, but that there is a subtle visual slippage that an acute reader of images must interpret. As evidence of the formal modification of a visual topos, he shows a group of pictures of Francis I, Henry II, and Henry III, in which the king changes from celebrated transvestite who combines the desirable qualities of male (in war) and female (in peace) to scandalous hermaphrodite, a woman who passes herself off as a man. But his fascinating case in point is a drawing by Giuliano Romano that appears to show Apollo making love to Hyacinthus or Cyparissus. A female witness to this male lovemaking holds her finger to her lips, a gesture traditionally thought to originate with Harpocrates, god of silence. Orgel notes its similarity to an emblem of Meditation or Revenge, where the finger is not simply touching the lips but is being bitten, and finds an identical gesture in a Romano sketch of Venus and Mars expelling a fury from a garden of putti. This turns out to be the gesture of the woman observing the adult god dallying with the young boy, whom Orgel now identifies as Orpheus, believed to have introduced pederasty into Greece after the loss of Euridice and killed by an enraged bacchante for the insult to womanhood. Not secrecy but vengeance is on the mind of the female voyeur. This is a brilliant demonstration of close reading, and Orgel uses it to make a pitch for recognizing the representational capaciousness of images: "beyond the silent woman lies the vengeful fury, beyond *Caritas* lies inhumanity, behind all of these lies the unspoken. The image, unlike the word . . . also represents what does not signify, the unexplained, the unspeakable—all those meanings we reject because we believe nobody in the Renaissance could have conceived them" (149). He is surely right, but I would press further. He has revealed a visual *system* of gestures in which one image slips beyond itself into another in a manner not unlike the phonemic variation with which we are familiar from structural linguistics, which suggests that built into the activity of interpretation was a differential recognition that invited just the kind of revisional reading activity he accomplishes in the essay: it is not only the capaciousness of Renaissance images that we must acknowledge but that of the acculturated imagination that fashioned and viewed them. This proves to be crucial in his discussion of a group of images relating to the queen, which adapt Catholic and specifically Spanish iconography to Elizabethan imperialist ends, and infuse them with an erotic content that was ostensibly lesbian, subliminally heterosexual, and chaste. Without an understanding of the multisignifying potential of sixteenth-century imagery and its reliance upon a corresponding interpretive power these images would make no sense.

The object of Nancy J. Vickers's inquiry is "the unauthored 1539 volume in which is printed the *Hecatomphile, The Flowers of French Poetry,* and *Other Soothing Things*," published in Paris by Pierre Sergent. This is a "tract" volume—a book of writings bound together, of independent origin but related thematically and culturally—consisting of a French prose narrative, translated without acknowledgment from the Italian of Leon Battista Alberti; a *florilegium* of French verses that bear traces of Italian forebears; and a collection of anatomical blazons. Vickers asks what the book tells about the way subjectivities can be formed by a savvy community of publishers attuned to the tastes of their customers. The poetry has the marks of coterie verse and stages itself as such, through ascriptions like "The Disciple begins to describe love," "Another author defines love," "A Lady answers," and so forth, conveying the sense that one is privy to courtly pastime—an impression also promoted by the promise of "*autres* choses solatieuses" in the third part. The poems have been variously ascribed to Frances I, Marguerite of Navarre, Claude Chappuys, and others, and probably are pieces exchanged in the French court.

Vickers is less interested in their authorship, however, than in their marketing. There were ten editions of the *Hecatomphile* betewen 1534 and 1540 published in Paris and Lyons by various booksellers, and they reflect a common understanding of what the volume was to be like, for they share both format and illustrations. The 1534 octavo edition of Galliot du Pre (a bipartite text without blazons) was downmarketed to a sixteenmo, handy to carry about, display, and present as a gift. Du Pre and Sergent (publisher of the tripartite 1539 text) had shops on the Ile de la Cite, where they produced a line of books—humanist works, law texts, classics, romances—for the edification of a class of nonscholarly professionals. Of the two men, Sergent was more the popularizer; his editions were cheaper and cruder. Vickers shows the ubiquity of woodcuts used in these books; one, presenting the painter Zeuxis collating the best parts of the world's most beautiful females on canvas to portray Helen of Troy, moved from Du Pre's 1531 edition of *The Romance of the Rose* to Sergent's *Hecatomphile* and then to his 1541 edition of *Controverses des sexes masculins et feminins*, but not before it appeared in the new *Les blasons domestiques* published in 1539 by Gilles Corrozet—who used the woodcut to blast its earlier users in a moral castigation titled "Against the blazoners of body parts." This, in a book that now contained praises of home furnishings! Vickers's witty point is that commodification is proceeding apace, as courtliness trickles down for the consumption of a rising class of commoners through a medium whose form and substance clearly reveal the way books can become fetishes: the volume itself opens the court to the urban gaze, the inventory of female body parts (a courtly, not an urban invention) caters to the desires of city males, and for readers who wish to distinguish themselves from emptors of amorous objects, desire can be aestheticized and moralized as it is displaced onto objects of domesticity. "Postulating greater solace in the pleasures of houses than in the pleasures of women, *The Domestic Blazons* stands as a revealing complement to the *Hecatomphile*," Vickers observes. "As objects assembled in the image of their consumers' varied desires, they materially shape those desires in the process" (183). The *blason du cabinet* says it succinctly: "Cabinet remply de richesses / Soit pour roynes ou pour duchesses." ("A chest stuffed full of expensive things / Be it for queens or duchesses.")

Spider women and their webs are foregrounded in "Dematerializations: Textile and Textual Properties in Ovid, Sandys, and Spenser," where Ann Rosalind Jones studies some Renaissance transformations of Ovid's tale of the contest between Athena and Arachne. Jones shows how the labor and skill of Arachne and Athena, emphasized in Ovid, undergoes sublimation and masculine appropriation in these later renderings. Her essay takes off from and concludes with a discussion of Velasquez's painting *Las hilanderas*—the spinners—a title that refers to the contemporary female figures in the foreground who are variously spinning, carding, and combing wool. The painting also goes by the name of

La fabula de Aragne, which identifies the scene in the background, where elegantly dressed women stand before a tapestry—one wearing a classical helmet—with the myth. This scene was framed squarely as on a stage in the original version but enlarged vertically by the addition of an arch some time between the painting's completion around 1654 and the year 1711, when it was willed to the royal collections. Jones sees the titles and the criticism that has gathered around the painting as symptomatic of "the process through which a physical substance—wool yarn produced by women's labor—and the object made from it—a tapestry—can be dematerialized into transcendent symbols" (189).

The issue centers on what Velasquez was up to in so dividing his painting between the close-up view of poor women making wool thread and the more distant display of the finished product to an appreciative audience of aristocratic ladies. Critics have argued that he was staking his claim as humanist by including the myth in what otherwise might have been a genre painting, that he was celebrating the superiority of art to mere manual labor, that in appropriating figures from Titian in the tapestry he was asserting his own artistic merit. Jones is not satisfied with these explanations. She points out that one of the painting's anomalies is the very presence of women in the tapestry workroom, since labor in the Spanish cloth industry was rigidly divided between women who spun wool into thread at home in private and workmen who wove their thread into tapestries in the public workplace. For her, Velasquez is *interested* in portraying women at work and (by implication) women as consumers, which is why he includes no men in the painting. Her excursion into the *fortuna* of Arachne and Athena in Ovid, Sandys, and Spenser, therefore, is a means of grounding the critical reception of the painting. The account she provides reveals the change in emphasis the myth undergoes from its treatment by Ovid, who expresses interest in the skill with which both Arachne and Athena weave images—the former of the gods seducing and raping mortal women, the latter of her contest with Neptune for the patronage of Athens—to Sandys, who in the second instance, masculinizes and disembodies Athena by seeing in her a pagan counterpart to the son of God, Jove's "pure mind," and sees in Arachne an envious female upstart. Whereas in the Ovidian myth, Athena tears up Arachne's tapestry and transforms Arachne herself into a spider for protesting at losing the contest, Sandys's Minerva justly destroys the work of a traitor who reveals the secrets of the gods. Spenser sinuously co-opts weaving in *Muopotmos* (where the contest is between Arachne's son, the sly Aragnoll, and the male butterfly Clarion), is alive to the details of craft, but subordinates the material feminine to the fictional masculine fantasy of the mock epic, and in *Amoretti 71*, epideictically fashions himself as a real-life Aragnoll, lovingly entrapping Elizabeth Boyle.

Jones offers shrewd analyses of these authors, revealing once again the penchant of Renaissance interpreters for cross-gendering and manipulating significant images—in this case for the purpose of containing the female by eliding or devaluing fabrication. (Her work should be read in conjunction with Parker's and Orgel's.) Less satisfying is her return to Velasquez, whom she credits with a concern for labor per se and for women's labor in particular. Earlier she remarked that "the painting is itself an object: oil on canvas, a material also made by women in its first stages. Women grew, soaked, combed, and spun the flax from which painters' canvases were made" (193). She returns to this observation at the end: "Women's work on flax made linen thread, which was woven into canvas; women's work on wool produced the yarn that was woven into a tapestry—before a painter's work in oil produced an image of weavers" (206). An intriguing concatenation, but how significant? To find out, she calls for study of the material circumstances of Velasquez's enterprise, though from the evidence presented, one wonders if this would reveal a Velasquez who identified with his materials or sought to dematerialize himself and transcend mere craftsmanship in homosocial competition with other masters. We will have to see.

In part 3, "Appropriations," Maureen Quilligan, Margaret W. Ferguson, and Gary Tomlinson turn to the role played by New World objects in European subjectification. Quilligan's essay, "Freedom, Service, and the Trade in Slaves: The Problem of Labor in *Paradise Lost*," draws attention to the connection between epic and slavery, whereby the conquered and enslaved enemy is traditionally the reified Other against which the heroic ethos is fashioned. Adapting Frederic Jameson's thesis that literary genres are fashioned to manage social contradictions and carry that ideological potential into new cultural situations, she questions the revival and appreciation of epic in a period that fostered the notion of the individual, and explores specifically its social resonance in an author known for his insistence on human freedom.

Slavery was an important element in European economies by the seventeenth century, and a fact invoked by Milton on several occasions. In *The Tenure of Kings and Magistrates*, he wrote that "to say, as is usual, the king hath as good right to his crown and dignity as any man to his inheritance, is to make the subject no better than the king's slave." His assertion was based on the assumption that king and subject are relative entities that mutually constitute one another: "if the subject, who is one relative, take away the relation, of force he takes away also the other relative . . . that is to say, the king's authority, and their subjection to it" (216). But he also assumed that the subject enjoys free authority over his own family and property that would be destroyed were he considered a part of the king's inheritance and not a contractual partner. Quilligan points out that this freedom was articulated within a contemporary discourse that differentiated the English both from black slaves and those who trafficked in slavery. In 1659, Parliament debated a petition from Cavalier captives who had been given a choice of death or slavery in Barbados, chosen the latter, and now complained bitterly of their abject condition. The argument in favor of the petitioners was that liberty must be secured to all Englishmen lest their lives be "as cheap as those negroes" already employed on the plantations (219). That is to say, men enslaved by conquest would become indistinguishable from those sold in trade, and Englishness would thereby lose its association with the heroic. Milton participated in this discourse not only in its political but also its racial register. In *Of Reformation*, he threatened the unregenerate with a hell where the damned would "exercise a Raving and Bestial Tyranny over them as their Slaves and Negroes" (220). Race and trade, then, distinguished contemporary from classical slavery by conquest.

With the slave population of Barbados growing exponentially in the seventeenth century because of the changeover from tobacco to sugar, the need for and dissociation from slavery was a fact of economic and psychological life. It was one of the elements, Quilligan argues, that shaped Milton's Satan, who comes to conquer "this new world" and enslave Adam and Eve, who as lords over their dominion enjoy the "sole propriety" of Paradise in mutual self-possession, as he envisions populating hell with their "numerous offspring." Given Satan's project of building an empire on Adam and Eve's seduction and enslavement, he cannot serve as Milton's epic hero. This reading richly complements Milton's explicit rejection of Satan as outmoded military hero (though one wonders if the specter of slave rebellion is not also informing Milton's portrait of Satan's enterprise), the better fortitude of patience and heroic martyrdom to sing. It also complicates our understanding of Milton's treatment of work in the Garden, for if manual agricultural labor is becoming associated with black slaves, it becomes necessary to dignify the labor that Adam and Eve have to perform. It is dignified, as we know, by refashioning it as horticulture but, Quilligan argues, it is also divided by gender and mode of production—Adam's associated with theological "good works" or intellectual labor and a "feudal" mode of service, Eve's with physical or reproductive labor and a "proto-capitalist mode" that includes an injunction that women "study household good." Thus *Paradise Lost* participates in a redefinition of work, influenced by New World experience, that is gendered and also racialized—explicitly in book 12, where the black descendants of Ham are identified as "servants of servants." Quilligan's account of the poem's part in this reconception and the way socio-economic modes, gender, and race are imbricated in one another, is illuminating and generally persuasive.

In "Feathers and Flies: Aphra Behn and the Seventeenth-Century Trade in Exotica," Margaret Ferguson is also concerned with the bad faith engendered by the English colonial experience in the second half of the seventeenth century and how one author dealt with it. Behn visited Guiana in the early 1660s and later drew upon her life in the novella *Oroonoko* and the play *The Widow Ranter*. What Ferguson is after is to see how the colonial model of male penetration into virgin lands described by Montrose in his study of Ralegh's *Discovery of Guiana* fares in a subject who is a woman, English, and professional. To gain purchase on Behn's subject position in regard to the New World she compares three accounts of native nakedness, in Columbus's letter to Gabriel Sanchez, Milton's initial description of Adam and Eve, and Behn's account of the natives in *Oroonoko*. All three present the natives as naked and not quite naked. Columbus first writes, "all go naked, men and women," then adds that "some women are covered in a single place by a leaf or net of cotton" (238), and contemporary print versions of the letter illustrate one state or the other. Similarly, Milton's Adam and Eve are "clad" only in "naked majesty," but shortly afterward Eve is described veiled to the waist by wanton ringlets, directing the male gaze (participating in Satan's) to her partially covered breasts, before asserting once more the mutual unconcealment of "those mysterious parts." Ferguson's point is that Milton, like Columbus, "revises a statement about a general human nakedness into the 'exception' of a specifically gendered veiling" that draws upon the noble savage trope "to create a split subject position—between

desire and guilt—for the male narrator and implied male reader,"
thus disrupting an easy binary division of "naked them/clothed
us," so as to complicate distinguishing between ontological states
(242). In Behn, the natives are first described as wearing beaded
aprons before them, "as *Adam* and *Eve* did the Fig-leaves," but
shortly after as naked, without the trace of an indecent action (243).
Ferguson offers a brilliant reading of all three uses of the Edenic
metaphor associated with the New World: "If the natives are naked,
then they are not only like Adam and Eve *before* the fall, but we,
the colonists, are either superfluous to their blissful state or, worse,
like Satan, filled with greed and desire to destroy it. If, however,
the natives, and especially the native women, are cinctured around
the genitals, then they are like Adam and Eve after the fall, and we
can legitimate our profit-taking desires under the guise of bringing
Christian salvation to the heathen" (245).

But there is a third position open to Behn, as a woman, writer,
collector, gift giver, and theater person: that is to *aestheticize* potentially moral categories by participating in the traffic in New World
luxuries. Behn indulges in a lengthy digression about the ornaments used by the Indians and connects these autobiographically
to the dress of an Indian queen she had given to the King's Theater,
which turns out to be the headdress worn by the actress Anne
Bracegirdle in Behn's own play, *The Widow Ranter*. To contextualize these negotiations, Ferguson points to the seventeenth-century
transvaluation of luxury, which had an ancient history of association with sin, and especially with female excess—as spices, cloths,
gems, feathers, and other items (including native Americans and
Africans) entered and circulated in the European market. Their
negative moral associations now had to compete with even stronger
mercantilist ambitions, and as a result the category of *necessary
luxury* was invented and objects were unabashedly collected for
display in curiosity cabinets, pageants, and theaters. The implications for subjectivity are especially intriguing. Not only were identities more strongly cathected onto things, but when those things
were exotic persons and exotic persons became fashionable objects
for display, the interflow between imitating or collecting subject
and imitated and collectable object excited an oscillation that destabilized identity. Ferguson shows a contemporary illustration of
Anne Bracegirdle in the role of Indian princess, adorned with
feathers and attended by two black children, also feathered, playing
her Indian attendants: whiteness and blackness meet in fictional
tertium quid—"redness"?—just as Behn herself, on a visit to a vil-

lage in Guiana, meets natives adorned with feathers not unlike the feathered headdress she is wearing. In *Oroonoka*, Ferguson concludes, "we have a partial representation, partial in both senses of the word, of a cultural system in which actors, white women, Native Americans and Africans of both sexes shared versions of a subject position we might define simply as that of 'being on display in and for the market'" (255). What she suggests is that the subject itself is now a necessary luxury, the reciprocal effect of aestheticizing the Other.

Gary Tomlinson's "Unlearning the Aztec *Cantares* (Preliminaries to a Postcolonial History)" explicitly articulates the issues involved in the attempt to perceive, understand, and represent an older, non-European subjectivity. His essay is a model of methodological awareness and cultural analysis. The aim of the postcolonial historian, he observes, is "not to create a docile past 'the way it really was' but to build a past that resists our intellectual attempts to occupy it even while it takes it shape from us" (261). In doing so, the historian will be aware that he must construct two dialogues—one between the present and the past, the other between subjectivities in the past. This second task is especially sensitive in the case where the voice of one communicant is transmitted by the other—an issue raised by Ferguson regarding the unrecorded subjectivities of Indians and Africans brought to Europe for display. Tomlinson further specifies the problem by observing that the dialectic of the familiar and the uncanny that informs historical assessment is particularly acute in the space between speech and song, for while Western analysis distinguishes a wide range of utterance between plain speaking and full-fledged singing, we are accustomed to a hierarchical binary of "words" and "music" that may distort our apprehension of ancient songs.

Tomlinson's exemplary instance is a sixteenth-century manuscript entitled *Cantares mexicanos*, or Mexica Songs, which preserves the texts of ninety-one Aztec songs in alphabetized Nahuatl. The very form in which the material has been transmitted—a book of poetry written in a phonetic alphabet—invites a familiar kind of reading, and much of the scholarship on the songs has assimilated the poems to Western concepts, seeing in them the expression of a stoic philosophy critical of warfare, human sacrifice, and cannibalism that is conveyed through an extensive use of metaphor. Their characteristic technique, according to this interpretation, is diphrasis, a joining of two metaphors to express a single thought, and the diphrasis *in xochitl in cuicatl*, which means roughly "flower and song," has been taken to refer to poetry and, more generally, to the poetic-philosophic worldview that is being articulated. While not denying the possibility of such a worldview, Tomlinson questions the attitude toward language and the habit of reading that has led to its stipulation. He focuses on the nature of spoken Nahuatl and the nearly invisible "songishness" of the recorded texts. Drawing upon the work of Serge Gruzinski, Inga Clendinnen, and other Mezoamericanists, he points out how Nahuatl differs from Western languages in its concreteness—its basic words are "sentence words" irreducible to grammatical abstraction—and suggests that before European contact "such irreducibility must have assured that every Nahuatl utterance reached outward to an external context" (268). The distance between word and thing or action was, he argues, simply not there, as it is in Western representational languages, and thus Nahuatl had a materiality that was contiguous to that of the world. Therefore the transcription of the native language into the abstract alphabet of a linguistic system thought to parallel—not to integrate—perceived reality effected a fundamental rupture that has influenced all subsequent interpretation. In particular, the notion of metaphor, a joining of separate phenomena, seems far less appropriate as a description of how the language works than metonymy, which emphasizes proximity, interflow, continuity. Extant glyphs resemble spoken Nahuatl insofar as they suggest the conflation of images and things, functioning as presentations rather than representations.

The "songishness" of the poems, which is virtually absent in the alphabetized texts, must be retrieved from the word/music dichotomy, Tomlinson argues, by expanding our notion of how sounds might have conveyed meaning in the Mexica culture—sounds including not only words but "introductory finger-whistling; the deep intonation of the *huehuetl*; the resonant wooden thong of the *teponaztli*; perhaps the rhythmic clatter of rattles, the scratchy whisper of rasps, the wail of conch trumpets" (273). Evidence in extant Aztec codices indicate that music was thought to have the same material powers as speech: volutes of varying size and ornamentation are shown flowing from singer's mouths and their instruments, some becoming flowers, which brings new meaning to the phrase *in xochitl in cuicatl*: song actually flowers, meaning is incarnational. The metonymic physical world, he points out, has critical bearing on the human subject who was part of it, less boundaried, more permeable, easily transmutable—the subject, one might say, from whom the Western subject had been detaching itself since

Aeschylus, and whose strangeness was so foreign to sixteenth-century Europeans that they objectivized and thus familiarized it. This essay, one-third shrewd scholarly caveat, two-thirds lucid analysis, is required reading not only for historians of colonialism but also for those of us concerned with the lingering? renascent? presence of magic in European linguistic thought during the age of exploration.

In part 4 of *Subjects and Objects* the editors have gathered essays by Peter Stallybrass, Jonathan Goldberg, and Stephen Greenblatt under the heading "Fetishisms," perhaps glancing at the European need to reanimate the world even as it was being objectified. Stallybrass's "Worn Worlds: Clothes and Identity on the Renaissance Stage," offers a convincing case that the London clothing trade was the locus of a complicated identity crisis in the later-sixteenth century, in which the theater played a central role. Contemporary anxieties about dressing across gender and class are now familiar topics of cultural criticism, but Stallybrass contextualizes these commonplaces so as to give us a sense of their material basis. The most salient fact he presents is that business in fabrics was booming. Citing Steven Rappaport's astonishing statistic that nearly twice as many young men were apprenticed to the four major cloth and clothing guilds between 1530 and 1609 than to eleven other London guilds, he shows that the theater was not simply engaged in "dressing up" and thus shaking up sexual and social identities but that it was up to its neck, so to speak, in clothing exchange. Many playwrights—including Webster, Middleton, Munday, and Heywood—were affiliated with the cloth guilds. Companies paid more for costumes than for scripts or props; they used these valuable costumes as collateral when they needed to raise cash and borrowed them, virtually *as* cash, when strapped for funds to commission their own. Philip Henslowe was in the thick of this trade; his account books reveal that he was in the clothes-pawning business himself, paying cash for the garments of private citizens and often loaning costumes on account to the players he financed. Not without reason was the pawning of clothes an activity frequently dramatized on the London stage.

Outside the theater and business, clothes were also an important medium of exchange. Liveries were part of a household servant's pay—usually the greater part—and gifts of clothing at court to ladies and gentlemen in waiting were common, and were recorded in detail. As important as clothing exchange itself was the signifying function of garments. Stallybrass makes the important point that

in the sixteenth century it was not the commodity that was fe-
tishized, as Marx describes the inspiriting of material goods at a
later stage in the history of production, but the distinctive object.
That is to say, even as clothing circulated in society as an apparently
fungible commodity, it might also retain or become imbued with
the aura of persons who owned and wore it or of the household or
noble in whose name it was worn. The theater, though it had a way
of displacing the memories and values inhering in garments by
staging them in new situations, also took seriously the identities
clinging to them. Stallybrass cites the outraged Sir Henry Herbert,
who penalized a pawnbroker for selling a church robe with the
name Jesus on it to the Salisbury Court Players for use in a flamen's
role, an extreme case of putting the meaning of a vestment in crisis.
And lesser violations were feasible onstage, as in Volpone's proposition that he and Celia act out the erotic possibilities enabled
by changing costume. "In the process," Stallybrass observes, "the
aristocracy becomes no more than one possible kind of style: a
style which one can adopt or drop according to the extent of one's
wardrobe" (308). Yet some of the most poignant and strange moments on the stage occur when a garment or accessory circulates
and retains its personal identity: Othello's handkerchief, Troilus's
sleeve, Posthumus's clothes. It is this dual potentiality of clothing
to attach old identities to new persons (Macbeth's "borrowed
robes") and to insist on the inherence of their original wearers that
renders them so problematic as a source of self in this culture.
"Clothes have a life of their own," Stalleybrass reminds us; "they
both are material presences and they encode other material and
immaterial presences" (313).

It may be difficult to conceive of a single poem as fetish, but that
is what Goldberg shows Mary Sidney made of Petrarch's *Trionfo
della Morte* in her translation, *The Triumph of Death*. "The Countess of Pembroke's literal translation" takes its title from a tradition
of criticism that praises this work on the basis of its fidelity to the
Petrarchan original and Sidney's capacity to "reproduce" the very
terza rima of the father of humanism. At the outset, then, the poem
raises not only the question of relationship between translator and
maker but the even more intricate issue of cross-gendering that
arises when a female writer turns a man's poem into a palimpsest.
This issue of cross-gendered voicing is not absent from Petrarch's
work. One of the features of his poem is the postmortem appearance of Laura, who informs the speaker that their relationship,
which had been the occasion for him to exhibit his mastery, had,

in fact, "been mastered by Laura, whose withdrawals and refusals, whose very silences, had produced their effects in him" (322). This has given some recent critics occasion to discover female agency in the poem and also female acquiescence, especially in view of the fact that even here, Laura's voice is Petrarch's.

The issue becomes even more complicated when one tries to locate Mary Sidney's "I" in her appropriation of Petrarch's double voicings. Is she, who also occasioned male effusions from the poets she patronized, finding her own voice in Laura's? If so, what is to be made of the identity of her "Petrarchan" speaker? Goldberg's sinuous analysis leads to the conclusion that Mary is both Petrarch and Laura in this poem, and he shows that the two figures are, literally, not clearly distinguishable. The initial speaker, whose gender identity in Petrarch remains stable, is female and male in Sidney's, insofar as "she" begins as a figure longing for death, apparently soon to be dead, and whose death is announced in the second part of the poem—announced to a figure who is still "me" but is now grieving the heroic death of a beautiful, courteous other self. In translating *Il Trionfo della Morte* into *The Triumph of Death*, Mary Sidney was thus animating Petrarch's poem with the spirits of her dead brother and herself in a transgendering fantasy that reflects the incestuous metaphorics through which Philip Sidney dedicated the *Arcadia* to her, substantiates the language of "Two, by their bloods, and by thy Spirit one," which Donne uses to praise brother and sister's translations of the Psalms, and gives a certain credence to Aubrey's salacious gossip that they were known to lie with one another. Goldberg weaves into his reading recent work by Ann Rosalind Jones, Judith Butler, Jonathan Crewe, and others to build a strong case for locating female agency at the site of disempowerment (women's last wills, for example) and of transgressive sexuality, which is reflected not only in the presence of women as screens for sister and brother but as homoerotic "chosen mates." As with much of the work of Jonathan Goldberg, the essay is nothing if not provocative, and sometimes exasperating in the teasing ways epithets used by other critics—for example, "preposterous"—are converted into charged terms in his argument. But it is also unremittingly intelligent and one feels microcosmically enlightened after attending it.

Leave it to Stephen Greenblatt to notice that people worried about what happens to crumbs from the sacramental wafer that are not consumed by the communicant. But as he demonstrates in "Remnants of the Sacred in Early Modern England," this material concern—and others like it—was shared by serious people in the sixteenth and seventeenth centuries, and was symptomatic of a growing anxiety about the borders of the self after the Reformation. Here—centrally, because of its eschatalogical implications—the anxiety focused on what Christ meant when he instituted the Eucharist by saying, "Hoc est corpus meum." Catholic doctrine interpreted the statement literally, insisting that the body and blood of Christ were really present in the bread and wine of the Mass, while Protestants denied this and proposed various representational readings. Zwingli and Calvin, Greenblatt records, emphasized the word *est* rather than the word *hoc*, which they interpreted as equivalent to *significant* by a trope in which "the sign borrows the name of the truth that it figures" (340). Reformer John Frith argued that "an alepole is not the ale self which it doth signifie or represent," and a person who seeks salvation in outward signs might just as well "goe and sucke an alepole, trusting to get drinke out of it" (341).

The linguistic issue, however, had ontological—and potentially scatological—implications. Whether Christ's assertion identified the sacrament with his body and blood or merely linked it metaphorically led to questions about its material progress in the body of communicant. According to Greenblatt, Catholics defended the position that one ate Christ's flesh even if one could not see or taste it, for God covered the corporal with bread, as John Rastell argued, "lest some horror & lothsomenes might trouble us, if it were geaven in visible forme of flesh . . . unto us" (341). Thomas Cranmer, on the other hand, insisted that we do not "eat Christ with our teeth grossly and carnally," for Christ is in heaven with God; the bread and wine are "tokens, significations, and representations" (343). Dispute on this matter descended to such questions as how deeply into the digestive system the body and blood of Christ reached before he departed, and whether a priest who became drunk after consuming too much sacramental wine was reacting to its "accidents" or "substance." If the former, why confuse faith by instituting the sacramental in a material way in the first place? Cranmer's pregnant answer was that human beings were ineluctably carnal creatures, and that seeing, touching, smelling was believing: "the eating and drinking of this sacramental bread and wine is, as it were, a showing of Christ before our eyes, a smelling of him with our noses, a feeling and groping of him with our hands, and an eating, chewing, digesting, and feeding upon him to our spiritual strength and perfection" (344). As Greenblatt observes, Cranmer's "as it were" marks the uneasy intersection of gross physicality and pure spirituality; but it also installs the worshiper in quite a different subject position than that held in the Catholic dispensation. If, as he suggests, the Eucharist was the Renaissance's "sublime object of ideology"—which, in Žižek's Lacanian formulation, is the Real that precedes and grounds the subject, and is unknowlable and unrepresentable by the subject—then culturally the Reformation moves the individual more deeply (superficially?) into the symbolic register that in granting meaning denies being, and literally sets the stage for that substitution of incarnation by theater that he and others have described so well.

The last section of the book is called "Objections" because, as the editors explain, the essays are more concerned with loss than with objects and implicitly deny the priority of objects in subject formation. Marjorie Garber's "The Insincerity of Women" borrows its title from Freud's note to Wilhelm Fliess concerning the symptomology of one of his patients, Frau P. J., who was suffering from anxiety, a sense of oppression, and abdominal ills: "The insincerity of women starts from their omitting the characteristic sexual symptoms in describing their states. So it really had been an *orgasm*" (356). For Garber this triumphant observation punctuates a long history of male exploration and attempted colonization of female pleasure, an effort dramatized and rationalized in the virginity test of Middleton and Rowley's *The Changeling*. Rationalized insofar as the drama itself mystifies its heroine's sexuality—an overdetermined secret compounded of excitement, aversion, fear, cunning, desire, and passion—while the virginity test purports to make that secret empirically evident by the use of pharmaceuticals. Critics have been puzzled at Middleton's allusion to Antonious Mizaldus's *De arcanis naturae* while apparently inventing the test himself with symptoms not found in Mizaldus—gaping, sneezing, and laughing if one is a virgin, apathy if one is not. Why these particular symptoms? she asks, and recurs to Freud, with the assistance of William Harvey, Robert Burton, Auguste Debay, and more recent theorizers of female psychology (both academic and pop) to come up with a fascinating account of the symptomology of the orgasm in which the gape, sneeze, and laugh play leading roles.

The implications for *The Changeling* and for male-female relations more generally are twofold. First, Middleton seems to be staging Alsemero's attempt to observe rationally what would be rationally unobservable were he engaged in sexual intercourse himself—the induced orgasm of a virgin. So the test objectifies his own sexual agency and satisfies his need to see his own power. In the play, however, it is evident that these symptoms can be *performed*—Diaphanta responds *au nature* to the contents of glass M, but the already deflowered Beatrice-Johanna, watching her maid "prove" that she is an acceptable bedtrick candidate, deliberately reproduces her symptoms before the audience of Alsemero and Jasperino. This act obviously compromises, indeed frustrates, the male quest, and demonstrates the power women possess to keep their secret and to manipulate men, but it also thematizes the theatrical nature of that power. As performed by male actors impersonating women who respond to men both *authentically* and *insincerely*, sexual pleasure is *only* faked—and it is only the fake that is in the control of males. Though Garber does not quite come out and say so, this in itself would seem to reinforce the misogyny that both founds and destabilizes male identity, and a male theater is a major donor to this cause. The essay widens the masculine problematic of knowing by adducing the materials of late-twentieth-century self-help books in which women are counseled to rehearse their pleasure in private—"for use can almost change the stamp of nature"—both to satisfy themselves and their male partners, but never to reveal whether the orgasm is real or counterfeit, since "the existence of the possibility of fakeness protects the privacy and control of pleasure" (366). Brilliant on its own, Garber's essay provides a useful complement to Stanley Cavell's reading of *Antony and Cleopatra*,[3] where Renaissance skepticism is read in the register of marital sexual relations.

In "Desire is Death," Jonathan Dollimore is concerned "with the perverse dynamic in western culture which binds together desire, death and loss (mutability), and especially the belief that desire is in a sense impossible, which is to say that it is driven by a lack inherently incapable of satisfaction; it is at heart, contradictory: the very nature of desire is precisely what prevents its fulfillment" (369). Though this has a palpably Lacanian ring, Dollimore is expressing an enduring sentiment that has taken different historical forms. If Aristophanes' myth of a race of doubly sexed mortals, cloven in two by a jealous Zeus and thenceforth doomed to strive in vain to repair their loss, explains desire as the consequence of splitting and division, Lucretius sings cryptically of the bitterness experienced even in the fruition of lovemaking. More explicit is Gregory of Nyssa's renunciation of physical pleasures in the belief that such joys produce grief because they make one vulnerable to the little deaths that are effected by mutability and thus "permit death to thrive inside life" (371). Drawing upon Peter Brown's work on Christian asceticism, Dollimore notes that "such writers sought not the repression of the sexual drive *as such*, but rather to be released from the devastating effects of death, mutability, and time on desire, and *as* desire," for "these things at once engender desire and render it impossible" (371). Time, that is to say, as the agent of death, and mutability, as the medium or activity of death, enable death to inhabit life from its inception, installing the desire for a consummation that ever ebbs before the reach of desire. This insight, Dollimore shows, lies behind the intimations that *in vita mors est* in such familiar material as Herbert's "Virtue" and "Church Monuments," Drummond of Hawthornden's "A Cypresse Grove," Castiglione's *Il cortegiano*, Shakespeare's sonnets, Ralegh's *History of the World*, and Wyatt's *Penitential Psalms*. In all these works the life process is vitiated by yet indistinguishable from dying, and there is a correlative attempt to bind the self-infected unstable subject to absolute coherences—to a homosocial order perceived to transcend mutable passion, to death seen as a sovereign, to the good or God. His argument, if not wholly new, gives new force to the poignancy that we hear in Renaissance writers' allusions to mutability—no longer merely voicing the dreaded passage of youth or the ephemeral joys of earthly goods, but the apprehended gap between desire and fulfillment that is the condition of the possibility of life. This leads him to a provocative and original reading of *Romeo and Juliet* as not a representation of an adolescent passion in which death and love are romantically linked but rather as a projected *adult* fantasy of the proximity of passion and death, in which there is both an idealization of a lost hope of consummation *in vita* and a recuperative vision of death *as* the unrealized consummation. "Adults behold adolescent desire ambivalently," he remarks; "theirs is a gaze socially sanctioned in the name of hope, yet haunted by loss. At its most intense, *Romeo and Juliet* takes this form: a barely unconscious wish that death—that which mutability serves—be summoned in order to end mutability: to banish one kind of loss (mutability), another kind (death) is embraced. Absolute loss cancels loss across time" (380). This is a moving insight into the tragic, and one can extend it easily to Shakespeare's later adult fantasy of *adults* attempting to secure themselves against mutability by imitating mutability itself in the polymorphic perversity of youthful passion until, unable to keep ahead of the real thing, they choose the consummation that "shackles accidents and bolts up change."

Subject and Object in Renaissance Culture is a splendid book. As I hope I have conveyed, its concerns are wide-ranging, and its authors liberally provide information as well as argument. There is relatively little in the way of rote formulation; critical positions are articulated and turn out to be remarkably large-minded. It is impossible even in a lengthy review to indicate the quality of detail that informs these essays. Perhaps the highest commendation I can offer is to observe that one would not ordinarily read an anthology like this one all the way through (unless one were reviewing it), but the essays complement and supplement one another so well that such a reading is incrementally more satisfying.

Notes

1. Louis A. Montrose, "Professing the Renaissance: The Poetics and Politics of Culture," in *The New Historicism*, ed. Abraham Veeser (New York: Routledge, 1989), 21.
2. All Shakespeare citations refer to *The Riverside Shakespeare*, ed. G. Blakemore Evans et al. (Boston: Houghton Mifflin, 1974).
3. Stanley Cavell, *Disowning Knowledge in Six Plays of Shakespeare* (Cambridge: Cambridge University Press, 1987).

Staging Reform, Reforming the Stage: Protestantism and Popular Theater in Early Modern England.
By Huston Diehl.
Ithaca and London: Cornell University Press, 1997.

Reviewer: Heather James

This lucid study examines Protestant strategies to reform the interpretive habits of English readers and their influence over the popular theaters of London. The range of passions, intellectual habits, and cultural practices that fall within Diehl's scope is wide: from the love, fear, or smashing of icons to sight, the gaze, the imagination and memory, and to anthitheatricality and gynephobia. Diehl presents these key terms, their histories, and their interrelations

with a painstaking care that should make this study valuable to
advanced undergraduates as well as to critics of the period.

The introductory chapters explore various representational tactics, developed by Protestant reformers, to teach English audiences
to reevaluate signs and guard against the idolatrous sensuality of
the gaze. After brief but attractive readings of northern paintings
by van Leyden, Dürer, and Cranach, Diehl turns to anecdotes from
Foxe's *Book of Martyrs* to illustrate Protestant efforts to turn skeptics into heroes and artists into iconoclasts, and thus to offer new
exemplars for English readers to emulate. Diehl works carefully
to dispel the stereotype of the reductive, pleasureless Protestant
interpreter. In fact, the reformers' new aesthetics and epistemology
have an unexpectedly Barthian feel: for Diehl, the conversion to
Protestantism of the reformed artist Rochus "does not shut down
his creative energies, despite Protestant hostilities toward sacred
images, but rather authorizes him to enter into and attempt to manipulate a new symbol system, one that is characterized by self-
reflexivity, arbitrariness, and the free-floating play of signifiers"
(38–39). As the example suggests, Diehl is as concerned with the
relationship of Protestant reform to models of human agency as
she is with its propagandistic aims.

The next chapter, on imagination, uses interpretations of *Dr.
Faustus* and *Hamlet*, termed "Wittenberg Tragedies," to advance
the idea that reformers are less concerned with inhibiting pleasure
than with constructing subjects who are skeptically aware of their
own love of visual pleasure and imaginative creativity. Diehl discusses the enigmatic religious theatrics and historical figures of
Marlowe's play in relation to the debates, waged between Reformation defenders and opponents of the stage, about whether plays
expose or enact theatrical ruses. Particularly intriguing are the possible implications of introducing a rival pope whose name may
recall the historical magician Giordano Bruno. Also appealing is
Diehl's discussion of the dramatic and imaginative course of the
Eucharistic wine figuratively spilled on Marlowe's stage: the wine
passes from friars' rituals to Faustus's secular banquet and finally
to the clowns who steal from a vintner. While providing tantalizing
observations and questions, Diehl moves warily through her suggestions about Marlowe, leaving his theological position as mysterious as his political loyalties and employment and as undetermined
as the text of his play.

Paired with Marlowe's tragedy is a reading of *Hamlet*'s Mousetrap that is contrastingly certain of Shakespeare's reformist inten-

tions. Diehl's Hamlet "articulates the qualities of an ideal *Protestant* theater" (original italics) by praising "plays that mirror nature, actors who refrain from exploiting their creative powers, and audiences who distance themselves from spectacle and focus on the meaning of the play" (82–83). Diehl then argues that the playlet serves to transform Claudius into a Calvinist "split subject" (William Bouwsma's term), theatrically aware of himself as "observer and observed, audience and actor" (91). The Calvinist split takes place when the players move from the dumb show to the jointly auditory and spectacular representation of the murder: the "combination of dramatic image, poetic text, and choral commentary" so affects Claudius "that he can no longer repress or conceal his guilt. Rather than privileging spectacle, Hamlet's play emphasizes the capacity of language to realize or bring into being, what the images signify" (111). Hamlet's play, however, does not "certainly" impel Claudius to contemplate himself and his sins in a Calvinist light (89). If the playlet's success depends on its capacity to lead audiences to "condemn and abhor our sin" (89), as Calvin characterizes good images, it fails miserably with Claudius: after a half-hearted attempt at prayer, he reconfirms himself as Gertrude's husband and Denmark's king, roles stolen from the brother he murdered. If anything, Claudius's failed encounter with penitential theater hardens him to crime, since he subsequently plots the murder of his brother's son. The Mousetrap's failure to revive conscience in Claudius—if that was its purpose—would seem to qualify the idea that Shakespeare defines drama's efficacy in terms of Protestant responses to images.

The following chapter rehearses the Eucharistic debates in Reformation England and in current criticism, and seeks to ground the conventions and preoccupations of revenge tragedy, Kyd's *Spanish Tragedy* in particular, in the Reformist concern with words over image, figurative over visual power. The chapter, which focuses on the literalizing, bloody spectacles that are the stock-in-trade of revenge tragedies, seeks a specifically Protestant cause for their ambivalence about words and spectacle. The Protestant perspective enables a splendid anti-Catholic interpretation of the blasphemous Pedringano's overconfidence in the pyxlike box he believes contains his pardon. It also reduces Hieronimo, who "blatantly violates the distinction between visible sign and the thing it signifies, turning the analogous into the identical, the symbolic into the literal, the represented into the real" (114), to a deluded Catholic. The example of Hieronimo suggests the occasional problem this book incurs of assuming rather than testing the idea of a Protestant agenda embraced by Elizabethan and Jacobean playwrights from Shakespeare to Jonson and Middleton to Webster, without differentiating among their attitudes toward the theater and theology. Since "skeptical, mediated, self-reflexive, analogical" perspectives are not "distinctly Protestant" in themselves—Montaigne, Ariosto, and Cervantes come to mind—it seems unlikely that English audiences would have found a specifically Protestant agenda in the encouragement of such perspectives in Kyd's stagecraft. It is even less likely that *The Spanish Tragedy*'s "repeated performance on the London stages surely must have contributed to the demystification of the Roman Mass in Elizabethan England" (119). One might point, for example, to questions of law, justice, and agency as factors in Hieronimo's enormous popularity in early modern London.

In chapters on ocular proof and on iconophobia and gynephobia, Diehl offers a beautifully written and conceived reading of *Othello* rivaling the finest studies of the play to date. The chapter opens with a meditation on Rymer's impatience with Othello's obsession with the magical handkerchief and the suggestion that *Othello* has become partially illegible because post-Enlightenment audiences find it easier to belittle the Moor's superstition than to accept the handkerchief for the mysterious object of contention that it would be to Jacobean audiences, steeped in Protestant doubts about the interpretability of signs and wonders. Diehl suggests that Iago's contemptuous attitude toward "trifles," as well as "his identification of the magical with the erroneous, his racist and misogynous sentiments," which serve to "rationalize and estrange the magical elements of the play" (127), relate historically to Protestant reformers' awkward grappling with the epistemological problem of determining whether a sign originates in the divine or in the human imagination. Diehl persuasively locates Desdemona's handkerchief in the context of Protestant responses to relics such as the handkerchief that the Apostle Paul sent to cure people in his absence—a troublesome, because biblical, sign. Othello's search for ocular proof in the "trifling" handkerchief takes on fascinating cultural significances when it is related to the nervous glosses that Calvin and Tyndale furnished to explain Paul's handkerchief as a visible sign and not a magical agent. What is a "trifle" to Rymer and many critics, Diehl demonstrates, was to the early reformers a token of a traditional and tenacious way of seeing, whose imaginative hold could not easily be dispelled: "Read in the context of the religious controversies of the Reformation, and in particular the radical reinterpretations of the validity of ocular proof in acts of faith, *Othello* may be said to rehearse the epistemological crisis created by the reformers when they deny the magical efficacy of images and relics and yet assert the power of visible signs" (134).

Diehl persuasively traces the handkerchief's passage through the play and Protestant discourses about epistemology and ocular proof. She shows how the handkerchief is estranged from its original significance as Desdemona's "first remembrance of the Moor" (134), no token of idolatrous affection but a "recognizance and pledge of love" (135). As questions of interpretability attach to the handkerchief—as "a magical totem, a potent sign, and an insignificant trifle" (147)—during its passage from scene to scene and character to character, specifically Protestant doubts about magic, faith, and ocular proof circulate through the play. In a comprehensive reading of the handkerchief itself, Diehl teases out a complex interpretation of its pattern, the strawberries on a white background: iconographically associated with deceit; the sexual and fertile female body; the Virgin Mary and fallen Eve; the slandered Susanna; and spotted wedding sheets. In short, the handkerchief confronts early modern audiences, along with Othello, with its web of incompatible and authoritative meanings. According to this reading, Othello's catastrophic fall into error renders him an extreme figure for problems of knowledge in Jacobean London. For Diehl, Othello is both Everyman and the "extravagant and wheeling stranger" Brabantio fears, since he represents "the 'othering' of the imagination in the theological discourse of the reformers" (152).

A final chapter uses the theme of martyrdom to connect the wrenching spectacles in Webster's *Duchess of Malfi* with a Calvinist understanding of witnessing. Noting the variety of responses to martyring spectacles shown in the woodcuts illustrating Foxe's *Book of Martyrs*, Diehl proposes an analogy between the indifference, pleasure, pity and horror, and pious submission to the divine spectator displayed in Foxe and the responses of Ferdinand, Bosola, and the Duchess to the cruel theatrical spectacles to which Ferdinand subjects the Duchess. For Diehl, Bosola serves as a vehicle for Calvinist ideas about introspection and conscience as an internalized spectator, and is tellingly unable to do good even when he has "a mind to it." Diehl associates the Duchess with Protestant ideas about authority and rituals (particularly the marriage ceremony), resistance to Catholic officials, and renunciation of the world and a concomitant "faith in an invisible God" (198). By refusing to respond to Ferdinand's abusive theater with fear, and instead renouncing worldly and sensual pleasure, the Duchess herself represents, for Diehl, a Protestant ideal in the face of torture. The Protestant look at Webster's play makes a good sense of the play's morbid props—including dead hands and ghostly waxworks—and landscapes of graveyards and a ruined monastery.

This study's most compelling chapters join powerful and detailed interpretations of plays to historical discourses that provoke specifically Protestant anxieties. Diehl's discussions of the Protestant reformers' exploitation of misogyny in order to rouse antipathy for images, for example, are riveting in themselves and illuminating of plays like *Othello* and other revenge tragedies that fetishize and torment female bodies. The onstage tormenting, repudiation, and even murder of women by their adorers have compelling links to Protestant desecration of images: "Iconoclasts almost never looted the images for material gain," Diehl points out, "instead preferring to deface or desecrate them in certain highly symbolic ways, gouging out their eyes, for instance, or piercing their sides. They decapitate, dismember, torture, disfigure, and even crucify the offending images," and because "they have constructed those images as seductive women, they symbolically kill women they believe are polluted in ritual acts of purification" (162). Drawing on Kenneth Burke's discussion of "dying dialectically," in which "'a man can "substantially" slay himself through the sacrifice of another who is cosubstantial with him'" (163), Diehl further relates iconoclastic abuse of images to male protagonists' self-mutilation through the symbolic, as well as literal, murder of the women they love. These readings are tenaciously feminist, historical, and philological.

Premodern Sexualities.
Edited by Louise Fradenburg and Carla Freccero.
New York and London: Routledge, 1996.

Reviewer: Nicholas F. Radel

In the introduction to *Premodern Sexualities*, Louise Fradenburg and Carla Freccero propose a collection of essays about medieval and early modern sexuality in Europe that, at least in part, questions "whether the observation of similarities or even continuities between past and present inevitably produces an ahistoricist or universalizing effect" (xix). They begin with the by now seemingly orthodox Foucauldian assertion that before the modern period understandings of the body and its pleasures were organized around acts and not identities. Then, without devaluing the importance of this insight (or its political implications), the editors question the validity and utility of constructing a past that is absolute in its commitment to cultural difference. This is perhaps one of the most pressing issues in gay and lesbian or queer studies at the moment, and Fradenburg and Freccero's introduction theorizes it with great subtlety. Nevertheless, *Premodern Sexualities* as a whole does not guide its readers toward any synthesis of ideas around the issue.

At best, *Premodern Sexualities* collects essays that contribute to our historical knowledge of early modern and medieval sexuality and that articulate clearly and carefully various (and sometimes contradictory) perspectives on historiography and theory. The collection is divided around four historical themes that suggest some of the different discourses in which the erotics of premodern bodies are played out: "The Erotics of Conquest," "Medicine and the Law," "Sexuality and Sanctity," and "Rhetoric and Poetics." These divisions, however, provide only a superficial thematics. They do not help adjudicate the questions of historiography that the editors take as the main focus of the anthology, and, in fact, sometimes obscure them.

Even the best and most unified section is problematic. In "Rhetoric and Poetics," three essays all touch, at least peripherally, on what Elizabeth Pittenger calls the "sexual politics of writing" (230). Taken together, they make a convincing argument for the discursive production of homoerotics through early modern and medieval pedagogy and literary production. In her essay on Alain de Lille's *De Planctu Naturae*, Pittenger shows how the material realm of medieval pedagogy and manuscript production produced and reproduced the ideological campaign against sodomy waged in "The Complaint" itself. Her argument usefully complements Patricia Parker's essay, "Virile Style," which focuses on the Latin *nervus* as a keyword in the transmission of the Roman literary tradition that valued a virile, masculine style over a more "effeminate," Ciceronion one. Parker illustrates the ways in which the debate over style was gendered throughout the early modern period, a point whose relevance she explores in Montaigne's essays especially. Although Parker's essay stops short at gender, bypassing the implications of its argument for sexuality per se, one might question how the homoerotics of pedagogy and writing that Pittenger reveals would actually expand and corroborate Parker's revelations about masculine anxiety in the debate over style.

The issues get more complex, however, when we consider Bruce Holsinger's "Sodomy and Resurrection: The Homoerotic Subject of the *Divine Comedy*." Holsinger argues convincingly that the poetics of the *Divine Comedy* inscribe the pilgrim Dante into both a homosocial world and a homoerotic one in his encounters with the sodomites of Hell and Purgatory. Among other things, the poem provides a meditation on the "homoerotics of literary paternity" (249) in Dante's encounter with his teacher Brunetto. Even more to the point, Holsinger argues that Dante inscribes homoeroticism itself into the *Commedia*'s eschatological vision, "queering" the end of time itself. Clearly, Holsinger's argument is made salient by its association with Parker's discursive histories and Pittenger's superb historicizing. Yet unlike either of these writers, Holsinger fabricates his argument as a search for a universalized "homoerotic subject position," which he conceives of "as historically contingent, fleeting, unstable, produced at certain moments, by certain texts, and through specific cultural practices" (245). In other words, he proposes a way of reading history that sees "sexual definition and homoerotic desire" as issues of continuing importance (245). Holsinger's essay is not necessarily inconsistent with Pittenger's and Parker's, but at heart it seeks a transhistorical queer identification that the others tend to ignore. What are we to make of the difference? Does it question Pittenger's or Parker's methods—or vice versa? There is nothing here to interrogate—or even note—the interrelationship of essays that may or may not be theoretically at odds.

In another instance the thematic organization of *Premodern Sexualities* actually obscures a potentially important opposition around ideas that the editors take to be the main focus of their collection. In the section "Sexuality and Sanctity" Simon Guant explores the Old French vernacular hagiographic narrative, *Euphrosine*. Guant's essay explicitly rejects elements of a social constructionist argument by showing that a transvestite text like *Euphrosine* produces homosexual desire only to displace its disturbing implications back into a heterosexual framework. What is important, Guant emphasizes, is the revelation of this desire as explicitly homoerotic, and, he contends, it is equally significant that the text reveals it in the dialectical relationship with heterosexuality that Judith Butler defines as constitutive of modern sexual identities. At the very least, Guant makes a strong argument for a seemingly modern rendering of sexual discourses in a medieval text.

But Guant's essay might be usefully read next to Jonathan Goldberg's "The History That Will Be," from the first section of the book, "The Erotics of Conquest." In this essay, Goldberg takes up Stephen Greenblatt's reading of the "invisible bullets" anecdote from Harriot to argue that we must invent a strategy with colonial narratives that does not reproduce their ontological assumptions, one of which inscribes history with a heteronormative slant in which the European man triumphs over the virgin land or the feminized native. His essay, thus, argues for a way of reading Harriot's "invisible bullets" as a heteronormative European fantasy, not as a prescient reminder of the much later discovery that it was actually germs and disease that helped decimate native populations. As becomes clear when we consider his long introduction on psychoanalytically inspired theory like Judith Butler's, Goldberg attempts to write a history that escapes inscription into what he sees as a culturally specific rule of heteronormativity. His addressing Butler's work is germane to Guant's argument, for it could suggest that Guant's sighting of a modern dialectic between homo- and heterosexuality may itself be a culturally specific, postpsychoanalytic fantasy. In a book devoted to raising questions about the historical relations of modern and "premodern" sexuality, then, Goldberg's and Guant's essays have much more to say to each other than to their companion essays in the historically thematized sections in which they appear.

The organizational problem in Premodern Sexualities plays itself out in yet another way in the section "Medicine and the Law," which contains three essays. "Ut cum muliere: A Male Transvestite Prostitute in Fourteenth Century London," by Ruth Mazo Karras and David Lorenzo Boyd, explores the peculiarities of a rare legal case describing same-sex intercourse and male transvestism in medieval England. "The Hermaphrodite and the Orders of Nature: Sexual Ambiguity in Early Modern France," by Lorraine Daston and Katharine Park, argues that French medical and judicial attitudes toward hermaphrodites change considerably in the sixteenth and seventeenth centuries. In an interesting sidelight, Daston and Park use their material to argue that the opposition between nature and culture that seems so illuminating to us must also be contextualized to provide useful historical information. These essays are both useful.

But only the third essay in this section seeks to make a significant intervention into the theoretical impasse that *Premodern Sexualities* stages. "Don't Ask, Don't Tell: Murderous Plots and Medieval Secrets," by Karma Lochrie, compares the strategies of the open secret in medieval gynecological texts to those of the American military's "Don't Ask, Don't Tell" policy. In doing so, it illustrates one way that the divide between premodern sexual acts and modern sexuality may be navigated: not by looking at sexual behavior itself but by exploring larger regulatory strategies such as secrecy. Although the "subjects" of this essay are medieval medical discourses, its larger point is about how to negotiate the divide between the modern and the "premodern." Again, the reader, the essay, and the collection itself may have been better served by placing Lochrie's work within a theoretical rather than a historical context.

Other essays in the collection are only tangentially related to the thematics and theory of historiography, but they nevertheless make superb contributions to our historical knowledge. In addition to Guant's essay, the section on "Sexuality and Sanctity" includes an excellent analysis by Kathy Lavezzo of the homoerotics of compassion in *The Book of Margery Kempe*. Lavezzo reads Kempe's confessions to define medieval spirituality as a place "where devout ends mingle with and possibly serve as a legitimizing cover for other, less decorous and patriarchal ends," especially homoerotic female bonding (191). The first section, "The Erotics of Conquest," contains three other essays in addition to Goldberg's. José Piedra writes on the uses of black eroticism in the creation of a Spanish hybrid culture between the eighth and the fifteenth centuries, and María M. Carrión attempts to "queer" *El burlador de Sevilla*, that most quintessential of plays about masculine erotic conquest. But it is the last essay in this section that will be of particular interest to readers of *Shakespeare Studies*, though it is, to my mind, one of the most problematic essays in the entire collection.

Richard Corum's paper on *Henry V* attempts to find a place beside the already superb "queer" essays on this play published elsewhere by Valerie Traub and Jonathan Goldberg. Corum strikes out in a new direction by looking at the ways in which Shakespeare's play participates in a larger historical debate about Henry V and aggressive masculine sovereignty. More specifically, he attempts to see Henry's actions in the play as efforts to exchange his former

sodomitical imaginary for a new homosocial one. That is an interesting and probably correct argument. But in making it, Corum
suggests that Henry never really gives up his sodomitical desire,
and so, in effect, acts out the suppression of that desire. It is an
argument that seems in some ways to confuse the early modern
sodomite with the modern homosexual, in particular because
Corum seems to suggest that the thing Henry wants always to suppress most is sexual desire for other men (though he equivocates
on this point because, as he knows, sodomy in the early modern
period is never simply a sexual crime).

Perhaps I would feel comfortable with Corum's argument if he
marshaled more convincing evidence from the play itself, but some
of his readings strike me as special pleading. For example, he suggests that it is Henry who authorizes the killing of the boys who
guard the luggage during the battle at Agincourt because one of
those boys is Falstaff's companion from Eastcheap, who could possibly identify him as a sodomite. To his credit, Corum does seem
to be teasing out the implications of a position articulated several
years ago by Gregory Bredbeck, who argued that Bray's description
of the sodomite as existing outside the social order was not perfectly inscriptive and left space for what he wanted to call a "sodomitical subjunctivity." Corum's reading of Henry V may provide
additional evidence for that position. It is also true that Corum
sees the play as Shakespeare's comment on some of the motives of
the historical Henry. He thus begins to make a case for reading the
play as a historical document in ways different from what we had
previously thought possible. But the suggestive possibilities of both
these theoretical enterprises need to be spelled out more carefully
to make this piece satisfactory.

Premodern Sexualities is important, then, because it raises significant questions about the continuities between sexual behavior
in the premodern and the modern periods. These questions have
been too easily dismissed in some recent scholarship, and in raising them, Fradenburg and Freccero's collection expands the
theoretical and historiographical presuppositions of works like
Jonathan Goldberg's Queering the Renaissance and Susan Zimmerman's Erotic Politics. Unfortunately, however, the attempt is only
partially successful, for those essays in Premodern Sexualities that
do reconsider the new history of sexuality are allowed to stand in
simple tandem relation to those that adhere to its orthodoxies.
There is too little editorial guidance around the complicated and
sometimes contradictory historiographical issues that this collec-

tion raises to make it wholly satisfying. The essays themselves add a great deal to our knowledge of medieval and early modern sexual history, but *Premodern Sexualities* does not quite supplant earlier theoretical formulations of the history of sexuality.

Things of Darkness: Economies of Race and Gender in Early Modern England. By Kim F. Hall. Ithaca and London: Cornell University Press, 1995.

Reviewer: Valerie Wayne

When Kim Hall reads Petrarchan poetry, an English lover's expression of desire for his mistress's golden hair can mask a pan-European avarice for foreign gold and an envy of Spain for having a competitive edge in recovering riches from the New World. When she encounters *The Tempest*, she finds colonial economies of desire producing the threat of miscegenation in the response to Alonso's marrying his daughter to an African king as well as to Prospero's fears about Caliban. Hall observes numerous black attendants in seventeenth-century portraits offering an admiring gaze or a prized object to a white master or mistress, but in all of the portraits she treats, the primary sitter never acknowledges the proffered gift, so the offerings take on the impersonality of a commodity exchange rather than forging a relation through a gift exchange. Kim Hall has written an extraordinary book, one that I hope will make it difficult to sustain aestheticized and deracialized readings of the fair/dark binary and tropes of blackness in early modern culture. Using an approach that "understands the 'multiplicative nature' of oppression" (257) and consistently reads cultural elements in relation to one another—race in relation to gender, poetic authority in relation to sunburn, elite literary culture in relation to its participants' support for the slave trade, Hall's methodology provides a brilliant alternative to the limited foci, whether traditional or political, of much current practice.

A concern with the critical effacement of evocations of blackness lies behind her entire study. When discussing the sonnets, for example, she comments on "literary criticism's traditional (and almost pathological) insistence that blackness means nothing beyond its antithesis to 'whiteness'; that is, in the absolute insistence on a merely aesthetic basis for blackness in the Renaissance, a practice that extends even to reading direct references to Africa as mere signs of physical beauty" (69). She refuses this approach by showing how notions of "self" and "other" were formulated in a wide range of texts through the language of dark and light in order to construct the modern—white, European, male—subject. The five main chapters deal with travel narratives, sonnets, drama, women-authored texts, and material objects (especially cameos and portraits) in early modern England. This generic diversity is extended by temporal variety: Hall begins by addressing texts from the 1550s and moves in a roughly chronological pattern through Elizabethan and Stuart literature, ending with portraits prepared after the Restoration. Again and again, while drawing on an impressive range of critical and historical knowledge, she shows how blackness is evoked in order to racialize whiteness, make it visible, and define white subjectivity.

Attention to language enables Hall's approach at every turn. Granting that she is "more interested in discerning the ways in which the Africanist presence is embedded in language than with proving the nature of the black presence in England" (14), she uses the term "black" to refer to Africans and African-descended peoples as well as to social practices and cultural categories, and she eschews scare quotes around the word "race" on the grounds that "language itself creates differences within social organization and that race was then (as it is now) a social construct that is fundamentally more about power and culture than about biological difference" (6). These strategies strongly enable her readings of tropes of blackness. Her own success in this work may justify her assertion that "the correct insistence on race as a construction seems at times to be used as a shield against talking about racism, which is no less painfully real just because it is based in a fiction" (255). By confronting directly the color codings of language, Hall deals with an ideological agent that is pervasive and obvious in the present as well as the past. She makes her readers conscious of these linguistic patterns because "acknowledging the power of that language and its material effects is a good place to address issues of race and to do antiracist work" (266). While she recognizes that the trope of blackness was applied in the early modern period not only to Africans but to native Americans, Indians, and Spanish, Irish, and Welsh groups, she asserts that "in these instances it still draws its power from England's ongoing negotiations of African difference and from the implied color comparison . . . that itself relies on an idea of African difference" (7). She supports this claim with accounts of England's involvement in the slave trade beginning in the 1550s and with travel narratives that enabled European readers to formulate their own identity in relation to foreign others.

Hall's work intersects in important ways with the projects of New Historicists and feminists, but her multiplicative approach also shows the limits of much of that work. Faulting the New Historicists for paying no more than cursory attention to gender and racial assumptions in identity formation, she grounds her approach in feminist practices and more specifically in black feminist criticism that "reads race as a dynamic category that can be understood only in its contact with a number of other categories" (258). She finds this approach particularly well equipped to intervene in Renaissance studies because of "the contingency of the interactive model" of race (258) in a place and time lacking a term or a coherent ideology to mark its racial preoccupations. Her aims and achievements become fully apparent in a strong personal epilogue, where Hall admits she has chosen to focus on one dominant strand of racial thought "so that I could play out the possibilities of multiplicity" (261), even though she concedes that "to discuss blackness in the Renaissance is for me to inhabit an uneasy and undetermined position in relation to my subject and my audience" (257). By the end her deliberate choice seems especially smart, because it has allowed her to illustrate through so many different texts and artifacts that "the language of fairness and darkness is always *potentially* racialized" (261) and to do the antiracist work that she most wants to do. "What damage do we do to students and history when we ignore the vital language of blackness that shaped the English as social subjects and that currently shapes our social relations today?" (265). Through her attention to pedagogy in the epilogue and her explicit articulation of her method, Hall makes the politics of her analysis available for others to appreciate and emulate: "I identify my project as black feminist literary criticism because it explores the interactions of race and gender in a specific cultural context, because it comes to the academy out of an oppositional consciousness, and, most important, because it is antiracist in its attempts to analyze traditional discourses and cultural assumptions that have been damaging to people of African descent" (263–64).

Hall's chapter on the drama, called "Commerce and Intercourse," extrapolates from Gayle Rubin's discussion of systems of kinship and economy with the observation that the exchange of goods across cultural borders also includes the possibility of other forms of cultural exchange. She posits that when England developed commercial ties across the globe, "associations between marriage, kinship, property, and economics become increasingly anxiety-ridden" (124). Commercial interaction also fostered the social and sexual relations underlying representations of interracial desire during the period. "Thus women's bodies become the site of struggle between, on the one hand, the need for both colonial trade and cultural assimilation through union and, on the other, the desire for well-recognized boundaries between self and other" (125). Noting that women are usually represented as fair or black in competition with or in relation to each other (a topic that she takes up at more length concerning women-authored texts), she discusses the *Masque of Blackness* in light of Queen Anne's estrangement from James, Anne's visible pregnancy at the time of the performance, and the relative powerlessness of female beauty in James's court. Although the masque "presents an idealized world in which normally intransigent blackness is subdued by a European order predicated on white, male privilege and power" (137), the performance by court ladies was itself a transgressive act, and some of those who participated in it—Penelope Rich, Lady Mary Wroth, Arbella Stuart, and Frances Howard—would exhibit more disruptive resistance to patriarchal power through producing illegitimate children, forging a secret marriage, and even planning a murder. Hall's analysis of the masque illustrates how social control is exercised through the violent and intimate intersection of sex and race.

In discussing *The Tempest* and *Antony and Cleopatra*, Hall sees both texts grappling with issues of cultural integrity and endogamous unions within imperial/colonial economies of desire. Caliban's desire to people the isle with others like himself licenses Prospero's anxiety about miscegenation, which then requires that he preserve Miranda's fair aristocratic body within a chaste marriage to a fellow aristocrat in order to ensure the orderly transference of power through European bloodlines and secure the state. His foil here is Alonso, whose willingness to marry his own daughter to a dark foreigner—he did "lose her to an African"—is described by Sebastian as the reason that Ferdinand was lost at sea and the occasion for the rupture of other European families. In *Antony and Cleopatra*, an African queen to whom Antony is lost threatens a European empire and evokes what Hall calls "Europe's primal fear: loss of identity in measureless expansion. Antony's absorption with Cleopatra is only the romantically reversed reading of Rome's political absorption" (157). Both Egypt and Caliban's island are then liminal spaces "in which the separations of dark and light, self and other, are momentarily broken down, and the anxieties over that collapse are displayed and explored" (160). As the plays end, Octavius Caesar is unable to control and display Cleopatra, and Prospero is pushed to acknowledge his connection to a "thing of darkness." Hall concludes her chapter with a discussion of Webster's *The Devil's Law-Case* and Richard Brome's *The English Moore*, both plays in which women disguise themselves as moors. All of these analyses affirm and document what she sees as the Jacobean fascination with otherness, which is described as the logical successor to Elizabethan insularity. Whereas Elizabeth twice tried to expel "Blackamoores" from England, the first entertainment for James and Anne as a royal couple involved "four young Negroes" who "danced naked in the snow in front of the royal carriage" and later died of pneumonia. The wedding pageant that followed featured "forty-two men dressed in white and silver and wearing gold chains and visors over blackened faces" (128). Fascination with otherness, indeed.

These summaries of select interpretations do not do justice to the complexity of Hall's individual readings or the diversity of texts that she takes up, which include Leo Africanus's *Geographical Historie of Africa*, Hakluyt's *Principal Navigations, Voyages, and Discoveries of the English Nation*, Sidney's *Astrophil and Stella*, the sonnet cycle *Zepheria*, the biblical Song of Songs, Aemilia Lanyer's *Salve Deus Rex Judaeorum*, Elizabeth Cary's *Tragedy of Mariam*, Mary Wroth's *Urania* in its published text and manuscript continuation, a re-creation of the coat of arms of Sir John Hawkins, the Gresley and Drake jewels and other late-sixteenth-century cameos, and eleven portraits of masters and mistresses with black servants. These last images are well reproduced and offer compelling visual evidence to support her verbal analyses elsewhere. An appendix called "Poems of Blackness" further confirms Hall's work by reprinting twenty-six poems, most of which are largely inaccessible today and were circulated privately at the time they were written. Included are William Dunbar's "Ane Blak Moir," three poems by George Herbert, two by Richard Lovelace and Richard Crashaw, and many more by less well known poets. It would have been helpful to provide the dates during which these poets lived or flourished, since they range over a 150-year period. In general the temporal locations of texts discussed in the book could be marked more specifically to avoid their blurring indiscriminately into the vast expanse of "the early modern period."

Hall worries in her epilogue that "our developing work on race might become merely another new frontier for literary criticism, yet another way to reanimate Renaissance studies rather than to produce antiracist criticism and politically forceful pedagogy" (255). This seems to me an especially important concern, and Hall does what she can to counter the recuperative effect through her turn to pedagogy in the epilogue and her attention throughout to language, which crosses the borders of history and academe. Had the book given more attention to the prose in which it presents its ideas, it might have succeeded even more fully. Political writing has its own reasons to want to communicate effectively apart from aesthetic criteria, and there is some opaque writing here that needs unpacking and revision. The epilogue is in this sense a welcome change in style from the earlier text, perhaps because Hall feels freer to express her intentions more overtly. She closes by affirming her desire to "give students the critical tools for a more meaningful and complex dialogue on race, one that comprehends the intersection of categories without disregarding our differences and that moves beyond racial guilt—but not beyond justice" (268). In its tone and texture as well as its trenchant analyses, her book achieves this very difficult goal by tracing the patterns of violence embedded within the language of color. This is a book for all who use language.

Alternative Shakespeares, Volume 2.
Edited by Terence Hawkes.
New York and London: Routledge, 1996.

Reviewer: Linda Woodbridge

Both Terence Hawkes in this volume's introduction and John Drakakis in its conclusion begin with the words "alternative to what?" It is a good question. Both see the essays in this collection as radical alternatives to what they seem to regard as the entrenched conservatism of "Shakespeare studies" (Drakakis, 238), but a glance at the table of contents makes a person wonder. Is it really a radical departure from the familiar, to find Brace Smith or Alan Sinfield writing on queer theory, Margreta de Grazia on print culture, Catherine Belsey on desire, or Ania Loomba on "empire, race, colonialism, and cultural difference"? These scholars made a name for themselves some time ago writing on just these topics, and legions have followed in their footsteps: every Renaissance conference features mainly essays on queer theory, print culture, desire, empire, race, colonialism, and cultural difference. Far from radical, this is mainstream. The question bears repeating: alternative to what?

The essays are thought provoking and useful; there's not a dud in the bunch. But most read like "state of play" updates, retailing the latest thinking on Shakespeare via queer theory, race theory, or the postcolonial. Useful as introductions or summaries, they are; radical departures they are not.

In his introduction, Hawkes gives an excellent summary of the conservative thinking that the book opposes: the idea that "Shakespeare is an all-wise, all-knowing genius," that his plays "present portrait galleries of individual human figures, exemplifying characteristic faults or virtues," that his work "is universally valid and speaks to human beings across the ages," that "to encounter his plays is . . . to come across ourselves," that his plays present us with "the truth," that "human nature is permanent, one and indivisible, regardless of place, race, creed and culture" (9–10). These ideas, admittedly, are pretty easy for us Shakespeare scholars to be against. But who exactly is for them? Drakakis, in the conclusion, gestures vaguely toward the menace of "academic institutions [which] have become huge bureaucracies" during the last decade (239)—really? only the last decade?—but Hawkes is more specific: the obnoxious beliefs he opposes can be traced to Dr. Johnson, Coleridge, Bradley, and Tillyard (9). The reader may be pardoned for doubting whether this crew comprises an immediate threat. They have the look, in fact, of straw men; and one recalls that essay after essay in this volume's forerunner, *Alternative Shakespeares 1* (Methuen, 1985; reissued Routledge, 1992) took arms against just this array of eighteenth-, nineteenth-, and earlier-twentieth-century bogeymen.

Yet the ideas anathematized by Hawkes—wise Bard, universal human nature—are definitely out there: one encounters unshakable faith in such ideas among undergraduates in English classes, local literary societies, and campaigning politicians. In the United States, an annual nationwide Shakespeare recitation contest strives to increase public awareness of "Shakespeare's universal message." The recent furor over the discovery that many United States colleges no longer require a Shakespeare course even of English majors reveals yet again the importance of Shakespeare, conservatively interpreted, to the political agenda of those who pledge allegiance to family values, the war on drugs, and an end to welfare as we know it. The radical challenge most needed is not to academic Shakespeare studies, already impeccably radical enough, but to the kind of thinking that aligns Shakespeare's universal message with messages like "put Father back at the head of the family" and "bring back flogging." The problem is that people who believe in All-Wise Shakespeare and Universal Human Nature do not read books like *Alternative Shakespeares*. What efforts do Hawkes and Drakakis envision, to get some queer theory, race theory, politically left literary interpretation, postcolonial reading out into the high schools, literary clubs, and politicians' speechifying? No easy task, granted; but still, when reading *Alternative Shakespeares*, the words "preaching to the converted" do come to mind.

Turning to the individual essays, Steven Mullaney in "After the New Historicism" offers not only a critique of New Historicism, but a critique of critics of New Historicism; not only a review article on New Historicism, but a review of review articles on New Historicism. (Is this topic reaching the omphaloskepsis stage?) Catherine Belsey fascinatingly suggests that paintings featuring both beautiful naked women and beautiful naked boys (such as Venuses and Cupids) imply unstable sexuality in the viewer, further evidence of the fluid sexual identities other scholars have noted in this period.

Margreta de Grazia discusses the revitalization, by print, of the ancient signet/wax trope signifying "both processes of conception: the having of thoughts and the having of children" (70); imaginatively ringing many changes upon this trope, she observes that "counterfeit coining, like usury, is frequently associated with sodomitic sex" (79) and that "letters could themselves be quite sexy, as they are in sixteenth-century embodied alphabets in which the body of the letter is represented by lusty human bodies in seductive poses and erotic positions" (87)—a far cry, one cannot help thinking, from the way children are wooed to love letters on Sesame Street. Bruce Smith, in "L[o]cating the Sexual Subject," notes that "carried to its logical conclusion, queer theory deconstructs the femina that gives feminism its very reason for being" (97), which might help explain the fact that queer theory almost entirely displaces feminist theory in Alternative Shakespeares 2—at least volume one had one feminist essay, Catherine Belsey's (and also, arguably, Jacqueline Rose's), while in volume 2, Hawkes manages to give a potted history of Shakespeare criticism through the ages without so much as a mention of feminism. Queer deconstruction or not, this still strikes me as leaving a "gap in Nature." It is interesting, though, that Smith defends deconstruction as politically and socially relevant ("queer theory has founded its critical platform on deconstruction" [97]), in contrast to Malcolm Evans's grumble, in Alternative Shakespeares 1, that "deconstruction permits a delirium of dissent which is also a babble of compliance," that it is "a-political" and "particularly in its North American forms, . . . a conservative rather than a progressive force" (89–90).

Alan Sinfield provides an unexceptionable if unexceptional reading of The Merchant of Venice via queer theory. It seems a bit of a stretch to call Launcelot Gobbo's change of masters a "traffic in boys" (132), but Sinfield is generally persuasive in declaring the play's culminating triumph of heterosexuality a "failure of nerve" (138). Keir Elam, dissecting the semiotics of "body criticism" of Twelfth Night—that which "adopts as its own universe of discourse the realms of early modern gastroenterology (the alimentary tract), uroscopy (great P's), gynaecology (the cut) and comparative reproductive physiology (one-sex/flesh)"—throws out the provocative suggestion that the physiological preoccupations of recent Shakespeare criticism comprise "a return to a Puritan aesthetic, or antiaesthetic, of the drama as pathology" (153).

The strongest essay, I think, is Ania Loomba's. Noting that "English contact with the East—India, the Spice Islands, Turkey, Persia,

China and Japan—has not become part of the working vocabulary of Renaissance scholarship" (169), which instead emphasizes New World contact, Loomba draws a distinction between Renaissance representations of Eastern enterprises, conceived as trade, and the colonizing enterprises involving the New World. The former produced powerful, autonomous literary figures—often queens—in contrast to the dominated Calibans of the latter. Dympna Callaghan, in "'Othello Was a White Man': Properties of Race on Shakespeare's Stage," says some very good things about blackface and whiteface, and retells a wonderful anecdote about Billie Whitelaw's white pancake makeup rubbing off on Laurence Olivier's "shiny black make-up" (202–3). And Philip Armstrong offers the insight that "psychoanalytic models of identity construction remain dependent for their development and representation upon drama; more specifically, upon Shakespeare; in fact, upon *Hamlet* itself. Lacan, for example, uses this play as a primary instance of the imaginary identification between the ego and its ideal image in the mirror" (224).

The essays, then, are well worth reading; but they are oddly framed by introductory and closing materials that make them out as more audacious and groundbreaking than they are, and also more narrowly political than they are. Hawkes in the introduction tells us that "as Steven Mullaney comments, . . . the 'aesthetic analysis of literary texts' can no longer constitute an appropriate project for literary criticism" (10); but Mullaney himself does not, in his article, put the case against aesthetics quite that baldly, and there are moments of aesthetic appreciation in several essays in the collection—for example, Belsey's essay posits seduction as something approaching the aesthetically pleasing. And it is hard to see why criticism needs to be as exclusionary as Hawkes decrees—must criticism limit itself to a relentless rehearsal of oppression? Is there no way aesthetics can coexist with political criticism? If nothing else, the aesthetic appeal of literature helps account for its seductive ability to oppress. And *must* the aesthetic necessarily be bourgeois? Does an interest in the beauty and skill of a play or a painting necessarily imply elitism and High Art? Would attention to the formal beauty of artisanal objects be similarly condemned? The rules that the editor sets forth, concerning what literary critics ought to be allowed to do, are too narrow, rigid, and prescriptive for my tastes. Happily, many of the contributors to *Alternative Shakespeares 2* have clearly felt free to ignore them.

The Texts of "Othello" and
Shakespearian Revision.
By E. A. J. Honigmann.
London and New York: Routledge, 1996.

Reviewer: MacDonald P. Jackson

More than thirty years ago, in The Stability of Shakespeare's Text (1965), E. A. J. Honigmann raised a minority voice against the stubborn propensity of the foremost Shakespearean textual scholars of the time to explain all variants between early Shakespeare texts as due to forms of corruption and to dismiss the possibility of authorial revision. He showed that authors copying their own manuscripts, including Renaissance playwrights, are apt to tinker with their wording, making many trivial changes, as well as some significant ones. He argued that at least some of the considerable variation between the Quarto and Folio texts of such plays as Troilus and Cressida, Othello, and King Lear had resulted from Shakespeare's indulging in second thoughts and replacing original words or phrases with new ones. Now that the idea of Shakespeare as reviser is widely entertained, Honigmann aims to correct an increasing tendency to regard all early printed versions as of equal status and to minimize the extent to which the plays have been distorted in transmission. He still believes that some of the differences between Quarto (1622) and First Folio (1623) Othello are due to Shakespeare's own rewordings, but his special concern is with the agents and processes that have intervened between the author and the two substantive texts that have been preserved. And for him, the preparation of a "critical edition" that draws on the evidence of Quarto and Folio in an attempt to recover "Shakespeare's final intentions" remains a worthwhile objective, however hard it may be to achieve.

The stemma that Honigmann proposes begins with Shakespeare's working draft, his "foul papers." The Quarto (Q) he sees as having been printed from a scribal transcript of these. The line of descent for the Folio (F) is more complicated: from the foul papers an authorial fair copy was prepared, and this in turn was copied by a scribe, F having been set from this transcript, but with

some "contamination" directly from Q. Except insofar as it postulates Q influence on F, this stemma is exactly the same as that
proposed in the *Textual Companion* (1987) to the Oxford Shakespeare. So in what sense is Honigmann's book "a groundbreaking
piece of scholarly detective work," as the dustjacket claims?

The answer is that Honigmann has reexamined all the variation
between Q and F and found patterns not remarked on before. F has
some 160 lines not in Q, the additional passages being scattered
through the play and ranging from 1 to 22 lines. Also, the texts
differ in about one thousand substantive (or verbal) readings. At
some point the F text was purged—by excision and substitution—
of more than fifty oaths that are preserved in Q and restored by
modern editors. Honigmann begins by looking again at the F-
only passages.

The Oxford editors' belief that F represents "an authorially revised text" owes a good deal to a chapter in Nevill Coghill's *Shakespeare's Professional Skills* (1964), where he detected a "strategy
of revision" that linked several of the longer F additions; he argued
that the added material strengthened the play's effectiveness in the
theater. The alternative theory that the passages had been deliberately removed from Q seemed to him to imply cutting so "stupid"
and "destructive" as to be scarcely credible. Honigmann is less
ready than Coghill to rule out the necessary degree of stupidity
and destructiveness as inconceivable in the Elizabethan theater,
and judges "that what Coghill saw as brilliant afterthoughts were
equally brilliant strokes of stagecraft when the play was first written" (10). As evidence that matter has been cut from Q rather than
added to F, he points to (a) the way that Q, like F, prints lines and
phrases that appear to lead into or out of the F-only passages, or
otherwise presuppose their existence, and (b) to cases where Q's
omission of material present in F disrupts the flow of the verse,
and especially the dovetailing of consecutive speeches. The fact
that sense or meter or both run more smoothly in F suggests that
these more substantial F-only passages were in the play as Shakespeare originally wrote it. Honigmann theorizes that "the manuscript behind Q was 'marked up' to indicate possible cuts by
someone asked to shorten the play" (13), and that either, the mark-
ings being "light and confusing," the printer made only a few of
the proposed deletions, or the marking up was sporadic and not
completed. A few Q omissions seem accidental, due to eyeskip by
a compositor or scribe. On the other hand, in many of the shorter
passages that differ in Q and F, Q is metrically regular and F irregu-

lar, and Honigmann finds other evidence that F in such instances displays minor additions to the text, along with associated rewording. Honigmann's conclusion, a slight retreat from the position he defended in an article in the *Library* in 1982, is that "Q and F *Othello* are examples of textual instability, not of large-scale revision" (21)—in other words, that Shakespeare introduced small variations into a fair copy of the play without making sizable interpolations.

"Metrical considerations, of course, must not be allowed to weigh too heavily in *Othello,* a play that contains many irregular lines," as Honigmann concedes (14), and it would not be surprising if Shakespeare, after first leaving a short line, later stitched it into the pentameter structure as he added phrases or sentences. So the argument from meter is inconclusive. But the case for believing the F-only Willow Song to have been original but omitted from Q, rather than composed as a late expansion of the play, seems strong. This is disconcerting for anybody who has admired John Jones's brilliant discussion, in *Shakespeare at Work* (1995), of divergences between Q and F *Troilus and Cressida, Hamlet, King Lear,* and *Othello* in terms of revision: assuming that not only the Willow Song itself but the substantial patches of F-only dialogue in 4.2 and 4.3 were added by Shakespeare, he gives an illuminating account of their function. However, Jones's critical insights remain no less astute, whether the longer F-only passages were created in the first fire of Shakespeare's imagination or when the fading coals flickered anew.

Honigmann's exploration of court archives reveals new grounds for suspicion of any text procured around 1620 by the "fascinating rogue" Thomas Walkley, publisher of Q *Othello.* He finds evidence of "false starts" suggestive of Shakespeare's foul papers, which he thinks were so hard to decipher that a scribe or scribes copying them were beguiled into an inordinate number of misreadings and sometimes resorted to guesswork or to omitting bits of text. There can be little doubt that Q was set from scribal copy, not from autograph: the frequency of 'em, ha', and tho is quite un-Shakespearean and unlikely to be compositorial, and the Oxford editors summarized other features suggestive of a scribe's intervention. In *Stability,* Honigmann gave grounds for thinking that Q was set by three compositors (one for 1.1–2.3, a second for 3.1–5.1, and a third for 5.2) working from manuscript in the hands of two scribes, who had copied alternate chunks of the text. Drawing on a University of Kansas doctoral dissertation by Millard T. Jones (1974), Charlton

Hinman, in his Clarendon Press facsimile of *Othello 1622* (1975) rejected Honigmann's findings in favor of the view that Q had been set by one compositor. Jones and Hinman based their conclusions on a thorough survey of "spelling peculiarities" tabulated by computer, and on type analysis, which revealed setting by formes from a single pair of cases. Hinman noted that "beginning with sheet H" the printing of Q "seems to have been interrupted frequently for the sake of getting on, more or less concurrently, with the printing of X," some unknown piece of work (xv). Honigmann now defers to Hinman's expertise as bibliographer, but points out that the number of scribes who prepared the manuscript behind Q is a separate issue, and implies that all the questions raised by the data he set forth in *Stability* may not yet have been answered.

I agree with him. Use of a single pair of cases need not preclude one compositor's having taken over from another. Jones whittles away at Honigmann's evidence for a meaningful shift in compositorial practices, and suggests that one man, without settled preferences, reacted variably to the demands of justification, type shortage, setting by formes, and other printing-house pressures. But hints of a pattern remain. And a simple statistical test, a Runs Test for Randomness, suggests that the clustering of variables that Honigmann cited in support of his claim that two scribes, working on alternate stints, prepared the manuscript from which Q was printed is unlikely to be due to chance. Moreover, the spelling *mistresse* (eight times) seems to be associated with Honigmann's Scribe B, *mistrisse/mistris* (nine times) with his Scribe A. A curious feature of the data is that Honigmann's Scribe B markers predominate up to F2r (A:21/B:38), whereas from F2v onward Scribe A markers predominate (A:52/B:25). This pattern is additional to the pattern of alternating clusters. Admittedly Q displays hundreds of variables, so there is considerable scope for finding apparently nonrandom patterning in a selection of them. But on the whole it is hard to believe that only two agents (one compositor and one scribe) intervened between Shakespeare's foul papers and Q. The matter turns out to be of some consequence to theories about the relationship between Q and F, as we shall see.

The casting-off of copy necessary for setting by formes is, as Honigmann notes, likely to have been responsible for some of Q's mislineation, and the Q compositor(s) may even have resorted to some omission or expansion of the text. This is also the case with F, set by Folio compositors B and E. Honigmann examines some of the other dramatic texts that issued, like F, from the printing house of William Jaggard, and also notes that an altercation between Jaggard and one of his authors, Ralph Brooke, shows that Jaggard's compositors regarded the correction of a writer's English as within their province. His conclusion is that "Jaggard's men took many liberties with the texts they printed" (57). But he later concedes that, as is clear from his setting of reprints, E was fairly faithful to the minutiae of his copy, except in so far as inexperience betrayed his eye, brain, or hand; B was more apt to make deliberate alterations.

Honigmann's most important chapter concerns their manuscript copy. In short, he argues that F was printed from a transcript by the scribe Ralph Crane, who is known to have worked on other Folio plays. An impressive variety of data is accumulated to prove that F "has many distinctive features" and that these "point to one man." For example, the total of thirty-four single words enclosed in brackets ("swibs") links F *Othello* with other Shakespeare texts thought to have been printed from Crane transcripts: there are none in Q *Othello* and very few in any of the Shakespearean "good quartos." Only two were added in Jaggard's Pavier reprints of 1619, probably at least partly the work of compositor B. The swibs appear at about the same rate in the F *Othello* stints of both compositor B and compositor E, the latter known to have been disinclined to add brackets of any kind to those he found in his copy. Spellings and oddities of presentation support the hypothesis that Crane prepared the copy for F. We must agree with Honigmann that "more detailed study of Crane's scribal habits ... is now urgently needed" (76).

He feels "uneasy about putting a label to manuscript B, the manuscript of *Othello* copied by Crane," but tentatively identifies it as Shakespeare's not very fair "fair copy" (80–81)—"not very fair" because, in Honigmann's view, Shakespeare's handwriting, both in his foul papers and his subsequent copy of them, caused numerous misreadings. Listing the most likely of these, he notes that the same kinds of misreading—errors due to the handwritten formation of the letters—tend to occur in each text, Q and F. He believes that those in F are due to Crane's having misread Shakespeare's script while creating a transcript from the authorial fair copy.

I think he is wrong about this. In an article in the *Library* in 1987 I showed, basing calculations on Kenneth Muir's eclectic New Penguin edition of *Othello* (1968), that a disproportionate number of F's most clearly identifiable misreadings occur within compositor E's stints: twenty-three out of twenty-seven, though setting was fairly evenly divided between E and B. This strongly suggests that most of the misreadings were compositorial, the naive and inept novice E being much more prone to such error than the experienced B. Honigmann's own lists (82–89)—in which he marks with asterisks "variants that are definitely or probably corrupt," though composed to show the likeness of Q's and F's misreadings, reveal a similar, though less pronounced, disparity: sixteen of twenty-four F misreadings fall within E's stints. The disparity would have been statistically highly significant had Honigmann enumerated and evaluated the "final -s errors" that he attributes to Shakespeare's carelessness in scrawling word endings. He counts over a hundred such variants, in which a final -s is present in one text and absent from the other. But I found that twenty-one of F's final -s variants rejected by Muir in favor of Q had been set by compositor E, only eight by B. However, the vast majority of these are probably due not to misreading but to simple compositorial ineptitude, since in setting his shares of Folio *Titus Anronicus* and *Romeo and Juliet* from known printed copy, E made forty-two such omissions or additions of -s. In short, I think that Honigmann classifies as misreadings in F several variants more plausibly attributable to other causes and that most of the remainder originated with compositor E.

This is important, because if Shakespeare's penmanship (even in a fair copy) was as erratic as Honigmann claims, there are implications for other plays. He admits that the putatively Shakespearean Hand D's famous three pages in *Sir Thomas More* "are really quite easy to read" (87), but he dates Hand D's contribution to *More* in 1593 or 1594 and suggests that by around 1600 Shakespeare's hand had become less legible. In my view, he is wrong about the date of the three pages too; the case, summarized in the Oxford *Textual Companion*, for an early-seventeenth century date seems to me sound.

Honigmann's belief that Crane often misread Shakespeare's fair copy is, at any rate, hard to reconcile with his notion that Crane had Q beside him to help him decipher the manuscript. Why should he so often prefer his own nonsensical misreading of Shakespeare's hand to the meaningful Shakespearean reading that he could find in plain print in Q? Honigmann offers his theory as "a compromise solution" to the problem of the physical relation between Q and F. Nearly fifty years ago Alice Walker persuaded the most influential textual scholars that F *Othello* had been set from a copy of Q that

had been annotated to bring it into line with an authoritative manuscript. She cited bibliographical links between Q and F, which
share not only errors in wording and lineation, but anomalies in
spelling. J. K. Walton's *The Quarto Copy for the First Folio of
Shakespeare* (1971) was largely successful in rebutting this evidence: he showed that in quantity and kind the errors shared by
Q and F *Othello* matched those to be found in independent prints.
Gary Taylor reinforced Walton's conclusions by his demonstration
that if compositor E set from annotated Q copy, his treatment of its
punctuation was utterly at variance with his normal practices in
setting from known printed copy. But the number of mistakes in Q
that are also made in F impresses Honigmann sufficiently to cause
him to postulate Crane's sporadic consultation of Q.

This is the most puzzling of all aspects of the *Othello* textual
problem. But Honigmann does not mention the piece of evidence
advanced by Walker that seemed to Greg "conclusive" and that
Philip Williams, reviewing Walker's *Textual Problems of the First
Folio* in *Shakespeare Quarterly* in 1953, pronounced "classic in
its simplicity and force" (482). This was her argument from the
pattern of -*t*/-'*d*/-*ed* endings of preterites and past participles that
are phonetically [t]. She argued that the variant spellings appear
arbitrarily in Shakespearean texts (Q and F *Lear*, for example, having "stopt" and "vsurpt," whereas Q and F *Othello* have "stopp'd"
and "vsurp'd"), that the tendency was for -*t* endings in the quartos
to be "modernized" as -'*d*/-*ed* endings in the Folio, that for the
seventy-two such verbs shared by Q and F of *Othello*, Q preferred
-*t* (47 instances) and F -'*d*/-*ed* (48 instances), and that every one of
F's twenty-four -*t* spellings was anticipated in Q. If Q and F were
independent prints, F should, she maintained, sometimes have
spelled -*t* where Q spelled -'*d*/-*ed*; the normalization must have
been progressive.

Walton countered this with the suggestion that Q exactly reproduced the endings in Shakespeare's foul papers (or perhaps in the
promptbook), from which F also, through however many intermediaries, derived, and that these agents in the transmission of F sometimes changed -*t* to -'*d*/-*ed*, but never changed -'*d*/-*ed* to -*t*. But
Walton postulated a single archetype, Shakespeare's foul papers,
whereas Honigmann postulates two authorial manuscripts. It
seems unlikely that Shakespeare, in making a fair copy of his own
foul papers—one into which he introduced various revisions—
would change no -'*d*/-*ed* endings to -*t* endings. After all, his ortho-
graphical instability equaled any textual instability that might be

imputed to him. This was a playwright who (in *Sir Thomas More*) could spell "sheriff" as "Shreiff," "shreef," "shreeve," "Shreiue," and "Shreue" within the space of five lines. And Honigmann's earlier theories about the origins of Q—theories now partially and hesitantly retracted, but not conclusively rebutted—would have put extra strain on our ability to believe that Q exactly reproduced the pattern of phonetically [t] preterite and past participle endings of Shakespeare's foul papers: if Q was set by three compositors from a transcript prepared by two scribes, we would hardly expect all five agents to be so conservative, particularly when Q displays so many other nonauthorial features. In fact, the prevalence of nonauthorial features in Q seems somewhat at odds with the notion that it preserved Shakespeare's original -*t*/-'*d*/-*ed* endings, however many scribes and compositors were involved. We also need information about Crane's habitual treatment of such endings. Walton's explanation of the evidence adduced by Walker would require that Crane never changed -'*d*/-*ed* to -*t*.

Occasional consultation of Q by Crane as he transcribed Shakespeare's fair copy is not in itself a very satisfactory explanation of the -*t*/-'*d*/-*ed* pattern observed by Walker. If Q influence on F created it, then that influence must have been quite consistently sustained. Since, the concentration of F's misreadings in E's stints reveals that they were largely compositorial, printer's copy for F must have been manuscript, as was also demonstrated by Taylor's analysis of F's punctuation and spelling. So Q influence on F would have to have been via a transcript of an annotated copy of Q. Yet it is hard to see why, in 1622/3, a quarto should have been marked up with corrections from Shakespeare's fair copy (or some other authoritative manuscript) and then transcribed, when the fair copy could have been transcribed directly. If, on the other hand, the pattern observed by Walker is to be attributed to a shared Q/F ancestry, then there seems no reason why errors common to the two texts should not be similarly explained. I could wish that Honigmann had set his mind to this particular puzzle and come up with a plausible solution.

Honigmann includes an interesting chapter on lineation and scansion in *Othello*. He believes that "the number of syllables per verse line was sometimes Shakespeare's first concern, not a strict adherence to iambic rhythms" (107), and accordingly attempts many novel rearrangements of series of short speeches to create ten- or eleven-syllable lines. The premise seems to me mistaken. The fact that a line of mature Shakespearean verse may have fewer than five "emphatic accents" is irrelevant to whether or not an iambic beat is maintained. If, for the sake of argument, we recognize four grades of stress, 1 to 4, of increasing weight, iambic feet may as legitimately consist of a syllable with the least degree of stress followed by a syllable with the second least as of two-syllable patterns involving degrees of stress 3 or 4. The *relative* degrees of stress within individual feet are the crucial factor. Honigmann's idea of Shakespeare's metrical practices would be more apt to William Rowley's. I find the old Cambridge lineation of 5.2.68–75 more convincing than that of Honigmann's Arden, for example (as set out on 107–8 of *Texts.*). But his discussion of the need for slurring and elision is useful. Modern editors should duly consider the question he raises, whether when Q or F *I have, I am,* and the like are metrically monosyllabic they should be replaced by the elided forms (*I've, I'm,* and so on). Honigmann also argues that F's heavy punctuation has had too much influence on later editors.

In a final chapter, headed "Some Conclusions," Honigmann surveys "indifferent variants" between Q and F in the hope that further knowledge of the habits of the agents of transmission will enable editors to make rational choices, rather than allowing a blanket preference for Q or (as has been customary) F to prevail. Neither Q nor F is in all departments "the better text". "F *Othello* is more reliable with 'substantive' variants and verse lineation, and less reliable with at least some indifferent variants, punctuation, stage directions and profanity" (143). Acknowledging the harm that may be done both by "copy-cat editors" and bold interventionists who back the wrong textual theory, he ends with a commendable warning about the limitations of all editorial endeavor. Scholars interested in Shakespeare's texts should read this book, which, as well as providing some challenging new evidence, is a provocation to further research and thought.

The Rhetoric of Concealment: Figuring Gender and Class in Renaissance Literature.
By Rosemary Kegl.
Ithaca and London: Cornell University Press, 1994.

Reviewer: Lorna Hutson

In conclusion to *The Rhetoric of Concealment*, Rosemary Kegl quotes Richard Halpern's expression of skepticism about the claims of certain versions of New Historicist criticism to be truly material-ist. Halpern is wary, Kegl explains, of those critics who argue, "that *everything* is an economy" and then "figure all the relations of culture as an expanded or general process of circulation." Though attributed to Halpern, there is a sense in which this reservation speaks for Kegl herself. Her book is a serious attempt to find a form of Marxist Renaissance criticism that would do justice to the developments in the last thirty years in the economic, social, and feminist history of the early modern period. What she emphatically refrains from, then, is any resort to the critical strategy of "figuring all the relations of culture as an expanded or general process of circulation." Rather, in each of her four extended analyses of Re-naissance texts, she keeps steadily in view a variety of detailed and nuanced historical accounts of emergent institutional formations and changing economic practices (such as that of the evolving role of the Tudor justice of the peace, or of the access of women to positions of skilled labor in the textile industry, or of the develop-ment of defamation as a legal action for material damages) that remain quite distinct from her analysis of the figuration of these institutional developments and practices in the texts in question. Her book therefore lacks the sense of teleological inevitability—the sense that a text's "subversion" in Greenblatt's famous formulation, has always already been "contained" by itself—that characterizes a great deal of New Historicist criticism. Indeed, Kegl's is a *utopian* work of criticism insofar as it uses the analysis of literary texts to uncover or reveal the historical moment of writing as one in which the future was not prescribed, as a moment in which resided the possibility for things to turn out differently.

The way Kegl goes about this might seem a little paradoxical. According to her analysis it is not the authors of the texts she chooses to explore—George Puttenham's *Arte of English Poesie,* Philip Sidney's *Arcadia* (both versions), Shakespeare's *Merry Wives of Windsor,* and Deloney's *Jack of Newbury*—who are drawn to imagine utopias; rather the contrary, for the "rhetoric of conceal- ment" in her title refers to what she sees as each author's attempt to foreclose certain "emergent utopian impulses" in the historical processes to which the text imaginatively refers and responds. The first text she approaches thus is the *Arte of English Poesie,* ascribed to the lawyer George Puttenham. This text is familiar to New His- toricism as exemplary of the courtliness of Renaissance literary production in general, and in particular of the literary text's thema- tization of its own courtly negotiations. Kegl, however, is critical of such readings, which she thinks collude with Puttenham's own rhetoric of concealment; gender and class struggles within the court are not homologies, as she points out, for such struggles within society at large. "By reinforcing a monolithic version of social struggle," she argues, "critics reaffirm Puttenham's attempt to obscure the relationship between a single institution and the larger society." The recurrent gesture that she identifies as typical of Puttenham's rhetoric of concealment is the transparent riddle, which allows the courtly poet to occupy contradictory positions simultaneously, thereby avoiding liability for his own, potentially offensive aspirations. The figure of the riddle, she argues, works to "replace process with simultaneity" and enables Puttenham's more general project of aligning the courtly poet with the aspiring crafts- man in order to effect a complicated dissociation between the two categories. "Puttenham," she suggests, "uses a complicated system of shifting affiliations between courtier and craftsman" in order to deny the political threat of either's social mobility. "By advising that poet-courtiers no longer dissemble the link between them- selves and craftsmen, Puttenham subsumes those laborers within the world of courtly artistry—ending their exclusion *from* the court so that he might reinstate them within royal control."

In Sidney's *Arcadia,* the next of Kegl's examples, the author's utopian impulse of imagining the grievances of rebels as a just criticism of the shortcomings of monarchical rule is checked by his characteristic homology of impassioned body and rebellious state, a homology that likens the ineffectuality of passionate self- division to the fatally divisive contradictions in political aims and allegiances among antimonarchical rebels. An episode that critics usually take to be indicative of Sidney's radical critique of monarchy—"This was a notable example how great dissipations monarchical governments are subject unto"—is thus interpreted by Kegl in terms of her sense of the "narrative inevitability of . . . disintegration" in Sidney's description of opposition to monarchy: "all agreeing in the universal names of liking or misliking, but of what especial points, infinitely disagreeing." By figuring such disintegration as an unstable architecture, Sidney (Kegl argues) makes it impossible to recognize the importance of divided alliances to the processes of social change. Moreover, Sidney's idiosyncratic version of the analogy between orderly household and orderly state— he allows women to be men's moral equals, but denies them political agency—subtends a rhetoric of consent, even while the real hierarchy of the rulers and the ruled remains undisturbed.

Kegl's analysis moves from popular critical conceptions of the courtly Puttenham and the anticourtly Sidney to equally popular conceptions of the bourgeois Shakespeare and the artisanal Deloney. In relation to both Shakespeare's and Deloney's texts her interest focuses on their representation of forms of collective speech— defamatory insults in the former, proverbial wisdom in the latter. Kegl demonstrates how critics of *The Merry Wives of Windsor* have colluded in the play's own defamatory rhetoric of concealment, insofar as they have imagined the inhabitants of Windsor to be a unified "middle class," united in their opposition to the aristocratic Falstaff. Rather, she argues, the language of insult highlights the unassimilability of Windsor's ecclesiastical and legal authorities— Evans and Shallow—to the local and regional interests of the "townsfolk." And where Shakespeare uses the language of defamation to constitute difference, Deloney, in Kegl's analysis, invents a proverbial wisdom that reconciles the interests of capital and labor in the sixteenth-century clothing industry: "Jack's commonsense appeal to all craftsmen who live by their hands acknowledges the difference between employers and their labourers without acknowledging that this difference is conflictual." The denial of conflict ultimately serves the purposes of employers at the expense of laborers.

The complex and patiently unfolded insights of Kegl's book will stimulate Renaissance critics to new ways of thinking about a whole range of early modern texts, and the book's distinctive method of detecting strategies of "concealment" will surely find imitators. My only reservation concerns the author's own over-recurrent gesture of sign posting the progress of her argument. I felt, as I read, that I was being informed rather too often of what the chapter had just done and was just about to do. Thus, for example, Kegl announces in the midst of her discussion of Shakespeare's *Merry Wives*: "I pause in my reading of *The Merry Wives of Windsor* to discuss the position of justices of the peace in late-sixteenth century England." Anticipation and retrospection of this sort, often adumbrating or recapitulating the argument in exactly the same words as used on nearby pages, drain Kegl's book of some of the vitality it might otherwise have had. These infelicitous repetitions, however, may have been adopted on the advice of an editor, and they certainly do not invalidate the book's subtle and powerful arguments.

Shakespeare and South Africa.
By David Johnson.
Oxford: Clarendon Press, 1996.

Reviewer: Thomas Cartelli

David Johnson's *Shakespeare and South Africa* is an ambitious and wide-ranging book that examines with uncommon insight the vexed positioning of Shakespeare studies in both the new and old South Africa. It is particularly effective at dissecting the postwar efforts of English-speaking South Africans to make Shakespeare a "third term that resolves the contradiction between the state and its disaffected subjects" (155), and will no doubt serve for some time to come as a controversial point of reference for broader debates about the future of English studies in South Africa.

Johnson is "interested in the central, symptomatic role played by Shakespeare . . . in South African literary studies" and sets out to "survey all South African literary criticism, and particularly Shakespeare criticism, produced from the beginning of the nineteenth century to the present," in addition to "educational journals, syllabuses, examination papers, set-work books and recommended reading–lists, school editions of Shakespeare plays, and study aids" (5). As he notes in his introduction, he also pays "particular attention" to the influential work of English critics like A. C. Bradley, F. R. Leavis, and G. Wilson Knight, which exerted "a defining influence on the versions of the Bard deployed in former colonies" (5). And he devotes a final chapter to an informed assessment of newer developments in Anglo-American critical theory and Shakespeare criticism that have been taken up in South Africa to greater and lesser degrees.

Johnson's primary subject matter is, then, the archive and its texts, the layers of commentary, criticism, encomia, school papers, and intramural debate that constitute the history of English studies in South Africa and, by extension, South African Shakespeare. I say "by extension" because although Johnson provides a detailed account of the development of South African Shakespeare studies, he often puts his interest in the "symptomology" of Shakespeare to work in a narrowly academic and formulaic manner, rarely staging the direct contention or dialogue between Shakespeare's texts and South Africa's readers and writers that his book's title leads one to expect.

Part of the problem is a matter of style. The writing throughout is more expository than elaborative, and seldom—with the significant exceptions of the theory chapter and chapter 5, "Shakespeare and Apartheid: The 1950s"—develops a sense of forward drive or momentum. At times it feels as if Johnson refuses to allow himself the pleasure of generating his own text, of pursuing for more than a few pages—or sentences—a matter that might be expected to engage a reader interested, say, in what Johnson calls "perhaps the most famous South African appropriation of Shakespeare," that is, "the one performed by Chris Hani" in a 1988 interview where he confesses, "I want to believe I am decisive and it helps me to be decisive when I read *Hamlet*" (201). Similarly frustrating is Johnson's failure, in a chapter nominally devoted to the exemplary "case" of Solomon Plaatje, even to mention what some readers may consider the more famous effort at appropriation witnessed in Plaatje's translations of Shakespeare into Tswana.

Johnson begins this chapter by quoting from Plaatje's contribution to Israel Gollancz's *A Book of Homage to Shakespeare*, an international collection of encomia published in 1916 in honor of the Shakespeare Tercentenary. He then offers a brief biographical sketch of Plaatje before extending the chapter's focus to other contemporaneous colonial subjects and to the state of Shakespeare in South Africa in 1916. Upon returning to Plaatje, Johnson finally delivers on his initial promise to focus "on how [four groups of] different thinkers have tried to make sense of Plaatje's relation with Shakespeare" (75). This promise, however, plainly confounds Johnson's own intentions with chronological and interpretive logic. None of the thinkers in question—"anti-imperialist writers" like Frantz Fanon and Albert Memmi; "Marxist theorists, including Marx himself"; "social historians in the E. P. Thompson mould"; and "First World" literary theorists—either knew, or were in the position to know, anything about Sol Plaatje, much less about his "relation with Shakespeare." What Johnson really means to say is that the "four groups" can provide us with ways "to make sense of Plaatje's relation with Shakespeare" from the vantage point of the present. They do so, however, only in the most distant and predictable ways. The "colonial subject's love of Western culture" is, in the first instance, equated with "political betrayal" (96); the "colonial intellectual" is, in the second, "seen as an agent and apologist for capitalism, a traitor to the African masses" (101). Plaatje emerges "as a reasonable black man trapped by impossible contradiction" (104) in the third, expressly "liberal" formulation and "as engaged in a strategy of mimicry" or incipiently postcolonial emulation in the fourth (109).

What is missing in all but the third of these formulations is any sustained attempt to give "the real Plaatje" his due. Unlike Brian Willan, who painstakingly records Plaatje's frustrated efforts to get his Shakespeare translations published, Johnson does not assume Plaatje capable of exercising any kind of agency over or amid his contradictions.[1] Despite Plaatje's well-known commitment to the sustaining of Tswana's viability as a spoken language and establishment as a written medium, Johnson never considers that Plaatje might have been attempting to exploit Shakespeare's alleged universality for his own purposes. The Tswana translations were, after all, undertaken not to promote Shakespeare but to promote Tswana and the black South African claim to cultural equality. Even at the conclusion of his discussion, Johnson eschews "offering the real Plaatje," providing instead what he no doubt considers an unanswerable parable about the complicity of all four Plaatjes in the De Beers company's endowment of a £30,000 "Chair of English Language" at the University of Cape Town "extorted from the labour of the 17,000 De Beers mineworkers" (110).

Johnson could have culled a richer postscript to his chapter from Willan's account of De Beers's refusal, in 1929, to grant Plaatje's modest request of £123 to pay for his Shakespeare translations: one that would have put Plaatje on the same level as the mineworkers instead of on the level of De Beers.[2] Plaatje's attempt, in the same letter quoted by Willan, to advertise to De Beers his opposition to communist organizers in exchange for the company's sponsorship no doubt does much to underwrite his marginalization by Johnson. But Johnson employs what he calls his "combative tone" (212) too peremptorily here, in a manner that gives him an unearned moral advantage over a figure he effectively renders invisible. This is especially notable given the prevailing imbalance in the book between his frequently voiced commitment to the struggle of black South Africans and the comparatively brief accounts of their engagement with Shakespeare that he supplies.

Part of Johnson's problem is that all the black South African references to, and appropriations of, Shakespeare he documents betray a positive association with the Bard at odds with Johnson's more critical stance. Given his persuasive rendering of the role assigned Shakespeare in an order-driven and racially divided educational system, it would, of course, be difficult for Johnson to applaud Can Themba's statement that "the world of Shakespeare reaches out a fraternal hand to the throbbing heart of Africa" (175). He could, however, certainly have done more with the moral on decisiveness Chris Hani drew from *Hamlet*, a transaction some readers are apt to find mystifying.

A few years before Hani made his remark, United States Secretary of State George Shultz observed, regarding the Reagan administration's efforts to subvert the Sandinista government in Nicaragua, that America did not intend to become "the Hamlet of nations," evidently drawing from the play the same moral about manly self-assertion that Hani drew but deploying it in the interests of a radically different political persuasion. Both "interventions" arguably constitute misreadings of Shakespeare sponsored by educational systems that present Shakespeare's plays "as lessons in manliness" (60) and that seek to indoctrinate students "in the values of competitiveness, respect for order, and individual responsibility" (67). But while Johnson convincingly shows how the association of Shakespeare with such values has effectively implicated his work in the South African "state's ideological project" (166) and thus made it a questionable "resource in the struggle against racism" (148), he fails to consider how Shakespeare may be reappropriated to serve the interests of new or different ideological projects.

Although Johnson's skepticism about Shakespeare's liberatory potential is understandable, he also dismisses with undue condescension the "struggle" of other avowed revisionists "to wrest the

Shakespeare text from the conservative grasp of traditionalist critics."[3] Positioning Martin Orkin's Shakespeare "as the sensitive and
politically astute Master ready to instruct anxious South African
students" (209), Johnson positions Orkin himself as an anxious
liberal seeking to sustain Shakespeare's viability in a new South
Africa: "In locating such value in Shakespeare, Orkin forestalls
the option, which might arise in a post-apartheid South Africa, of
choosing a different set of texts" (209–10). The framing of this option is, however, posed as little more than an afterthought in Johnson's own book, which shows considerably less engagement with
such texts than Orkin does in Drama and the South African State.[4]
Indeed, in the last chapter of Orkin's book, entitled "The Shakespeare Connection," one may find distilled and articulated several
of the arguments and assessments Johnson develops at greater
length in Shakespeare and South Africa. Among these, one finds
Orkin remarking that "the determination of apartheid education in
the teaching of literature to choose especially the Shakespeare text
and literature mainly from England indicates . . . an active uninter-
est in fostering in pupils awareness of South African literature."[5]
In the light of such statements, and of Orkin's earlier call, in Shakespeare against Apartheid, for "the development of readings of
[Shakespeare's] texts that will free them from ruling class appropriation," Johnson's assertion seems strangely disingenuous.[6]

What motivates Johnson here, as elsewhere, is the drive to claim
a higher ground than "liberals" like Orkin can presumably command. But the drive requires from Johnson more candor than he
seems willing to supply. On the one hand, Johnson wants to argue
that Shakespeare and English studies in South Africa has, from the
start, been collaborative with and productive of colonial racism
and, hence, that its effect has been been almost entirely pernicious.
From this point of view, its perpetuation in any form would be
highly suspect. As Johnson writes, "Whether Shakespeare is adequate to the task of 'challenging inhumanity' has yet to be decided"
(204). On the other hand, Johnson does not want black South Africans to lose the opportunity to make decisions of their own about
Shakespeare's viability. He appears, in this respect, to give contemporary expression to fears voiced by blacks in the late 1950s that
"Shakespeare would disappear completely from Bantu education
syllabuses" as a result of the "dilution of the 'standards' established
for white schools" (170).

Johnson negotiates this disparity by contending that "Shakespeare's vulnerability [to erosion or disappearance] rests less in his

capacity to change his identity and start serving the new nation than in the difficulty of the language in the plays for second-language English speakers" (202). And it is, in the end, the connection between the "failures" with Shakespeare of this same group and the "much larger histories of imperial violence, in which the Bard plays a central and deeply compromised role" (214) that Johnson most seeks to emphasize. That a "recoded and democratized" Shakespeare (202) might serve as something like a third force in the new South Africa becomes thinkable for Johnson only in the context of "a reformulation of English studies" (213) and that greater reformulation of South African society which would provide access to literacy to more than 30 percent of the adult population. As Johnson writes, "to continue teaching Shakespeare as before to relatively small numbers of students, seems particularly unlikely to make a positive impression . . . on these entrenched patterns of exclusion" (213).

Johnson may, however, underestimate the exchange value of a writer who continues to serve as "something like the gold standard of literature."[7] In a *New York Times* article published the same week of the 1996 conference on Shakespeare and postcoloniality in Johannesburg, one Tiro Matshoe, a trainee patrolman with the Soweto Traffic Department, is described as wanting to secure an edition of the complete works in order "to expand my knowledge" and "because I think of being a leader someday."[8] Matshoe identifies the ability to "quote Shakespeare" with aims that are generally indistinguishable from those Johnson describes and decries throughout his book. But for Officer Matshoe, Shakespeare constitutes a reliable commodity in a society in a state of flux, if not a third term or third force, then at least a resource that can help him negotiate the distance between failure and success. Although he is presumably unlike David Johnson's students, for whom "this book stands as a long answer" to their "failures" with Shakespeare (214), I would like to think that Johnson would neither begrudge Matshoe access to his dream nor consider it woefully misplaced.

Notes

1. Brian Willan, *Sol Plaatje* (London: Heinemann, 1984).
2. Ibid., 328.
3. Martin Orkin, *Shakespeare against Apartheid* (Craighall, South Africa: A. D. Donker, 1987), 184.
4. Martin Orkin, *Drama and the South African State* (Manchester: Manchester University Press, 1991).

   5. Ibid., 240.
   6. Orkin, *Shakespeare against Apartheid*, 184.
   7. Rob Nixon, "Caribbean and African Appropriations of *The Tempest*," *Critical Inquiry* 13 (1987): 560.
   8. *New York Times*, 3 July 1996.

Unediting the Renaissance: Shakespeare, Marlowe, Milton.
By Leah S. Marcus.
London and New York: Routledge, 1996.

Reviewer: Lois Potter

Since the early 1980s, an intriguing conjunction of technology and literary theory has moved bibliography and textual criticism from the margins to the center of literary study. Anyone who composes on a computer soon develops a heightened awareness of the writing process. One idea literally jostles another for room on the screen, or is superimposed on it; ideas vanish and (if one is lucky) are retrieved, like characters at the end of a Shakespearean romance. Traditional editions of Renaissance texts, with their emphasis on discriminating between good and bad versions and standardizing inconsistencies, seem increasingly out of place in this world. When one's own writing exhibits such apparently infinite potential, right up to the moment of printing out, it seems absurd to insist that someone else's writing should be made fixed and finite. And there is no need to: a growing body of opinion now attributes the variations among multiple texts of a work not to corruptions of a single "correct" original but to revision by the author or others—revision, perhaps, for a specific occasion rather than with a view to creating a definitive text. So why reject any reading, any text? Why edit at all? Or rather, why not offer multiple editions, all available at the push of a button? Or why not scan in all the early versions and let the readers do the editing themselves instead of trying to decipher the textual notes? Modern printing technology, which makes the incorporation of illustrations into a book much simpler and cheaper than it used to be, is already transforming even the printed edition, as in T. W. Craik's Arden *Henry V*, which prints a photographic facsimile of the entire quarto text of the play. It is not clear which came first, the seductive theoretical vocabulary or the technology that supports it, but indeterminacy, deferral, and desire are all available on the computer menu.

It is against this exciting if unsettling background that Leah S. Marcus positions her book. Its main point is that any edition of a Renaissance text inevitably falsities it, both by imposing an official, "correct" version of words or meaning and by eliminating the elements—typeface, frontispiece, layout, and so forth—that formed part of the original reading experience. Most of the book is concerned with plays that exist in two or more versions: Marlowe's *Dr. Faustus*, *The Merry Wives of Windsor*, *The Taming of the Shrew*, *Hamlet*. A final chapter on the publication of seventeenth-century poetry analyzes the different stages in the presentation of the author (Donne, Shakespeare, Herbert, Herrick, Milton) via typography, title page, and frontispiece. Her examination of the different strategies adopted in reissues of works by the same author is particularly interesting, but for the purpose of this volume, I will concentrate on the chapters that deal with drama.

Marcus is widely read in the extensive recent literature on theories of editing and synthesizes it entertainingly. Her argument—as in her initial discussion of the various attempts to explain Sycorax's description as a "blue-eyed hag"—is not so much that previous editors have been wrong as that their choices, whatever they were, frequently closed off interesting possibilities. The two *Faustus* texts, for instance, seem to differ on the spelling of Wittenberg, but in fact they are talking about two different places, one of which, Wertemberg, was part of an alternative tradition about the historical Faustus, with a ruler well known in the late sixteenth century as a radical Lutheran. The differences between the Shakespeare texts, she maintains, are equally significant.

Others of course have thought so too. It is not surprising that modern editors in recent years have taken a liking to the quartos. As Marcus herself admits, part of their attraction is that they are short; one might add that their very sketchiness makes them good material for actors trained in the modern, subtext-based style of acting. These versions often read very well if taken in isolation, but for anyone who already knows the fuller text they will naturally seem to "lack" something. This is presumably why Marcus suggests that "the bad quartos are gendered as feminine" (102). Like a number of other scholars, she would prefer to see them as early versions to which more was added, rather than later versions that have been cut or misremembered. She occasionally forgets these chronological assumptions—or maybe decides to ignore them—when saying, for instance, that the quarto of *A Shrew* "implicitly rejects the folio argument" (120), which, on this theory, cannot yet have been written.

Undoubtedly, much of what is said of these "bad quartos"—that is, quartos supposedly derived from texts put together by short-hand or memory or some other method not based on the author's own manuscript—has been the result of what Ernst Honigmann calls "editorial inertia."[1] Once we accept that the author himself was responsible for both versions, what looked like errors become puns, alternative readings, indices of a different conception of the play. We can imagine him producing a short text for acting pur-poses and then expanding it for readers more easily than imagining him cutting down his play to the bare bones of *A Shrew* and the quarto *Merry Wives*. For instance, the dialogue between Mistress Ford and Mistress Page, after the disguised Falstaff has been chased offstage by Ford, goes thus in the folio:

> *Mistress Page.* Trust me, he beat him most pitifully.
> *Mistress Ford.* Nay, by th' mass, that he did not; he beat him most
>   unpitifully, methought.
>
> (4.2.186–88).[2]

It is hard to imagine anyone who had written that exchange being willing to settle for the quarto reading:

> *Mrs. Ford.* By my troth, he beat him most extreamly.
> *Mrs. Page.* I am glad of it.

It is not only that the folio text is livelier and more verbally witty; for a supposed reading text, it also conveys a far stronger sense of the spoken rhythm than the quarto—and far more direct address to the audience. The quarto makes Falstaff address the audience on "you know the water swells a man," but the speech's best line, "you may know by my size that I have a kind of alacrity in sinking," becomes, in the quarto's "They might know," a reference to Ford's servants who heartlessly dumped him into the river. Marcus argues that the folio is more "literary" than the quarto—but perhaps, one might add, one object of the folio was to convey the experience of performance more vividly than performance itself could do.

It is when Marcus starts considering the reasons for the critical preference for one text over another—usually for the folio over one of the earlier quartos—that she gets onto more treacherous ground. Her method is to show that the less favored version is more feminist, or popular, or theatrical, than the alternative, then to argue that those who have preferred the latter are actuated by unconscious antifeminist, elitist, or antitheatrical priorities. Thus, she thinks, the general editorial preference for the folio Merry Wives over the quarto has to do with the fact that the former provides a more "gentle" Shakespeare and a less threatening vision of female empowerment. In the case of The Shrew, with a little shuffling, she manages to make A Shrew look somewhat less misogynistic, on the grounds that it depicts Katherine's final submission to her husband as a way of winning the wager rather than as a sign that she has internalized the doctrines of patriarchy. Marcus builds a good deal on the fact that the actors depicted in The Shrew are clearly more sophisticated and on more familiar terms with the Lord than are their barely literate predecessors in A Shrew. Thus, if one assumes that the live actors identified themselves with the stage actors in both plays (rather than enjoying a feeling of their superiority to mere strolling players), the logical conclusion is that "the actors triumph by putting women down" (114). So, if A Shrew is largely ignored by editors of The Shrew, it is because it is "perceived as a danger to the editors' own manhood" (109)—an argument which it would be interesting to apply to Ann Thompson's New Cambridge edition.

In the Hamlet chapter, with three texts to compare, Marcus finds a number of examples where typical editorial practice can be said to reinforce twentieth-century ideas of good taste and consistency; these are also, she suggests, Hamlet's own ideas, so, in an Escher-like effect, we can imagine the play's hero not only the product of but the producer of the textual difficulties of his story. She points out, for instance, that editors make the Ghost say "Adieu" only twice, as in the folio, because Hamlet in all three texts repeats the word only twice though the Ghost of both quartos says it three times. After providing alternate scenarios for the order of composition of the three texts of the play, she suggests that the first quarto—the one that most develops the theme of the improvising clown who belongs to oral tradition—might itself be an essentially oral, semi-improvised version of the play, as opposed to the "literary" texts of the second quarto and folio. This is an attractive idea. To prove it, we would need to know not only how actors learned their lines (was it "as I pronounced it to thee"?) but also how strictly they were expected to stick to the text that had been submitted for licensing by the Lord Chamberlain.

In fact, as Marcus herself occasionally has to admit, the plays do not always differ in a consistent way: while the folio *Merry Wives* is more genteel in that it associates Fenton with Prince Hal and Poins and the quarto does not, the quarto contains a reference to the Prince that is lacking in the folio. Similarly, although the women may perhaps dominate slightly more in the early Falstaff scenes of the quarto, the folio wives decide independently to continue playing tricks on Falstaff, while the quarto wives decide first to tell their husbands, after which the two couples work out their final stratagem together. And it is fortunate that Marcus does not try to include *Othello* in her argument, since the quarto text, also usually rejected, is the one that "lacks" Desdemona's willow song and the "equal rights" speech by Emilia.

Though at times it may seem that Marcus is trying to do to earlier editors what Terence Hawkes's *That Shakespeherian Rag* did to earlier scholars, she is less aggressive than some of the above examples may suggest. Her book really works something like a computer menu, offering a series of different arguments without necessarily committing itself to any one of them. I am not sure that this is exactly what the "new bibliography" advocates. It is one thing to let scholarship be informed by theory, but another to become so interested in the theoretical implications of each conclusion that one abdicates the task of making a rational decision among them. The book is likely to become what I think it aspires to be, a text to be recommended to students as a synthesis of "the new bibliography." Readable, clear, and comprehensive in its presentation of multiple arguments, and full of insights, it is more useful in this role than as a contribution to the argument about the status of the Shakespeare texts. But if Marcus really intends to follow up her final comment—that those who complain about the shortcomings of earlier editors ought to become editors themselves—she will have to make some real choices. In that case, one can look forward to some lively and controversial work.

Notes

1. Ernst Honigmann, *The Texts of "Othello" and Shakespearian Revision* (London, Routledge, 1997), 120.

2. Quoted from *The Merry Wives of Windsor*, ed. by T. W. Craik (Oxford: Oxford University Press, 1990).

Textual Intercourse: Collaboration, Authorship, and Sexualities in Renaissance Drama.
By Jeffrey Masten.
Cambridge: Cambridge University Press, 1997.

Reviewer: Bruce R. Smith

Since Zeus produced Athena out of his own forehead, males in European culture have been "conceiving" ideas and "giving birth" to works of art. The locus classicus for this trope of artistic creativity is the contrast Socrates draws in the *Symposium* between children and "deeds of beauty" as alternative means of achieving immortality. To Alcibiades and the other men present at Agathon's banquet, Socrates reports what Diotima of Mantineia has taught him about love:

> Those who are pregnant in the body only, betake themselves to women and beget children. . . . But souls which are pregnant—for there certainly are men who are more creative in their souls than in their bodies—conceive that which is proper for the soul to conceive or contain. And what are these conceptions?—wisdom and virtue in general. And such creators are poets and all artists who are deserving of the name inventor.

The union that produces such offspring, Socrates assumes, will happen between men. The relationship between these men is, in fact, a kind of marriage. A young man who has had "the seed" of temperance and justice planted within him will go through life looking for beauty. When he finds someone who possesses beauty in both body and soul,

> he embraces the two in one person, and to such a one he is full of speech about virtue and the nature and pursuits of a good man; and he tries to educate him; and at the touch of the beautiful which is ever

present to his memory, even when absent, he brings forth that which he had conceived long before, and in company with him tends that which he brings forth; and they are married by a far nearer tie and have a closer friendship than those who beget mortal children, for the children who are their offspring are fairer and more immortal. (secs. 208–9)

Shakespeare is thus drawing on ancient tradition when, in the course of dedicating *Venus and Adonis* to the earl of Southampton, he modestly refers to the finished poem as "so weak a burden" and vows to honor Southampton in the future "with some graver labor." Before the gaze of "so noble a godfather," he fears that "the first heir of my invention" will appear "deformed." If in this part of the conceit Shakespeare flirts with playing the mother to Southampton's godfather, he quickly reverts to a male role in promising that he will henceforth be more careful where he casts his seed and "never after ear so barren a land for fear it yield me still so bad a harvest."

The dedicatory address before *Venus and Adonis* is beyond Jeffrey Masten's purview in *Textual Intercourse*—his attention is limited to theater—but Masten's book makes it impossible to read such passages hereafter without sharp awareness of the social, political, and sexual issues that the idea of artistic parthenogenesis entails. "Dramatic writing" is Masten's subject, in two senses of the word: as a *process* (the practice of collaboration as the main mode of textual production in professional theater) and as a *product* (the dramatized fictions themselves). Masten is concerned, in his own phrase, with "the collaborative writing of Renaissance drama, and the dramatization of Renaissance collaboration" (37). The thoroughgoing materialism of Masten's approach is registered in the fact that quotations are transcribed as closely as possible from the original printed texts. In addition to eleven reproductions of title pages and frontispieces, three facsimiles of typefaces are dropped into the text as quotations, so as to show exactly the size and spacing of words in dedications and the spatial use of brackets in framing Beaumont and Fletcher's names in one of the poems prefacing the 1647 folio of their dramatic works. Arranged in roughly chronological order, each of the book's five chapters studies a different aspect of collaborative authorship, as exemplified in one, two, or three printed texts. "Seeing Double," the first chapter, uses *The Knight of the Burning Pestle* to argue that collaboration, not single authorship, ought to be seen as the primary form of textual production in early modern theater. The insinuation of sexual discourses in this process of collaboration is studied in the second chapter, "Between Gentlemen," through particular attention to *The Two Gentlemen of Verona* and *The Two Noble Kinsmen*. Political discourse is added to sexual discourse in the third chapter, "Representing Authority," which traces the emergence of presiding authority figures in the persons of Gower in *Pericles*, Gobrius and Arbaces in *A King and No King*, and Prospero in *The Tempest*. The book's longest chapter, "Reproducing Works," studies the prefatory matter to the 1647 folio of *Comedies and Tragedies Written by Francis Beaumont And Iohn Fletcher, Gentlemen*. In a brief final chapter, "Mistris Corrival," Masten contemplates the intrusion of a self-styled *female* author, Margaret Cavendish, duchess of Newcastle, into the formerly all-male world of printed authority. Masten's treatment of these diverse texts is an act of creative synthesis. He draws on already published scholarship—Gerald Bentley on the organization of playwriting and play production in the early-seventeenth century, Alan Bray on the homoerotics of the Renaissance cult of male friendship, Margreta de Grazia on the construction of Shakespeare's authority in the first folio, Lois Potter on the publishing and reading of plays in the 1640s as a form of royalist political activity—but brings to this established knowledge a deconstructionist alterness all his own, a sexual-political agenda, and a talent for brilliant close reading.

Instances of such reading are to be found in every one of the book's five chapters. Armed with the *OED*, Masten never leaves a strange or editorially contested word unexamined. Take, for example, the close of Emilia's remembrance of her friend Flavina in *The Two Noble Kinsmen*: "This rehearsall / . . . has this end, / That the true love tweene Mayde, and mayde, may be / More then in sex individuall" (quoted on 51). Without fail, modern editors have emended "individuall" to "dividual." In doing so, Masten argues, they have obscured the early modern sense of "individual" as "indivisible"—precisely the opposite of the word's modern meaning. Thus, Emila may be suggesting one of two things: either that the love between maids is more than the love between man and wife as one flesh or that the love between maids "is indivisible *in more than simply sex*" (52, Masten's emphasis). This is not the only instance in which Masten, as a materialist critic, defends a text as originally printed. In larger matters Masten proves to be just as astute. He provides an especially circumspect reading of Prospero's authority in *The Tempest*. In the moment when Prospero remembers the conspiracy of Caliban, Stephano, and Trinculo and dispels the wedding masque, Masten points out, Prospero is simultaneously an author and a collaborator. As the author of the masque and of all else that the island's spirits perform, Prospero may control representations, but he does so only as a collaborator with others. In Prospero's eyes, and in their own, the spirits are "fellows," the commonest word for actors in a professional theatrical company. "I and my fellows / Are ministers of fate," says Ariel at 3.3.60–61; "Thou and thy meaner fellows your last service / Did worthily perform," Prospero declares at 4.1.35–36; "Two of these fellows you / Must know and own. This thing of darkness I / Acknowledge mine," Prospero tells the Italian nobles at 5.1.277–79. When Prospero exchanges his magician's garb for the costume of a duke, he reveals that he is not outside the realm of representation over which he presides. As the script printed first in the 1623 folio, *The Tempest* helps to establish authority over plays printed later but written earlier, when single authorship was still an inchoate idea, but it is wrong to assume, Masten argues, that "authorship" in the modern sense of the word is firmly established in the text: "To the extent that authorship is emergent in the 'authorial presenters' of this and other plays, *The Tempest* displays the range of authorship's intersection with and implication in other discourses of the period: the rhetoric of patriarchal reproduction, the language of political authority, the discourse of a global imperialism and colonization" (112). Through scrutiny of individual words and entire plays alike, Masten manages to sustain a certain arch affability that keeps *Textual Intercourse* eminently readable from page to page. From start ("I begin with the desire to sleep with the dead" [1]) to finish ("we may never get, or set, the authorship of this canon straight" [155]) the text is full of parodies and puns that delight all the more without benefit of footnotes or the underline key.

For many readers, the most original aspect of *Textual Intercourse* will be the attention Masten gives to sexuality as one of the discourses informing early modern ideas about textual production. Numerous quotations from the poets who contributed verses to the 1647 folio of Beaumont and Fletcher's plays attest to how readily contemporaries found in homoerotic images a way to celebrate the two men's collaboration as writers. In studying these images Masten's concern is not with biographical facts—with the question of whether Beaumont and Fletcher were "gay" *avant la lettre*—but with discourses. Sexual language is used by Beaumont and Fletcher's peers to talk about artistic creation, specifically about collaborative artistic creation between men, and Masten sets out to discover why: "The point, then, is not to bring the Renaissance out of the closet, but to bring the closet out of the Renaissance—to account for the abiding differences in the ways this period represented sexuality and its connections with modes of textual production" (7). With Alan Bray, Masten agrees that "sodomy" (which Masten takes to be sexual acts between males of different social classes) and "pederasty" (sexual acts between males of different ages) fail to exhaust the range of possibilities of same-sex eroticism in early modern England. With respect to *The Two Gentlemen of Verona*, for example, Masten demonstrates that "Homoeroticism . . . is not always and already a disruptive and unconventional deconstruction of a sex/gender system. In this play, and in the highly class-inflected context of gentlemen's conduct books and essays, homoeroticism functions as part of the network of power; it constitutes and reflects the homogeneity of the gentlemanly subject" (48).

Readers who attempt to fix *Textual Intercourse* as the "outing" of Beaumont and Fletcher will be missing the point. In the course of investigating the conjunction of textuality and sexuality, Masten charts the emergence of "author" as a modern concept. The strange publishing history of *The Two Noble Kinsmen* indicates, as Masten points out, a continuing uneasiness about collaboration. Described on the title page of the 1634 quarto as "Written by the memorable Worthies of their time; M^r. John Fletcher, and M^r. William Shakspeare. Gent.," the play had not figured among *Mr. William Shakespeares Comedies, Histories, & Tragedies* eleven years before, nor was it to be included in the first folio of plays ascribed to Beaumont and Fletcher thirteen years later. Only recently has *The Two Noble Kinsmen* begun to find a secure place in modern editions of Shakespeare's complete works. Even so, the play usually comes equipped with scholarly apparatus that applies the rational methods of "the new bibliography"—tests of diction, syntax, pronomial forms, punctuation—in an attempt to distinguish just which scenes were written by Shakespeare and which by Fletcher. Masten sees such anxieties as anachronistic and seeks to avoid them by treating authorship as a historical construct. Authorship, he maintains, is not an entity that exists *prior to* published texts; rather, it is a phenomenon constructed *by* published texts. Training his critical eye on the prefatory matter to the King James Bible of 1611 and to James's collected works of 1616, Masten distinguishes a range of early modern meanings of *author*: "father," "begetter," "divine Creator," "instigator," "ruler," and "authority," as well as "writer." Authorship was thus grounded in discourses we now would separate and label as sexual, textual, political, and (although Masten does not pursue this) theological. In all its senses, authorship was predicated on patriarchal absolutism; hence paternity as a recurrent metaphor for artistic creation. Between 1590 and 1650, Masten argues, two things happened to the cultural construction of authority: single authors emerged as the expected norm at the same time that textual, sexual, and political discourses devolved into the separate conceptual categories they remain today. Material evidence of those changes is to be found in printed playtexts.

The compilers of the "authorized" version of Shakespeare's collected plays in 1623—all of them professional actors—were entertaining a different idea of authorship, Masten contends, than they had when the plays were in production. Theater, after all, is fundamentally a collaborative medium—a fact registered in sixteenth-century printings that generally specify the name of the acting company even in the absence of the scriptwriter's name. In general, Masten observes, quarto printings of playscripts emphasize theatrical genesis of the text; folio printings, following the example of Ben Jonson's collected *Workes* (1616), emphasize authorial genesis. By the 1620s and 1630s, however, quartos begin to include the more elaborate apparatus of literary texts. Arthur Marotti in *Manuscript, Print, and the English Renaissance Lyric* (1995) has argued that print in general bestowed an authority lacking in manuscripts; Joseph Lowenstein, Margreta de Grazia, and Leah Marcus have made similar arguments about the construction of authorship in Jonson's collected works of 1616 and in the 1623 folio of Shakespeare's plays. Where these scholars have sited a definitive "birth of the author" Masten finds continued negotiation of authority. The most sustained analysis of the entire book is devoted to the prefatory matter to the 1647 folio of Beaumont and Fletcher. This material, Masten argues, presents Beaumont and Fletcher as the "authors" of the volume but not entirely as its "writers." In Moseley's preface and in the thirty-seven commendatory poems Masten finds "inscriptions of a particularly pivotal moment in English cultural history—a moment when collaboration (and the attendant lack of concern, in certain discourses, over authorial attribution) has not yet been fully supplanted by the regime of the singular, proprietary author within which we now write" (126). The Beaumont and Fletcher folio may attribute authorship to the men whose names appear in brackets on the title page, but it is in fact a collaborative endeavor: in addition to a number of plays in which writers other than Beaumont and Fletcher are admitted to have had a hand, it contains a statement from one of the printers about the provenance of the texts and no fewer than thirty-seven commendatory poems from almost as many writers, not to mention the names of the two printers who manufactured the book as a physical object. In sum, "Collaboration and authorship . . . are not only in contention in descriptions of prior textual productions, but in those of the volume's present moment as well" (139). The commentatory poems, Masten demonstrates in a series of acute close readings, attempt with varying degrees of finesse to negotiate inconsistencies between old ideas of collaboration and new ideas of individual authorship. As part of these negotiations, changing ideas of sexuality come into play: "Here Beaumont and Fletcher begin to register as 'queer,' in the more recent sense of that term" (133).

In a book full of smart argument and clever reading there is only one disappointment: the limited ambitions of the last chapter. In an analysis of two printed folios of her collected plays (1662 and 1668) Masten presents Margaret Cavendish as self-consciously adapting the rhetoric of male parthenogenesis to serve her own protofeminist ends: insisting on the primacy of her own authorship, specifying just what her husband's few collaborative contributions are and "heterosexualizing" them in images of companionate marriage, situating her labors in an ostensibly pastoral, incipiently bourgeois locale within "A Cottage warm and clean, though thatch'd and low" (quoted on 160). Masten's closing gambit, a witty reading of the sexually ambiguous figures of Apollo and Mercury that frame the frontispiece to Cavendish's *Plays, Never before Printed* is fully supported by a work not cited here: Joseph Porter's investigation of the phallic iconography of herms in *Shakespeare's Mercutio* (1988). The draped torsos of Apollo and Mercury in the Cavendish frontispiece each ends at the waist in a herm, making them, literally, hermaphrodites. By limiting his attention only to title pages, prefatory texts, and the 1668 frontispiece, Masten stops short of considering the fictions presented by the dramatic texts themselves—an exercise that has inspired some of the book's most compelling reading earlier on. That is a shame, since Cavendish's plays are full of appropriations of male-authored plays—appropriations that complicate the question of paternity and authorship in provocative ways. *The Convent of Pleasure*, for example, re-presents the plot situation of *Love's Labor's Lost*, this time with a household of women who have sworn off men. This convent, in the words of its founder Lady Happy, "shall not be a Cloister of restraint, but a place for freedom" (7). The intruder into the fiction's gendered space is not, as in Shakespeare's comedies or Beaumont and Fletcher's, a maid in male disguise but a male in maid disguise. In the context that Masten provides, the play's flirtations with same-sex dalliance are all the more intriguing. Some of the women, the male trespasser tells his friends, "do accoustre Themselves in Masculine-Habits, and act Lovers-parts" (22). Masten's presentation of Cavendish as a female author who situates herself with careful calculation vis-à-vis male authority in general and her husband in particular suggests that Lady Happy's eventual marriage to the wooer-intruder might be something more than the capitulation to patriarchy it otherwise seems. *The Sociable Companions; or, The Female Wits*, another play included in the 1668 folio, ends with a young lady choosing an old suitor and defending her choice in a public assembly, in a self-aggrandizing appropriation of the patriarchal terms that Masten has investigated:

> Concerning the Church and State, since they do allow of buying and selling young Maids to Men to be their Wives, they cannot condemn those Maids that make their bargain to their own advantage, and chuse rather to be bought then sold, and I confess I am one of the number of those; for I'le rather chuse an old Man that buys me with his Wealth, then a younge one, whom I must purchase with my Wealth. (95)

William Cavendish, it is worth noting, was thirty years Margaret Lucas's senior when she married him to become duchess of Newcastle—and a lady with means to write.

Let regret for the last chapter's brevity stand as a measure of how thoroughly and serviceably Masten has otherwise mapped the intersection of textuality, sexuality, and political power in the construction of early modern authorship. In more ways than one, the subject of authority will never be the same.

Works Cited

Cavendish, Margaret. *Plays, Never before Printed.* London: A. Maxwell, 1668.

Plato. *The Dialogues.* 2 vols. Translated by B. Jowett. New York: Random House, 1937.

Shakespeare, William. *The Complete Works.* Edited by Stanley Wells and Gary Taylor. Oxford: Clarendon Press, 1988.

Inwardness and Theater in the English Renaissance.
By Katherine Eisaman Maus.
Chicago and London: University of Chicago Press, 1995.

Reviewer: Patricia Fumerton

In an important contribution to the ongoing investigation into early modern notions of inwardness and subjectivity, Katherine Eisaman Maus offers us *Inwardness and Theater in the English Renaissance.* Maus begins her study by situating herself in opposition to recent cultural critics who argue that interiority in the English Renaissance was either nonexistent or only publicly rendered. Instead, she finds evidence in the period of a widespread and urgent preoccupation with inwardness and with "the discrepancy between 'inward disposition' and 'outward appearance'" (13). Maus attributes this preoccupation primarily to the disruptions caused by the English Reformation and sees it best enacted and explored in the culture's drama.

Obsession in Reformation England over the divide between internal truth and external manifestation, Maus argues in the second chapter, further leads to a general "paranoia about hypocrisy and surveillance" (36). Since God alone can verify internal truth, Machiavellian hypocrisy is equivalent to atheism and opposed to God-sanctioned social hierarchies and kinship networks (although at the same time the Machiavel problematically mimics the true believer's detachment from such worldly obligations). Shakespeare's *Richard III* and Kyd's *The Spanish Tragedy* both stage the need to expose Machiavellian inwardness, she observes, but Kyd recasts the issue in terms of a pressing class conflict that makes subterfuge or seditious inwardness more justified. Maus goes on to consider in the third chapter the knotty question of "conscience" in relation to perceived "boundaries between inside and outside, between soul and body, between self and other" (92). She here specifically looks at methods of interrogation employed by the English state to extract hidden "truth" from suspected dissidents. Crossing an inner/outer boundary in progressing from persuasive speech to physical torture in the 1580s, such inquisitorial strategies themselves called into question the nature of truth so exposed. Marlowe, she finds, stages similar problematics of examining a "heretical conscience" (87) in theatrically maintaining and dissolving divisions between the interior and exterior self as well as between self and other in *Dr. Faustus* and the *Tamburlaine* plays.

In perhaps the most exciting chapters, four and five, Maus next turns to the special difficulties juries faced in trying to discover the inward truth in crimes of witchcraft and treason as well as in questions of impotence. She explores the literary representation of such perplexing "trials" of discovery in Shakespeare's *Othello* and *Measure for Measure* as well as in Jonson's *Volpone* and *Epicoene*. While Jonson's plays more fixedly stage the problem of "proving" impotency and of promoting the satirist as judicial examiner of such human failing, Maus finds that "in both Jonson and Shakespeare sexual experience becomes a *topos* of unknowable inwardness" (131). In her final chapter, Maus focuses on the body itself as conceptualized by contemporaries in terms of boundaries between inside and outside. Drawing on medical notions of woman's secret parts and the social idea of woman as hidden, she shows how male poets such as Sidney and Milton appropriated images of the female womb to project authorial independence. Milton's *Comus*, however, questions this imagining of an impenetrable inward spirit through the staged contestation between the seducing Comus and the chaste Lady. Maus concludes that "For the English Renaissance, it is a commonplace that spectacle depends upon, sometimes betrays, but never fully manifests a truth that remains shrouded, indiscernible, or ambiguous" (210).

What makes Maus's book truly important? Why is her study more than just another drop in the subjective bucket already filled to brimming by Stephen Greenblatt, Jonathan Goldberg, Francis Barker, Catherine Belsey, Ann Jones, Peter Stallybrass, and Kay Stockholder, among many others? It is not simply that the book is extremely clearly written, always intelligent, consistently interesting, historically well grounded, and highly sensitive to nuances between the authors she studies (Kyd, Marlowe, Jonson, Shakespeare, Milton, et al.). Many of the above scholars have claims to such admirable qualities as well. Nor is it that Maus has the courage to champion early modern inwardness as separate from outer, public or political forms and practices—rather than as always socially defined—though to take such a stand is to go against the trend of the last fifteen years of cultural studies and to risk her book being seen as, in her own words, "regressive or misconceived" (2). We all admire a rebel. But in my mind what makes Maus's book so important is a twofold contribution it offers to the inwardness issue.

1.) Maus foremost brings to the discussion of inwardness the pressure of religion, which has so often been largely absent as a social factor from earlier studies of interiority, whose bias has most definitely been secular. In this sense, she joins ranks with a small group of scholars, led by Debora Shuger, in her *The Renaissance Bible: Scholarship, Subjectivity, and Sacrifice* (University of California Press, 1994), followed by Elizabeth Hanson, in her *Discovering the Subject in Renaissance England* (forthcoming Cambridge University Press, 1998), and recently advanced by the panelists in the 1997 Modern Language Association special session, "Religion and Subjectivity in the English Renaissance": Jeffrey Knapp, Debora Shuger, and Ramie Targoff. Maus's study is closest to Hanson's (clearly the two were generating their books at the same time and, indeed, cite each other's work). Both authors look to religious dissension and interrogation/torture as active factors in the formulation of an early modern notion of inward mystery (which Hanson more outrightly than Maus calls "subjectivity") and both turn their historical investigations to, among other literary works, Shakespeare's *Othello* and *Measure for Measure*. Both authors also recognize the network of cultural factors that intersect with such religious issues. Hanson, for instance, has a chapter on Thomas Harman's interrogation of rogues and another on Sir Francis Bacon's discovery of Nature. Maus casts her net even wider than Hanson, extending her study of interrogation to include judicial practices and their representation (not only of heresy trials but also of witchcraft, treason, and impotence trials) and looking at the impact of religious inwardness on historical and literary attitudes to societal and personal obligations as well as to the human and sexualized body. I am oversimplifying Maus's argument, however, in using the word *impact*, since Maus is more than aware that cultural ideas float freely in any given period. Nevertheless, she does tentatively uphold the Reformation as a causative, if not always visible, force in shaping versions of inwardness in late sixteenth- and seventeenth-century England. As she guardedly puts it, "Inward truth, as it is conceived in the Renaissance may be an intrinsically or originally theological concept, but not all of the settings in which it becomes important are explicitly religious ones" (211).

2.) Maus's second important contribution to inwardness/subjectivity issues is a highly sophisticated awareness that such notions are discontinuous: in other words, different understandings of inwardness or subjectivity might operate at the same time. We thus should not expect every contemporary to hold to a single (or particularly modern) definition of self. "'Subjectivity,'" she declares, "is often treated casually as a unified or coherent concept when, in fact, it is a loose and varied collection of assumptions, intuitions, and practices that do not all logically entail one another and need not appear together at the same cultural moment" (29). Thus Maus argues that "both Kyd and Marlowe dramatize what might be called 'individualism,' but they differ drastically in what they consider an individual to be. Likewise, Jonson and Shakespeare both construe the sexual domain as a kind of metonymy of inward truth, but their notions of what that inwardness comprises are radically at variance" (30).

The slight qualms that I have about Maus's study are interestingly side effects of its important strengths. First, in regard to her admirable flexibility of approach: because Maus rightly sees inwardness and subjectivity—and related concepts such as individualism, unity of the subject, and privacy—as loosely defined and not necessarily equivalent terms, her study at times seems overly broad in its reach and too ready to slide between a statement about inward truth and a claim about subjectivity (so that, ironically, the concepts often seem quite easily interchangeable). Second, in regard to her valuable religious perspective. The originary source of inwardness and subjectivity in Maus's interpretation, of course, is God. Early modern inner truth in her reading can exist and be confirmed only in the eye of God and, for this reason, the Renaissance subject is both God-centered and a mystery to others, whose penetrating gaze must always be limited and hence vulnerable to deception, Machiavellian distortion, and other forms of false mimicry. My problem—and Maus would probably say it is indeed my problem, and my particularly modern problem at that—is that I find it hard to entertain a notion of interior self that is akin to, if not identical to, subjectivity when that interiority is defined primarily in theological terms. If we look inside ourselves and find God, how can we be said to find ourselves? In other words, the kind of self Maus is describing is relational to a transcendent being, not reflexive of a mortal subject, and thus has a lot to do with truth/Truth but little to do with notions of interior human subjectivity.

Now, a similar complaint might be made about the work of other cultural critics who see early modern subjectivity as self-defining only through external forms and practices, whether physical, social, or political. A closet, one might point out, is as much an external other as God—more so, one might continue, in being a "thing," not a "being." But I would counter that such is not the case precisely because a room *is* a thing and specifically, a secular, man-made thing or space that can be inhabited in the here and now. This is why, in my own restricted foray into religion in *Cultural Aesthetics*—in looking at the shift from Byzantine iconic representations of the Annunciation to Renaissance perspective renderings of the event—I found that the subject materializes as private and interior precisely when the mystery of the Godhead (previously represented as the gold lux or written word occupying the background of icons) is minimalized to golden halos, a lighted dove, dialogue, or the like in the foreground and thus no longer made the visual source/end point of the picture; in its place stands the man-centered perspective plane of receding columns, interior rooms, or walled gardens that mortal man/woman occupies in this world and that image (in their own closedness—recession, walls, shut doors) *human* privacy or interiority (*Cultural Aesthetics: Renaissance Literature and the Practice of Social Ornament* [University of Chicago Press, 1991], 143–54).

One of the most interesting facets of Maus's study is that, although it consistently promotes a God-based inward subject separate from outward expression, it also turns primarily to secular forms of discovery—foremost trials and plays—as revealing (and thus erasing) this closed or invisible truth: "But inwardness as it becomes a concern in the theater is always perforce inwardness displayed: an inwardness, in other words, that has already ceased to exist. The cultural institutions with which I shall concern myself, then, are those which share the peculiar drawbacks and anxieties of the theatrical situation: they are highly public procedures of revelation, and the interiors they unveil often seem to be structured as much by those procedures as by their prior hidden content" (32–33). Maus sounds a lot like Jonathan Goldberg here—"the private sphere is mystified, politicized, made into an ideological construct," says Goldberg of a Caroline masque (*James I and the Politics of Literature: Jonson, Shakespeare, Donne, and Their Contemporaries* [Johns Hopkins University Press, 1983], 97)—and it is precisely such moments where her articulation of the discovery of inward truth as mystery appears to dovetail with other cultural

critics of subjectivity that I find especially telling. Such a convergence of positions would suggest that there might also be a similar
convergence or coexistence of the two modes of thinking in the
early modern period itself. I would go so far as to suggest that
slippage between two notions of inward truth—on the one hand,
as divine-sanctioned and separate from observable outer forms; on
the other hand, as secularly seen to be apart, closed, or mysterious
precisely through such externals—is necessary for the discovery of
subjectivity. This slippage involves the transference from God as
other that sanctions the mystery of self to man-centered or human
others (closets, walled gardens, lyrics, juries, players) that do the
same thing but in more human and thus *self*-referential ways. Of
course, the early modern period would itself have slipped back
and forth between such imaginings of inwardness in the typically
fluid and unstable cultural thinking of which Maus is fully aware.
But in my reading, a secularly defined inwardness that is the same
as subjectivity would occur alongside of, and even *in spite of*, not
because of the religious issues of the Reformation.

Finally, I would like to conclude by reflecting further on the
parameters of Maus's wonderfully expansive and highly nuanced
argument and where it might point us. There is much sophisticated
historical grounding of Maus's study: in religious controversies,
trial practices, gynecological treatises, and so forth. But given her
interest in the relation of inwardness to outer forms like the body, I
wonder why she does not turn to other contemporary physicalities,
such as city spaces (only fleetingly and incongruously discussed
in her introduction), or private meditational spaces, such as closets,
or chapels, or enclaves in churches, etc., which might further
ground her position and make more manifest the historical presence of inwardness as a fact/problem. Furthermore, though Maus's
readings of historical texts and practices are very sophisticated,
the fine nuances that she finds in contemporary understandings of
inward truth lie mostly in the literary readings she offers. Kyd,
Marlowe, Jonson, Shakespeare, and Milton explore inwardness and
its relation to the external or public in many often subtly different
ways. But, interestingly, Catholics, Protestants, Anglicans, sectari-
ans, and skeptics, in Maus's reading, mostly share the same belief
when it comes to inward truth. In this respect, we might contrast
Maus's position with that of Debora Shuger, who sees Catholics and
Protestants of the early modern period developing very different
notions of subjectivity. Along these lines, we might further inquire
whether attitudes to inner/outer relations might not differ between

the sexes as well (Maus examines the appropriation of female wombs by male poets—metaphorically speaking—but never suggests what the attitude of women or women poets to their own inwardness might be). Lastly, is the question of class. Like many other cultural critics of subjectivity, Maus's study draws on an educated selection of early modern culture as representative of attitudes of the whole. But what about the illiterate or barely literate lower orders? Or the mobile poor and vagrant? Would they or could they hold to the same notions of inward truth or subjectivity as their social superiors? Or should we not yet again take up Maus's notion of unstable and diverse meanings of subjectivity in the early modern period and *hit the streets*.

The Purpose of Playing: Shakespeare and the Cultural Politics of the Elizabethan Theatre.
By Louis Montrose.
Chicago and London: University of Chicago Press, 1996.

Reviewer: Lawrence Manley

Louis Montrose begins *The Purpose of Playing* by noting that "during the course of the 1980s, literary studies in the American academy came to be centrally concerned with the historical, social, and political conditions and consequences of literary production and interpretation" (1). This is both understated and modest: Montrose has been one of the most influential innovators in what are probably the most pervasive developments in the Renaissance literary scholarship of the past fifteen years. In a series of articles on the politics of Elizabethan pastoral (including a 1979 essay on Spenser's *The Shepheardes Calendar* that, along with similar essays that same year by Richard Helgerson and David Lee Miller, helped to redefine the study of Spenser's career for the 1980s), in articles on the cultural genetics and generativity of Shakespeare's major comedies, and above all in the occasional theoretical formulations that include his seminal *Helios* article (1979) on the anthropology of dramatic playing and his essay "The Elizabethan Subject and the Spenserian Text" in David Quint and Patricia Parker's *Literary Theory/Renaissance Texts* (1986), Montrose has shown, in both theory and practice, how the works of Shakespeare and his contemporaries, integrated with the formative and transforming functions of politics and culture, participate in the historical process. A whole generation of English Renaissance scholarship has been influenced by Montrose's example, and it is good to have several of his widely scattered articles and conference papers on Shakespeare and the theater—augmented, updated, and argumentatively revised—within the covers of this book.

In a prologue with the significantly plural title "Texts and Histories," Montrose reformulates his work for the 1990s by situating recent New Historical and cultural materialist paradigms not only in relation to the Anglo-American New Critical model of midcentury (as others have done) but also in relation "to the intellectual ferment of the past two decades . . . summed up in the word *theory*" (2). Montrose has always been one of the most theoretically articulate in a school of studies not generally distinguished for its systematic precision or coherence, and his deft chiastic formulations (e.g., "the historicity of texts and the textuality of history") continue to epitomize a mode of dialectical thinking that is particularly rich, flexible, subtle, and inspiringly suggestive. If there is a new theoretical note in this volume, it comes from the author's debt to the "theoretical field of poststructuralism," a field "inhabited by a multiplicity of unstable, variously conjoined and conflicting discourses" (2). Among earlier New Historicists, Montrose has always been one of the most receptive to the currents of deconstruction and feminism, though this can be hard to spot—most self-respecting New Historicists take a nominally pluralistic stance when (with Montrose) they disavow "a general suspicion of closed systems, totalities, and universals" (2), particularly the standard "humanist" universals. But *The Purpose of Playing* also develops a case for suspicion toward New Historicist totalities, if that is what Montrose means by pitting his own "inconclusive conclusions" against the "sheer excitement" of "the bold assertions that have become commonplace in the critical literature on the Elizabethan theatre" (104).

The Purpose of Playing is divided into two parts. The first, "Drama, Theatre, Society and the State," drawing on Montrose's earlier writings on the stage, makes a case for the powerful and complex cultural influence of the Elizabethan theater. Montrose traces the complex social affiliations of the theater to a moment of transition between declining popular religious performance and the appropriation of theatrical techniques by the emergent Tudor state. By exploring the differing attitudes of the Elizabethan court and the City of London magistracy and clergy toward the stage, Montrose situates the emergent institution of professional theater at the boundary between hierarchical and exchange-based modes of social organization. Revisiting the much-explored performance of *Richard II* by the Lord Chamberlain's Men on the eve of the Essex rebellion, Montrose goes on to suggest that the performance was motivated by "the unstable conjunction of patronage-based and market-based modes of production . . . characteristic of the public and professional theatre" (75). In keeping with his aim of showing how Elizabethan politics, society, and culture "*complicate* the ideological positioning of the professional theatre and its repertoire" (87), the first half of the book ends with a deliberately inconclusive note on "The Cross-Purposes of Playing."

These "cross-purposes" are then developed in the second half of the book, a much-expanded version of an earlier essay on *A Midsummer Night's Dream* ("Shaping Fantasies: Figurations of Gender and Power in Elizabethan Culture," *Representations* 2 [1983]) that also alludes to Montrose's other early work and includes much new material. Here Montrose shows how the play's patriarchal treatment of sexuality and gender works paradoxically to complicate and undermine as well as reinforce the ideology of the Elizabethan state and how, in turn, this destabilizing power of the play, contemplated metatheatrically in the performance of Bottom and his fellow artisans, is linked to the complex social position and historical moment of Shakespeare and his fellow professionals.

To readers by now familiar with terms like these, *The Purpose of Playing* will nonetheless offer some interesting differences in both nuance and overall import. Montrose has quite properly undertaken to revise and refine his work in response to criticism, to the differently inflected use that others have made of his work, and to his own changing sense of the place of the theater in the Elizabethan age. I will single out three related areas of elaboration where it seems to me that Montrose has sought to clarify (and perhaps to change somewhat) the tenor of his work. The first of these is a renewed but reinflected insistence on the *secularity* of the professional theater. Such an insistence was already explicit in Montrose's early distinction (in the *Helios* article on "The Purpose of Playing") between the premodern traditions of popular religious performance and the practices of the emergent commercial theater. But in seeking to explain how the latter absorbed and transformed the former, Montrose's early work relied heavily on anthropological theories of "liminality" in order to argue for the communally based "affinities" between "theatrical performances" and "religious services," between "magic" and "fiction," that in his view helped to make "the play itself . . . a rite of passage, created by the playwright and the players for their audience." Montrose always insisted that in the professional theater the transitions being acted out were not the calendrical ones of traditional religious observances but those transitions in the life cycle—birth, puberty, marriage, death—in which conflicting social demands and allegiances come most powerfully to bear on both individuals *and* the community. But in *The Purpose of Playing*, his anthropological account of "magical" affects and communal psychology has been almost entirely eliminated, resulting in a stronger emphasis on the theater's *intellectually* enabling approach to the "quotidien experiences," the unfilled secular needs and problems, that confronted individuals as the influence of traditional religion and local society was usurped by the centralizing Tudor state. By subjecting their protagonists to "vividly represented experiences of cognitive and ideological dissonance," Montrose suggests, Shakespeare's plays could serve "as a cognitive and therapeutic instrument," functioning, in the most ideologically "enabling" way, "to stimulate the intellect and to promote . . . emotional well-being" in their audiences (39–40). It is through this insistence on the "public and profane" (32) nature of the professional theater, then, that Montrose is able to enter into more recent debates about "the nature and the scope of the agency available to subjects of the early modern state" (7), and to conjecture that the Elizabethan theater "may have helped some in its heterogeneous audience not only to adjust but also to manipulate to their own advantages the ambiguities and conflicts . . . arising from the contradictory realities of change" (40).

   In this view that the *secular* function of the theater is addressed to individual agents (who are at the same time tightly circumscribed by posthumanist theories about the ineluctable reciprocity of "subjectification and structuration," 15) lies the basis for a second revisionary feature of the book: a renewed and strengthened emphasis on the *power* of the theater as a cultural institution. There are different kinds of arguments about the powerlessness of the theater, of course, but Montrose initially addresses himself to a recent argument by Paul Yachnin, who maintains that the social marginality of the theater and the social heterogeneity of its audience made it not just politically impotent but politically irrelevant. For Montrose, these are precisely the features that contributed to the power of the Elizabethan stage, enabling it to produce the kind of situations in which being "*within* or *among* ideological formations may make it possible for us . . . to read, as in a refracted light, one fragment of our ideological inscription by another" (16).

In concluding that "a reflexive knowledge so unstable may, nevertheless, provide subjects with a means of empowerment as agents" (16), Montrose lays down the premise of a third and most important revisionary position in the book: a strenuous and frequently reiterated assertion that the secular power of the theater was not in any ultimate sense more ideologically "containing" than it was "subversive." Of the four possible ways in which these two now-familiar terms can be digitally combined, only two ("both/and," "neither/ nor") can hold much serious interest. In making a case for the former of these (Yachnin would probably endorse the latter), Montrose places heavy emphasis on the capacity for "subversion," thereby redressing what he and others have seen (perhaps too reductively) as an undue emphasis on ideological "containment" in the work of Stephen Greenblatt. The case for "subversion" is made at points throughout the book, but most forcefully and interestingly in a largely new chapter on "The Power of Personation," where Montrose links the possibilities for subversion to *formal* qualities of the drama. Such familiar formal traits as argument *in utramque partem*, self-reflexive performativity, and metatheatrical exploitation of the *theatrum mundi* trope are interestingly connected to the contemporary analysis of human motivation in Tacitean realpolitik and, in less satisfactory shorthand, to "other material and ideological developments" like "capital accumulation, market calculation, and 'possessive individualism'" (92). It would take many good books to spell all these connections out; the point of this one is to underline a shift of "playing dimensions . . . to the horizontal plane, upon which human characters interact within an imagined social space." For Montrose, the "social dialectic" of *mimesis* in the Elizabethan theater, by using "personation" to imply "that the temporal and mutable realm of second causes had become the locus of dramatic action," helped audiences to see that alternative perspectives and courses of action were possible (93). In what is the centerpiece of the chapter (and, in a way, the book), Montrose returns to the soliloquy of Henry V on the eve of Agincourt, the episode with which Stephen Greenblatt concludes the case for sub-version in his famous "Invisible Bullets" essay; but he concludes (even while he follows Greenblatt in glossing Shakespeare with Marlowe's *The Jew of Malta*) that the metatheatricality of the scene, in the spirit of the play's prologue, gives visibility "to the imaginative authority of the common subject in constituting the political authority of the sovereign" (82).

Montrose has always favored dialectical complexity, but never more so than in *The Purpose of Playing*, where he finds new, historicizing reasons for admiring the qualities that so many others have valued in Shakespeare: "multiplicity of perspective," "ambiguity and complexity," and "objectivity" (88, 98). Because of its efforts to give a historicized account of these qualities, the book will be useful not only to the official record keepers of late-twentieth-century scholarship, but also to our students. Like many of the recent classroom handbooks that the work of Montrose has helped to inspire, *The Purpose of Playing* contains a great deal of useful documentary material (much of it from E. K. Chambers's *The Elizabethan Stage*) and wide reference to recent scholarship; but it has the additional merit of engaging these materials in just the kinds of original arguments and formulations that—to go back almost a generation, now—first made us want to think about them again.

Shakespeare from the Margins: Language, Culture, Context.
By Patricia Parker.
Chicago and London: University of Chicago Press, 1996.

Reviewer: *Margreta de Grazia*

The margins from which Shakespeare is read in Patricia Parker's *Shakespeare from the Margins* are hardly typical. They are not tidy, white borders; they are busy, teeming spaces. They do not enclose the text they surround; they stretch it beyond its dramatic confines into other discourses, other practices. They do not uphold the text they flank by glossing it; rather they throw its centrality into question.

So what is in the atypical margins from which Parker reads Shakespeare? Shakespeare, but not familiar Shakespeare. It is, in the main, the Shakespeare that has over the centuries been slighted or ignored. Parker looks to the margins for what the critical tradition has largely overlooked: minor plays like the farcical *Comedy of Errors*, minor characters like bombastic Paroles, minor scenes like Williams's comical Latin lesson, minor passages like Othello's "close dilations working from the heart." And minor, above all, is the linguistic feature pervading the book: wordplay. As Parker demonstrates, however, wordplay is hardly incidental to Shakespeare's work.

The rhetorics of Shakespeare's time distinguished a number of different kinds of phonetic, semantic, and syntactic overlapping, for example, *paronomasia, antanaclasis, asteismus,* and *syllepsis*. In modern usage, we lump all these verbal effects under the nineteenth-century coinage *wordplay*. The shift in terminology itself suggests something of a fall in stature. If words *play* instead of *work*, how can they be anything but trivial, decorative, and tricky? Shakespeare, however, was writing in a period before such biases had set in: before lexical regulation, before neoclassical prescripts, before scientific and philosophical attempts to make words exactly correspondent to things. Parker, reading without these biases, succeeds in demonstrating just how serious this type of linguistic activity can be. Indeed, in light of her demonstration of the power and force of wordplay, we might want to introduce a modifier. *Radical* wordplay better characterizes the verbal effects she charts. They run deep and spread out wide—not only through Shakespeare's work but through early modern culture at large.

It might be said that Parker has discovered a way to read closely without subscribing to the formalist fantasy of a monadic text, self-contained and self-reflexive. While New Criticism saw homonyms, for example, as integral to the literary work, Parker's readings trace them outside the boundaries of the text into a range of discourses. The *joinery* that is the craft of one of the rude mechanicals in *Midsummer Night's Dream*, for example, moves from the fittings of carpentry to the constructions of rhetoric, grammar, and logic, to the couplings of matrimony, to the order of the social formation. Similarly, in several of the plays the term *dilation* (also spelled *delation*) links various kinds of rhetorical expansion (narration, bombast, amplification, garrulousness) to juridical accusations, to anatomical openings of the body, to disclosures of New World exploration, to displays of the exotic and sexually "monstrous." In addition, Parker suggests that these semantic links extend beyond discourse to contemporary issues and events. Her exploration of *joinery*, for example, leads to the question of the players' social status; in following the semantics of *dilation/delation*, she lights upon a range of topical issues and practices, ranging from the inflation of titles and currency to the emergence of a proto–secret service, to Elizabeth's notorious stalling tactics in her marriage negotiations.

In her attention to how words cluster around complex cultural formations, Parker is indebted to Raymond Williams's still remarkable book, *Key Words: A Vocabulary of Culture and Society* (1976, rev. ed. 1983). The glossary was prompted by Williams's conviction that our understanding of social order and cultural value was dependent on a historically variable network of words. The words Williams selected as "key words" were urgent and necessary. We need words like *art, individual, democracy, criticism, psychological, sex,* and *work* in order to think, speak, and act in the world of the present. We could easily, however, do without Parker's "key words": *conveyance, dilation/delation, increase, preposterous, joinery,* and *breach.* Dispensable to modern use, they were basic to early modern Shakespeare. And yet Parker's key words lead to some of the same social and cultural issues Williams was committed to clarifying. Had she traced the movement of any of Williams's words, most of which acquired their modern senses in the eighteenth century, it is doubtful that she would have gotten very far, certainly not to the questions of rank, status, priority, right, and order to which her own key words repeatedly return.

It is more than Parker's selection of words that makes her readings unmodern. It is also the way the material properties of these words appear to be directing conceptual linkages. The discursive ties she traces are motivated by orthographic and phonetic likeness. If words look alike and sound alike, there appear to be grounds for an ideational link. It is as if the material resemblance between *dilation* and *delation,* for instance, prompted a semantic kinship between concepts as ostensibly diverse as "opening up" and "bringing charges against." The material overlap between the words appears to secure a relationship between them. And indeed, there *is* one to be found between these two cognates, in at least three areas: (1) the legal, in the expanse of time between accusation and sentence (the proverbial "law's delay"); (2) the dramatic, as in the prolonged interim in *Othello* between the accusation of adultery and the "bloody period" with which it ends, and (3) the eschatological, in the span of history extending from the Fall to the Last Judgment. Similar kinds of material likeness seem, sometimes absurdly, to call for a shared semantics between what we deem two entirely different words. What do the *leaks* in a container have to do with the *leeks* that are eaten? Parker's discussion of the *Henriad* makes the connection surprisingly plausible. The leeks the Welsh customarily wear in their caps trigger the Lancastrian fear, especially acute when Henry is at war with France, that a *leak, breach,* or *fault* will be found through which to invade the English *continent,* particularly from the bordering Welsh *marches,* the land of Henry's rival for the throne, Richard's named successor, Mortimer, the Earl of *March.* (The italicized words all radiate out from the *leek/leak* merger, 40–45.)

The phonetic slurring and graphic blurring of words as distinct to us from one another as *Moor* and *more, clothes* and *close, seams* and *seems* allow for a play of sounds and letters that sets into motion meaningful connections. We have no theory by which to understand this dynamic. It seems particularly to characterize the early modern period before language was brought under the rule of later systems of correctness, decorum, and accuracy. In its conflation of sound and sense, signifier and signified, it bears some resemblance to the imagined Adamic language in which words contained in themselves knowledge and power over what they named. So, too, it seems related to its classical Cratylean counterpart in which the material form of words led back to original and transparent truths. Yet the difference between these mystical ideal words and radical wordplay may be more telling than the similarity. Later in the seventeenth century, Adamic and Cratylean words inspired attempts to construct philosophical and scientific languages in which words possessed perfect referentiality: an exact correspondence between word and thing. But the key words ranging through Shakespeare's work have no such aim. They are at once fascinating and frustrating because they have no telic end point of signification. They sprawl out laterally, making discursive connections that lead deeper into the verbal maze.

To a remarkable degree, Parker's writing takes on the features of the writing that is her subject. It is, above all, nonteleological. It does not move linearly, developing as it proceeds and gradually reaching a conclusion. It dilates and increases, swelling in swirls and swerves, spreading out before us its copious materials. She herself is aware that her subject cannot be pursued via the conventions of efficient and purposive exposition, "Circling, backtracking, or revisiting from another perspective is, therefore, integral to treating the accretive associations through which Shakespearean wordplay works" (19). It is for this reason a difficult book to read. We are after all modern readers who expect to get somewhere for our labors and travails. Reading Parker, however, is strangely disorienting. We do not quite know where we are or remember the detours and byways by which we got there. It is, then, like the way she reads early modern texts, what she terms "reading without a map" (18). Her unconventional writing makes the book difficult to write about as well as read. A review, for example, customarily gives abstracts of the book's individual chapters. But it is hard to reduce any unit of Parker's prose to a nutshell—not so much because it is rich and full (and it certainly is that), but because it is unschematic. Yet even this difficulty is instructive, revealing how even as simple a critical exercise as a review follows conventions devised to satisfy modem standards of organization and intelligibility.

If *Marginal Shakespeare* is a hard book to read and to review, one can only imagine how hard it must have been to write. Anyone who has tried to explain the workings even of a single pun in Shakespeare knows the difficulty of charting its generative course. Parker has numbers of them resonating at once, and she falls back on no critical categories (work, author, plot, character, theme, imagery) to contain their activity.

There is one device, however, Parker does rely on to give form to her subject. It is the metaphor of her title, *Marginal Shakespeare*. It is a witty title, to be sure, naming the book for its margins rather than for its contents, itself an example of inverted priority that might fall under the category of another of her key words, *preposterous*. But, of course, there is more to the title than that. The metaphor applies to several different kinds of early modern physical space: the margins of the page but also the *platea* skirting the *locus* of the medieval stage, the liberties outside London, and the borderlands girding England. To a contemporary sensibility, it is easy—too easy—to identify these spatial margins with the political margins drawn along lines of race, class, and gender. Parker does not always push the metaphor into the realm of ideology, but when she does (as in her introduction and her discussion of *Midsummer Night's Dream* and the *Henriad*) her project starts to look suspi-

ciously familiar and modern. The critical and historical project of
giving voice to ostensibly minor linguistic effects becomes inexpli-
cably equivalent to the political project of entitling marginal peoples. Early modern wordplay ends up having a telos after all: it
aims at subverting the ruling formation, particularly by the ingenious tactic of drawing attention to the artifice of what the dominant center would pass off as true by nature (12–15).

The metaphor of the margin, when pressed too far, produces a
problematic political configuration and one that, as Parker knows,
lends itself too readily to the deadlocked subversion/containment
debate. It addition, it introduces a problematic textual configuration. It leaves us with a hegemonic textual center that is static,
staid, and dull, with all the challenging verbal activity occurring
on the sidelines. But is it only wordplay that probes surface stability? Is it only, for example, the wordplay in the *Henriad* on *breach*,
march, and *conveyance* that registers the Lancasters' guilt and their
attempt to cover it up? Does not the text proper quite openly dramatize that guilt and its protective strategies, beginning at the moment
of Richard II's assassination with Henry IV's resolution to voyage
to the Holy Land to wash the guilty blood off his hands and ending
with his son's tortured anxieties before the battle of Agincourt?
The kind of profound interrogation performed by radical wordplay
also takes place at the heart of the text proper.

It may be helpful to suggest that early modern wordplay is radical
more in its semantics than its politics. It gets to the notional and
practical roots of the discourses it pervades, but not necessarily to
undermine them. It is precisely in the delineation of the elusive
reticulations of these semantic networks that Parker's skill is so
breathtaking. She demonstrates prodigious linguistic agility, theoretical sophistication, and deft familiarity with a staggering array
of early modern texts. As with any strongly original work, it will
take time to absorb and assess the book's importance. There is no
greater proof, however, of the validity of her reading practice than
the experience of seeing inert stretches of the Shakespearean text
come alive with new energy and consequentiality. It leaves us with
the disquieting but stimulating feeling that we have not fully appreciated the difference the four centuries separating us from Shakespeare has made. It leaves us, too, with much to ponder regarding
how language is working in these plays, and to what effect. The
six blank pages at end of the book, providing ample space for the
reader's notes, are a nice materialization of Parker's desire "to open

up rather than foreclose possibilities" (19). Needless to say, they
have no margins.

The Body Emblazoned: Dissection and the Human Body in Renaissance Culture.
By Jonathan Sawday.
London and New York: Routledge, 1995.

Reviewer: Karen Newman

This book is big, hefty in size, ambitious in its claims. Sawday
argues that the practice of early modern anatomy produced a "culture of dissection" that had a profound impact on human subjectivity and what philosophers have subsequently termed the mind/
body problem. According to Sawday, that "culture of dissection"
refashioned "the means by which people made sense of the world
around them in terms of their philosophy of understanding, their
theology, their poetry, their plays, their rituals of justice, their art,
and their buildings" (ix). Specifically he claims that anatomy as a
mode of knowledge produced the idea of human interiority. Sawday's aim is to show that the imaginative arts, which are now
widely perceived as alienated from empirical science, were in early
modern Europe allied with science. Sawday's is a historical argument that traces the shift from what he calls "the *discovery* of the
Vesalian body" to "the later *invention* of the Harveian or Cartesian
body," or from divine workmanship to mechanistic rationality.
    The book is made up of eight chapters that range widely; a short
first chapter sets up the claims made on behalf of anatomical science. Sawday reads the Perseus and Medusa myth as an emblem
for the culture of dissection/partition he analyzes. In chapter 2, he
outlines the shift from the microcosm/macrocosm analogical view
of the relation of body to world to the modern Cartesian silenced
body, a "mechanism, a contrivance" subject to medical/scientific
discourse. From these initial general claims, Sawday moves on to
consider anatomical theaters, the spectacle of early modern anat-

omy, and its links with popular theater. Chapter 3 surveys the relations between the anatomists and public execution, the growing demand for corpses and the various means—legal, quasi-legal and illegal—undertaken to meet that demand. In chapter 4, Sawday explores what he terms "sacred anatomy" and the conflict between theology and the new science; in chapter 5, he interprets Rembrandt's *The Anatomy Lesson of Dr Nicholas Tulp* as a response to Cartesian dualism and an assertion of civic and social order; this section ends by reading the House of Alma episode from the *Faerie Queene* using Freud's theory of the uncanny. The last two chapters are concerned more particularly with questions of gender: chapter 7 a survey of the allegorical figure of *Anatomia* and the poetic tradition of the *blason*; and chapter 8, the Royal Society's attack on metaphorical language, its exclusion of Margaret Cavendish from its ranks, and an original and provocative reading of her work as a precursor to "scientific journalism" in which metaphor works to explain scientific ideas to the lay reader (254).

This lengthy outline only gestures at the wide and impressive array of texts—verbal and visual, early modern and modern—Sawday considers. Not only well-known canonical works including Vesalius's *Fabrica*, Spenser's *Faerie Queene*, Shakespeare's *Romeo and Juliet* and *Henry V*, much of Donne, prose and verse, Bacon's *Advancement*, Milton's *Paradise Lost*, Rembrandt's *The Anatomy Lesson of Dr Nicolas Tulp*, even Joyce's *Ulysses*, which is included because Joyce is said to have described it as an "epic of the human body" (141) modeled after Phineas Fletcher's somatic epic *The Purple Island*. But Sawday also considers a host of lesser-known texts by Marot and the French *rhétoriqueurs*, Cowley, Crashaw, Carew, Cavendish, Rochester, Traherne, and others. Though "blurbed" by Roy Porter as "a major event in the cultural history of the early modern era," *The Body Emblazoned* owes more to cultural studies than to the more traditional practice of cultural history. It brings together widely disparate materials from different epochs and national cultures and, methodologically, somewhat awkwardly yokes together Freud and Foucault.

This book's wide sweep is both its strength and its weakness. It usefully brings together in one volume materials on anatomy scattered in articles and books in the history of science, the history of medicine, and social and cultural history and it overflows with provocative and subtle readings of both well-known and little-known texts; but it occasionally plays fast and loose with its historical argument. Though Sawday claims, for example, that partition and, as the book's title suggests, the blazoned body, is produced by the practice of scientific anatomy, he makes no attempt to account for the blazoned body of Petrarchan lyric, which predates his "culture of dissection." And though Sawday is certainly right in claiming, as many recent commentators have in reading the *blason*, that the form represented a male arena of competition and mastery of the female body, women poets in France and Italy did emblazon the male body, and his argument, since it already uses French evidence, would have been strengthened by a consideration of *blasons* by women including Louise Labé, Veronica Franco, and Gaspara Stampa. In reading the great frontispiece to Vesalius's *De Humani Corporis Fabrica* (mistakenly labeled "title page"), Sawday argues that its central point is "an opened womb," which he glosses anachronistically as "a demonstration of the structural coherence of the universe itself, whose central component—the principle of life concealed within the womb—Vesalius is about to open to our gaze" (70). Sawday here seems to assume a transhistorical view of human reproduction and a male fear of the reproductive female body that ignores the still dominant Aristotlean and Galenic theories of human generation that denied any generative power to the female reproductive organs. And there are occasional startling historical lapses as in the claim, in reading a 1491 gravida figure from de Ketham's *Fasciculus Medicinae*, that the "human foetus acknowledges the sin of Adam and Eve by covering *her* [italics mine] face" (105). I know of no example, from the earliest Soranian fetal images until well into the eighteenth century, of a fetus sexed female in any anatomical rendering.

Jonathan Sawday writes with missionary zeal about the anatomical culture of early modern Europe, and though we learn a great deal, readers are unlikely to be fully converted. The claims for anatomy's explanatory power are somewhat overstated; anatomy is not Casaubon's key to all knowledge, and little is served by seeing every aspect of early modern culture through the lens of anatomical dissection. When Hamlet is a new scientist and Elizabeth I an anatomist, anatomy has become so metaphorical as to lose its analytic specificity. But *The Body Emblazoned* is filled with powerful and arresting readings that take into account not only contemporary fashionable preoccupations with gender, status, and colonial exploration, but the learned traditions of religious iconography and the memento mori and the wider contexts of European poetics and the visual arts. It is a major contribution to early modern cultural studies, to the history of sexuality, and to the burgeoning corpus of writing on the body in culture. No one working in these fields or on Renaissance poetry can afford to miss it.

Feminist Readings of Early Modern Culture: Emerging Subjects.
Edited by Valerie Traub, M. Lindsay Kaplan, and Dympna Callaghan.
Cambridge: Cambridge University Press, 1996.

Reviewer: Georgianna Ziegler

The past dozen or so years have seen the publication of a number of fine anthologies of essays attempting to recover the life, writings, and social milieu of early modern Englishwomen. I find it appropriate that the anthology—largely edited and written by women— has become the preeminent genre for this project of recovery, because its form recapitulates the group structure of much of women's work throughout social history. This current collection of essays, edited by Valerie Traub, Lindsay Kaplan, and Dympna Callaghan, continues the tradition of recovery as a group dynamic, but complicates the project by mapping varieties of feminist theoretical approaches over an inquiry into the diverse ways in which gender and subjectivity were constructed in the early modern period. The contributors to this fine volume represent a new generation of scholars who work from the assumption that there is not one but many "feminisms" and that these may be more richly evocative when held in dialogue with each other, while recognizing the inherent "difference" between postmodern and early modern intellectual constructs.

While broadening the field of feminist engagement, these essays also reflect the variety of ways in which the early modern subject was constructed by the state, the church, the court, the "middling" groups of society, and the stage. They query a broad range of texts including travel narratives, anatomies, witchcraft trials, plays, cookbooks, and legal, ecclesiastical, and scientific treatises in an attempt to identify and examine some of the "diverse kinds of knowledges" "through which subjects became invested with various modes of signification, a range of material embodiments, and new forms of authority" (5). The essays are organized in subgroups that create a logical progression of topics from considerations of representations of the gendered body to attempts by women to create a space for their own writing or intellectual pursuits; the implications of gender and race in early colonial projects; and considerations of marriage, divorce, rape, and same-sex relationships as constituted in church, legal, and theatrical venues.

The first group provides a fascinating view of the visual construction of the gendered body. In a highly original approach, Denise Albanese invites us to view the series of "History Portraits" by the modern photographer Cindy Sherman, who inserts herself into well-known historical portraits as a way of forcing the viewer to think about questions of difference and anachronism. Albanese then looks at ways in which the earlier and later Renaissance humanists (specifically Petrarch and Bacon) read their classical past and how they defined "the supreme male European subject" (35) against a counter or different subject comprised of the barbarian/female other. Specifically, Albanese focuses on the portraits of the Algonquin and Pictish male warriors from Harriot's *A Briefe and True Report* . . . (1590), noting that the sixteenth-century point of view distanced the North American native both in space (on the other side of the world) and time (like the ancient Britains). But this quasi-ethnographic construction of an English past was joined by a quasi-classical one that identified the progenitor of the English race among the Trojans. Albanese's point is that "the past is made, not found—manufactured according to ideological interests" (28). Though she is interested in issues of gender in the ways in which we—and they—construct the past, Albanese does not consider in her discussion the portraits of the Algonquin woman or of the Pictish warrior woman and young girl that also occur in Harriot. The latter two, in particular, physically reproduce classical models of female beauty, but are overlaid with "barbaric" tatoos and implements of war. The inscription on the picture equates the Pictish woman with the man as a generic type of "warrior." It would have enriched her discussion of the female "other" to have included these further images.

This is the sort of book that opens spaces for the reader to engage in her own dialogue between and with the essays. S/he may, for example, carry some of Albanese's remarks on the relationship of humanism with its classical past into the discussions of anatomical illustration by Traub and of the wounded Roman body by Marshall that follow. In a necessarily limited but evocative survey, Traub examines sixteenth- and seventeenth-century anatomical illustrations to argue that while the traditional male body was seen as impermeable and the female body as permeable, anatomies reveal the physical, mortal body, dissecting it until traces of gender are removed and implicating the anatomist in his own demise. In the works of Vesalius and later of Charles Estienne, the male body is ever more virulently implicated in its own dissection, but Estienne counters this violence with his depiction of eroticized female bodies enclosed in comfortable domestic spaces and designed to evoke a sense of virility on the part of the male voyeur rather than fear of his own death. By the time of Johann Remmelin's "pop-up" anatomy, the female body is depicted "as the source of sin," on which are projected "both the ontological problem of meaning posed by physical matter and the epistemological failure of dissection to resolve it" (83).

While Traub examines the anxieties inherent in contemplating the destruction of the physical subject, Marshall investigates the construction of the subject through the representation of the physical body onstage. Specifically, she uses the case of Coriolanus's refusal to show his wounds to the Roman public as a means of investigating what is implied by the creation of self-hood in the early modern period, and how theatrical representation invites the audience to participate in this construction. Marshall points out that critics have read Coriolanus's thoughts, assuming that he does not show his wounds because he wants to control his identity himself, not make it vulnerable to the reactions of the people. However, his thoughts on this decision are not actually given in the play but are dependent on the reaction of the audience to the actions of the actor and to the display of the body. Like the wound-man in medieval medical illustration, Coriolanus is in danger of having his identity be subordinate to his wounds. Marshall sees Coriolanus as an example of Kristeva's "subject-in-process" as he "attempt[s] to define himself in relation to his mother and, by extension, to Rome" (111). She also offers a corrective to Cavell's argument that the play "'raise[s] the question . . . what it is to know that others, that we, have bodies'" (113, from Cavell, *Disowning Knowledge* [1987], 176) by injecting the consideration of gender into this question and suggesting that "the play forces its audience into a confrontation" (113) with the diversity of physical bodies with which we exist.

The other two Shakespeare essays in this volume use feminist strategies that equally compel us to ask new questions of familiar plays. While critics have noted the absent mother in *The Tempest*, Jyotsna Singh points to the absence of gender itself in the newer colonialist discussions and appropriations of the play. Caliban has been adopted "as a colonial subject or an embodiment of any oppressed group" (193), but especially in Césaire's popular version of the play, Miranda assumes her marginalized role as an object of gift-exchange to maintain a white/European/male power network, while no space is made at all for any "'physiognomically complementary mate'" (quoting Wynter, in *Out of the Kumbla* [1990; edited by Davies and Fido], 360) for Caliban (206). Singh's argument is finally with the colonial liberation movement itself: "if resistance movements are 'imagined communities,' then such imaginings are frequently based upon particular, and often disempowering, constructions of women's sexuality" (206). In a closely argued companion essay, Laura Levine strips away our romantic illusions about *A Midsummer Night's Dream* to show the play's "heart of darkness." She takes as her text the statement by Theseus that having wooed Hippolita with violence, he will wed her "With pomp, with triumph, and with revelling" (I.i.19), and she asks what evidence there is that theater *can* transform sexual violence. She shows that in the play itself, sexual violence "is actually aggravated" rather than healed, both through the actions of Theseus against Helena and of Oberon against Titania and Bottom (216). Furthermore, the theatrical, as represented within the play by the mechanicals and the fairies, is equally incapable of transforming sexual violence. While each of the three essays devoted to discussions of Shakespeare's plays takes a rather narrow frame of reference, together they demonstrate forcefully how reading with a feminist eye can force us to ask awkward but important questions, not only of familiar literary texts, but of other theoretical approaches as well.

Another fine essay that, like Singh's, considers gender, race, and the colonial project is by Kim F. Hall. While Singh is concerned with querying the contemporary colonialist project, Hall uses a novel approach to argue a connection between culinary texts and British colonial history. She shows the importance of sugared cakes and creations made of sugar to upper-class feasting, as revealed in seventeenth-century cookbooks such as Plat's *Delightes for Ladies*, suggesting that confectionary was considered part of a gentlewoman's art. Then she discusses Richard Ligon's early *History of the Island of Barbados*, showing how his travel narrative is informed with the language of cookbooks so that the foreign, the native, the raw food products are tamed within a domestic setting. Her point is that "the shaping of the English woman's role in the household was necessary; not only for maintaining domestic order, but for the absorption of the foreign necessitated by colonialism" (170). Hall's work is part of a larger project in which it would be useful for her to look at the continent as well, where convents of nuns were known for their production of sweetmeats in a country such as Portugal, adding a religious dimension to the colonial project.

Laura Levine's essay on sexual violence in A Midsummer Night's Dream is linked with three others by Lindsay Kaplan, Theodora Jankowski, and Dympna Callaghan that investigate different aspects of early modern sexuality. Kaplan's well-argued essay, based on a reading of political and religious legal systems, discusses the early development of a divorce law in Britain, and the close relationships between this development and British politics from Henry VIII's break with Rome to the Royalist versus populist debate of the mid-seventeenth century. She shows that support for the developing Protestant/parliamentarian concept of a dissoluble marriage came from their study of Hebrew law in the Old Testament. But though the "marriage" of the king and his subjects was dissolved with the death of Charles I, divorce on the domestic level never completely became law because, Kaplan argues, it would have meant that "a wife could 'unsubject' herself from her husband" (244), taking along her property and assets.

While Kaplan's essay looks at legal aspects of heterosexual love, the pieces by Jankowski and Callaghan investigate possibilities for same-sex desire in early modern England. A number of recent scholars have explored the social construction(s) of what we term male homosexuality in the early modern period, but the possibilities for same-sex female relationships— perhaps more difficult to define in early modern discourse—are still under investigation. Both Jankowski and Traub have elsewhere made important contributions to this discussion, and in her current essay, Jankowski furthers this work by asking whether there was a space for virginal same-sex relationships outside the patriarchal definition of "virginity" as a state of physical "perfection," a means toward the end of a marriage contract. She finds such a space in Lyly's play Galathea, where two girls are disguised as boys and thrown in with Diana's nymphs to save them from being sacrificed to a monster. Though the gender boundaries are complicated in this play by the double cross-dressing of the boy actors, Jankowski argues that Diana's company creates such a community outside the patriarchy that allows the two girls to pledge undying love for each other, just before one of them will be arbitrarily turned into a boy. The notion is attractive and I want to be persuaded by this argument that there *was* a space for virginity outside the patriarchal social boundaries, but I also want to know more about how this literary/theatrical space, defined by a modern eye, might have been construed within a society ruled by the court of a virgin queen.

Callaghan's essay, on the other hand, explores a relationship already coded as same-sex desire; that between Edward II and Gaveston. Beginning like Albanese with a modern photograph, she posits that we cannot really separate concepts of sex and gender in our society, since the position of the subject is still largely determined by patriarchal forces. While Callaghan is aware that we should not read our modern constructs onto early modern society, she looks at Edward II's story as told by Marlowe and by Elizabeth Cary to find their perceptions of the relationship between sexuality and gender. In Marlowe's version, "male homoerotic bonds are represented . . . as within rather than outside patriarchy, and making them is acknowledged to be one of its most pervasive practices" (284). In this play Isabella may be seen as a manipulator of access to power, but she loses this power and is silenced once she takes Mortimer as a lover. In Cary's version, "Isabel is a warrior queen who frequently outwits the men around her, and whose paramour is barely mentioned" (292). Rather than subverting patriarchy, however, Callaghan sees Isabel's maneuvers as really supporting a strong patriarchy against a society in crisis because of a weak king. Callaghan uses these examples from early modern texts to argue against what she sees as a current critical fallacy to pit femininity against homoerotic masculinity when both submit to patriarchal notions of "order." While Callaghan is clearly conversant with current work in "queer" studies, she curiously overlooks two pieces by Bruce Smith that deal with *Edward II*: his book *Homosexual Desire in Shakespeare's England* (1991), and an essay in *Erotic Politics* (1992; edited by Susan Zimmerman).

Two other essays in the volume also deal with writings by women; Rosemary Kegl looks at Margaret Cavendish's *Blazing World*, and Frances Dolan examines the literacy and illiteracy of women accused of witchcraft. In the first part of her essay, Kegl astutely describes Cavendish's views on the possibility of an equal intellectual life for women: that women need not only the *concepts* for such a life, but also and just as importantly, the contemplative *habit* that makes scientific/intellectual inquiry possible. The latter parts of Kegl's essay take up other issues associated with the *Blazing World*, including the (im)possibility for a material as opposed to spiritual relationship between women, economies based on barter versus money, and questions of race and species. While these are all fruitful topics which Kegl evidently engages elsewhere in a larger work on Cavendish, their relevance to what seems the central query of this essay is not always made clear.

Dolan's strong essay is based on careful reading and interpretation of printed evidence from Catholic and witchcraft trials. Her main point is to query the ways in which we have customarily construed literacy in women. The ability to write one's name has generally been taken as a sign of literacy, but Dolan points out that there were probably many women who learned to read but not to write, since that was taught as a separate skill. Furthermore, both reading and writing could be dangerous for women. Using material from trials of women expected to be Catholics and witches, Dolan shows that "criminal women's reading ability did not confer the same legal benefits that men's did, [and] their writing ability carried equal risks: in court the prosecution could use handwritten documents to incriminate them" (146). Dolan marshals her evidence in a clear and persuasive manner to argue, finally, that literacy was an ambiguous skill for women, construed "as virtuous when it aided social control and as criminal when it aided self-determination" (159).

Though some of these essays present their arguments more clearly or forcefully than others, the strength of all of them taken together is that they invite us to query and define the late-twentieth-century assumptions we bring to the study of early modern culture, and to ask new questions that will make us rethink our own readings of the past and help us to a better understanding of that culture.

ERRATA

Errata List for "Allegorical Commentary in The Merchant of Venice," Shakespeare Studies, 24 (1996)

Judith Rosenheim

BECAUSE of special circumstances attendant on the preparation of this article, *Shakespeare Studies* has made this space available to the author for listing the following significant *errata*.

page 159, line 11 from top. For *work;* read *work";*.

page 159, line 15 from top. For *refer to* read *refer the.*

page 161, line 5 from bottom. For *clowns,* read *clowns.".*

page 162, line 7 from top. For *invites.* read *invites.".*

page 162, line 3 from bottom. For *lucid* read *ludic.*

page 164, line 21 from bottom. For *younger.* read *younger.".*

page 167, line 4 from bottom. For *money;* read *money:.*

page 169, line 15 from top. For *monitory* read *monetary.*

page 170, line 13 from top. For *usury,* read *usury;.*

page 170, line 14 from bottom. For *then* read *them.*

page 171, line 19 from bottom. For *become* read *becomes.*

page 173, line 4 from top. For *resign* read *design.*

page 174, line 19 from bottom. For *unwisdom* read *unwisdom,.*

page 174, line 5 from bottom. For *"good [Gobbo],* read *"good [Gobbo],".*

page 175. The last 5 lines should be expanded to read:

flight and contempt both express alienation, albeit in significantly different ways. Flight is an action and can thus be said to express alienation physically or carnally; while contempt is a state of mind and can thus represent alienation psychically or spiritually. Thus if the alienation of flight expresses prodigality, so too may the alienation of contempt express prodigality, the one expression being carnal while the other is spir-

page 176, line 2 from top. For *expressions of prodigal expressions of prodigal* read *expressions of prodigal.*

page 177, lines 7-6 from bottom should be expanded to read:

who plays the harlot or "strumpet wind" to her bark. Like the Prodigal whose riotous living leads him into "necessitie" (Luke xv.14), the bark returns "Lean, rent, and beggar'd by the strumpet wind"; and like the bark, Jessica is beggared by her riot with Lorenzo.

page 180, line 13 from top. For *conducting* read *conducing.*

page 180, line 10 from bottom. For *The* read *This.*

page 189, line 9 from top. For *decries* read *descries.*

page 194, line 14 from top. For *his* read *this.*

page 198, line 6 from bottom. For *her* read *his.*

page 200, line 12 from bottom. For *comprises* read *compromises.*

page 201, line 7 from bottom. For *father* read *father,.*

page 202, line 13 from top. For *yo* read *you.*

page 204, line 7 from top. For *scent* read *scant.*

page 206, line 10 from top. For *Spenser* read *Spencer.*

page 208, line 21 from top. For *Levin these* read *Levin sees these.*

Index

427